The Art of Dress

The Art of Dress

CLOTHES AND SOCIETY 1500–1914

Jane Ashelford

Special Photography by
Andreas von Einsiedel

THE NATIONAL TRUST

Distributed by Harry N. Abrams, Inc., Publishers

First published in Great Britain in 1996 by
National Trust Enterprises Limited,
36 Queen Anne's Gate, London SW1H 9AS

Text copyright © Jane Ashelford 1996
Archival material copyright © The National Trust 1996

Distributed in North America in 1996 by
Harry N. Abrams, Incorporated, New York
A Times Mirror Company

Acknowledgements

Cecil Beaton, *The Glass of Fashion*, Weidenfeld and Nicolson, 1954
By kind permission of his Literary Trustees and Rupert Crew Ltd.
Jane Austen's Letters, ed. R.W. Chapman, Oxford University Press, 1952
Alice Fairfax-Lucy, introd., *Mistress of Charlecote*, Victor Gollancz Ltd
and Tigerliliy Ltd, 1983
The Lisle Letters, ed. Muriel St. Clare Byrne, Martin Secker & Warburg Ltd
and the University of Chicago Press, 1983
The Diaries of Samuel Pepys, ed. Robert Latham and William Matthews,
Bell & Hyman, an imprint of HarperCollins Ltd, 1969-1983
Gwen Raverat, *Period Piece. A Cambridge Childhood*, Faber and Faber Ltd, 1952

Library of Congress Cataloging-in-Publication Data

Ashelford, Jane.
     The art of dress : clothes and society, 1500-1914 / by Jane Ashelford ;
photographs by Andreas von Einsiedel.
          p. cm.
     ISBN 0-8109-6317-5 (clothbound)
     1. Costume—Great Britain—History. 2. Fashion—Great Britain—History.
3. Dress accessories—Great Britain—History. 4. Great Britain—History.
5. Great Britain—Social life and customs.
I. Einsiedel, Andreas. II. Title.
GT730.A68 1996
391'.00941—dc20   95-44103

Picture research by Caroline Worlledge, Sophie Blair and Cerys Byrne
Wigs made by Margaret Harrold
Mannequins made by Museum Casts
Designed by Newton Engert Partnership
Production by Bob Towell

Phototypeset in Monotype Sabon Series 669
by Southern Positives and Negatives (SPAN), Lingfield, Surrey
Printed and Bound in Hong Kong
Mandarin Offset Limited

The Snowshill Costume Collection is currently in store at Berrington Hall, Hereford & Worcester. Several of the most interesting garments were put on mannequins and photographed specially for this book to provide an opportunity for those who are interested to see something of the collection.

The National Trust has provided a facility to enable scholars to study the costumes at Berrington. Anyone wishing to pursue this should write to the Assistant Historic Buildings Representative, National Trust Severn Regional Office, Mythe End House, Tewkesbury, Glos GL20 6EB, specifying the articles they would like to see and giving details of their research purpose. All visits must be organised in advance. It is the National Trust's intention to put some of the garments from the Snowshill collection on display when funds are available, and a suitable building can be found.

1 (*frontispiece*) Detail of a sack-back gown, 1760-74, from the Killerton collection. The elbow-length sleeves, weighted with coins so that they hang properly, are finished with braid-trimmed, gathered flounces and engageantes. Engageantes, used to decorate cuffs, were mostly of fine lace, often in double and treble layers, though this example is fine cotton embroidered with whitework.

The blue silk taffeta, patterned with white stripes and black flecks, was woven by the *chiné à la branche* technique, whereby the pattern was printed onto the warp prior to weaving. Such fabrics are light and pastel in colour, with an attractive blurred appearance. They found particular favour in France, and were also known as 'Pompadour taffeta' because Madame de Pompadour had a preference for them.

Contents

Introduction

When the photographer Cecil Beaton wrote an account of fashion and the decorative arts in the first half of this century he felt he had to defend himself against the charge of being a 'propagandist of frivolity', for the author of such a work will 'certainly discover that, both in England and America, fashion is viewed with a jaundiced eye, feminine enthusiasm notwithstanding'. At the time of writing, 1954, Beaton thought that it was 'France alone' who had 'laboured to elevate both fashion and *les arts mineurs* to a degree of perfection comparable with the purity of its literature and painting'. Endeavouring to resolve the essential paradox that 'fashions are ephemeral but fashion is enduring' he concluded that 'changes in fashion correspond with the subtle and often hidden network of forces that operate on society – political, economic and psychological factors all play their part. In this sense fashion is a symbol.'[1]

During the four hundred years covered by this book, fashion was a symbol of the power of the monarchy, aristocracy and the upper classes, dictated by their lifestyle and moulded by their taste. The six chronological sections of the main text illustrate how the monarchy gradually lost its position as the unchallenged arbiter of taste and instigator of fashion, and how the court's status as the ultimate arena in which to exhibit fashionable dress was eroded. It was a process which did not, however, diminish the importance of ceremonial at court or the social cachet that continued to be attached to presentation there. Princess Alexandra of Denmark, acknowledged as an innovative leader of fashion and a style-setter in the early and middle years of her marriage, changed the image of British royalty when she was crowned Queen in 1902. Her choice of an increasingly ornate and formal style of dress, whatever the occasion or time of day, 'removed her from reality and only helped to increase the aura of distance that one associates with the court'.[2] Even as she did this, deeply entrenched attitudes were being questioned, and it was no longer thought desirable or necessary to emphasise distinctions of class by means of clothing. The First World War wrought a social revolution in attitudes, but the underlying circumstances that gave rise to these changes were already in place in the years before 1914.

Rapid technological advances during the Industrial Revolution had enabled factories to produce fashionable but inexpensively priced materials. With the invention of the sewing machine, ready-made clothes could be manufactured and distributed on a massive scale and were cheap enough to be bought by all classes, thus reducing the exclusive influence formerly exerted by fashionable society. The beginnings of the ready-made industry can, in fact, be traced right back to the late sixteenth century, when the lower and middle classes were able to purchase items like hats, girdles, neckwear and

2 The Prince of Wales depicted opposite his host, Sir William Armstrong (in a top hat) at Cragside, Northumberland. In deference to the rural setting, the Prince wears a stylish suit of heavy country tweeds, thick socks and a bowler hat. The last became a fashionable item after he wore his first bowler as a student in 1859. (H.H. Emmerson, 1884, Cragside)

children's clothing from the chapmen's shops that were scattered all over the country. In order to appreciate subsequent developments in the eighteenth century, the rise of warehouses with their 'ready money' policy, and, in the nineteenth, of the department stores and mail order catalogues, there is a section at the end of each of the six chronological chapters which explores the way in which the fashion industry operated and how ordinary people, as well as the very wealthy, did their shopping and made their clothes.

Two general chapters supplement the main chronological text: children's clothes and servant's dress. Apart from a brief period of freedom at the end of the eighteenth and the beginning of the nineteenth centuries, children were dressed as miniature replicas of their parents. In its collection of costume at Killerton House, Devon (see p.10), the National Trust owns a number of items of children's dress, and several are illustrated in this book. Anyone interested in the clothes and lifestyle of Victorian and Edwardian children should also visit the National Trust's Museum of Childhood at Sudbury Hall in Derbyshire, where there are comprehensive displays reflecting changes in family life, the care of children and the ways in which young people have played, learnt and worked over the generations.

The next chapter describes the clothes worn by those who worked as servants in country houses and on estates, charting in particular the development of livery. This was the distinctive uniform style of dress worn by male servants, based on the colour and symbols of the family's coat-of-arms. Provision of livery was expensive; usually made from good quality fabric and trimmings, it was renewed on a regular basis to those servants entitled to wear it. As livery was the property of the family (and a servant who left employment was expected to relinquish it) its chances of survival were relatively good, unlike the dress of the rest of the working classes. Men and women at the bottom of the social scale wore correspondingly old and tattered versions of what had originally been fashionable garments, and if they did not have the means to replace them, these eventually disintegrated into rags. Hence this comment made by a visitor to London in 1872: 'An English crowd is almost the ugliest in the world; because the poorer classes are but copyists in costume of the rich. . . . Observe this lemonade vendor. His dress is that of a prosperous middle-class man . . . gone to shreds and patches.'[3]

The collection of clothes under the care of the National Trust is unique, for a significant proportion belongs to families for whose ancestors the clothes were originally made. Such provenance is invaluable, allowing the clothes to be related to the specific and individual circumstances of the original owner, thus enriching and enlarging our knowledge. Unlike a museum, which has the ability to build up a collection in a systematic and ordered way, and has the option to concentrate on a particular category of dress, these clothes are similar in only one respect – each reflects the personal taste of its original owner. Fortunately, successive generations did not discard or cut up these clothes once they were no longer fashionable, but chose to pack them away carefully, protected from the damp and moths. Their foresight has resulted in a random but remarkable collection that spans three centuries.

There are three major collections of costume and accessories owned by the Trust: Killerton, Springhill and Snowshill. Charles Paget Wade built up his extensive collection of costume and accessories at Snowshill Manor, Gloucestershire, for a comparatively practical purpose. He was an enthusiastic organiser of amateur theatricals and his

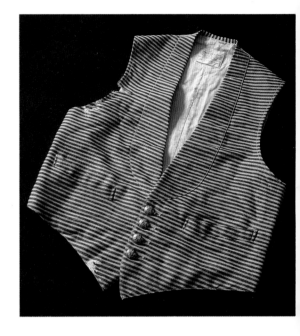

3 This gold and black striped silk waistcoat is all that remains of the livery purchased by Thomas Agar-Robartes, 6th Lord Clifden, for the staff of Lanhydrock in Cornwall in the late nineteenth century. The last footman to wear it has inscribed his name on a label sewn inside, while a second label shows it was purchased from one of the specialist livery shops in London, Simpson & Son, 63 South Audley Street.

The direction of the stripes on footmen's waistcoats indicated whether they were worn by indoor or outdoor staff: this waistcoat with horizontal stripes shows it was indoor wear.

4 (*above*) Charles Paget Wade on the steps of Snowshill Manor in Gloucestershire, wearing one of the two sets of Cromwellian armour from his collection over an original buff leather coat. Both sets of armour and the coat are displayed on the Old Stairs leading up to Ann's Room. The similarity in uniforms worn by the opposing sides in the Civil War is apparent when this suit is compared with the sleeveless jerkin and breastplate worn by the Royalist Newport (**41**).

5 (*above right*) A detail of the pocket from a 1780s court coat in the Snowshill collection. The matt surface provides a perfect foil to the naturalistic flowers and grasses embroidered in silk. So subtle are the gradations of colour, highlighted by sequins and spangles, that an almost three-dimensional effect is created.

collection furnished him and his visitors with endless opportunities to dress up in the clothes of the past, with all the relevant props. James Lees-Milne, who was responsible for negotiating the transfer of houses to the care of the Trust, found that Wade (**4**) was 'the most eccentric' of all the owners he had to deal with: 'Wearing square-cut, shoulder-length, Roundhead hair and dressed in trunk and hose this magpie collector would, while showing visitors over the house, suddenly disappear behind a tapestry panel to emerge through a secret door on a different floor level.'[4]

The Snowshill collection is impressive, comprising some 2,000 items of male and female dress, of which nearly 200 are eighteenth-century. A number of these are embroidered coats and waistcoats of exceptionally high quality (**5**), but Wade did not only concentrate on grand, formal clothing. His taste was broad and included country-men's smocks, livery, military uniforms and jockeys' shirts and caps. He wrote in 1945 that he bought things for their 'interest as records of various vanished handicrafts', an acquisition policy applauded today by curators of costume museums, who find that they have few examples of these less glamorous, but much rarer garments. The collection is currently in store at Berrington Hall, Hereford and Worcester (see also p.124).

The second major collection of costume is lodged at Killerton House in Devon, where the exhibitions featuring the costumes, and related illustrative material, are changed every year. The actress Paulise de Bush, daughter of an American opera singer and an Englishman who had been made a baron of the Holy Roman Empire, began assembling this collection almost by accident during the Second World War. Paulise was then living in a cottage near the village of Aston Tirold in Oxfordshire. One day, when walking past a Tudor house, she saw a lady throwing old clothes from its upstairs window onto a bonfire. The niece of the owner of the house had come to the village to escape the London Blitz, but found that nothing had been thrown away since the eighteenth century. Unable to gain access to the upstairs bedrooms, she was burning the obstacles.

Paulise gradually acquired the entire collection and, rejecting the idea of using it for her own theatrical activities, decided to store it carefully, hence its excellent condition. Like Charles Wade, she could not stop collecting and subsequently made many purchases from Christies and Sothebys. Before she died in 1973 Paulise had asked her friend, the stage and costume designer Atherton Harrison, to advise her trustees on the collection. Atherton approached the National Trust, who suggested that it be lodged at Killerton and that Atherton herself should supervise it, which she did until her retirement in 1993. The collection now contains over 8,000 items of dress ranging in date from the mid-seventeenth century to the present day, and including a number of extremely fine eighteenth-century gowns and accessories and the comprehensive collection of children's clothing already noted.

At Springhill in Northern Ireland the outbuildings, the Old Laundry and the East Pavilion, house a collection of 2,300 items of costume from the eighteenth century to the present day. The original collection made by the Pack Beresford family has been supplemented by local donations and loans. The displays are changed annually.

Many houses display individual items of clothing or small collections, but other National Trust houses with significant costume holdings include Felbrigg Hall in Norfolk. In 1969 the estate at Felbrigg was bequeathed to the National Trust by Robert Wyndham Ketton-Cremer, described by James Lees-Milne as a 'squire, historian, man of letters, moral guardian of his Wyndham ancestors' treasures, and recondite conversationalist'.[5] Ketton-Cremer had packed away a number of items discovered in the house he had inherited. These clothes, now stored in the Trust's Conservation Workroom in Blickling Hall, Norfolk, include an unusual collection of eighteenth-century clothes in excellent condition, probably worn on the estate for shooting and riding (see 109). Also stored at Blickling are a number of clothes from Ickworth in Suffolk that belonged to the wives of the 3rd and 4th Marquesses of Bristol, and some miscellaneous items, including a 1660s mirror in an embroidered case (see 9).

The exceptional collection of needlework, lace and costume made by the Hon. Rachel Kay-Shuttleworth (1888–1967) is kept at Gawthorpe Hall, Lancashire and is administered by a board of trustees. 'Miss Rachel', as she was widely known, had lived at Gawthorpe for most of her life, managing affairs for her ageing father, the 1st Lord Shuttleworth, in the 1920s and 30s, and for her nephews during the Second World War. Her own creative talents were strongest in the field of embroidery and during the 1950s and 60s she assembled the great collection. She envisaged it as the basis of a 'craft house', where the many different forms and techniques of textile crafts might be learnt and practised, but out of a total of more than 14,000 items only about 500 can be

6 Paulise de Bush, photographed with her grandmother, 1905. Paulise is dressed in her best party frock, with an oversized hair-bow and new satin shoes. The crinkly, shiny appearance of her dress suggests it was made from accordion-pleated silk often used for tea-gowns. Girls' dresses, whether for everyday or a special occasion, were usually cut with a deep yoke, to which was attached a frill or other form of trimming. In this example, the frill has created a cape-like effect over extremely flared sleeves.

displayed at any one time. Those currently on view include samplers, quilts, needlecraft tools and garments and accessories demonstrating the different embroidery techniques of the eighteenth and nineteenth centuries. Application to view the collection is by prior arrangement with the custodian.

The clothes that have been selected for illustration here have been photographed in a way intended to highlight the intrinsic beauty of each garment and to convey the essential style of the period. To this end, display dummies with stylised features and non-naturalistic wigs have been used as they do not conflict with, or distract from, the garment. Presentation of the clothes is also governed by one essential difference between the appearance of men and women today and those of previous generations – that of size. Very few of the garments, ranging in date from an early seventeenth-century gown at Hardwick Hall, Derbyshire, to a beaded evening dress made in 1914, would fit a dummy with the figure of an average Englishwoman of the 1990s. At 5ft 4in, 36B–25.5–36 and 9st 9.4lb, today's woman has added two inches to her bust in just twenty years and nearly half an inch to her height in a decade. She is also two inches taller than a century ago and has gained a stone in weight. Moreover, by receiving the proper calcium intake during her formative years, she has a thicker and stronger rib cage than her predecessors. This change in the density and size of bones is also true for men, and is particularly noticeable in the way that old clothes have been cut to accommodate much narrower shoulders and smaller backs. The tightness of cut is sometimes so acute that a garment will not even fit a dummy specially designed for display.

Choice of illustrative material has also been determined by the condition of the garments. Clothes that might appear to the inexperienced eye to be in a robust condition could be subjected to unacceptable stress if placed on a dummy, so all the garments were examined and given the appropriate treatment in the Trust's conservation workrooms before they were photographed. Even then, some garments were too frail to be placed on a dummy. One such was the wedding dress that Mary Elizabeth Williams wore when she married George Hammond Lucy in 1823 (7). Writing in the 1950s, Alice Fairfax-Lucy observed, 'It would hardly fit a well-grown child of twelve.'[6]

Photographs of these existing clothes have been supplemented by portraits from the magnificent collections found in National Trust houses. These provide essential information about the way in which the clothes relate to the human body and the image that the sitter wished to have recorded for posterity. An exceptional selection of portraits from the National Portrait Gallery is on permanent display at three National Trust houses – Montacute House, Somerset, Gawthorpe Hall, Lancashire and Beningbrough Hall, Yorkshire – and a number of these have been included in the book. The display at Montacute illustrates the reigns of the Tudor monarchs and the early Stuarts. Portraits of leading courtiers and literary figures from the second half of the seventeenth century are featured at Gawthorpe. At Beningbrough, portraits, sculptures, pastels and engravings 'form a history in miniature of national life from the time of the "Glorious Revolution" in 1688 which signalled the end of the Stuart dynasty, up to and beyond the succession of George III in 1760'.[7]

Complementary visual material has been provided by family albums in Trust houses, a collection of cartes-de-visite and fashion illustrations from Killerton and photographs from the Fox Talbot Museum of Photography at Lacock, Wiltshire. But, inevitably, in a

7 Detail from the wedding dress worn by Mary Elizabeth Williams when she married George Lucy of Charlecote in December 1823. Although it is no longer snow white and in a very delicate condition, the beautiful applied decoration of vine leaves and bunches of grapes is still intact, as are the puffed sleeves with their elaborate overlapping crescents of silk outlined with sewn piping.

Martij 12
Anno Domini
1614

No Spring Till now

8 Mary Throckmorton, Lady Scudamore. It was fashionable in the early seventeenth century to combine garments embroidered or patterned in different ways, and in this portrait the dark red and black brocaded silk of her sleeveless, full-length gown is contrasted with a much lighter red and black figured velvet skirt. Her button-fastening linen jacket is decorated with a delicate, scrolling design in blackwork. Her plain ruff, with tasselled strings, contrasts with the magnificent edging of cutwork and lace on her cap of wired linen and matching cuffs.

A very popular fashion in jewellery for men and women was a black ribbon bracelet: Lady Scudamore wears one on her right hand. Strings of black silk also served as ear-rings – the silk would be threaded through the lobe of the ear and left to dangle (50), although if worn long, it could be tied at the end.
(Marcus Gheeraerts, 1615, Montacute)

book covering such a span of time and subject matter, the National Trust has not been able to provide all the illustrative material and this shortfall has been filled by photographs, engravings, prints and drawings from a variety of other collections.

It has also proved possible to illuminate the lifestyles of the men and women who

9 This salmon-pink brocade case would have been an elegant addition to a 1660s dressing-table. It contained a flat mirror backed with the same material, and a brush (now missing). Richly embroidered with a coiling pattern in silver thread and seed pearl, it is just the sort of fashionable accessory that would have tempted Pepys on his shopping excursions. Cases of a similar shape were used to store combs: these were tucked into the pockets, the rest of the case then wrapping around them.

originally wore these clothes by quoting pertinent extracts from family papers. These have survived in many forms and include correspondence, inventories, accounts, diaries and other documentary material. Such papers have been transcribed and published at different times and some have been edited, and the spelling modernised, whereas others have been left in their original form. Where possible I have acknowledged all the sources, in whatever form or edition they took.

Many people have helped with the writing of this book. Margaret Willes, the National Trust's Publisher, initiated the project and she, and Dr Aileen Ribeiro of the Courtauld Institute of Art, made numerous corrections and unfailingly helpful and constructive suggestions.

I am also extremely grateful to Andreas von Einsiedel for taking such beautiful photographs. We were able to include these through the generous support of Laura Ashley, who have given the National Trust funds towards the conservation of the costumes and their photography. This was a particularly appropriate sponsorship, as the late Laura Ashley was very interested in the history of textiles and a tireless researcher into the subject. We hope that this book will serve as a tribute to her memory.

The project would not have been possible without the help and co-operation of many staff members of the National Trust both in London and the regions. I would particularly like to thank Alastair Laing, Oliver Garnett, Diana Lanham and the staff of the Photographic Library, all of whom responded to my endless requests for information with good-humoured tolerance. Thanks also to Caroline Worlledge, whose enthusiastic support and administrative skill was much appreciated. I am very grateful to those regional representatives of the Trust who not only supplied information, but also arranged for items from their collections to be photographed. Thanks are also due to Kysnia Marko and Jacinth Rogers for showing me the collection of costume at the Textile Conservation Workroom at Blickling Hall, Jilly Newby the Kay-Shuttleworth collection at Gawthorpe Hall and Kvetia Gidney the Snowshill collection. Pamela Clabburn, Judith Dore and Atherton Harrison gave me invaluable help and advice and Shelley Tobin, custodian of the collection at Killerton House, searched out garments, accessories and information with indefatigable enthusiasm.

Jane Mathews and the team at the Textile Conservation Workroom at Hughenden Manor deserve special thanks for ensuring that the costumes from Snowshill, Sizergh, Blickling and Gawthorpe were displayed in an attractive and sympathetic way. My thanks are due to the staff of the following: The London Library, The University of London Library, The Witt Library, The Courtauld Institute of Art, The National Art Library and The British Library. I would particularly like to thank Penelope Ruddock, not only for the invaluable resource of the Research Centre, the Museum of Costume, Bath, but also for letting me include photographs of some items from that collection.

Special thanks are due to the Stricklands at Sizergh, Edmund Fairfax-Lucy at Charlecote, Sir Ralph Verney at Claydon, and Lady Floyd of Landue for allowing us to photograph items from their family collections of costume. Also to Janet Arnold for her photographs of the collection at Claydon.

I would like to thank my editor Libby Joy for her patience and her reassuring ability to create order out of chaos. Finally I must thank my husband Paul for his immeasurable support and encouragement.

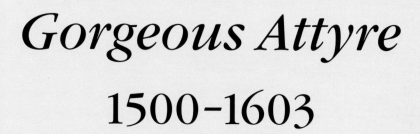

CHAPTER ONE

Gorgeous Attyre

1500–1603

I

The austere and pious man who was crowned Henry, King of England, in 1485 subsequently enjoyed a reputation for being a surly miser who 'seems never to have laid out any money so willingly as on what he could never enjoy, his tomb – on that he was profuse . . . '.[1] This is rather unfair, as Henry VII actively patronised the arts and had a high regard for learning. In personal matters of dress, however, Henry had no interest in finery; portraits of the King show him wearing plain and unflamboyant clothes in the style that had prevailed for over a century, with centre-fastening doublet reaching below the knees, and a fur-lined gown, whose heavy folds swept along the ground. But Henry VII, like his Tudor successors, never begrudged spending money on displays to impress his own people and foreign visitors with the splendour of his court.

Henry VII consolidated victory over Richard III on Bosworth field by marrying the dead king's niece, Elizabeth, thus uniting the warring houses of York and Lancaster and bringing to an end the Wars of the Roses. The subsequent establishment of the Tudor dynasty allowed him to centralise his authority and to create a new nobility directly dependent on his patronage. When his son succeeded to the throne in 1509 as Henry VIII, he inherited not only a united country, but also a full exchequer, which he immediately set about spending. At the age of eighteen, Henry VIII was the paragon of a Renaissance prince, being 'extremely handsome . . . very fair, and his whole frame admirable proportioned'. Well endowed with 'the noble qualities of his royal estate',[2] he was also very athletic, believing that idleness was the 'chief mistress of vices all'. His vanity would have been rewarded by the observation made by the Venetian Ambassador, Giustinian: 'He is extremely fond of tennis, at which game it was the prettiest thing in the world to see him play, his fair skin glowing through a shirt of the finest texture.'[3]

The perfect Renaissance gentleman was expected to place as much emphasis on the mastery of learning and the arts as on the physical virtues of sport, or of military success. Henry was a major patron of the visual arts and of music, where he displayed talent as both a performer and a composer. Literature also benefitted from his interest – again, he was a writer himself. Though intensely chauvinistic, he was not insular, and could converse and write fluently in French, Italian and other languages.

Henry's determination to keep abreast of developments in the arts was fuelled by a desire to create a court as sophisticated and splendid as that of his admired 'brother', François I of France. In France the Renaissance style of architecture and the decorative arts had been established for more than a decade, so Henry, desperate to keep pace in matters of taste, invited Italian, French and Flemish craftsmen to work in England. Competition between the kings reached its climax in the spectacle that took place on the Field of the Cloth of Gold outside Calais in 1520. Ostensibly the reason for this meeting was to cement an alliance, but it became a contest in which each tried to outshine the other by the magnificence of his appearance and that of his followers. Every part of the retinue was affected, from the horse-trappings, one of which was 'a marvellous vesture of a new devised fashion of fine gold . . . pounced and set with antique work of Romayne

10 (*previous pages*) James V, King of Scots, with his French wife, Mary of Guise, the parents of Mary, Queen of Scots. This double portrait shows Mary wearing a French hood and a kirtle bodice of rich brocade with matching sleeves slashed to show puffs of the smock underneath. Massive ermine cuffs are folded back over the sleeves. James is depicted in a low-cut doublet over a shirt, and a gown with exaggeratedly-sized fur revers and slashed sleeves. (Unknown artist, 1539, Hardwick Hall)

11 Sir Thomas More in a loose black velvet gown with an ample collar of sable, whose sleeves end above the elbow in a matching fur cuff, thus disclosing the rich red velvet of the doublet sleeve underneath. His white linen shirt can be glimpsed at the neck and wrist. On his head he wears a hat of black blocked felt, its broad side flaps tucked up onto the crown. (After Hans Holbein, 1527, Montacute)

figures', to the gilded pennants flying from the army of tents. Henry dazzled spectators with rapid and increasingly elaborate costume changes.

One of the many foreign artists who accepted the King's invitation to England was the German, Hans Holbein the Younger. Although his official title was that of the King's Painter, his work was not limited to portrait painting, but embraced jewellery and metal design, book illustration and decorative schemes. His involvement in these spheres had a profound influence on the course of fine and decorative arts in England.

A vivid impression of the dress of leading members of Henry's court may be obtained by a visit to Montacute House in Somerset, completed in 1600 for Sir Edward Phelips. Its splendid Long Gallery is now filled with a selection of sixteenth- and early seventeenth-century portraits on loan from the National Portrait Gallery. One of the earliest is a sixteenth-century copy of Hans Holbein's portrait of Sir Thomas More (11); the original was painted in 1527 when More was Chancellor of the Duchy of Lancaster.

Erasmus, the Dutch humanist, wrote in 1519 that his friend More liked to 'dress simply and does not wear silk or purple or gold chains excepting where it would be decent not to wear them'.[4] This observation is borne out by Holbein's portrait, in which More, as a royal and loyal servant, wears a collar of linked Ss. In the fifteenth century, this collar had signified allegiance to the house of Lancaster. Henry VII restored its use with the addition of Tudor badges like the pair of portcullises for fastening, and a pendant rose.

12 This portrait of Henry VIII, a contemporary variant to Holbein's original image for the Presence Chamber at Whitehall, shows an increased preoccupation with decoration in his dress: application of interlaced gold braid, liberal distribution of jewels on the surface of the doublet, and slashes through which puffs of the shirt underneath are drawn. The massive width across the shoulders is emphasised by the broad fur revers of the gown, the puffed-out upper section of which is also decorated with bands of interlaced gold braid.
(After Hans Holbein, 1537, Blickling Hall)

In contrast, Henry VIII's love of jewels and flamboyant display is immediately apparent in the many depictions of him, but it is Holbein's full-length portrait that presents the most familiar and powerful image. The prototype was a wall-painting in the Presence Chamber at the Palace of Whitehall executed by Holbein in 1537 to celebrate the birth of Henry's son, Prince Edward, and thus the perpetuation of the Tudor dynasty. Behind the King are shown his parents, Henry VII and Elizabeth of York, while Jane Seymour, his third wife and mother of his heir, stands on his right hand. This wall-painting was destroyed by fire in 1698, but there are many copies and variants of the image (12).

In 1537, although Henry was still in early middle age, he was in great pain from a chronic bone infection, thought to be the result of an earlier jousting accident, which

13 Edward Hall, writing in 1540, described this type of garment as a 'coate of purple velvet somewhat made lyke a frocke all over embrodred with flat gold of damaske with small lace mixed betwene of the same gold'. It must have suited the King in the last years of his life as he became increasingly stout and immobile and, as this portrait shows, used a walking-stick. Lined with fur, the sleeves continue as false hanging sleeves, while the doublet sleeves beneath have been cut so that puffs of the shirt alternate with rubies set in gold. Jewelled clasps are distributed across the sleeves and front opening of the gown, and a large collar of pearls and jewels is draped across the King's chest. (Unknown artist, *c*.1542, Montacute)

affected both his legs. The King had been obliged to give up the sports which he had so much enjoyed, but his gargantuan appetite was not diminished, with the result that he became grossly overweight (13). Undisputed evidence for the expansion of his figure comes from his made-to-measure suits of armour, preserved in the Royal Armouries. They reveal that Henry's chest measurement when he was still physically active was 45in, with a waist measurement of 38in, but by 1540 his chest measured 58in, and his waist 54. As his girth increased, he sought to disguise it by adopting the hugely over-padded styles popular in Germany.

A fashion innovation in this early part of the sixteenth century was the division of the hose, which covered a man's body from waist to feet, into two separate garments. The upper stocks, slops, trunk hose or breeches, covered the area between the waist and mid-thigh. The nether stocks or lower hose consisted of woollen stockings that were attached to the upper hose by means of points (ties with metal tags). The codpiece was a separate item of dress, usually cut from the same material as the trunk hose, and was laced to hose and doublet with points. At Henry's court the codpiece was heavily boned and padded so that it jutted out between the breeches and the skirts of the doublet. This blatant display of masculinity did not survive in the more refined atmosphere of his daughter Elizabeth's court, and after 1580 it was no longer fashionable.

The basic elements of female dress during Henry VIII's reign were the kirtle and the gown. Until about 1545 the word kirtle denoted a garment with a square décolletage which fitted the body closely to mid-thigh and then fell in folds to the ground. After that date, when bodice and skirt were made separately, the term kirtle was applied to the skirt alone, the gown becoming an optional overgarment worn for warmth or on formal occasions. The bodice then was referred to as a 'pair of Bodies' because it was made in two parts – the back and front being joined together at the sides. Sleeves were made separately and attached to the bodice by means of ties. In the 1530s, massive oversleeves with turned-back cuffs were worn over stiff, often quilted, undersleeves. Movement of the arms must have been very restricted, inhibited by the very tight cut of the upper part of the sleeve and by the combined weight and volume of the two sleeves. The rich fabric used to make a bodice was protected from perspiration and dirt by the shift or smock, a fine linen undergarment worn next to the skin. Its trimmed edge appeared above the edge of the bodice and through the slashed decoration on the sleeves.

In the early years of the sixteenth century, ladies of the court wore the distinctive English hood, called a gable or pediment head-dress (14). This was usually made of velvet and was given its gable shape by means of a wired or stiffened framework. Beneath would be worn an undercap, allowing the centre parting of the hair to be displayed – though after about 1525 the undercap hid the hair completely. It was superseded by the French hood, which English court ladies found more flattering (10). This style of head-dress was adopted by Henry VIII's second queen, Anne Boleyn, who had been educated at the courts of Margaret of Savoy, the Regent of The Netherlands, and of François I of France, and thus it became the fashionable style of the 1530s in England. The French hood was small and semi-circular, set on a stiff foundation and worn on the back of the head. It had jewelled upper and lower borders (called upper and nether billiments), the lower edges of which curved forward onto the ears and were trimmed with crimped cypress (a black transparent material like crape).

When Anne Boleyn fell from grace in 1536, the King charged her with adultery and she was executed on 19 May. The next day Henry was betrothed to one of her ladies-in-waiting, Jane Seymour, and they were married on 30 May. Jane was far more conservative in her taste than Anne, preferring to wear the English hood (15). Perhaps it was felt that this traditional head-dress would be more suitable for the restrained atmosphere that the new Queen brought to the court.

An excellent written source for this period of transition can be found in the letters of the Lisle family. About 3,000 of these were written between 1533 and 1540 when Arthur Plantagenet, Lord Lisle (an illegitimate son of Edward IV), was Lord Deputy of Calais, where he and his wife, Honor Greville, lived in great state. Much of the correspondence is with John Hussee, 'my Lord Lisle's man', who spent a good deal of his time in London

14 A portrait of Henry VII's queen, Elizabeth of York, shows her wearing the distinctive English hood. Her hair is framed by a border of gold set with rectangular rubies, and two sets of lappets, one plain, the other decorated with pearls and jewels, that fall in front of the shoulders. The rest of the hood hangs down behind. The Queen's costume comprises a bulky gown with a low, square neckline narrowly edged with ermine and decorated with rich bands of pearl-studded brocade. The fullish sleeves end in turned-back cuffs of ermine. Positioned just above the bodice is a hefty jewelled collar of interlaced links set with pearls, a ponderous design typical of late Gothic taste.
(Copy, Anglesey Abbey, of original, 1500–3, National Portrait Gallery)

coping with the family's legal, financial and personal affairs. He also kept them informed of the latest news from court and his letters contain references to political events and public gossip juxtaposed with domestic details. A letter written to Lord Lisle on 19 May 1536 is typical: 'Anne the late Queen suffered with sword this day, within the Tower, upon a new scaffold; and died boldly. . . . Your hosen shall be sent within this vi days. And touching Mr Page [Sir Richard Page, Comptroller of Customs] and Mr Wyat [Sir Thomas Wyatt the Elder, poet and courtier, who was suspected of an improper relationship with the Queen, but was later cleared and released], they remain still in the Tower. What shall become of them, God knoweth best.'[5]

Lady Lisle's daughter by her first marriage, Anne Bassett, had just taken her place as one of Queen Jane's Maids of Honour when Hussee wrote this letter to her mother on 17 September 1537:

> My Lady of Sussex [her cousin] hath given Mrs. Anne a kirtle of crimson damask and sleeves to the same . . . the Queen's pleasure [is] that Mrs. Anne shall wear out her French apparel, so that your ladyship shall thereby be no loser. Howbeit, she must needs have a bonnet of velvet and a frontlet of the same. I saw her yesterday in her velvet bonnet that my Lady Sussex had 'tired [dressed] her in, and me thought it became her nothing so well as the French hood; but the Queen's pleasure must needs be fulfilled.[6]

Hussee's belief that Anne would be able to wear out her French clothes at court was ill-founded, for on 2 October he wrote to say that 'Mrs. Anne shall wear no more her French apparel' and that she must have 'a bonnet or ii, with frontlets and an edge of pearl and a gown of black satin, and another of velvet, and this must be done before the Queen's grace's churching'.[7] Churching was a combination of a service of thanksgiving and of purification for the mother after a successful childbirth. Jane Seymour gave birth to Prince Edward, the longed-for male heir, on 12 October 1537. Lady Lisle delayed in granting permission for the two new gowns for Anne to be made, so Hussee had less than twenty-four hours to complete the commission before the Prince's christening on 16 October. Only by enlisting the help of John Young, another member of the Lisle household, was he able to present Anne with her finished gown in time for her to take her place with the rest of the royal household.

Lady Lisle had obviously economised on the quality of linen used to make her daughter's smocks, for in the same letter (2 October), Hussee explained that he would have to buy new cloth because her existing ones had been deemed to be 'too coarse'. It was essential that the gentlewomen attached to the court were dressed 'according to their degree', that is, commensurate with their status at court. As Anne was a Maid of Honour, a paid position, she wore finer clothes than her sister Katherine, who was a Gentlewoman to one of the Queen's ladies.

Queen Jane's triumph at having produced a prince was short-lived, for she died twelve days later on 24 October, apparently of septicaemia. This meant that the entire court had to exchange their brightly-coloured clothes for black mourning dress. Although Anne had a place in the funeral cortège, the death of the Queen meant that her post at court was at an end. However, her cousin Lady Sussex took her in, enabling her to remain on the edge of court life. On 14 December 1537 Hussee informed Lady Lisle

15 Jane Seymour, Henry VIII's third queen, wearing the final variation of the English hood. One section of material is folded into an elongated triangle secured on top of the head; the remaining half being allowed to fall behind the shoulders. The front edge of the hood, the frontlet, decorated with gems, clamps the hood tightly against the sides of the face. Both the frontlet and the tucked-up lappets are much shorter than those worn by Elizabeth of York (14). Jane's hair is masked by two bands of material stretched across the forehead.

The square neckline of the smock, clearly visible above the closely-fitting crimson velvet bodice, is delicately embroidered with black silk. The skirt has an inverted V-shaped opening filled with a decorative triangle of gold braid called a forepart. It would have been attached to the underskirt by ties. As it was a separate accessory, it was often made with matching sleeves. Here the back seams of the brocade sleeves are left undone, but are joined at intervals by jewels so that the smock sleeve can be pulled through.
(After Hans Holbein, 1536, Knole)

that Lady Sussex had suggested that she should have a 'gown of lion tawny satin, turned up with velvet of the same colour'[8] made up for Anne. Lady Lisle immediately questioned the idea, believing it unnecessary when the court was still in mourning. However, Hussee assured her on 19 December that it was essential, for Lady Sussex thought 'it was uncertain how long the King's pleasure should be that they should wear black', and one never knew 'what sudden chance so ever might happen'.[9] The King remained a widower until 6 January 1540 when he married the German princess Anne of Cleves. Although the marriage lasted just six months it allowed Anne to resume her post at court, and she retained it throughout the reigns of his last two wives, Catherine Howard and Catherine Parr.

Hussee's letters provide an invaluable source of information about the type of clothes worn at court, for he set about finding the correct material and trimming for a new outfit and instructing the tailor on how to shape it into the latest fashion with great diligence and dedication. Two garments which are frequently mentioned in his letters are nightgowns and waistcoats. These were informal garments, the latter shaped like a jacket, worn by men and women in the privacy of their home, rather like dressing-gowns today. As they were lined with fur they must have been an indispensable garment in cold draughty houses. We learn in one letter dated 6 March 1537 that Hussee had just bought $10\frac{1}{2}$yds of black damask, 3yds of black velvet and just over $2\frac{1}{4}$yds of white satin to make a nightgown and waistcoat for Lady Lisle. Hussee stood over the tailor when he cut out the material to make sure that there was no wastage: 'There was no piece therof saved worth taking up, for I was at the cutting therof.'[10] On 9 March the garments had been made and he sent them to the skinners to be lined with fur. On the 18th he sent the finished nightgown, two waistcoats, one furred with ermine, and two ermine bonnets to Calais accompanied by the plaintive assertion: 'By my faith, Madam, I have made hard shift for it!'[11] The whole process had taken twelve days, but when Lady Lisle received them she was not satisfied and must have written to Hussee asking him if he was sure that they were indeed the latest fashion. On 2 April Hussee replied that they were 'the very fashion that the Queen and all the ladies doth wear, and so were the caps'.[12]

Hussee's life became unbearable if Lady Lisle thought he had been cheated by a mercer or a tailor, so he went to great lengths to ensure that this did not happen. On her part, Lady Lisle was extremely slow to pay any bills and relied on Hussee to keep everyone happy by giving them quails especially sent over from a poulterer in Calais. This ploy was usually successful with the royal tailor Skut, but on one occasion the Lisles had run up such huge debts that Hussee dared not call on Skut with 12yds of satin because the accompanying gift of quails had not arrived.

In 1540 the Lord Chancellor, Thomas Cromwell, struggling to retain his own position, accused Lord Lisle of being an enemy of reform. Lisle was sent to the Tower of London and all the family goods (including the correspondence) were confiscated and a careful inventory made. When the auditors opened the locked chests in which the Lisle's jewels and jewelled dress trimmings were stored they must have been amazed by what they found. The quantity of jewels and other ornaments sewn onto separate items like sleeves, head-dress borders and partlets (yokes) was staggering. A pair of crimson satin sleeves was decorated with 800 pearls, and a pair of black velvet sleeves was adorned with 573 pearls and 84 'paired stones' of gold. A long gold girdle made up of 43 pieces of

16 Henry Howard, Earl of Surrey. His doublet
has a low waistline, giving a slightly swollen
appearance, and short skirts. The surface is
decorated with an intricate pattern of gold braid
encircling areas of velvet appliqué. The codpiece
matches the breeches, which are an early form
of trunk hose, with the breech, paned
diagonally, distended in an oval shape from the
fork to be closed at mid-thigh with bands of
matching material. The fur collar of a sleeved
cloak rests across his shoulders.
(After William Scrots, *c.*1550, Knole)

gold was found in a black box, and amongst the jewels were a 'hawthorn of gold' set with 20 diamonds and a gold rose set with 3 diamonds and 3 pearls.[13]

While Lord Lisle languished in the Tower Thomas Cromwell lost favour with the King. When Henry married Catherine Howard, the niece of Cromwell's enemy Thomas Howard, 3rd Duke of Norfolk, in 1540, his fate was sealed and he was executed for high treason. In March 1542, the King finally ordered Lisle's release, but he was so delighted and relieved by this news that he died the next day in the Tower 'through too much rejoicing'.[14]

One of the last judicial victims of Henry's reign was Henry Howard, Earl of Surrey, eldest son of the Duke of Norfolk. This 'foolish proud boy' was famous for his extravagant taste in dress and one of the charges against him at his trial for high treason in 1546 was that he wore a doublet and hose of purple silk and gold tissue, the prerogative of royalty. In a posthumous portrait by William Scrots, *c.*1550 (16) we see him wearing the latest Italian fashion as he leans languidly against a broken classical pillar. His spectacular Order of the Garter collar was returned to the Crown and was worn by Edward VI when he was crowned.

Henry VIII died in 1547 safe in the knowledge that his son would succeed him as Edward VI. But the delicate child reigned for only seven years, and at his death in 1553 the throne passed first to Mary, Henry's daughter by his first wife, Catherine of Aragon, and then to Elizabeth, daughter of Anne Boleyn. Although the Catholic Mary and the Protestant Elizabeth were very different in character and outlook, they shared the Tudor love of dress. Even when Mary was in disfavour with her father, she was entitled to her own clothes allowance as a royal princess, and the Privy Purse expenses for the period 1536 to 1544 show that she had an impressive collection of clothes and jewels.[15] However, her marriage to Philip II of Spain in 1554 had a marked effect on the English court. The vibrant colours worn by Henry VIII and Edward VI were replaced by the more sombre colours favoured by the Spanish. Philip's brief stay in England introduced courtiers to the Spanish cloak, hooded and hip-length, sleeveless paned jerkins, and the superior quality of Spanish leather and gloves. By 1557, when the Duke of Mantua visited, he noted that Englishmen had discarded Italian fashion (see 16) in favour of the Spanish. Here is the paradox: the Englishman was fiercely chauvinistic and disdainful of all foreigners, but he was susceptible to foreign fashions.

By the 1550s women had a choice of two styles of gown to wear over the bodice and skirt. The loose gown (see 18) fitted across the shoulders to fall in set folds spreading outwards to the ground, leaving an inverted V-shaped opening in front from neck to heel. The gown could be closed by means of buttons, bows and aglets (ornamental metal tags used either as fastenings or as decorative trimmings). The closed gown (see 17) fitted to the waist and then extended over the hips to fall in folds to the ground.

The area between the throat and the edge of the bodice could be covered by a decorative yoke, a partlet, made either of embroidered linen or a rich fabric studded with jewels or spangles. It would be attached to the bodice by means of pins. A letter written to Lady Lisle in November 1533 shows that even at this early date the partlet was embroidered. Leonard Smyth (the Lisle's agent before Hussee) explains that he had 'delivered your frontlet to the Queen's broiderer. . . . Also I delivered the measure of your neck for your partlet collar, which you shall have within x days.'[16]

The French hood remained in fashion, particularly for older ladies, until Mary Queen of Scots popularised the heart-shaped hood in the 1560s. In the mid-1550s, hair was parted neatly in the middle to puff out slightly on either side of the head, but during the next five years that puff of hair became much more pronounced.

One of the most talented artists to work in England after the death of Holbein in 1543 was the Fleming Hans Eworth. His known works cover the period 1549 to 1570, but signed and dated works are rare. A full-length portrait by his circle, *c.*1555, is thought to be of Lady Mary Sidney, sister of Robert Dudley, later Earl of Leicester, and mother of Sir Philip Sidney (17). Lady Mary's costume, despite the luxurious nature of its components, gives an overall impression of elegant severity and sobriety that was very much the style favoured at Queen Mary's court. She is depicted wearing the type of bodice, skirt and closed gown preferred by the Queen – when the Venetian ambassador met her in 1554, the year she married Philip II of Spain, he noted that she favoured the close-bodied style of gown: she wore 'a gown such as men wear, but fitting very close, with an under-petticoat, which has a very long train; this is her ordinary costume, being also that of the gentlewomen of England'.[17] The smooth, bell-shaped lines of skirts like this were dictated by the Spanish underskirt, the farthingale or vertugado, worn underneath. This undergarment is what gave the sixteenth-century female such an inflexible and exaggerated silhouette. First recorded in the royal accounts in 1545, when one was ordered for Mary's half-sister Elizabeth, the farthingale remained in fashion, with a number of variations, for over seventy years.

The loose gown is shown in a portrait of Elizabeth Hardwick, known as 'Bess', later Countess of Shrewsbury (see 18). In 1547 Bess of Hardwick had married the second of her four husbands, Sir William Cavendish. Their union had important dynastic consequences as, through their sons, the couple were the founders of the ducal families of Devonshire, Newcastle and Portland. Cavendish died in 1559, the year that Elizabeth Tudor was crowned, and he left Bess of Hardwick a life interest in Chatsworth in Derbyshire and a substantial proportion of his property. Bess, through her Protestant connexions at court, had been a friend and supporter of Princess Elizabeth, whose position during her Catholic half-sister's reign had always been perilous. When Mary died in 1558, Bess's loyalty was rewarded when she became a lady-in-waiting to the new Queen. The portrait of Bess – now hanging at Hardwick Hall, Derbyshire, the house she built in the 1590s – is erroneously inscribed 'Maria Regina' and dates from the time of her appointment to Elizabeth's court.

The accession of Elizabeth to the English throne marks an important period in the history of costume. Never has there been an English monarch with such an interest in dress and in the impact that dress can have upon image. At the same time, the prosperity established by Elizabeth's grandfather, Henry VII, was bearing fruit, creating a society with an unprecedented degree of mobility.

The costumes described above have been very much the dress of the most privileged. But the increased expenditure on dress was not confined to courtiers, as fashions spread from the court into London society and out to the rest of the country. This Tudor achievement is alluded to by William Shakespeare in his play, *Henry VIII*. Thomas Cranmer, Archbishop of Canterbury, predicts at the birth of Elizabeth Tudor in 1533 that when she comes of age:

17 Lady Mary Sidney's bodice has a high standing collar, derived from Spanish fashion, turned outwards to display the richly-embroidered lining. This replaced the low, square neckline that had been popular in England for the previous thirty years. The triangular shape of the stiffened bodice is balanced by the inverted triangle of the skirt, and yet another triangle is created by the forepart of richly-patterned brocade worn under the parted skirt. The collar of her smock has been left undone, the area filled with an elaborate pendant. Embroidery on the sleeves of the chemise, visible as puffs pulled through the aglet-decorated slashes on the bodice, matches the collar.

Lady Mary's wealth and status are indicated by the variety and quality of her jewellery: the pendant pinned to the opening of the bodice and the long jewelled girdle defining the waistline and ending in an elaborate pomander.
(Circle of Hans Eworth, *c*.1555, Petworth)

18 Bess of Hardwick, in a portrait painted *c.*1560. Her loose gown is lined with soft white fur and fastened down the front with aglets. The fur is also revealed through aglet-decorated slits on the short upper sleeves and sides of the gown, and it forms a neat collar. The bodice sleeves are embroidered in a geometric pattern of interlaced circles, and this design too is visible on the standing collar of what is either her smock or partlet. The ruff is still in its earliest state, merely an embroidered frill attached to the collar. Her French hood has a nether billiment of pearls, set on a border of crimped cypress, wired so that it curves onto the side of the face, whereas the curve of the top edge of the hood is defined by a billiment of engraved gold set with gems.

Bess always wore a rope of pearls in her portraits; in this one they are twisted around her neck, as dictated by the fashion of the time. Two interesting accessories are the enamelled link bracelets worn around the wrist. Bracelets of this type often appear in Elizabethan portraits, and a number of examples survive. (Follower of Hans Eworth, *c.*1560, Hardwick Hall)

> . . . every man shall eat in safety
> Under his own vine what he plants; and sing
> The merry songs of peace to all his neighbours.[18]

Inevitably, increasing social mobility brought with it words of warning from conservative observers. William Harrison, in his *Description of England*, 1577, looked back wistfully to a time when:

> an Englishman was known abroad by his own cloth and contented himself at home with his fine kersey [rough woollen cloth] hosen and a mean slop [wide breeches], his coat, gown and cloak of brown-blue or puke [blue-black], with some pretty furniture of velvet or fur, and a doublet of sad tawny [dark orange-brown] or black velvet or other comely silk, without such cuts and garish colours as are worn in these days and never brought in but by the consent of the French, who think themselves the gayest men when they have most diversities of jags and change of colours about them.[19]

There was also concern that dress should reflect the wearer's class, rank and profession, as it had done in earlier centuries. A series of ten proclamations, sumptuary legislation, was issued by Elizabeth I between 1559 and 1597. (See also p.289.) These divided society into nine groups, with Dukes and Earls at the top, and servingmen at the bottom, the levels in between being determined by annual income and the value of property owned. This legislation sought to define exactly what fur, fabric and trimming could be worn by each rank, but it is doubtful whether such stipulations could be enforced. Sir John Harington, the Queen's godson, wrote an epigram about the ineffectiveness of the law:

> . . . Apparells great excess;
> For though the laws against yt are express,
> Each Lady like a Queen herself doth dress,
> A merchaunts wife like to be a barroness.[20]

That the English loved a show is apparent in many contemporary descriptions. The equation of ostentatious display with strength and power gave rise to ceremonial occasions at which the hierarchical system was clearly shown by the style of dress worn by the participants. A person of importance proclaimed his status by his choice of dress and jewels and by the number of liveried servants who accompanied him in public – the assumption being that the greater the number of retainers, the more important the man. The most common livery was broadcloth trunk hose and coat with the badge or 'cognizance' of the household embroidered on the left sleeve. When the noblemen and their retainers were all gathered together in their brilliantly-coloured liveries it made 'a goodlie sight . . . which doth yeeld the contemplation of a noble varietie unto the beholder, much like to the shew of the peacockes taile in the full beautie, or some meadow garnished with infinite kinds and diversitie of pleasant floures'.[21]

In 1595 Breuning von Buchenbach visited the English court at the head of an embassy from Duke Frederick of Würtemberg. He noted the many 'earls, lords, and knights. They all wore gold and silver dress and their raiment embroidered with precious stones and pearls. At no other court have I ever seen so much splendour and such fine clothes.'²² (See also **257**.) This blatant and indiscriminate display of jewels and shimmering luxury fabrics not only had the desired effect of confirming the strength and wealth of the country, but it also meant that a visit to court was expensive. Many changes of wardrobe were required, and any reduction in the quality of the outfits or any repetition of them would soon be noticed and commented on.

The court was a compact society comprising all the officials of the Royal Household. Technically, any gentleman could be admitted to the court, but to be noticed, and thus in a position to gain preferment, it was essential to be introduced by a father or uncle already present at court, or to be a member of a family with an established tradition of service to the crown. Any man who was not fortunate enough to have such family ties would have to find a patron, for being at court without a friend was like being 'a hop without a pole'. The wives of some of the great men held posts as Ladies of the Bedchamber or Privy Chamber and they would endeavour to find positions for their daughters and nieces as Maids of Honour to the Queen.

Many writers deplored the fact that men would squander the revenues of their estates in order to buy new clothes. Ben Jonson in his play *Every Man out of his Humour* (1590) writes: 'twere good you turned four or five hundred acres of your best land into two or three trunks of apparel'.²³ When Arthur, son of Sir Nicholas Throckmorton of Coughton Court, Warwickshire, went to court in 1583, he recorded in his diary that he financed his new clothes by selling part of his land and by borrowing his brother's legacy, on which he had to pay interest for many years.

During the first two decades of Queen Elizabeth's reign, fashion for men and women moved at a much faster pace, replacing the dignified sobriety of the 1550s with a softer, less rigid style in the 1560s. This favoured much brighter colours (see p.31) and an enlivening of plain surfaces again, with applied decoration like embroidery, pearls, gems and braid. Surfaces could be 'pinked' – that is they were cut in small holes or slits arranged to form a pattern; 'paned' – when a vertical slash exposed material of a contrasting colour underneath; and 'puffed' – a decorative effect produced when material was drawn through slashes and panes in 'puffs' (**19, 20** and **21**).

A comparison between a portrait of Sir Nicholas Throckmorton painted early in 1562 (**20**) with one of Robert Dudley, Earl of Leicester, painted *c.*1575–80 (**21**) shows the later proliferation of decorative detailing and the change in the male silhouette after padding was used to create the swollen appearance of the doublet and hose. Throckmorton was Elizabeth's ambassador to France when his portrait was painted. Leicester was the Queen's supreme favourite for more than twenty years, until his death in 1588. His intense love of finery earned him a respected position as an arbiter of taste amongst the fashionable men at Elizabeth's court, but he ran up enormous debts with mercers, tailors and other suppliers in the process.

During the second two decades all the garments in these portraits were to become the subject of exaggeration, but in the portrait of Leicester they are in a state of perfect balance, with their volume equally distributed between the doublet and the hose. After this date each garment developed independently and the balance broke down: the doublet belly swelled out and under, into the curious peascod shape; and the hose shrank to a mere pad around the hips. The ruff, previously so carefully contained above the collar, was destined to extend far beyond it so that the head effectively became

19 (*right*) Pinking and paning have been employed on the doublet worn by Thomas Radcliffe, 3rd Earl of Sussex, in this portrait of the early 1560s. Gems have been scattered over the cloak and also form a hatband on the bonnet. As a Knight of the Garter, the Earl proudly displays the Lesser George around his neck. (Follower of Antonio Mor, 1560s, Anglesey Abbey)

20 (*far right*) Sir Nicholas Throckmorton wears a suit – a matching set of garments – consisting of a doublet, trunk hose and a cloak draped across the shoulders. His doublet has a small standing collar, and is fastened down the centre with little gold buttons. A roll of stiffened fabric, called a wing or epaulette, hides the join between the sleeve and the armholes of the doublet, and the sleeves and the doublet body are both decorated with alternate pinked bands of material producing a striped effect. A ruff edged with bobbin lace matches the ruffs round the wrists. A handkerchief, a fashionable accessory, is prominently displayed in a pocket suspended from a matching girdle, the dagger and sword echo its finely worked gold frame. (Unknown, probably French artist, 1562, Montacute)

disconnected from the body. The ruff was pinned to a wire frame called an under-propper or supportasse, which held it at the required angle. Decoration, whether pinking, slashing, braid, lace or embroidery, became more prolific as the garments filled out and increased in volume.

Decoration also took on an important role in women's fashions. A portrait of Katherine Vaux (22), Sir Nicholas Throckmorton's mother, dated 1576, shows a wonderfully complex and exuberant costume, an example of the experimentation with surface decoration that took an almost *trompe-l'oeil* form in the 1570s.

In contrast was the smock, worn under these highly-decorated garments. It was usually made and embroidered by the lady of the house herself. It consisted of two pieces of lawn or linen joined at the sides and could have a square neckline or small collar. Sleeves were always long and the area nearest the hand, 'the sleeve hand', was usually embroidered, as were the collar, hem and neckline.

Men's shirts were cut in a very similar way to women's smocks and were also decorated with embroidery. In John Eliot's *The Parlement of Prattlers*, 1593, a book

21 The cream satin doublet worn by Robert Dudley, Earl of Leicester, shares the same waistline as Throckmorton's but has a much higher standing collar and is decorated with narrow bands of gold braid alternating with bands of pinking. His trunk hose has the onion shape typical of the 1570s, cut into panes that disclose the gold satin lining. The limited range of colours – black, white and gold – creates a dramatic background for the Earl's splendid Garter collar with its enamelled Great George. Elegant square-cut black gems set in gold form a central seam down the sleeves of his short, fur-lined black cloak (it could also be a gown), and round the brim of his bonnet.
(Unknown artist, c.1575–80, Montacute)

intended to help children learn how to converse in French, there is a dialogue between John and his servant in which the boy brings John a smock by mistake:

Boy: Pardon me sir, if it please you, I am deceived it is my mistresse smock.
John: Wretchlesse boy thou wilt make me smell of the smocke all today and tomorrowe.[24]

John was annoyed because his wife's smock, unlike *his* shirt, would have been perfumed.

Embroidered shirts could be very expensive if bought ready-made from a seamstress. The Puritan pamphleteer Philip Stubbes complained in 1583 that you could buy shirts covered in 'needleworke of silk, and curiouslie stitched with open seame, and many other knackes beseydes . . . some ten shillings, some twentie, some fortie, some five pound, . . . some ten pounds a peece.'[25]

In the Elizabethan period elevation in status was often celebrated by commissioning a portrait, for which the acquisition of new clothes was essential. When the astrologer Simon Forman married in 1599 he spent £50 on a new gown, breeches, cloak and cap for himself and new clothes for his wife and then they both sat for their portraits.[26] If the sitter held a distinguished office the artist would give the symbols of that position a prominent place in the portrait: an officer of the Royal Household would carry his white wand; if the sitter was a military commander he would be shown holding his baton; and a Knight of the Garter would invariably wear the Lesser or Great George, jewelled pendant badges of the order (see **19** and **21**).

An artist commissioned to paint a portrait knew that it was intended to be a record of wealth and status and that he would be expected to portray the sitter's clothes and jewellery in as precise and detailed a way as possible. Painters adapted their style of painting in order to satisfy the demands of their patrons. It was a trend strengthened by the Queen's preferred manner of portraiture, and her choice of the miniaturist Nicholas Hilliard, a brilliant colourist, endorsed a style that lasted for nearly forty years. Her first sitting for Hilliard in 1572 took place in 'the open alley of a goodly garden where no tree was near, nor any shadow at all'.[27] The two-dimensional impression that resulted from this sitting reduced the face to an impassive mask, but it gave the artist the freedom to concentrate on the intricacy and complexity of decorative detail that was such a characteristic of this flamboyant period in costume history. An example of this style can be found in George Gower's 1577 portrait of Elizabeth Knollys, whose mask-like face is but one part of an interlocking pattern of lace, embroidery and jewels (**23**).

It is difficult now to understand the importance of colour for the Elizabethans, for the brilliant colours that we see in embroidery are not only indicative of an intense love of the natural world but they also speak a language of their own, as each colour had a particular meaning. Richard Robinson's translation of an Italian treatise on the symbolism of colours was published in 1583, and explains, for example, Queen Elizabeth's insistence that her six Maids of Honour should wear a white and silver costume when at court: 'white indicated faith, humility, and chastity: silver, purity'.[28]

Colours with negative values were black, which signified grief and constancy; grey for despair and ash for trouble and sadness. Yellow was a positive colour as it represented hope, joy and magnanimity, whereas yellow-red was deception. Russet,

22 The top garment in this portrait of Katherine Vaux is a gown, the high collar of which has been turned back to create revers. Its lining, displayed as revers, the sleeves and the partlet are all made from a semi-transparent, gauzy material embroidered with a delightful pattern of roses and strawberry plants. Above the curved line of the bodice, underneath the partlet, can be seen the embroidered edge of the smock. A pendant attached to a ribbon is worn in the fashionable way – off centre – and a pearl collar rests under the collar of the partlet. Aglets are scattered all over the gown.
(Unknown artist, 1576, Coughton Court)

23 Elizabeth Knollys, Lady Layton, one of the Queen's Maids of Honour, showing outdoor clothing for a wealthy lady. Her short-sleeved gown is decorated with aglet-trimmed bows and tasselled bands of braid. The liberal display of jewels, commensurate with her position in society, consists of a rope of pearls and gems draped across the chest, and a pendant of a dove and a snake – emblems of mildness and prudence – attached to a loop of twisted braid. Her high-crowned hat has a magnificent jewelled hatband, ostrich feather and large jewel in the form of a starfish and coral.
(After George Gower, 1577, Montacute)

with its association with country values, was prudence. Green was the colour of love and joy, but turquoise (from the French *pierre turquoise*, Turkish stone) was jealousy. As red was associated with courage it was not surprising that both Mary, Queen of Scots and Robert Devereux, Earl of Essex, chose a colour scheme of red and black with which to meet their end on the executioner's block.

To extend the range of colours available new dyes had to be found – a matter of some importance for those in the textile trade. Sources in other countries were eagerly sought out and experimented with. In 1579 a dyer, Morgan Hubblethorne, was sent to Persia to learn of 'great colouring of silks'. He was told to 'have great care to have knowledge of the materials of all the countreys that you shall passe thorow, that may be used in dying, be they hearbs, weeds, bark, gummes, earths or what els soever'.[29]

Materials were available in a wide range of colours, for the primary colours were divided into a number of subtly different tones, each of which had a particular name. The most vivid tone of red, for example, was lustie gallant and the palest was maiden's blush. Between these two extremes there was a choice of Catherine pear, carnation, incarnate, sangwyn, stammel, flame, gingerline, murrey and peach. The new colours that proliferated during Elizabeth's reign were assigned picturesque and 'fantastical' names that are, nevertheless, self-explanatory, like 'gooseturd green, pease-porridge tawny, popinjay blue'.[30] A refined sense of colour led to an appreciation of the different effects of light and shade on fabrics when varying textures like satin, velvet, taffeta and fur were combined in a single outfit. Further displays of great beauty and richness were created when the pile of velvet, woven on a ground of a contrasting colour, was cut away to create a pattern of opulent richness. A surface could be further embellished by embroidery with coloured silks, gold or silver thread and the application of seed pearls, spangles and oes (small rings or eyelets).

One of the more obvious problems in studying dress of this period is the scarcity of extant garments, those that have survived being mostly embroidered jackets, gloves, coifs, partlets and forehead cloths. These tend to represent a selection of the labours of the domestic embroiderer, who was creating garments to be worn at home and whose work does not necessarily illustrate contemporary high fashion. Of the magnificent clothes worn at the court of Elizabeth absolutely nothing remains, and we can only imagine their appearance by looking at portraits (24, 31 and 257).

The eighteenth-century chronicler and historian, Horace Walpole, dismissed late Elizabethan dress as a 'vast ruff, a vaster farthingale and a bushel of pearls',[31] but to its contemporaries exaggeration was an end in itself, and creating a style that to our eyes might be excessive would have elicited admiration and respect from their peers. The process of starching and then arranging the 'vast ruff' was perhaps the most time-consuming activity, and one that men and women alike had to undertake.

Starch was introduced into England in 1564 by a Dutch lady, Dinghen van den Plasse. It was usually made out of wheat and had to be boiled before use. This was a tricky process and the starch often burned or thickened too quickly. (A soluble starch, made from rice, was not developed until the 1840s, when the potato famine in Ireland forced up grain prices and starch manufacturers had to find a cheaper source.)

Securing the immense circle of starched material and then tilting it at the appropriate angle resulted in the 'burning out many pounds of Candle',[32] and the end result would be completely ruined if one was caught in a shower, when it would 'goe flip flap in the winde, like rags flying abroad, and lye upon their shoulders like the dishcloute of a slut'.[33] The extent of the circular ruff worn in the 1580s can be seen in a version of the famous 'Armada' portrait of Queen Elizabeth – painted to commemorate the defeat of the Spanish in 1588 (24). The Queen's ruff, made of cutwork, has been arranged over an underpropper so that it is tilted at an acute angle.

24 In this version of the 'Armada' portrait, the original of which is at Woburn, Queen Elizabeth's bodice is front-fastening, ending in an extended point. The wings, where the sleeves join the bodice, are decorated with bands of pearls and gem-studded bows, and the white satin sleeves and matching petticoat have been embroidered with golden stars and set with gems. (By or after George Gower, *c*.1588, Montacute)

As every part of female dress was stiffened at this time, an extremely unnatural shape was created, but it presented endless opportunities for embellishment and decoration. The bodice could either be front-fastening and end in an extended point, or it could have a V-shaped opening in front filled with a stomacher. This was an inverted triangle of material, lined with pasteboard or canvas and stiffened with whalebone busks (strips of wood, whalebone or metal inserted into the casing), that bypassed the waist and extended right down the skirt. The greatest wish of one fourteen-year-old girl in 1597, the daughter of a gentleman from Lancashire called Starkie, was to have a bodice 'not of

25 Hardwick Hall has a very rich collection of Elizabethan embroidery, including a cushion depicting the Judgement of Solomon, recorded in the 1601 inventory as being in one of the windows of the Long Gallery. This detail shows the exaggerated styles worn in the 1580s at the court of Henri III of France, many features of which were incorporated into English court dress. The man on the right wears a cartwheel ruff of immense size, a heavily padded doublet, the short flared French cloak, minimal trunk hose, close-fitting canions and, on his feet, backless pantofles or overshoes. His companion wears Venetians (full breeches closed at the knees) that match his doublet, a rope of pearls and an elegant lace falling band.

whalebone for that is not stiff enough but of horne, for that will hold it out . . . to keep in my belly'. Sleeves were also distended, with wire and whalebone, and padded so that they reached an enormous width. The same girl wanted 'sleeves set out with wires for stickes wil break, and are not stiffe enough'.[34]

The French farthingale that appeared in 1580 gave the skirt a tub-shaped hang and this in turn was replaced at the end of the decade by the even more extreme shape of the wheel farthingale (see 30). This structure carried the skirt out at right angles from the waist to a width varying from 8 to 48in before falling vertically to the ground. To avoid the hard line made by the rim of the wheel farthingale the skirt was given a circular frill or flounce, the pleats of which radiated out from the centre to the edge of the rim. The whole skirt was then tilted at the waist so that the hem was raised at the back and lowered in the front. Wearing the farthingale at this angle enabled the wearer to rest her hands on the ledge-like surface of the flounce, a stance that the same fourteen-year-old wanted to adopt, as she requested a 'French farthingale laid low before and high behind and broad on either side so that I may laye mine arms on it'.[35]

Hair has now 'curled, frisled and crisped, laid out (A world to see!) on wreathes and borders from one eare to another . . . underpropped with forks, wyers and I can not tel what'.[36] No longer neatly parted in the middle, hair was raised over a wired support which gave it a dip in the centre with a widening at the temples. After about 1590 it was brushed up from the forehead into a bouffant style, still supported but without the dip. The Queen popularised the wearing of false hair when she lost her own after catching smallpox in 1562 and had to resort to an auburn-coloured wig.

An insistence on wearing fashions that were 'farre-fetched and deare bought'[37] led the upper-class Elizabethans to flit excitedly and indiscriminately from one exaggerated foreign style to another, adding to them a love of glittering surface decoration. The end result, according to the satirist Thomas Nashe, writing in 1593, was a disastrous one that left England as 'the Players stage of gorgeous attyre, the Ape of all Nations superfluities, the continual Masquer in outlandish habilements'.[38] His use of the word 'masque' in connection with contemporary fashion is illuminating, suggesting that fashionable dress resembled the exotic costumes that would be worn in a theatrical masque and, as such, were quite unsuitable for normal everyday life. This element of fantasy is characteristic not only of dress but of architecture, painting, sculpture and the decorative arts, endowing them with the unselfconscious exuberance and vitality that are their outstanding qualities.

In his play *Midas*, first performed in 1590 and published in 1592, John Lyly wrote: 'Traffic and travel hath woven the nature of all nations into ours, and made this land like arras, full of device, which was broadcloth, full of workmanship.'[39] It is an interesting simile that suggests that increased trade with other countries, and travel abroad, had enriched rather than diminished England. Philip Stubbes wrote more censoriously in 1583: 'But now there is such a confuse mingle mangle of apparell in Ailgna [England] . . . that it is verie hard to know who is noble, who is worshipfull, who is a gentleman and who is not.'[40]

The Tudors perceived that visitors equated lavish display at court with national strength and power. For many it was more important to have seen Queen Elizabeth than to have seen England, an attitude which underlines the success of the Tudor propaganda machine. One such was Baron Zdenek Waldstein of Moravia, who visited England in the summer of 1600 and was granted an audience with the Queen at Greenwich Palace. In his speech he explained he 'had hoped and prayed for nothing so much' than that he should 'one day set foot in this glorious Kingdom of England, and that at the same time I might come face to face into the presence of your Majesty' thus achieving 'the greatest object of my journey'.[41] The figure of the Queen 'glittering with the glory of majesty and adorned with jewellry and precious gems', and those of her equally resplendent courtiers had become a symbol of England's national unity and international success.

However, we know that Queen Elizabeth also enjoyed wearing the dress of other countries. In 1577, Dr Thomas Wilson, ambassador for England in Flanders, told Don John of Austria that Elizabeth wore 'diverse attires, Italian, Spanish and French, as occasion served'[42] and that he would be sent a portrait of the Queen wearing Spanish dress. Even the subsequent war against Spain did not cause Elizabeth to throw out the Spanish gowns in her wardrobe, and many are recorded in the 1599 inventory (see below).[43] Nor was there any interruption to the importation of Spanish leather from Cordoba during the hostilities. It was the finest quality leather in Europe and continued to be used to make the most expensive gloves, boots and jerkins.

Queen Elizabeth also used dress to make political points and on one occasion she attempted, in a very clandestine way, to obtain the services of a tailor who worked for the French Queen Mother, Catherine de Medici. So William Cecil, Lord Burghley,

26 An extremely rare example of a loose gown dating from between 1600 and 1610. Made from rich mulberry-coloured satin and lined throughout, it is thought from its style and size to have been worn by a man, though tradition links it with Bess of Hardwick, who died at Hardwick Hall in 1608 at the grand age of 88. This detail, the top of the sleeve and the wing, shows that the wing was composed of a series of tabs, each edged with a strip of satin.

instructed the English representative at Catherine's court in Paris of Elizabeth's intentions: 'The Queen would fain have a tailor that has skill to make her apparel both after the French and Italian manner and thinketh you might use some one as suiteth the Queen [Catherine de Medici] without mentioning any manner of request in the Queen Majesty's name . . . as she does not want to be beholden to her.'[44] Her ploy must have succeeded for in 1582, when her marriage negotiations with Catherine's son, the Duc d'Alençon, were at their height, a full-length portrait of Queen Elizabeth was painted for Catherine and displayed at the Valois court. 'The ladies marvelled at the size of the pearls on her dress and noted with satisfaction that she was attired all over *à la Française.*'[45]

These royal clothes were ordered from the Great Wardrobe, a separate government department. It maintained and stored the huge stock of costumes accumulated by the crown and purchased and made up new outfits for the monarch and officers of the court when ordered to do so. It had a separate budget and every year the accounts were presented to the Exchequer and the Treasury by the Master of the Wardrobe. In 1599 an inventory was made of the Great Wardrobe, showing that the Queen owned some 1,326 items, including robes that had belonged to her predecessors, Edward VI and Mary. The staff of the Great Wardrobe included seamstresses, tailors and embroiderers working full-time remaking and mending existing garments and keeping the stock clean and aired. It took one man a whole day just to beat and air the Queen's muffs, for example.

To be noticed at Elizabeth's court it was certainly essential to be dressed in the height of fashion – whether this meant being the 'ape of fashion' was irrelevant. Every aspiring courtier knew that the Queen expected him to look immaculate and fashionable at all times, so that if he was to make an impact much effort, imagination and money would have to be spent on his appearance. Even if one had to 'lie ten nights awake, carving the fashion of a new doublet', then so be it.[46]

When Arthur Throckmorton went to court in 1583 a note at the end of his diary for that year states that cloth of tinsel (an extremely expensive material of silk or wool interwoven with gold or silver thread) was purchased for a cypress silk suit, with silk ribbon for a matching cloak, and a payment of £6 1s was made for eighteen gold buttons to decorate it. This was in addition to a new suit of tawny velvet decorated with tawny satin and taffeta, matching silk stockings, a beaver hat, two dozen points, ruffs and bands and the silvering of his rapier. He also bought liveries of purple cloth with crimson and yellow velvet guards for his band of retainers and spent the considerable sum of £12 on a jewel to present to the Queen.[47]

On 8 November 1584 Arthur recorded that he 'came and dined at Hampton Court. My sister was sworn of the Privy Chamber.' This was an event of great importance for the family as his sister Elizabeth had been made a Maid of Honour and so was admitted to the Queen's inner circle. Unfortunately, by 1591 Elizabeth Throckmorton had fallen in love with one of Queen Elizabeth's favourite courtiers, Sir Walter Raleigh. She became pregnant and on 19 November they were secretly married. On 29 March 1592 Arthur wrote that 'my sister was delivered of a boy between 2 and 3 in the afternoon' and that on 27 April she returned to Court as if nothing had happened,[48] the baby having been dispatched to relatives in Enfield in Middlesex. Failing to inform the Queen of these events was tantamount to treason, as those holding office at court had to seek her

27 Sir Walter Raleigh's choice of black and white, liberally embellished with pearls, for his outfit was deliberate, as they were the colours of the Queen. Another possible allusion to the Queen is to be seen in the top left corner of the portrait, where a damaged Latin motto signifying 'by love and virtue' is accompanied by a crescent moon, a reference to Elizabeth as Cynthia, goddess of the moon. Slung nonchalantly over Raleigh's shoulder is a beautiful black velvet cloak lined with sable fur, its surface embroidered with sun rays worked in seed pearl ending in a pearl trefoil. He has chosen to wear the alternative, and simpler, style of neckwear to the ruff – a triple-layered falling band of plain lawn.
(Monogrammist H, 1588, Montacute)

permission before they could even contemplate marriage. Needless to say she soon discovered the couple's guilty secret. Raleigh was sent to the Tower of London for five weeks and was only released so that he could command a fleet sailing to the West Indies. Elizabeth remained in the Tower until the end of the year.

Raleigh was a very good-looking man who loved fine clothes and his dramatic taste in dress can be gauged from a 1588 portrait (27). When this portrait was painted the doublet had acquired its characteristic peascod shape, achieved by stiffening it with pasteboard or whalebone busks, and was so heavily padded at the extended point of the waist that it almost curled back on itself. Writing about these 'monstrous' garments Stubbes observed that the padding is so dense that the wearers 'hardly eyther stoupe downe, or decline themselues to the grounde, soe styffe and sturdy they stand about them'.[49] Sleeves are similarly padded, but, the swollen trunk hose worn by Leicester (see 21) in the previous decade has shrunk in shape and is cut into pearl-decorated panes.

A comparison of the portrait of Sir Robert Carey, 1st Earl of Monmouth, painted *c*.1591 (28), with that of Sir William Herbert (created Lord Powis in 1629), painted in 1595 (29) reveals a gradual deflation in the male silhouette as the taut, tense line of padded doublet and minimal trunk hose gave way to a more relaxed and romantic style. Thomas Middleton wrote in the preface to his play *The Roaring Girl*, 1611, written with T. Dekker, that 'The fashion of play-making I can properly compare to nothing so naturally, as the alteration in apparell: for in the time of the great-crop-doublet, your huge bombasted plays, quilted with mighty wordes to lean purpose was only then in fashion.'[50] The dramatic equivalent of the padded doublet was the verbose and long-winded play of the period.

The companion portrait of Sir William's wife, Lady Eleanor Percy, daughter of the 8th Earl of Northumberland, also painted in 1595 (30), shows the development of female fashion, and in particular of the farthingale. In Peter Erondell's French/English phrase book *The French Garden*, 1605, there is an exchange between Lady Ri-Mellaine and her maid while she is being dressed in the morning which gives an idea of the amount of time involved in placing so many garments on the body, the intricate task of pinning and tying them together, the arrangement of the lady's hair and accessories and the application of cosmetics.

Her maid's first task was to warm her smock. When she had put it on it was covered by the whalebone-stiffened bodice of her petticoat, which was tightly laced in position, to be followed by a petticoat skirt of 'wroughte [embroidered] Crimson velvet with silver fringe'. Her stockings were secured by garters and the maid then tied her Spanish leather shoes – chosen because the lady wanted to go out for a walk. The next task was to arrange the lady's hair, so a cloth was placed over her shoulders while the hair was combed thoroughly. The maid was told to bring some jewels to decorate her hair and some laces to bind it, and to sort out the head-dress – a French hood with a border of rubies. She then used a piece of scarlet cloth to 'scour' her face with paste of almond and dried it with a napkin. Once a carcenet (a heavy necklace resembling a collar) had been arranged round her throat, and agate bracelets round her wrists, the tailor was ordered to bring an 'open gowne of white Sattin layed on with buttons of Pearle'.

The next stage of dressing was the most tricky – the selection and fixing of neckwear. After some deliberation Lady Ri-Mellaine chose a cutwork rebato (a shaped collar wired to stand up around the back of the head) which was carefully pinned to the bodice at the appropriate angle. Her cuffs were secured with 'small pinnes' from the pincushion – without which the process of dressing would have been impossible. After the farthingale and gown had been put into position a girdle was placed around her waist and a variety of useful items were attached to it. These included scissors, pincers, a knife to open letters, a penknife, a bodkin, an earpicker and a seal. Other accessories brought to her were a comfit-box, a mask, a fan, a handkerchief, gloves and a rope of pearls. On the completion of her dressing the maid was bidden to pick up her discarded night clothes and 'put them in the cushen cloth'.[51]

This daily ritual was even more elaborate when applied to the Queen as each of her ladies-in-waiting had a specific task allotted to her. One of them, a Gentlewoman of the Privy Chamber, had the responsibility of keeping a Day Book in which she recorded all items leaving the Wardrobe and listed any jewels worn by the Queen or sewn onto her costumes that had been mislaid at the end of the day. Hence an entry for 1578 which reads: 'Item loste from her Majesties backe the xxxith of Marche at Grenewich from a

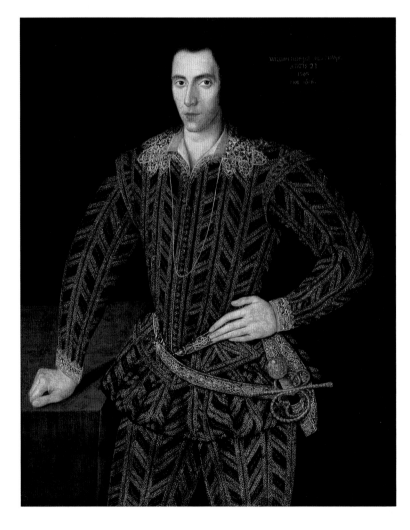

28 (*left*) Robert Carey, later 1st Earl of Monmouth, in an outfit that is a striking illustration of the last stage of the peascod-bodied doublet, now so exaggerated that it turns in on itself, while the trunk hose has been reduced to a pearl-studded roll. Like Raleigh (**27**), Carey obviously loved pearls and has, unusually, chosen to wear ropes of them across his body like a sash, and there is beautiful pearl embroidery on his cloak.
(English School, *c*.1591, Montacute)

29 (*below far left*) Sir William Herbert in a matching doublet and hose decorated in a chevron pattern of braid. In keeping with the more comfortable style, he wears his shirt undone, with its lace-trimmed collar lying on his shoulders.
(Unknown English artist, 1595, Powis Castle)

30 (*below left*) Lady Eleanor Herbert is depicted in a wheel farthingale under a red velvet flounced skirt. Her stomacher and matching sleeves have been embroidered in a pattern of foliating flowers, with the surface given extra interest by a covering of ruched gauze. This delicate transparent material is framed by heavy braid-edged hanging sleeves that match the bodice. Her elaborate ruff is composed of deep cylinders of sheer lawn edged with gossamer-fine lace and hanging spangles that lie on top of one another in magnificent profusion.

Lady Eleanor indicates her allegiance to the old faith by wearing a jewelled cross. Other jewellery includes three elaborate pendants: one pinned to her bodice, another fixed to a sleeve, and a third worn in the hair. A long jewelled chain is attached to either side of the bodice, and a gem- and pearl-studded band encircles her left arm. She holds the latest accessory – a folding fan.
(Unknown English artist, 1595, Powis Castle)

Gowne of clothe of golde with roses and honysuckles one dyamounde oute of a Claspe of golde.'[52]

When Thomas Platter saw Elizabeth I in 1599 he found she was 'most lavishly attired in a gown of pure white satin, gold-embroidered . . . in short she was most gorgeously apparelled'.[53] As we have seen, nothing has survived of her 'inestimable wardrobe', but a portrait of the Queen at Hardwick Hall gives some idea of her appearance (**31**).

Opinion has always been divided as to whether her flamboyantly-patterned white satin forepart and stomacher, with their extraordinary diversity of life-like motifs, were actually embroidered or stained (ie painted), but it is now thought that the skirt was embroidered and that it was Bess of Hardwick (by then Countess of Shrewsbury), who masterminded the design, and possibly worked on it herself, intending it to be a spectacular New Year's Day gift to the Queen.[54] It is typical of the extravagant and sometimes bizarre late-Elizabethan style of embroidery which mixed together all manner of motifs taken from the natural world, whatever the discrepancies in scale. A variety of flowers, including roses, irises and pansies, are interspersed with a lively depiction of insects, animals and fish, amongst which are fearsome sea-monsters, a crab and a whale spouting water (**32**). Sources for these motifs could be found in illustrations in natural history books, emblem books and herbals, the most famous of which was John Gerard's *Herbal or General History of Plants* published in 1597. Flowers and embroidery were apparently linked together in the Elizabethan mind, as suggested by a passage in Gerard's dedication to Lord Burghley: 'For if delight may provoke men's labour, what grater delight is there than to behold the earth apparelled with plants, as with a robe of imbrodered works, set with orient pearles and garnished with great diversitie of rare and costly jewels.'[55]

On New Year's Day everyone in the Queen's household, from the noblest to the most humble, was expected to give her a gift, in return for which they would receive money, or its equivalent in plate. Jewellery was a popular choice of gift and in 1584 they ranged from Sir Christopher Hatton's spectacular 'Attyre for the head containing vii peeces of golde, iii of them being Crownes of golde emperyal garnished with smale dyamonds, Rubyes, Perles and opalls on the one side and the other being Victoryes [allegorical figures holding an olive branch, probably made from enamelled gold and depicting Victory] garnished with diamonds Rubyes perles and opalls', to Mr Newall's gift of a tiny gold spade, set with mother of pearl and diamonds, that could be pinned onto a ruff.[56] Embroidered sweetbags, filled with sweetmeats or money, were another popular and less expensive choice, and when embroidered with gold and silver thread, pearls and spangles made extremely attractive accessories (see **37**).

In *The Parlement of Prattlers*, 1593, there is a dialogue set in a goldsmith's shop between the proprietor, Smith, and Jane, a customer. Jane asks Smith if he has either a pendant made of jet 'after the manner of France' or a topaz set in gold. Smith replies that he has neither, but he can show her a 'verie faire Turqouis'. After expressing her approval of the stone Jane wants to know where it came from and is surprised to learn that it originated in far-off 'Quinzay [Cathay] the imperiall State among the Chinos'. She then asks the goldsmith if he could create a ring similar to those sold in Venice, with a 'faire christall' under which is set a 'little Scorpio of iron wagging his tail very artificially'. Smith replies, 'I have been in Italy and have seene many of the same making',

31 In this portrait of Queen Elizabeth even her shoes and gloves are encrusted with pearls – symbol of virginity – and gold jewels. Pearls of varying sizes, arranged in different patterns, dominate the decoration. A massive jewel, suspended on a red ribbon, has been pinned to the skirt. It comprises a spire or obelisk of six diamonds, with a base of a large square diamond and three square diamonds, each with a pendant pearl. There is also a female figure in gold on either side of the spire.

Elizabeth was very proud of her long elegant fingers. She draws attention to them by positioning one hand on a pair of gem-encrusted and gold-fringed gloves, whilst the other holds a white ostrich feather fan set in a sumptuous gold frame studded with rubies. Gloves, often perfumed, were an essential article of finery and conspicuous mark of rank for men and women. (Nicholas Hilliard and Rowland Lockey, *c.*1599, Hardwick Hall)

32 A detail from the Queen's portrait (**31**) showing a pansy from the hem of her skirt. Also known as love-in-idleness, heartsease and cupid's flower, the pansy (much smaller and less floppy than today's version), with its elegant leaves, made it a popular motif with the sixteenth-century embroiderer. It was one of Elizabeth's favourite flowers, frequently appearing on her clothes, together with the eglantine rose representing the honour of virgins.

and he offers to fashion one for ten crowns.[57] This brief interchange is interesting as it not only reveals how merchants would trade with the most distant areas of the known world to procure luxury goods, but also underlines the ease with which ideas could be transferred from one country to another.

Throughout the sixteenth century the craft of the goldsmith was one of the most international. Their close involvement with the financial affairs of their clients (see p.48), the assurance of princely patronage and the circulation of published designs meant that their work was never confined within the borders of a single country. They also had access to extraordinary sources of raw materials. The gold and silver bullion that flooded into the Hapsburg Empire from the Americas via Spain and Portugal was then fashioned by craftsmen in its Central European territories in Nuremberg, Munich, Frankfurt, Vienna and Antwerp into glittering jewels, studded with diamonds from India, rubies from Burma, sapphires from Ceylon and emeralds from Colombia. Pearls, those quintessential Elizabethan jewels, were grown in oyster fisheries on the Persian Gulf and the Gulf of Manaar, off the north-east coast of Ceylon, to reach Europe via the trading cities of Alexandria in Egypt and Madras in India.[58]

Increased demand for goods that were 'farre fetched and deare bought' meant that merchants must be men of great resilience and determination, risking their money to gamble on the safe arrival of goods over difficult land and sea routes. Whether they used the sea passage to India round the Cape of Good Hope (discovered by Vasco da Gama in 1498) or the overland route to the Far East through the Eastern Mediterranean and Asia, the duration of such journeys and their inherent dangers meant that a high profit had to be guaranteed when the goods finally reached their destination. From the twelfth century raw silk and woven silk fabrics had been one of the most valuable imports from China, but by the sixteenth century these were supplemented by silks, brocades and damasks from the Middle and Near East. Italy was famous for its wide range of silks, designed and woven in centres like Florence and Genoa, and these were exported throughout Europe via the marketing cities of Venice, Leghorn and Genoa. London mercers such as Sir Baptist Hicks (see p.82), whose shop at the sign of the White Bear, Cheapside, was frequented by all the luminaries of Elizabethan London society, made his fortune by employing representatives in Italy. Negotiating directly with the suppliers meant that Hicks was guaranteed a regular and secure supply of the very finest silks.

In 1606 Thomas Dekker the playwright, who was noted for his portrayal of daily life, wrote that the clothes of a fashionable Englishman are '[like] a traitors bodie that hath beene hanged, drawne, and quartered, and is set up in seuerall places: his Codpiece is in *Denmarke*, the collor of his Dublet, and the belly in *France*: the wing and narrow sleeue in *Italy*: the short waste hangs ouer a *Dutch* Botchers stall in Utrich: his huge sloppes speakes *Spanish*; Polonia gives him the Bootes'.[59] This description, though somewhat exaggerated, reflects the eclectic style of Elizabethan dress, which borrowed fashions from many countries. The fact that the English were famous, or rather notorious, for their constant and restless desire for new fashions and their apparent inability to create their own national style was a source of annoyance to some observers. But it also ensured the continuing success and expansion of the London fashion trade, enabling the customer to find an impressive display of materials and accessories that were 'farre fetched and deare bought'.

II

Shopping in sixteenth-century London must have been an exhilarating, though physically uncomfortable experience. Packed within the City walls and already spilling out into the suburbs were nearly a quarter of a million inhabitants, busily involved in buying and selling, manufacturing and finance. Although most of the wealth of England was concentrated in London it was shared by many people and was constantly changing hands. The city's position as an international trading centre was confirmed by the reports of many visitors from the continent. One remarked in 1599: 'This city of London is so vast and nobly built, so populous and excellent in crafts and merchant citizens, and so prosperous, that it is not only the first city in the whole realm of England, but is esteemed one of the most famous in the whole of Christendom.'[60] Unprecedented economic expansion had led to an increase in demand for fashion goods and a proliferation of the luxury fashion trades. The contemporary historian John Stow pointed out that items like starched ruffs, worsted stockings and embroidered and perfumed gloves, unheard of at the beginning of Queen Elizabeth's reign, could easily be purchased in London forty years later.[61]

A visit to London would not be undertaken lightly, however. Travelling anywhere in England was a very slow and hazardous business and, until the construction of coaches improved in the seventeenth century, would have been on horseback. Coaches had first appeared in England in the 1550s but were too flimsy to withstand the rigours of a long journey on a rough and narrow country road. They were also extremely uncomfortable, for they were no more than an unsprung wooden box on wheels with only a curtain hanging across the open side to keep out the elements (33, 34).

The only sturdy wheeled vehicles were the lumbering waggons that were used to transport goods all over the country. The first carrier service was started by Tobias Hobson in 1568 and was conducted between Cambridge and the Bell Inn in Bishopsgate, London.[62] Inns served a twofold purpose, providing both accommodation and stabling for the traveller and a collection point for the carrier. Goods could be left at an inn to await collection by the carrier who, for a substantial charge, would deliver them to any location in the country.

There were three main routes into London and journey's end was determined by the area of the country served. If one's journey originated in Kent, Surrey or Sussex one either stayed south of the river in one of the Southwark inns, or carried on over London Bridge (35), along Fish Street and up the steep gradient of Fish Street Hill to the Mitre Inn or the Sun Inn. This road was the main thoroughfare to the City, giving access to the gates through which travellers from the northern, western and eastern provinces of England entered the City. To the Bull and Mouth Inn in St Martin's Le Grand and the inns of Aldersgate came travellers from the Midlands and the North, while the Saracen's Head at Aldgate and the inns in Bishopsgate were the terminus points for travellers from East Anglia.

A visitor arriving in London from a small, sleepy country town or village must have found the intense concentration of people and incessant noise an overwhelming and

33 and 34 These two manuscript illustrations dated 1597 show how uncomfortable travelling must have been at the end of the sixteenth century, and that a face-mask was essential to protect against the weather and dirt. Progress in the top vehicle, a wooden box with a curved roof supported on poles harnessed to the two horses or mules, would have been extremely slow. The other vehicle, driven by a coachman, is more substantial with its half-door and what appears to be internal upholstery, but the lack of springs and the large studded wooden wheels would have produced a most unpleasant jolting motion over rough terrain.

35 When Visscher engraved this picture in 1616, London Bridge was the only one to span the Thames. He provides a vivid impression of the traveller's first view of London, passing by the huddle of shops, with their projecting signboards and tall narrow frontages, on the South Bank, and entering the bridge through an imposing gateway. In Elizabeth's reign the gory practice of displaying the heads of traitors on poles was transferred from the gate at the City End to the Southwark end, which subsequently became known as the Traitor's Gate.

intimidating experience. The deafening noise is vividly described by Thomas Dekker:

> . . . in euery street, carts and Coaches make such a thundring as if the world ranne upon wheeles: at euerie corner, men, women, and children meete in such shoales, that postes are sette up of purpose to strengthen the house, least with iustling one another they should shoulder them downe. Besides, hammers are beating in one place, Tubs hooping in another, Pots clincking in a third, water-tankards running at tilt in a fourth: here are Porters sweating under burdens, there a Marchants-men bearing bags of money.[63]

Inside the City walls there was a maze of dark and narrow streets where the overhanging storeys of the wooden houses contributed to the claustrophobic atmosphere. When Fynes Moryson visited London in the 1590s he found that the houses of the citizens of London were 'very narrow in the front towards the street, but are built 5 or 6 rooves high'.[64] This type of construction caused the houses to lean at such bizarre angles that they provided 'umbrellas of tiles to intercept the sun . . . where the garrets (perhaps not for want of architecture, but through abundance of amity) are so made that opposite neighbours may shake hands without stirring from home'.[65] Unpaved muddy streets, criss-crossed by fetid streams of household refuse and the contents of chamberpots, ensured that any walk through the streets was an obstacle course.

In the centre of the City were the richly-decorated houses of the merchants, the trade of each denoted by a painted and gilded – usually wooden – sign which projected out from the façade of the building. As the symbol on the sign did not necessarily have any connection with the contents of the shop (and the same sign could be used by different trades) it was essential to know which street a particular shop was located in. As houses were not distinguished by numbers, addresses had to be related to the nearest shop sign or other distinct landmark. Philip Gawdy's address in 1588 was the 'next house in fleat street to the hanging sword at Danyelles a tayler'.[66]

An apprentice would stand outside the shop and try to gain customers for his master by informing passers-by of what was available inside: 'What lacke you Gentlewoman? What seeke you Gentleman?' The proprietor and his family would live above the premises and use the back of the shop as a workroom, leaving the ground-floor area for storage and display. The wooden shutters over the windows would be let down during the day to form a counter, covered with fabric, on which to place the shop's most enticing goods.

Shop interiors were dark and, even when lit by candles, inferior goods were often palmed off onto the unsuspecting customer, so it was generally forbidden to sell goods by candlelight. John Florio's proverb of 1578 – 'Neither a woman, nor lynnen, chuse thou by a candle' – was probably prompted by personal experience.[67] As there were no set prices the customer was expected to bargain – a lengthy process that often ended in recriminations and insults on both sides. Tricks were also played with money: if, for example, the customer offered a worn silver coin it would be placed on the scales with more coins until the true weight was made up; and customers were advised to check their change for counterfeit money.

Each trade or craft congregated in a specific area of London. The most exclusive mercers, haberdashers and goldsmiths were centred in Cheapside, the widest and, judging from the comments of visitors, the most impressive street in London. That was the place to visit to buy material for an expensive and fashionable outfit. Ordering a complete set of clothes would be reserved for a special occasion, like a wedding or elevation in social position, and would require a substantial financial investment, so would only be an option for a very wealthy family. For the wedding of Mary Kytson to Lord Darcy in 1583, for example, her parents spent the enormous sum of £203 5s on 'divers parcells of silke' in Sir William Stone's shop in Cheapside.[68]

Mercers specialised in costly, imported fabrics. A dialogue from a French/English phrase book of 1593 demonstrates the range available. The mercer explains that he has 'good wrought velvet of Geanes [Genoa], Sattins of Lucques [Lucca] and of Cypres [Cyprus], Chamblet [camlet, a fabric of mixed yarns – usually silk and camel hair] without waues [unwatered], cloth of gold, cloth of silver, damaske for damsels, Spanish taffatae, Millan fustians, Worsteds of Norwich'.[69]

Worsteds, in fact, would normally be found in the draper's shop, along with high-quality woollen goods woven in England – 'fine cloth, of serge, of bays, of kersey'. Worsteds were made from long wool that was prepared for spinning by combing, a process which produced a smooth, fine yarn and a lightweight cloth. Woollen cloths, on the other hand, were made from short, fine wool which was prepared for spinning by carding – working the wool between wooden bats set with wires. After it had been spun and woven on a broad loom, the resultant cloth was fulled (shrunk) in water to produce a thick dense cloth, exported to cold countries as it was virtually impervious to weather.

The draper gathered his cloths from all over England. The North produced the rougher types of woollens, like kersey, worn by ordinary people in town and country. The South West specialised in high quality broadcloths (so called because they were woven on a broad loom). East Anglia was famous for worsteds, and for 'the New Draperies' produced there after the 1550s by 'Strangers', immigrant Huguenot and Flemish craftsmen. Their skills in silk-weaving enabled them to produce the new draperies of grosgrain – a silk or half silk; serge – a mixture of wool and worsted; and shalloon – a cheap, twilled worsted used for dress linings and upholstery.

36 An elaborate gold pendant embellished with enamel, pearls and square-cut jewels, made in Germany, *c.*1600. The height of the pendant is only 8.5cm, yet the central standing figures, flanked by oarsmen and lute-players, are extremely detailed and life-like.

Another importer of fine fabrics was the linen draper. The best quality came from Flanders, with holland being the finest and the most expensive. Different types and grades of linen were often named after the town or district in which they were made: cambric from Cambrai; dowlas, a coarse and cheap fabric, from Doulas in Picardy. An exchange between Sir John Falstaff and Mistress Quickly, hostess of a tavern in Eastcheap, in Shakespeare's *1 Henry IV* illustrates the difference between the two cloths, holland and dowlas:

HOSTESS: . . . you owe me money, Sir John, and now you pick a quarrel to beguile me of it. I bought you a dozen of shirts to your back.
FALSTAFF: Dowlas, filthy dowlas: I have given them away to bakers' wives; and they have made bolters [cloths for sifting meal] of them.
HOSTESS: Now, as I am a true woman, holland of eight shillings an ell.[70]

In his late-sixteenth-century *Description of England* William Harrison states that linen was measured by the ell (45in), whereas woollen cloth and other fabrics were measured by the yard (36in), but this does not appear to have been a hard and fast rule. A large quantity of fabric was sold not by the yard or ell but by the piece, whose length varied with different cloths.[71]

Finished cloth was sent by packhorse to the cloth market, Blackwell Hall in Basinghall Street, near Guildhall, in London. There the bales were weighed and inspected by examiners called aulnagers. Dealers, known as 'factors', fixed the prices for the different grades of materials. The lighter-weight 'New Draperies' were sent to another part of the complex, Bay Hall. Once the quality, length and breadth of cloth had been established, and the excise duties had been paid, seals would be attached to it by the merchant and the aulnager. At the time of the Great Fire of London (September 1666), Blackwell Hall was full of stocks of cloth and linen brought there by weavers from all over the country for sale at Michaelmas. The building and its contents were lost in the fire – and the stock belonging to the weavers of Coventry alone, for example, was valued at about £2000.

The jewellers and goldsmiths were concentrated in Goldsmith's Row, an imposing edifice built in 1491 on the south side of West Cheap. It contained fourteen shops 'all in one frame, uniformly builded foure stories high, beautified towards the street with the goldesmith's arms . . . richly painted ouer with gilt'.[72] Goldsmiths and jewellers fulfilled two functions in the sixteenth century, the first being to design and make objects for sale, the other being to act as bankers. Using the client's own jewels as security, money would be loaned at an interest rate which varied between ten and twelve per cent, and if the client wanted to travel abroad the goldsmith could provide him with letters of credit and foreign currency.

Many women would use a husband's or a relative's visit to London as an opportunity to ask them to buy trimmings or accessories with which to alter or improve existing garments, and to purchase the imported fabrics that were not easily available outside London. Trips to London were not always determined by the exigencies of business: judgement on the legal quarrels in which the country gentry were so often embroiled meant that their presence was often required at the Westminster Courts; the duration of a Parliamentary session was another occasion when men from the shires and boroughs of England sought accommodation in London.

It was also common practice to send a son to the Inns of Court at London as an alternative to University. One such student, Philip Gawdy, who stayed on in London to practise law, was entrusted with the task of informing his sisters of the latest fashions worn at court, and then of buying and dispatching them. He found his task a somewhat onerous one. In 1587 he informed his sister Anne that he could 'assure you bothe the queene and all the gentlewomen at the courte weare the very fashion of your tuff taffata gowne with an open wired sleeve and suche a cutt, and it is now the newest fashion. For cappes and frenche hoods I fynde no change in the world all whatsoever els you shall undoubtedly be provided of.'[73] On 11 April 1589 he wrote to his youngest sister to let her know that he was experiencing some difficulty in deciding which head-dress he should buy, for he found 'nothing more certayne than their incertaynty, which made me forbeare to send you anything further of myne owne devise until I heare further from you'.[74] When he sent his brother a doublet made of fustian (a thick imported cloth) in 1597 he knew that his brother would question the style of the garment and the material he had chosen, so he assured him 'my Lord Admirall and some others suche haue had suites of the same, and trymmed in the same kind . . . . In one word I have made choyse of all these thinges as waryly and well as a theife at the gallowes wold keepe him self from hanging.'[75]

The Royal Exchange in Cornhill was built by Sir Thomas Gresham and opened by Queen Elizabeth in 1571. This prestigious building was the hub of commercial activity in the City. It had been built in the form of a 'quadrate with walks round the mayne building supported with pillars of marble; over which walkes is a place for the sale of all kinds of wares, richly stored with varietie of all sorts'.[76] The stalls of the milliners, haberdashers and many other purveyors of fashion were located in the Pawn on the south side of the Exchange.

Haberdashers and milliners both sold ready-made fashion items. The former sold hats, stockings, lace and a variety of trimmings. The latter, whose name derived from his merchandise which was originally imported from Milan, sold bracelets, brooches, jewels, fans, garters, perfume and a certain number of ready-made garments. The

37 This sweetbag of purple velvet is exquisitely embroidered in gold and silver thread and seed pearls, with a reclining stag amidst roses, a carnation, acorns and honeysuckle leaves. Its tassels and strings, worked with precision and care, are in excellent condition considering the fragility of such vulnerable trimmings.

milliner's association with such intimate feminine articles gave him a rather effeminate image, hence Shakespeare's description in *1 Henry IV*:

> He was perfumed like a milliner
> And 'twixt his finger and his thumb he held
> A pouncet-box, which ever and anon
> He gave his nose, and took't away again.[77]

The Pawn contained many well-lit shops which were originally let out at 40s rent per shop per year. It was the place to visit to buy presents as well as personal adornments, and inexpensive items like pincases, combs and points were available, alongside expensive ready-made garments like embroidered waistcoats.

Seamstresses specialised in the making and sale of linen garments and those in the Exchange were renowned for their sewing skills and for their reputation as 'both better workwomen and will afford a better penniworth than their French counterparts'.[78] According to Thomas Heywood's play *The Faire Maide of the Exchange* (1607), the seamstresses who worked there could offer the customer:

> Of lawnes, or cambrickes, ruffes well wrought, shirts
> Fine falling bands, of the Italian cut-worke,
> Ruffes for your hands, wast-coates wrought with silke,
> Nightcaps of gold, or such like wearing linen.[79]

There were many types of lace available there, too, from the inexpensive bone lace, an openwork lace, whose name was derived from the bone bobbins or pins used in its making – also available from street sellers – to the expensive 'cut-work' imported from Italy. Fastidious Brisk, a character in Ben Jonson's play *Every Man out of his Humour* (1599) boasts that he paid £3 in the Exchange for an Italian cut-work collar edged with purl (embroidery in gold or silver thread).[80] Other stalls in the Pawn included those of the starchers, the suppliers of the spangled and jewelled hat feathers and the 'attyre makers' – the Elizabethan term for a hairdresser. The starchers offered a specialised fashion service, starching any accessories of lace or linen.

Supplying a fur, or lining a garment with fur, was a specialist service available in Budge Row where the skinners worked. The road got its name from the fur called budge, which was a lambskin with the fur dressed outwards. The Worshipful Company of Skinners controlled and regulated a large and complex trade, for a skinner could be

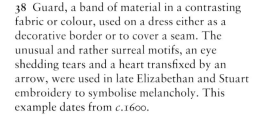

38 Guard, a band of material in a contrasting fabric or colour, used on a dress either as a decorative border or to cover a seam. The unusual and rather surreal motifs, an eye shedding tears and a heart transfixed by an arrow, were used in late Elizabethan and Stuart embroidery to symbolise melancholy. This example dates from *c*.1600.

anyone involved in the manufacture and sale of fur for clothing, accessories or household articles. In the early Tudor period furs had been the chief symbol of rank and wealth and, as such, were strictly governed by sumptuary legislation (see p.27). Although these laws continued to be in force throughout the sixteenth century, they were generally ineffective and the supremacy of fur as the ultimate status symbol began to be challenged by imported luxury fabrics such as silk and velvet. Furs were also becoming scarce and expensive because the wild animals in Britain that supplied them had been hunted to extinction, and the sources in northern Europe were also becoming exhausted. According to the 1620s inventory of a chapman's shop in Great Yarmouth, Norfolk, it could provide the following native – and therefore cheap – furs: polecat, cat, black and grey rabbit, squirrel, fox and otter. 'Very rare and precious skins', like sable, mink and miniver, were imported from northern Russia. Sir Henry Sidney's account for 1570–1 with the Queen's skinner, Adam Bland, shows that one had to be very wealthy to buy furs of the highest quality for, during that two-year period, he ran up a large bill of £66 6s 11d for linings – mostly imported – of lynx, Spanish fox, black coney (a kind of rabbit) and white lamb.[81]

The Guild of Shoemakers was one of the earliest in England, issuing its first Ordinance in 1272. It was then called the Guild of Cordwainers, a name taken from a corruption of Cordova, the town in Spain from which came the best leather (cordovan), and it was originally established in Cordwainer Street in London. By the end of the sixteenth century the two trades, that of the shoemaker and the 'currier' (who would 'dress' or treat the raw leather), had transferred to St Martins le Grand and Lothbury respectively. Shoemakers would have sold ready-made as well as made-to-order shoes and the variety that would have been on offer is illustrated in a dialogue in *The Parlement of Prattlers*, 1593. A customer asks to see 'two soled or three soled shooes, some pumps or pantofles of Spanish leather. Let me see some bootes.' The customer is insistent that he does not want a shoe with a single sole but requires the more elaborate two- or three-layered style.[82]

The price of a shoe would have been determined by the quality of the leather employed and the amount of decoration, like pinking or slashing, on the upper. Imported Spanish leather was the most expensive, but there would have been a range of cheaper leathers made from the hides of native animals such as deer, goat, sheep and cattle. Pantofles, unlike the pump, which had a thin sole and soft upper, were backless shoes. If worn outdoors as an overshoe they would be made from leather and have a cork sole that could be as much as two inches deep. When worn indoors as slippers they could be made from a rich material like velvet, decorated with embroidery and trimmed with lace and spangles.

'Martin's chain' – jewellery made from a counterfeit or base metal – also came from St Martins Le Grand. Wigs, false hair and even false eyebrows were on sale in Silver Street and in 1600 Shakespeare lived in the house of a French wig-maker called Mountjoy on the corner of Silver Street. Second-hand clothes were on sale in Birchin Lane, but to admit to buying anything there was a mark of social inferiority: 'His discourse makes not his behaviour but he buyes it at court, as country men buy their clothes in Birchin Lane.'[83] The range of garments on sale was enormous, for it was possible to buy clothes which had belonged to men of all classes and professions. Those

39 Early tailoring practices are shown in this German engraving of 1568: the material is cut out with a pair of shears; a wooden ruler, used as a measure, lies on the table. The large box under the table is full of odd pieces of material – cut-offs – which the customer did not want, or did not know about, and which would later be sold off. Hence the comparison of a tailor with an alchemist, for he can 'turn your silkes into golde'. The tailor's two assistants, one of whom sits in the typical cross-legged position, are busy sewing on a raised platform in the shop window.

who could not afford the prices in the Lane would frequent Houndsditch and Long Lane where the 'fripperer' sold older, more tattered clothes.

Tailors (39) made clothes for men and women and would charge for the labour involved in making them and for any extra materials (usually lining, trimmings and fastenings). They had a reputation for dishonesty as it was believed they promoted the eccentricities of fashion to boost trade; also that they kept a portion of their customer's material for their own profit. But tailors were not highly paid, whether they worked in town or country, and they often experienced great difficulty in extracting payment for their work. Their labour charge was approximately a quarter of the cost of the material and they were expected to deliver an order within a few days or, at the most, a week.

A garment was cut by taking a pattern from existing clothes or by giving the tailor one's measurements, although this method involved certain problems. A letter from the son of a Shrewsbury tailor, dated 1594, explains 'for the other gownes yo'r measures were so ill taken that the tailor sayes he cannot tell what to make of them'.[84] Even Henry VIII's tailor Skut got it wrong and was often accused by Lady Lisle of poor cut and shape. On 30 May 1536 Hussee told Lady Lisle that he would 'not fail to shew Skut of the misordering of your gowns, and how ill they be ordered, much worse than they were before'.[85] The tailor could circumvent this problem by dispatching the clothes unstitched so that they could be made 'fit for wearing' at home.

There was a time lag of about five years between a fashion originating in London and its appearance, albeit in a less extreme form, in the provinces. When Bridget Manners, the daughter of the Countess of Rutland, was accepted as Maid of Honour to Elizabeth I in 1589 her mother felt that, as she lived so far from court, at Belvoir Castle, she was quite out of touch with fashion and unable to choose her new clothes. Bridget had been sent to the house of the Countess of Bedford to complete her education in London, so Lady Bedford was given the responsibility of spending £200 on clothes for Bridget's appearance at court.

Four-fifths of the population of England lived in the country and the dress worn by the various classes and social groups of country people was quite distinctive and often the subject of scathing comment in fashionable circles. The easily-recognised costume worn by a country man when he visited London marked him out as easy prey for the 'connie-catcher', the Elizabethan version of a con-man. In his pamphlet 'The Art of Cony-Catching', 1591, Robert Greene describes how they would lie in wait for a 'plain country fellow well and cleanly apparelled, either in a coat of homespun russet or of frieze [a coarse woollen cloth] as the time requires, and a side pouch at his side.'[86] This contrast between the home-spun cloth breeches worn by a yeoman and husbandman, and the imported velvet worn by a gentleman, was an association clearly endorsed by Shakespeare when, in *Love's Labour's Lost*, the native materials russet and kersey are associated with simple honest values:

> Taffeta phrases, silken terms precise,
> Three-piled hyperboles, spruce affectation . . .
> I do forswear them; and I here protest . . .
> Henceforth my wooing mind shall be expressed
> In russet yeas and honest kersey noes:[87]

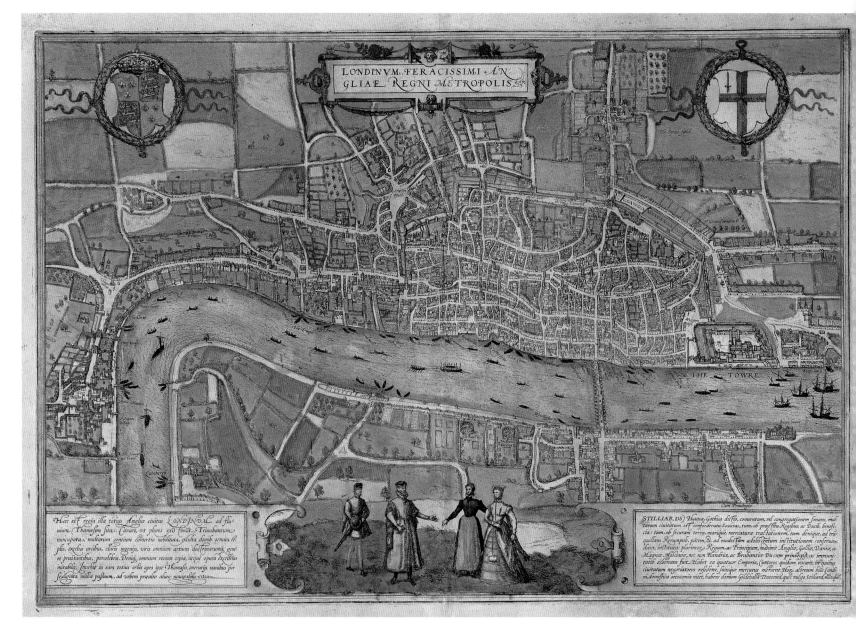

Such differentiation, determined by annual income and property owned, was supposed to be maintained by sumptuary legislation, but the disparity in dress between the wives and daughters of well-to-do yeomen and of the gentry had narrowed somewhat by the end of Elizabeth's reign. The yeoman's wife was expected to make her own and her family's clothes from home-spun wool and flax, but her best dress and her husband's best suit would have been made by a local tailor – who would also make everyday clothes for the gentry if they weren't being made in London or in a neighbouring big town or city.

Accessories could be bought in the weekly-held markets and at annual fairs, and were also sold by the pedlar. These itinerant salesmen were immortalised by Shakespeare when he created Autolycus in *The Winter's Tale*. His pack contained:

40 The limited extent of London in 1572 can clearly be seen in Braun and Hogenberg's map. In the foreground a merchant and his wife are shown with their servants. The merchant has a long gown trimmed with fur, with a high collar and long sleeves hanging open from above the elbow. His wife wears a close-bodied gown with a single vertical slash on either side of the bodice, and a miniver bonnet.

> Lawn as white as driven snow;
> Cyprus black as e'er was crow;
> Gloves as sweet as damask roses;
> Masks for faces and for noses;
> Bugle-bracelet, necklace-amber;
> Perfume for a lady's chamber;
> Golden quoifs and stomachers,
> For my lads to give their dears;
> Pins and poking-sticks of steel;[88]

Another group of travelling salesmen were the petty chapmen, who travelled on foot or on horseback selling textiles, haberdashery and ready-made clothing for working men and women. Operating in a designated area of the country, they sold to a regular clientele and at the local fairs and markets. They purchased their goods on credit in London and by the end of the sixteenth century, successful chapmen had started opening shops – which were, in essence, general stores. One such was William Davis of Winslow in Buckinghamshire. The 1588 inventory of goods sold in his shop divided the stock into six sections: linen cloth; woollen cloth; mercery; hats; grocery; and small haberdashery wares. Currants, knives, pens and ink-horns jostled for space beside rolls of holland cloth, mockado (a plain or patterned imitation velvet) and taffeta. His three main suppliers in London were a haberdasher, a grocer and a hatter, who together were owed the considerable sum of £20 at the time of Davis's death.[89]

There were few retailers in London to be found outside the walls of the City in the sixteenth century. The Strand, destined to become an important shopping area in the next century, was the location for the grand houses of the nobility, whose extensive gardens stretched down to the banks of the River Thames and their private landing stages. The walled area of London, only two miles across, was completely surrounded by open countryside, but there were constant arguments as the townspeople encroached upon the open land for cultivation and for the building of new houses and private gardens complete with summer-houses. A proclamation was passed in 1580 which forbade any new building within three miles of the City, but it proved to be ineffective. However, at the end of the century Islington, Hackney, Hampstead and Chelsea were still isolated country villages, the 'pimpernall rose' grew 'in a pasture as you go from a village hard by London called Knightsbridge unto Fulham' and 'wilde buglosse' grew in the 'drye ditche-bankes on either side of Pickadillie'.[90]

CHAPTER TWO

Careless Romance

1603–1660

I

When Elizabeth I died on 24 March 1603 her Stuart cousin, James VI of Scotland, was proclaimed King James I of England. Leaving Edinburgh on 3 April he travelled southwards to inherit what he called the 'promised land', followed by a motley collection of Scots who thought that the presence of a Scottish king on the throne of England would enable them to make their fortune. This doggerel verse is supposed to refer to their arrival in London:

> Hark, hark,
> The dogs do bark,
> The beggars are coming to town.
> Some in rags,
> And some in tags,
> And some in velvet gowns.[1]

The customary celebrations that accompanied James's coronation had to be delayed as there was a particularly virulent outbreak of the plague between May and December that year. Nobody wanted to have new clothes made for fear of infection, so gentlemen were to be seen 'in ruinous suite of apparrel'.[2] But as soon as it was safe to do so all the gallants were ordering new clothes to parade in at the new King's court, prompting an anonymous pamphlet writer to observe that those who wore 'old taffeta doublets yesterday, are slipt into nine yards of sattin today'.[3] The stage was set for a period of brash and lavishly-decorated fashion.

Like their Tudor forebears, the Stuart monarchs placed great emphasis on the public and flamboyant display of clothing and on the setting in which to 'publish one's clothes'. Throughout the seventeenth century the monarch, his family and his courtiers formed the circle where new fashions were generated. Even if the monarch was not interested in his personal appearance, he actively encouraged public ceremonies and private parties where a lavish display of fine clothes and jewels was expected.

Visitors to the court of James I were surprised by his unregal appearance for 'from his dress he would have been taken for the meanest among his courtiers, a modesty he affects, had it not been for a chain of diamonds round his neck, and a great diamond in his hair'.[4] James might have been indifferent about his own appearance but his susceptibility to the charm of young men meant that he was particularly interested in, and easily impressed by, the appearance of his courtiers, a preoccupation that acted as a catalyst and created court fashions of great extravagance. Sartorial competitiveness led to an enormous expenditure on dress at the court of James I and, to a lesser extent, of his son Charles I. As in Queen Elizabeth's reign, the insistence on 'fashions lately brought from foreyne lands' proved a source of irritation to contemporary observers. The 'noble ways at court' involved attendance at masques, tilts, the theatre, bowling alleys, cock fights and horse races – all activities at which a 'courtly show' was expected.

Putting together a fashionable outfit was a complicated business requiring the involvement of many different suppliers and specialists. A print of 1625–30 entitled *The*

41 (*previous pages*) Mountjoy Blount, Earl of Newport, and George, Lord Goring, Royalist commanders during the Civil War. Both wear that essential military garment, the buff leather jerkin. Newport's sleeveless version is worn over a white satin doublet with serrated slashes and turned-back cuffs. Although the jerkin offered some protection, an even more impenetrable layer is provided by the waist-length breastplate, the metal studs of which can be seen curving round the armhole, to disappear under Newport's sword-belt. The full sleeves of Goring's jerkin have been slashed vertically, disclosing the voluminous sleeves of his fine linen shirt. Van Dyck shows, by the way the jerkin hangs, that it is much tougher and more rigid than the soft, malleable leather used to make Newport's perfectly-fitting glove, for instance. In keeping with their military dress, both men wear plain linen collars and cuffs rather than the elaborate lace required at court.

Identification of commanders on the battlefield was determined by their scarves and sashes. A page is engaged in draping across Goring's jerkin a red and gold striped silk gauze for his sash, securing it at the side of his body lest it impede access to his sword.
(Sir Anthony Van Dyck, *c.*1639, Petworth)

funeral obsequies of Sir All-in-New fashions depicts a funeral procession consisting of those people who had supplied the dead knight with garments and accessories. It included the laundresses and their maids, a spur-maker, a cutler, four tailors, a goldsmith, a shoemaker, a painter, a feather-maker, a barber and a haberdasher, all following the coffin, which is carrying his entire wardrobe 'and other toyes where with he used to swagger'.[5] The final lines of the inscription make the point that the clothes on which the knight had expended so much money and effort were merely 'the trophies of his pride', and were destined to hang on a second-hand clothes stall in Houndsditch or Long Lane.

But excesses in fashion were not confined to the aristocracy and courtiers – the adoption of extreme fashions was apparent anywhere in London. Thomas Middleton makes fun of this trend in *Father Hubburd's Tales* of 1604, in which he describes how the landlord of a London inn changed himself into a 'French puppet' by wearing clothing that 'amounted to above two years rent'.[6]

James I and his queen, Anne of Denmark, spent large sums of money on their children's clothes. Their elder son, Prince Henry, had a particularly lavish wardrobe. In 1608, for example, the bill for clothing the thirteen-year-old totalled £4,574 14s, a thousand pounds more than Queen Elizabeth's annual bill.[7] It was said of the Prince that 'he loved to goe handsome and well cloathed; yet without any maner of superfluity or excesse',[8] but it is evident from a letter written in 1611 that the Prince had a direct influence on court fashion and enjoyed variety and change for its own sake: 'Carr [Robert Carr, Earl of Somerset, James I's favourite until 1624 when he was displaced by George Villiers, 1st Duke of Buckingham] hath changed his taylors and tiremen many times and all to please the Prince who laugheth at the long grown fashion of our courtiers and wisheth for change every day.'[9]

When Henry was created Prince of Wales in June 1610, amidst scenes of great festivity, he was given a separate household with its own officers, the whole establishment numbering about four hundred people. Its leading members shared Henry's passionate interest 'for new architecture, for pictures and bronzes, for coins and medals, for splendid court festivals'.[10] His attempt to 'transform the aesthetic milieu of his father's court'[11] led to a burst of artistic activity and patronage that was noticed by a Venetian visitor to Henry's court in 1611: 'His Highness . . . attends to the disposition of his houses, having already many gardens and fountains, and some new buildings. He is paying special attention to the adorning of a most beautiful gallery of very fine pictures, ancient and modern, the larger part brought out of Venice. He is also collecting books for a library he has built.'[12]

All was cut short by Henry's sudden and unexpected death on 6 November 1612 at the age of eighteen. There followed an enormous outpouring of national grief, for Henry had captured the hearts of the English and was perceived to be 'the Flower of his House, the Glory of his Country, and the Admiration of all Strangers; which in all Places had imprinted a great Hope in the Minds of the well affected'.[13]

The new heir, Prince Charles, had been rather outshone by his glamorous and charismatic older brother, but he shared his artistic interests. Their sister Elizabeth was destined to become the romantic 'Winter Queen' through her marriage to Frederick, Elector Palatine, in February 1613. James spent a fortune on Elizabeth's trousseau and wedding outfit of 'rich white Florence cloth of silver . . . embroidered all over in flowers with silver purl, purl and plate, lined with taffeta and trimmed with rich purled lace with goldsmith's work'.[14] But such expenditure strained the finances of the Great Wardrobe.

Unfortunately, the first Master of the Wardrobe in James's reign, George Hume, Earl of Dunbar (one of the King's unpopular Scottish favourites), realised that he could make some extra money out of his post by selling its contents. This he proceeded to do by 'wickedlie' transporting the clothes and accessories in the 'inestimable wardrobe' to the Low Countries, where they fetched more than £100,000. He sold the 'ancient cloathes of our English Kings which were worn on great festivals so that this Wardrobe was in effect a Library for Antiquaries, therein to read the mode and fashion of garments in all ages'.[15]

It was inevitable that a court with a royal family and a crowd of hangers-on would require more from the Wardrobe than the small, carefully-controlled court of Queen Elizabeth, although she, too, had encountered problems in financing this department. But during James's reign control of the Wardrobe was so lax that employees were able to enrich themselves by overcharging for the material and other goods supplied to the crown and pocketing the difference. This systematic cheating led to debts to mercers, linen drapers and other suppliers spiralling to such an extent that normal credit was no longer available to the crown. When Anne of Denmark died in 1619 her funeral had to be delayed because the Wardrobe could not buy black cloth for the mourners: 'The Master of the Wardrobe is loath to wear his own credit threadbare, or be so ill an husband as to use the King's credit and so pay double the price, which is now become ordinary because they stay so long for their money.'[16]

Anne had had a separate household, run on the same lines as that of Queen Elizabeth, with the responsibility for her daily dressing and undressing falling on her Gentlewomen of the Bedchamber. She also displayed a distinctive taste in art, patronising artists of the calibre of Inigo Jones, Paul van Somer and Isaac Oliver, but she was deemed frivolous, extravagant and empty-headed by her subjects.

> On the whole Anne lived for pleasure, passing her time moving from one of the palaces assigned to her to the next. She and her household made up what might be categorized as a second court based on Somerset House in London and Greenwich on the Thames. In the summer there were progresses to aristocratic houses, the occasion for alfresco *fêtes*. Anne set style. Immediately on her arrival in the south, fashion changed under her aegis, as the excrescences of her predecessor's dress were jettisoned in favour of a simpler silhouette with a lavish use of ribbon rosettes in pastel colours.[17]

However, Anne of Denmark's insistence that the farthingale should be worn at court, even when it was no longer a part of fashionable dress, meant that the ladies there had an awkward and ill-proportioned shape. At one court event in 1613 ladies were allowed to attend without farthingales 'to gain the more room', but they were not entirely discarded until Anne's death in 1619.

Her overriding passion for jewellery caused her to spend enormous sums of money, whether she could afford them or not, acquiring the pieces she wanted. Her bill for jewellery during the ten years of her reign as Queen of the Scots was £50,000.

Contemporary comments about Anne suggest that her taste was not particularly discerning, as she appeared to be more impressed by novelty of design rather than its aesthetic value. When the King's cousin, Lady Arabella Stuart, had to give Anne a New Year Day's Gift in 1604 she based her choice on the fact that 'the Queen regarded not the value, but the device' and that she 'neither liked gown nor petticoat so well as some little bunch of rubies to hang in her ear. I mean to give Her Majesty two pairs of stockings lined with plush, and two pairs of gloves lined if London afford me not some daft toy I like better.'[18]

Many of Queen Elizabeth's clothes were altered for Anne as 'nothing new could surpass them',[19] and some were 'translated' into costumes for the participants in a masque, *The Vision of the Three Goddesses*, performed at Hampton Court in 1604. Originating in Italy, the masque was first mentioned in England in 1512 when King Henry VIII and his guests were 'disguised, after the manner of Italie in garmentes long and brode wrought all with gold, with visers and cappes of gold'.[20] It was usual to perform a masque at the end of the banquet, or final course of dinner, when a group of masked people would enter the hall and, after a show of verses, singing and dancing, invite the assembled company to join them in a formal dance.

The masque occupied a central position in Stuart court festivities, encouraged by Anne, who loved spectacle and dancing and performed regularly in them herself. Her employment of Ben Jonson, Thomas Campion, Samuel Daniel and others as writers ensured that the masques had a strong literary content to balance Inigo Jones's superb scenic and costume designs.

The costumes designed by Inigo Jones (see **42**) were a mixture of antique and modern dress, being 'taken from the antique Greek statues, mixed with some modern additions'.[21] But his desire to dress the performers, all ladies of aristocratic birth, including the Queen, in semi-transparent draperies shocked many older, more conservative members of the court. The costumes were also 'excessively costly'.[22] *Tethys' Festival*, written by Ben Jonson and designed by Inigo Jones, was performed to celebrate the creation of Prince Henry as Prince of Wales on 5 June 1610. The mercer's bill was £668 0s 8d, the silkman's £1,071 5s 0d and the embroiderer requested payment of an unsettled account which included £55 for embroidering the costumes with silver and sea-green silk and gold oes.

When James came to the throne in 1603 men were still wearing the exaggerated fashions of the late Elizabethan period. The natural shape of the body was disguised by a padded doublet and trunk hose, and the projecting layers of the ruff and, 'later, the standing band effectively separated head from body. By the 1630s a slimmer and more elegant style had evolved. Raising the waistline of the doublet and lengthening its skirts, and reducing the bulkiness of the ungainly breeches created a more graceful and unified silhouette. Although decoration was still lavish it was made up of less expensive materials, as bows, braid and buttons replaced the gem-studded materials so beloved of James's courtiers. Wide collars of linen bordered with lace, and fine white linen glimpsed through the slashes in the doublet sleeves served to offset the uniform colour of the satin suit. The waistcoat and nightgown continued to offer men a comfortable alternative to formal dress, though these informal garments could be very elaborate and therefore expensive. When an inventory was made in 1614 of the contents of the

42 Inigo Jones' costume design in pen and ink for a winged masquer. The costume resembles that depicted by John de Critz in a portrait of Lucy Harington, Countess of Bedford, now at Woburn Abbey, recording her appearance in Ben Jonson's marriage masque *Hymenaei*, performed on 5 January 1606. In Critz's portrait she wears a billowing veil flowing down from a coronet, horizontally braided sleeves and a layered striped skirt. If this drawing is indeed a preliminary design for one of the costumes, the wings would refer to the central spectacle of the masque, the descent from the clouds of Juno and her ladies, confirming the union between the Earl of Essex and Lady Frances Howard.

wardrobe of Henry Howard, Earl of Northampton, a white taffeta waistcoat embroidered with vine leaves and grapes was valued at £8.

Collars at this time could either have a deep border of lace or be made from transparent lawn, in which case a number of collars could be placed one on top of another and called a falling band (see 43). In the play *The Honest Whore*, 1604, Middleton wrote: 'I wouldst thou wouldst give mee five yards of Lawne to make my Punke some falling bands a the fashion, three falling one upon another: for that's the new edition now.'[23] There was also the standing band (see 44), which was in fashion from about 1605 until 1615, when it attained its maximum width. It was a semi-circular collar with the curved edge standing up round the back of the head while the straight horizontal edges in front met under the chin and were tied by band strings. It retained its shape by means of a wire frame called an underpropper. This would be attached to the doublet and if the standing band was made of a transparent material the outlines of the support could be seen. The shoulder wings of the doublet tended to follow the same sloping lines as the neckwear, hence the description of a fashionable man's wings in 1604 as being 'as little and diminutive as a puritan's ruff'.[24]

Edward Herbert, brother of the poet George, was a kinsman of the Powis Herberts (see p.39) and lived at nearby Montgomery Castle. He was created Lord Herbert of Chirbury in 1629. A portrait of him painted *c*.1603–5, and perhaps after Isaac Oliver (43), is interesting as it depicts him wearing informal dress.

Lord Herbert was also a poet and scholar, famous for his *Life* and a philosophical treatise *De Veritate* (1624). Another portrait (44) by Isaac Oliver, painted in 1613 or 1614, depicts him both as an active soldier and man-at-arms and as a melancholy knight and lover, meditating in the leafy solitude of a wood. 'What is more pleasant than to walk alone in some solitary grove, betwixt Wood and Water, by a Brook side, to meditate upon some delightsome and pleasant subject,' wrote Robert Burton in *The Anatomy of Melancholy* (1621).[25] Melancholy was a fashionable affliction and those who felt they were suffering from it could express their state by their choice of dress and pose, appearing 'untrust and unbuttoned, ungartered, not out of carelessness, but care'.[26] The Renaissance theory of physiology proposed that men were divided into four distinct types: sanguine, choleric, phlegmatic and melancholic. As the last humour was most closely linked to genius, anyone with intellectual or artistic pretensions was quite happy to be called a melancholic; melancholy could also be induced by the pangs of unrequited love.

The unusual pose adopted by Lord Herbert demonstrates how much more relaxed the style of male dress had become, with the sleeves allowing ease of movement, unlike those worn by Sir Robert Carey (see 28) and Raleigh (see 27). The doublet was no longer distended into an unnatural shape, but finished at the waistline in a tabbed border, and breeches had become loose and baggy and closed at the knee. The fashionable tightly-fitting boots, worn over boothose, tended to be of Spanish leather, especially valued because it creased very easily. This creased effect was admired, for the 'good wrinkle of a boot and the curious crincling of a silke stocking'[27] showed that the wearer had bought the finest quality available.

One of the most splendid costume portraits of James's reign is that of Richard Sackville, 3rd Earl of Dorset (45). Painted by William Larkin, probably in 1613, it is

43 (*above*) Edward Herbert in informal dress, with both his doublet and shirt undone, and the inside of the shirt revealing the neckband with its attachment to the linen falling band. His doublet, richly embroidered with a floral pattern, has tabbed shoulder wings. Elizabethan and Stuart men never wore their cloaks in the way they were designed to be worn: Herbert wears his in the fashionable way – that is, draped across his body.
(After Isaac Oliver, *c*.1603–5, Montacute)

44 (*right*) A later portrait of Edward Herbert with allusions to his military activities. In the background an attendant is shown hanging up his armour, plumed helmet and surcoat, while Herbert lies at full-length in a melancholy pose under a tree, beside a stream. His doublet is undone and the band strings of his standing band are also unfastened, both clues to his frame of mind.
(Isaac Oliver, 1613–14, Powis Castle)

possible that it depicts the outfit he wore to the wedding of Princess Elizabeth and the Prince Palatine on 14 February 1613. The master of ceremonies at that event wrote that 'The bravery and richese of that day were incomparable . . . above all the King's Favourite, Viscount Rochester, and Lord Hay, Lord Dingwell and Lord Dorset dazzled the eyes off who saw the splendour of their Dress.'[28] There exists at Knole Park in Kent an inventory of the Earl's wardrobe, taken in 1617, and it is possible to match the

45 (*far left*) Richard Sackville, 3rd Earl of Dorset. Everything about his costume is lavish and exaggerated. Black honeysuckle flowers embroidered in gold form an almost harsh pattern against the white satin background of his doublet and extended cuffs to his gloves. His baggy black silk breeches were lined with white cloth of silver according to a 1617 inventory of the Earl's wardrobe, and this would have been glimpsed through the irregular small slashes on their surface. The breeches have been embroidered with a more delicate version of the honeysuckle motif, worked in gold thread. Even the shoes, with their pronounced curved heel and massive rose of lace and droplet spangles, are patterned with a honeysuckle flower, and the white silk stockings are embroidered with an exquisite pattern of vines in silver, gold and black.

A heavy black velvet cloak, casually thrown over his left shoulder, is lined with 'Shagg of black siluer and gold'. (Shag was a thick-piled cloth, sometimes woven with fur, used to provide a warm lining for garments like cloaks and nightgowns.) The girdle, matching hangers and garters, and the embroidered, lace-encrusted hatband on the table behind Lord Dorset, are all listed in the inventory. One of the most expensive items must have been the imported lace that forms such a dramatic edging to his standing collar. Here it has attained its maximum width, and completely encircles the Earl's face.
(William Larkin, 1613, Ranger's House)

46 (*left*) The rich gold and red Italian brocaded silk of Mary Curzon's bodice and skirt contrast with the heavy gold fringed underskirt. False serrated hanging sleeves tend to extend the shoulder line, while the small waist is emphasised by the wide oval neckline and circular flounce of the farthingale. Three ribbon rosettes on the neckline, the ribbon rosette tied on the arm, and the fan made from a massive ostrich feather are all standard accessories for the formal, highly decorated dress that Anne of Denmark expected her ladies to wear at court.
(William Larkin, *c*.1610, Knole)

garments that he is wearing in this portrait with the entries. This spectacular outfit perfectly expresses the Earl's exuberant and self-indulgent personality – he was a 'man of spirit and talent, but a licentious spendthrift'.[29] Sackville financed his gorgeous finery and hospitality by selling off not only family land and property but also attempting to do the same with the great inheritance based in the North of England brought to their marriage in 1609 by Lady Anne, the only child of George Clifford, 3rd Earl of Cumberland. By the time of Sackville's death in 1624 Knole had also been mortgaged.

During their marriage Lady Anne Clifford kept a diary which chronicles an increasingly unhappy relationship. Remaining at Knole whilst her husband amused himself at court, Lady Anne's life was a very lonely one. Her husband went 'much abroad to Cocking and Bowling alleys, to Plays and Horse races . . . [while] I stayed in the country, having many times a sorrowful and heavy heart, and being condemned by most folks because I would not consent to the agreements [about the disposal of her lands]'.[30] The entry for 20 November 1616 reads: 'All the time since my Lord went away I wore my black taffety night gown and a yellow taffety waistcoat and used to rise betimes in the morning and walk upon the leads [the flat leaden area on the roof of the house] and afterwards to hear reading.'[31] Her choice of the colours black and yellow is a deliberate one, as they signified sadness at the departure of a loved one.

However, Lady Anne's extensive estates in the North, and her endless legal battles, meant that she had to travel a good deal. In 1616 she wrote that she bought 'a cloak and a safeguard of cloth laced with black lace to keep me warm on my journey'.[32] A safeguard was a protective skirt worn over the lower clothing when out riding, while the cloak protected the upper half of the body. The two garments are usually listed together in inventories and accounts. If one was travelling in a wheeled conveyance extra warmth was provided by a lap-mantle which, as the name suggests, was a blanket or rug placed over the knees.

When Lady Anne was in London she would be expected to attend court and to wear very formal dress – similar to that in a splendid full-length portrait by William Larkin, *c*.1610 (**46**). The sitter is Mary Curzon, who married Anne's brother-in-law Edward Sackville in 1612: on the death of Richard Sackville, Edward became the 4th Earl of Dorset. Although the farthingale had ceased to be fashionable some years before, Anne of Denmark insisted that it be retained for formal court dress and a comparison between this one and the farthingale worn by Queen Elizabeth (see **31**) shows that it is now tilted at a more acute angle, so that it is up at the back and down in the front, an arrangement which meant that the radiating pleats of the skirt completely surrounded the waist. The bodice has retained its elongated shape and is set square onto the tilted farthingale but the hem-length has shortened and the general impression is that the outfit is a size too small for the wearer – an impression exaggerated by the rather shaky perspective in many portraits of this period.

On 25 May 1617 Lady Anne noted in her diary: 'My Lord St. John's tailor came to me to take measure of me and make me a new gown.' On 13 June she tried on the 'sea water green satin gown and my damask embroidered with gold, both which the Tailor . . . sent from London . . . made fit for me to wear with open ruffs after the French fashion'. That the damask gown was made to be worn at court is apparent from an entry made on 2 November in the same year: 'All the time I was at the Court I wore my green damask gown embroidered without a farthingale.'[33] Looking at the bizarre shape of the farthingale worn by Mary Curzon, one imagines that Lady Anne and the other ladies of the court must have felt some relief when it was eventually discarded.

On 28 December 1616 Lady Anne 'dined above in my chamber and wore my night-gown because I was not very well', and on the same day the next year, when she was pregnant, she wrote in her diary, 'went to Church in my rich night gown and petticoat, both my women waiting upon me in their liveries'.[34] From these entries it is apparent that the nightgown, worn by men and women, though essentially a garment that was worn in the privacy of one's home, could also be worn in public if it was sufficiently elaborate.

At Claydon House in Buckinghamshire there are a number of extremely rare seventeenth-century garments that belonged to various members of the Verney family. The earliest is a loose gown or nightgown, with a matching nightcap and slippers (47).[35] It is thought to have belonged to Sir Francis Verney and could have been left at Claydon after his last visit there in 1608. He was the black sheep of the family, having chosen to pursue the dangerous and reckless career of a pirate in the Mediterranean. In 1615 he was found living in a state of abject poverty in the Hospital of St Mary of Pity in Messina and the family were informed that 'Here in Missina I found the sometime great English gallant, Sir Francis Verney, lying sick in a hospital.'[36] He died there soon after. As befits a 'sometime great English gallant', the gown is splendid and opulent.[37]

Another development, this time in women's fashion, during the first decade of the seventeenth century was the elevation of the jacket or waistcoat. This had been worn informally during the Elizabethan period but now became a fashionable and comfortable alternative to the rigid busked bodice. It fitted closely to the waist and then flared out by means of a series of gussets. Ribbon ties were a common form of fastening, but hooks and eyes and buttons were also used. It could be bought as a ready-made garment in milliner's shops and in *The French Garden* Lady Ri-Mellaine bids Master Du Vault-l'amour to bargain on her behalf for one that she had found in a shop in the Royal Exchange in London.[38] The jacket was generally lined and usually heavily embroidered with a circular coiling stem that enclosed birds, flowers, fruit, small animals and insects (48).

The exquisite portrait of Mary Throckmorton, Lady Scudamore painted by Marcus Gheeraerts in 1615 (8) shows her wearing informal dress. Although it might be more comfortable than formal dress, it is just as elaborate and richly decorated.

The clothes worn by Sir Thomas Parker in a 1620 portrait, also by Marcus Gheeraerts (49) are no longer a rather haphazard collection of individual and exaggerated garments, but have a degree of grace and harmony new in male fashion. The elegance that is the hallmark of this style is reflected in the wearer's poise, for he is confident that he would be judged well-dressed not only by English, but also by continental standards. The doublet now curves to a sharp point just below the waistline, and is united with the breeches by ribbon points. Cloaks continued to be used to make flamboyant and extrovert gestures, a trend that is made fun of in Jonson's *The Devil is an Ass* (1616) in which one of the characters spends £50 on a velvet cloak so that 'all London' can see him in it. When he goes to Blackfriars Theatre he deliberately stands up between acts so that his cloak will fall gracefully from his shoulders and display his rich suit.[39]

47 A loose gown or nightgown, thought to have belonged to Sir Francis Verney. It is made from a rich purple silk damask, with a deep grey silk lining of shag that has faded – its crinkly and crushed surface now has the appearance of fur. On the shoulders there are wings consisting of tabs cut from pieces of the damask, stiffened with black buckram and held together by lines of gold braid. The splendid hanging sleeves have been worked with bands of gold metal braid set diagonally across the surface. They are fastened at the top with a hook and eye and with closely-set buttons with matching loops along the outer seam. This arrangement enabled the wearer to choose a hanging sleeve, if the hook was undone, or a wearing sleeve, when the hook was fastened and the arm emerged at the elbow, where the buttons and loops would be unfastened.

48 In this portrait of Elizabeth Craven, Lady Powis, painted in the early 1630s, the jacket has the same diminutive sloping wing and flared basque as the more formal bodice, embroidered with a coiling pattern encircling a delightful variety of flowers, insects and fruit. The larger scale design on the skirt, executed in brilliant colours, comprises pineapple trees and a generalised pomegranate pattern on which are perched birds, butterflies and flowers. (Unknown English artist, early 1630s, Powis Castle)

49 Paning on the breast and sleeves of the male doublet is seen here in its early, unexaggerated form. Sir Thomas Parker also wears full, loosely-gathered breeches which finish in a band just above the knee, where his stockings are secured with garters trimmed with spangled lace and tied in a floppy bow, while his open-sided shoes have matching shoe roses. The gently-sloping lines of the doublet are complemented by a falling ruff, parted slightly to show the tasselled strings. The cloak is thrown over his shoulder, then carefully wrapped round the waist to reveal the lining.
(Marcus Gheeraerts, 1620, Saltram)

50 The Lucy family of Charlecote: Sir Thomas, Lady Alice and some of their children provide a gallery of early seventeenth-century dress. (Unknown artist, *c*.1625, Charlecote)

Charlecote Park, Warwickshire, has been the home of the Lucy family since at least the twelfth century, though the present house dates from the sixteenth century. There is an impressive anonymous portrait, *c*.1625, of the third Sir Thomas Lucy, his wife, Lady Alice, and seven of their thirteen children hanging above the fireplace in the Great Hall (50). (See also 241.) It gives a very detailed picture of male and female fashion at a transitional period.

Female dress in the early 1620s had a narrower and more elongated line, emphasised by a higher waistline, less bulky skirts and long hanging sleeves. Brocaded silks tended to have a regular geometric design or a small stylised floral/plant design rather than the busy floral embroidery of the previous decade. This is apparent in Lady Lucy's bodice and skirt, which are made from a lustrous spotted silk. The clothes worn by the two eldest girls, Margaret and Constance, contain the characteristics of fashion from previous years yet look forward to the fashionable shape of the late 1620s and early 1630s. Although the deep oval neckline and the higher waistline distort the balance of bodice and skirt, the body is no longer pushed into an awkward and clumsy shape and the skirts

51 George Villiers, 1st Duke of Buckingham, and his family. A new style of collar and sleeve has evolved. The Duchess's pale yellow satin, high-waisted bodice serves as a perfect foil to the delicate lace collar spreading out over her shoulders. Embroidery of spangles and metal thread decorate the sleeves, which are paned from shoulder to elbow, the blue ribbon fastened round them allowing the panes to puff out slightly. The tiered effect of the sleeves is echoed in the style of cuffs, composed of layers of delicate lace. Softness of effect is also apparent in the simpler, more natural hairstyle, and the single rope of pearls.

Notorious for his extravagance in clothes, the Duke wears a paned doublet decorated with silver braid in a chevron pattern, and the very latest lace-edged collar and cuffs. Although it has a normal waistline, the skirt of it is lengthened into a deep basque. The bulk of his fur-lined cloak has been thrown over one arm, and the star of the Order of the Garter is embroidered onto the cloak.
(After Gerrit van Honthorst, 1628, Montacute)

are allowed to fall in natural folds to the ground. There was no agreed style of collar or neckwear at this time and this portrait illustrates the options that were available, from the old-fashioned ruff worn by the nurse to the lace falling band worn by Sir Thomas. The discreet paning on the girls' sleeves became an exaggerated feature of male and female dress by the end of the 1620s. It is also used as a decorative device on Sir Thomas's otherwise rather sombre black doublet and hose, but the restrained elegance of his outfit, and of that worn by his eldest son Spencer, looks forward to the fashions worn at the court of Charles I. Although display of jewellery is more discreet at this time, the two older girls wear very striking gold and pearl necklaces, and the blue enamel pendant attached to Lady Lucy's bodice would probably have contained a miniature.

When Charles I married Henrietta Maria of France a few months after his accession to the throne in 1625, it was not surprising that the main influence on fashion at their court was French. Although Charles's Wardrobe accounts show that he had a strong interest in fashion, his taste was not as flamboyant as his brother's and was characterised by a restrained elegance.[40] The French were not only responsible for popularising slashed or paned doublets, large-brimmed hats and long tapering breeches at the English court, but also for the distinctive way of wearing them. The effect was intended to be one of calculated untidiness, with the shirt billowing out of an unbuttoned doublet, breeches left unfastened, a feather-trimmed hat perched nonchalantly on the side of the head and crumpled soft leather boots with wide floppy tops.

Henrietta Maria introduced the ladies of the court to a short-waisted bodice, usually made with a basque that was tabbed on the lines of the male doublet, the tabs being deep, squared and very occasionally sewn together or laced across. Bodice sleeves were

52 Running across the bottom of this portrait of Alexander Carew of Antony is a line of crude stitching. Legend has it that this repairs a rip made when the painting was torn from its frame and banished to the cellar by Royalist relatives, furious that Alexander had declared for Parliament in the Civil War.

Carew's buff leather jerkin, still preserved at Antony, has been cut in the same style as the doublet – both have become fuller and looser in cut. Made of ox-hide dressed with oil, the buff jerkin was a functional and protective garment. The centre fastening is decorated with what appears to be red shag or thick fringing, and with a number of decorative points on the shoulder. Moderately full red breeches have been left unbuttoned at the knee, where there is a cluster of matching ribbon loops. Leather boots are folded back into deep tops, the front flap of the boots providing an elegant strap to which spurs could be fastened.
(Unknown artist, *c*.1630, Antony House)

SIR ALEXANDER
CAREW Bt

paned or slashed like men's doublets. Elegance of line was ensured by the plain silks and satins that replaced the heavier, densely-patterned materials of the Jacobean period. Garments from the male wardrobe were adopted by women for hunting and riding, much to the disgust of many writers who deplored 'the insolencie of our women, and theyr wearing of brode brimd hats, [and] pointed dublets'.[41]

The lax moral standards and dissolute behaviour that had been apparent at the court of James I were not in evidence at Charles's court, but beneath its refined and elegant surface the same tensions over finance and corrupt court practices remained. Charles was a discriminating and learned patron of the arts, anxious to shed England's image of being an artistic backwater. Despite the crown's patronage of foreign artists like Paul van Somer and Daniel Mytens, English portraiture remained provincial and relatively old-fashioned. Charles was determined to find an artist who could create an image of the monarchy and his court that was as sophisticated as any on the Continent.

His patronage of the arts took two forms: one was the systematic acquisition of masterpieces for the Royal Collection; and the second was to attract the finest living artists in Europe to work for him. The second part of his plan bore fruition in 1629, when the Flemish Peter Paul Rubens agreed to paint the ceiling of the Banqueting Hall in Whitehall, and again in 1632, when Anthony Van Dyck, also from Flanders, finally agreed to return to England. Charles rewarded him with a house, a gold chain, a pension and, three months after his arrival, a knighthood, but if Van Dyck had hoped to be involved in large-scale design and decorative commissions after all these honours he was disappointed. The increasingly precarious state of the crown's finances and the deteriorating political situation precluded the King from embarking on any major schemes and Van Dyck made his livelihood almost entirely out of portraits.

In this field he was outstandingly successful. His English clients, used to the stiff, meticulously-painted portraits of earlier court artists, were amazed by a fluid, illusionistic style that created a shimmering, almost breathing, image of themselves. A few years after Van Dyck's death in 1641 a contemporary writer observed that he was the 'first painter who e'er put ladies dress into a careless romance',[42] for the silks and satins that flow over his sitters have a timeless quality that ignores the heavy boning and structuring that were still demanded by fashion. Another, more modern, account comments:

> In a visual sense Van Dyck created, if not the English gentleman, at least the English aristocrat. It is quite true that if, in an English country house, you survey the portraits of its successive owners through the eighteenth and nineteenth centuries you will find again and again recurring that typical Van Dyck cast of features, high and proud . . . superbly uninterested in defeat.[43]

Choosing a Van Dyck portrait is difficult (there are several portraits of famous beauties at Petworth in Sussex alone), but at Kingston Lacy in Dorset there are particularly beautiful portraits of Sir John and Lady Borlase painted soon after their marriage in 1638 (53 and 54). Sir John's proud and haughty expression is that of a man who is in total command of himself and his destiny, while the soft billows of white and blue silk which flow over Lady Borlase invest her figure with a 'careless romance' that has little to do with fashion.

If the keynote of Van Dyck's portrait of Sir John is an understated elegance and

53 Sir John Borlase wears a falling band that
has widened into a full, laced-edged collar
extending so far that it almost resembles a
shoulder cape. By the end of the 1630s, mens-
wear had become so much looser and less formal
that the voluminous shirt spills out of the slashed
sleeves of the doublet and its lace frill cascades
from the front opening. In common with other
young courtiers of the time, Sir John is clean-
shaven and his long hair falls in wavy curls.
(Sir Anthony Van Dyck, 1638, Kingston Lacy)

54 Lady Borlase's costume, in a companion
portrait to **53**, is intended to be a modern
version of classical drapery, conveying a
timeless quality. The exigencies of fashionable
dress are ignored and the costume creates its
own rules. The scalloped edges of the low
décolletage are thus not masked by the wide lace
collar demanded by fashion, and the awkward
set of bulky sleeves into the high waistline of the
bodice is avoided by clasping it together with
brooches, disclosing the lace-trimmed sleeve of
the smock beneath. Lady Borlase's hair,
however, is arranged in the fashionable style
introduced from France to the Stuart court by
Queen Henrietta Maria.
(Sir Anthony Van Dyck, 1638, Kingston Lacy)

55 (*left*) Queen Henrietta Maria preferred a high-waisted, square-cut bodice, but the natural waistline of her costume in this portrait is indicated by a rope of pearls. A deep lace collar attached to the neckline is masked by a fine gauze kerchief folded diagonally and fastened with a jewelled button at the throat. Her smock sleeves with their lace cuffs have been turned back over the bodice sleeve. Delicate bands of gold braid are the only decoration on the matching red satin skirt and bodice. Such a low and visible décolletage would only have been worn at court.
(Unknown artist, *c.*1640, Penrhyn Castle)

56 (*below*) Margaret Spencer's blue satin bodice is shaped into the waist and is decorated, like the rather bulky matching skirt, with lines of wavy gold braid. A plain linen kerchief has been draped across her shoulder and fastened at the centre with a heart-shaped brooch. Unlike the Queen's smock sleeves, which have been turned back as close-fitting and gathered lace cuffs (55), Margaret's are plain and wide.
(Unknown artist, *c.*1645, Charlecote Park)

sophistication, the opposite is true of Edward Bower's portrait of an unknown Cavalier painted in 1638 (see **65**). Bower was an English artist about whom very little is known. His clientele came mostly from the ranks of the country gentry, though his masterpiece is acknowledged to be the sombre portrait of Charles I, painted while he was awaiting trial in London (a copy of which can be seen at Antony House in Cornwall). The portrait of the Cavalier has a curious nervy energy; the elaborate background, with its great swags of drapery and dramatic stormy sky, provides a suitably theatrical setting for this unknown man and his flamboyant finery, so despised by the Puritans, which he wears in a rather self-conscious way.

Van Dyck's double portrait (**41**), *c.*1639, of Mountjoy Blount, Earl of Newport and George, Lord Goring, two Royalist commanders, is an interesting and unusual one, as both men are wearing military dress with the same degree of elegance and panache as courtiers swathed in shimmering silks and satins.

Men and women's fashions had assumed an elegant and dignified line by the middle of Charles's reign, as a higher waistline, softly rounded contours and a lack of superfluous ornament replaced the restrictive rigidity and excessive fussiness of the previous period. The head, emerging from the gentle curves of the opulent lace-edged collar, was no longer isolated from the rest of the body and had once again become the focus of attention.

In a portrait of Queen Henrietta Maria by an unknown artist (**55**), painted *c.*1640, the artist's more linear style clearly shows the layered dress and accessories that were popular in women's fashion before the Civil War – in this case a high-waisted bodice with a square-cut neckline. An alternative to the high-waisted front-fastening bodice was one with a tightly-laced stomacher and a waistline that dipped to a low, rounded point. Margaret Spencer, who married Robert, Sir Thomas Lucy's second son, wears a bodice of this type in a portrait of *c.*1645 (**56**).

The appearance of Englishwomen was meticulously recorded between 1636 and 1646 by Wenceslaus Hollar, a Bohemian artist who had specialised in landscape studies before he came to England from Prague under the patronage of the Earl of Arundel. His passionate interest in the details of women's dresses and furs inspired him to publish in 1640 a series of 26 prints, based on his own drawings, showing English ladies wearing a style of dress that is associated with Van Dyck. Entitled *Ornatus Muliebris Anglicanus* the series was followed three years later by *Theatrum Mulierum*, a set of 36 prints depicting the women of Europe. It was later expanded in scope to a hundred prints with the title *Aula Veneris*. His drawings embrace all social groups and show a subtle distinction in dress between the classes. In 1643–4 a series called *The Four Seasons*[44] was published, in which Hollar placed a full-length figure of a woman in the foreground with a view behind. The lady representing 'Winter' (**57**) is of particular interest because she wears fashionable outdoor winter costume.

Despite repeated attempts at reform, the department of the Wardrobe continued to drain the limited financial resources of the Crown. Abuse of the system was uncovered in 1633 when a Commission discovered a 'persistence of old "scams" – tailors' bills, for instance, had been grossly inflated by unauthorized addition of travel costs'.[45] Attempts were then made to implement the findings of the Commission and expenditure was reduced to an average of £22,000 a year. But Charles continued to order many new

57 The lady representing 'Winter' in Wenceslaus Hollar's *The Four Seasons*, 1643-4, is wearing outdoor winter costume consisting of: a half-mask to protect the complexion; a chaperon, a soft hood worn over a linen coif and tied under the chin; a fine sable tippet over a lace-edged kerchief; and a ribbon-trimmed muff, also made of sable. Rather provocatively, she holds up her bulky velvet gown to reveal a petticoat and an elegant high-heeled shoe with a rosette.

She stands at the junction of Poultry, the east end of Cheapside, and Cornhill in the City of London. Behind her can be seen the tower and façade of the Exchange (see also **61**), and a number of wooden houses whose window shutters have been let down to provide a display area for shops. Painted signs identifying each shop are also visible. All these buildings were destroyed in the Fire of London, 1666.

clothes for everyday and ceremonial use. The Wardrobe Accounts for 1634–5 reveal that he received 30 suits (the most expensive cost £226 18s 8½d), 2 tennis suits, 1 coat, 2 cloaks, 4 riding coats and 1 chamber gown. All these garments were accompanied by a range of accessories, including protective calico covers for the most splendid embroidered suits, 98 pairs of shoes, 44 pairs of boots and 19 pairs of 'Tennis Socks'. Charles's belief in the importance of the 'outward trappings of royalty' was such that when he was held in captivity on the Isle of Wight in 1647 he ordered a new velvet suit, embroidered in gold, in anticipation of his transference to London. But the King's execution in 1649 was followed by a systematic destruction of the symbols of sovereignty: the coronation regalia was broken up, the metal was sent to the Mint and the jewels sold. The Queen's linen and clothes, stored in a large number of chests at Somerset House, were also dispersed when the Council of State sold the royal furniture.

During the Civil War the difference in dress between those who supported the Royalist or the Parliamentary cause was not as rigid as might be imagined, with plainness and severity in dress being less a distinction of religion than of social class. Portraits of some of the leading Parliamentarians and their wives certainly show them dressed in as much velvet and lace as their opponents. There were also varying opinions amongst the Parliamentarians as to what constituted sober apparel and there was scope for wide interpretation. In 1650, for example, when the Spanish ambassador was received in the House of Commons, the leading Parliamentarian soldier Colonel Hutchinson had shoulder-length hair and a suit that was 'pretty rich but grave', whereas his colleague, the Puritan General Harrison, wore a 'scarlet coat and cloak both laden with gold and silver lace, and the coat so covered with clinquant [metal foil] that one could scarcely discern the ground'.[46] The word puritan 'was a term very loosely applied to anyone who opposed the views of the court party',[47] and included a wide range of religious and political views. Only the extreme Puritans cut their hair short, hence the origin of the derisive term 'roundhead'. Lucy Hutchinson, for example, wife of the Colonel, was highly critical of such a hair-style in her *Memoirs of the Civil War*, denouncing those whose hair was cropped 'close round their heads, with so many little peakes as was something ridiculous to behold'.[48]

Another Puritan, Lady Brilliana Harley, whose husband Sir Robert was a leading Parliamentarian, was a keen needlewoman and very interested in fashion. Her letters to her beloved son Ned, an undergraduate at Oxford, express her concern that he should be well dressed. In a letter of 1638 she writes that she is unhappy about the colour her son has chosen for his new outfit, 'but the silk chamlet [camlet, see p.46] I like very well, both the cullor and stuff. Let your stockens be allways the same culler of your cloths and I hope you now weare Spanish leather shouwes. If your tutor does not intend to bye you silk stockens to weare with youre silke shurte send me word and I will, if please God, bestow a peare on you.'[49] A letter written a year earlier makes the point that he should be equally happy wearing 'plaine' or 'better' clothes and that if wearing fine clothes, one must 'not to thinke one self the better for them'. This attitude highlights the fact that for a Puritan the sin was not the clothes themselves, but being too preoccupied with one's own appearance.

Much has been written about the armour and uniforms worn in the Civil War and the activities of the Sealed Knot and other groups who re-enact the War have familiarised

58 Thomas Killigrew's portrait is interesting as he is wearing the informal fur-lined nightgown and nightcap, a combination which continued to be worn for comfort or before dressing. His satin gown, with its relatively narrow sleeves, is buttoned down the centre and tied with a sash at the waist. Its lining of brown fur has been turned back to form cuffs, and there is a matching turned-up fur flap on his cap. (William Sheppard, 1650, Dyrham Park)

people with a misleading stereotyped appearance. For example, as we have seen, the term 'Roundhead' originally denoted the short Puritan hair-style and not the rounded helmet, which was worn by the soldiers of both sides. Indeed, one of the problems encountered by soldiers was identification on the battlefield, as a recent book on the Civil War points out: 'Both sides looked very similiar and were only distinguishable by their scarves and sashes, or field signs, such as feathers or oak leaves which were often worn in hats, or by the use of field words, similar to passwords. The fact that both armies looked and dressed similarly and of course spoke the same language, made orientation on the battlefield difficult.'[50]

It is beyond the scope of this book to describe the uniforms worn by Cromwell's New Model Army, but an enthusiast is advised to visit Snowshill Manor in Gloucestershire (see p.9). On the Old Stairs which lead to Ann's Room are two sets of Cromwellian armour, one of which has its original buffcoat. It is rare for both to have survived, and extremely fortunate that the coat and a pair of leather riding boots of the same period are in such good condition (see 4).

The military turning point in the Civil War was Charles's crushing defeat at the Battle of Naseby in 1645, although military defeat did not necessarily mean that the King was prepared to concede political defeat. However, in November 1648 the Army's General Council finally decided that it must act against the King himself and 'purge' Parliament of members unsympathetic to its position. On 1 January 1649 the remaining members of the House of Commons passed an ordinance for the trial of Charles I. The execution of the King on 30 January and his son's humiliating defeat at the Battle of Worcester in 1651 forced Royalists into exile in Europe. One such was Thomas Killigrew, who had been a page of honour to Charles I. When Charles II made his first escape to the Continent Killigrew was appointed his Resident in Venice. In the portrait painted by William Sheppard in 1650 (58) he is holding his letter of appointment, and a portrait of the King hangs on the wall behind him. After the Restoration of Charles II in 1660 Killigrew was made Groom of the Bedchamber and Master of the Revels and was given a patent to build and manage the Theatre Royal in Drury Lane.

The foundation of 'The Commonwealth and free state' in 1649 resulted in a decade during which time-honoured customs and institutions disappeared. Christmas Day and May Day, with their attendant festivities, were abolished and country pursuits which involved communal dancing, singing and general merry-making were banned. Theatres were also closed, and a general air of dullness and sobriety engulfed the country. It is perhaps surprising that there was no legislation against extravagance in dress, and although a bill was proposed in 1650 'against the vice of painting, wearing of black patches and immodest dress'[51] it was never enacted. In fact, there is little difference in dress in the portraits of Royalist families and of the female relatives of leading members of the Commonwealth, some of whom were portrayed in a quasi-royal way.

But it was one thing to wear fine clothes in the privacy of one's own home and a different matter to flaunt them in London, a situation which Sir John Reresby discovered to his cost when he visited London from France in 1658:

The citizens and common people of London had then so far imbibed the customs and manners of a Commonwealth, that they could scarce endure the sight of a gentleman, so that the common salutation to a man well dressed was 'French dog' or the like. Walking one day in the street with my valet de chambre who did wear a feather in his hat, some workmen that were mending the street abused him and threw sand upon his clothes; at which he drew his sword, thinking to follow the custom of France in the like cases. This made the rabble fall upon him and me, who had drawn too in his defence, till we got shelter in a house, not without injury to our bravery and some blows to ourselves.[52]

59 Colonel John Russell, a Royalist officer in the Civil War. This portrait illustrates how fashionable dress retained certain military characteristics during the Commonwealth period of the 1650s. Russell's substantial sash, trimmed with thick gold fringing, is draped across a buff leather jerkin which has a natural waistline when compared with the looser fashion adopted by Alexander Carew (52). It is fastened down the front by means of lacing, and the same lacing is used to decorate the armholes. In both places the elongated points of the lacing are left to hang free. The wide lace collar, as worn by Sir John Borlase (53) and the unknown Cavalier (65), has now shrunk in size to a shallow collar raised in front to disclose its ornate tassels. Full shirt sleeves billow out of the divided sleeve of the doublet, and the movement of fabric is further accentuated by a bow tied on and above the wrist, so that the shirt flops over. A stiff lace cuff echoes the circular shape. Russell wears his hair very long and full. (John Michael Wright, 1659, Ham House)

II

The period leading up to the Civil War was one of expansion for the retail trade in London and signalled the move away from the confines of the area inside the City walls. Early in the seventeenth century the large mansions on the Strand were gradually replaced by smaller houses for the well-to-do citizens as the large estates were sold and redeveloped, their owners moving to more rural surroundings outside the City. Soon shops appeared to service this new community. One such, according to a letter written in 1603 by Frances, Countess of Hertford, was owned by a Mrs Price, who sold the finest embroidered nightcaps in London.[53] On the south side of the Strand, on the site of the stables of Durham House, Robert Cecil, Earl of Salisbury, James I's chief minister, built the New Exchange. When Count Lorenzo Magalotti visited it in 1669, on a private visit to England with Cosimo III, Grand Duke of Tuscany, he described it as having 'a façade of stone, built after the Gothic style, which has lost its colour from age, and is become blackish. It contains two long and double galleries, one above the other, in which are distributed, in several rows, great numbers of very rich shops of drapers and mercers filled with goods of every kind, and with manufactures of the most beautiful description.'[54] It was opened on 11 April 1609 with an entertainment written by Ben Jonson.

60 (*left*) The interiors of the Old and New Exchanges must have looked very much like Abraham Bosse's engraving of a similar establishment in Paris in the 1640s. The stock – linen, falling bands, collars and gloves – is displayed behind the lady standing at her counter. Her assistant busies himself placing the customer's purchases into a box: hence the origin of the expression 'band box'.

61 (*right*) The role of the Royal Exchange as a prestigious trading centre with an international reputation is vividly conveyed by Hollar's 1644 engraving. The entire ground floor is filled with a seething mass of merchants, foreigners and fashionable men engaged in animated conversation and negotiation. Some wear low-crowned, wide-brimmed beaver hats, others the latest style – the high-crowned hat. There is only one female figure, a ballad seller (left, foreground), in the conical, wide-brimmed hat of the lower classes, a bodice with a deep basque, a plain kerchief and a moderately full skirt and apron. The outside appearance of the entrance to the Exchange on the left-hand side, and the Tower above it, are clearly visible in the background of Hollar's 'Winter' (57).

The King and members of his court were present and 'over £96, or more than half the total cost of the royal visit, was spent on various Indian commodities, China commodities, and gold rings with poesies in them'.[55] Shops that imported oriental goods like silk and porcelain were called 'china houses', and they soon became a favourite resort for fashionable women who used them as places of assignation. That china houses were in existence on the Strand is apparent from the following line from Jonson's play *Epicene* (1609–10): 'He hath a lodging in the Strand for the purpose, to watch when ladies are going to the China-Houses or the Exchange that he may meet 'em by chance and give 'em presents, some 2 or 300 pounds worth of toys.'[56]

Even after the second Exchange was built, the original Exchange in the City remained the centre of commercial activity until the Fire of London. Its role as an international trading centre is vividly conveyed by Wenceslaus Hollar's engraving of 1644 (61), in which a mixed group of merchants and foreigners entirely fills the ground-floor area.

Thomas Heywood's play *The Faire Maide of the Exchange* (1607) (see also p.49), gives a very detailed picture of the way the different fashion stalls in the old Exchange operated and of the services they offered to their customers. The 'Faire Maide', Phyliss Flower, is an apprentice to a seamstress in the Exchange and is pursued by Cripple the 'Drawer'. A drawer was a professional pattern-drawer, who would adapt patterns from various pattern-books, or create a design to suit the customer's specific requirements. His patterns would have been suitable for clothing and accessories as well as cushions and hangings. We know from the Lisle letters a century earlier that Hussee was commissioned to find a drawer to execute complex patterns on some of Lady Lisle's cushions.

One of the characters in the play, Moll Berry, asks Cripple to create a design for a handkerchief embodying the following imagery:

> In one corner of the same, place wanton love,
> Drawing his bow shooting an amorous dart,
> Opposite him an arrow in a heart,
> In a third corner, picture forth disdaine
> A cruel fate unto a loving vaine:
> In the fourth draw a springing Laurel-tree,
> Circled about with a ring of poesie: and thus it is:
> Love wounds the heart, and conquers fell disdayne.[57]

Moll would embroider this design herself and then present the handkerchief to her lover, so that he might know by looking at it what her feelings for him were, hence the meaning of the phrase 'printing my thoughts in lawn'.[58]

Colours could also convey visual expressions of one's emotions, and the connection between the two is apparent in a poem of the period entitled 'A gentlewoman that married a young gentleman, who after forsooke hir, whereupon she took hir needle, in which she was excellent, and worked upon hir sample thus':

> Give me black silk, that sable suites my hart,
> And yet som white, though white words do deceive,
> No green at all, for youth and I must part,
> Purple and blew, fast love and faith to weave.[59]

Drawers did not only operate in London. We know, for instance, from the letters that Lady Brilliana Harley wrote to her son Edward, that there was one in Oxford. In a letter dated 14 March 1639 she asks her son to 'tell George Griffithes that I haue received the petticoates wch Mr. Nelham did drawe, and the silk and the wyre, for which Mr Nelham shall have money, when I receive the piece of greene cloth from him'.[60]

Not everyone would want to pay someone to create embroidery designs for them and would invent their own. Grace, Lady Mildmay, the daughter of Sir Henry Sharington of Lacock Abbey in Wiltshire, was a prolific embroiderer and she recorded in her Journal, written between 1570 and 1617, that 'every day I spent some tyme in works of myne owne invention, without sample or pattern before me for carpett or cushion worke, and to drawe flowers and fruitt to their lyfe with my plumett [quill] upon paper'.[61]

There were also embroiderers who travelled from house to house embroidering furnishings and garments during their stay. One such was John Rofe, who worked for the Bacon family in 1593: '. . . at one point he was working on the hangings for a bed and at another working on gowns and stomachers. He received as wages 16d a day', and for working on three gowns and stomachers £4 7s. He also drew patterns for the family and in 1591 received 12d for drawing a pattern on a cushion cloth and in 1593 3s 4d for 'drawinge your things'.[62]

The complex style of Jacobean embroidery design and the lavish use of rich gold and silver thread and spangles ensured that ready-made garments could be very expensive, with 'rich and curious embroydered waistcoats' costing as much as £20 or £40. In 1608 the Royal embroiderer charged Henry, Prince of Wales £45 for decorating a jerkin and a pair of panes of perfumed leather and £50 for embroidering two waistcoats 'wrought verie curiously in colour silke'.[63] The total bill for his clothes that year was £4,574 14s but, according to the Governor of his Household, the embroiderer, Mr Palmer, was not paid and was 'ready to perish for wante of money'.[64] On 14 February 1613 when Princess Elizabeth married the Elector Palatine, many of the guests wore sumptuously-embroidered clothes. According to one eyewitness: 'It were to no end to write of the curiositie and excesse of braverie both of men and women, with the extreme daubing on of cost and riches, only a touch shall serve in a few for a pattern of the rest.'[65] One guest, Lady Wotton, 'had a gown that cost 50 pound a yard the embrodering' – an astonishing sum, as a gown usually required six to twelve yards of material.[66]

The anonymous author of the play *Sir Giles Goosecap*, 1606, pokes fun at the fashion for life-like and expensive embroidery. One of the characters in the play, Lord Tales, boasts that he knows of an embroiderer who can 'worke you any flower to the life as like as if it grew in the verie place' and can make a bedcover embroidered with glow-worms that are so 'perfectly done, that you may goe to bed in the chamber, doe anything in the chamber, without a candle'.[67]

The variety and range of materials and trimmings that could be found in London meant that precise instructions were essential if someone was buying on your behalf. When Sir Edmund Verney of Claydon was appointed Knight-Marshal to Charles I, he was frequently required to be in attendance at court, but as he did not possess a suitably grand town house he leased the last two houses in the newly-built Piazza at Covent Garden. When in residence there he received endless requests for fashion items and accessories from Lady Sussex, who lived at Gorhambury House near St Albans. In one letter she needs a silver lace trimming and some ribbons for a sweet bag (37): 'If you woulde plese to imploye somebody to chuse me out a lase that hath but very littell silver in itt and not above a spangell or to in a peke i thinke woulde do will; i woulde not have it to hevy a lase; about the breth of a threpeny ribinge very littill broder will bee enofe; and desier Mrs Varney i pray you to chuse me out some ribinge to make stringes; six yardes will be enofe.'[68]

Covent Garden, originally the Convent Garden Estate, the property of the Abbey of Westminster, was granted to John Russell, 1st Earl of Bedford, in 1552. In 1585 Edward, the 3rd Earl, rebuilt Bedford House, the gardens of which later formed the southern boundary of the market there. In 1631 Francis, the 4th Earl, on payment of a fee of £2,000, was given a licence to build a number of houses suitable for the nobility and

62 *The Common Cryes of London* dating from the 1630s is one of the earliest broadsheets to illustrate the variety of goods that could be purchased from street sellers in London. As this detail suggests, they sold a huge variety of goods, from second-hand doublets and coney (rabbit) skins to foodstuffs of all kinds. The householder's requirements were also well met by items such as mats, glasses and 'kitchen stuffe' or the services of chimney sweeps.

wealthy gentry. The licence was granted on the proviso that the King's Surveyor of Works, Inigo Jones, should approve the plans. This was done, and a terrace of three elegant brick houses, each with a frontage of either 30 or 50 ft, was built on three sides of a central piazza between 1631 and 1639. There were elegant arcades, with a walkway 21-ft wide, on three sides, and on the western side Inigo Jones designed a new church, St Paul's, the first to be erected in London since the Reformation. Although traders were originally banned from the area, from the 1640s they began to gather in the Piazza on the south side and in 1670 the 5th Earl was granted a royal charter to establish a market that sold fruit, flowers and vegetables.

Another area famous for its concentration of shops selling high-quality fabrics and dress accessories was London Bridge (see **35**). This extraordinary bridge was the only one across the River Thames, and on either side of its narrow twelve-foot-wide thoroughfare wooden houses four storeys high were crowded together. The projecting backs of these houses overhung the water and had to be supported on great wooden beams, while the upper storeys were tied together by iron bars to stop them toppling backwards into the water. The houses were very narrow at street level and it was this dark ground-floor area that was used as shops. When the bridge was nearly destroyed

63 In this 1640s' engraving by Hollar, the new, spacious Italianate buildings of the Covent Garden Piazza are grouped around Inigo Jones' St Paul's Church (later depicted by Hogarth in his painting, *Morning* (**131**)). The ladies in the foreground would appear to be moderately wealthy, with their chaperons, plain kerchiefs and skirts carefully pulled round to the back to create a bustle effect.

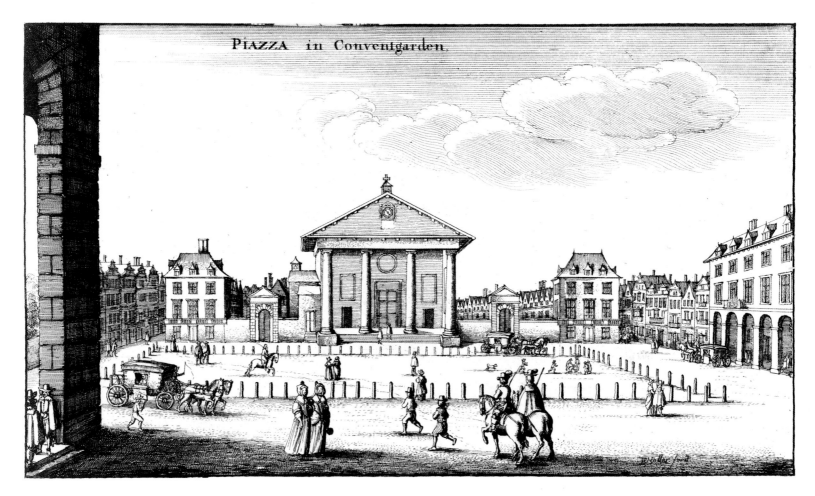

PIAZZA in Conventgarden.

64 Hollar was fascinated by ladies' dress and accessories, and many of his extraordinarily detailed engravings were concerned with these. This is one of seven illustrations of muffs and furs, dated 1647. In addition he shows a folding fan with a delicate ribbon bow, a feather fan, lace-trimmed kerchiefs and, resting on a striped pin cushion, a pair of gloves and a half-mask.

by fire in 1633 a list was made of the shops that had been lost. There were 41, including seven haberdashers of small wares, six hosiers, four haberdashers of hats, two glovers, three silk men, two woollen drapers, two mercers, one shoemaker, one girdler, one linen draper, one milliner and one needle maker, in whose shop the fire started. In the centre of the bridge there was a small square and on its west side was a shop with the sign of the Blue Boar. At the time of the 1633 list the shop was empty, but in the eighteenth century, when it was owned by Coles Child, it was famous for the enormous variety of goods that could be bought there.

The bridge consisted of nineteen small arches supported by eighteen solid stone piers, varying from 25 to 34ft in thickness. These piers rested on an outwork of piles that projected into the water, forcing it into narrow and dangerously fast-flowing channels. The river current was so strong that it was impossible to 'shoot the bridge' on a flood tide and dangerous on an ebb tide, and many passengers preferred to get out of the ferry boats at the Old Swan Stairs on the north bank of the river, walk along Upper Thames Street and rejoin the boat at Billingsgate Stairs. An average of fifty watermen were drowned attempting to pass under the bridge every year, and many passengers died after being tipped into the river and either drowning or swallowing too much of the heavily-polluted water. In July 1641 a log banged into the Royal Barge as it passed under the bridge, and overturned it. On this occasion all but one of the occupants were rescued – Mrs Anne Kirke, one of Queen Henrietta Maria's Women of the Bedchamber, was drowned.[69]

The sartorial competitiveness of King James's court created an insatiable demand for imported luxury fabrics. The desire 'to be the first and principle in all fashions: precede all the dames at court by a fortnight'[70] ensured a huge financial outlay on fashion. The mercers were quick to respond and their representatives scoured the cities of Europe for the most spectacular fabrics. The cosmopolitan taste of the *nouveaux riches* was satirised by John Webster in his play *Anything for a Quiet Life*, 1621, in which Lady

Cressingham complains that the silks the mercer shows her are not exciting enough, and requests that new patterns be ordered from Italy: 'The rich stuffs which my husband bought of you – the works of them are too common. I have got a Dutch painter to draw patterns which I'll have sent to your Factors; as in Italy, at Florence and Ragusa, where these stuffs are woven, to have pieces made for my own wearing of a new invention.' When the mercer replies that it would be very expensive, Lady Cressingham retorts that the cost is unimportant and she will employ her own agents in France, Italy and Spain so that they can gather 'intelligence of all new fashions'.[71]

Sir Baptist Hicks was the most successful mercer of the period. His shop, at the sign of the White Bear, was at the junction of Sopers Lane and Cheapside. It was established by the 1580s and he was still running it in 1618. He supplied goods to Queen Elizabeth, Robert Cecil, 1st Earl of Salisbury, Arthur Throckmorton, and Charles Howard, 1st Earl of Nottingham, the Lord High Admiral. We also know that Sir Francis Bacon, the Lord Chancellor, patronised Hicks's shop, and one belonging to another mercer, Edward Barnes. John Chamberlain wrote in April 1618 that he saw Bacon attending a sermon in the Mercers' Chapel in Cheapside 'in all his pompe of the counsaile [Council], which was not so straunge as (not a moneth) since to see him in the same state go to Sir Baptist Hicks and Barnes shops to cheapen [bargain] and buy silkes and velvets'.[72] By 1595 Hicks had a representative at Leghorn in Italy, and one in Florence by 1602. Trading in this way without recourse to an intermediary meant that Hicks ensured that the goods sold in his shop were of the highest quality. When James I came to the throne Hicks was chosen to be the main supplier to the Great Wardrobe, and he was knighted soon after.

The King ordered enormous quantities of fabrics from Hicks and in one year, between Michaelmas 1608 and August 1609, he was paid £14,083 for 'wares'.[73] The profits he made from the business enabled him to build the imposing Campden House in Kensington in 1612 in what was then open countryside. An engraving of the house, made by Hollar in 1647, shows that it had a magnificent and imposing façade with Hicks's coat-of-arms emblazoned above a large bay window. The house was considered grand enough to accommodate Charles II, who stayed there soon after the Restoration, and it was purchased in 1690 by Princess Anne (later Queen Anne) as a home for her delicate only surviving son, the Duke of Gloucester, who died in 1700, hoping that he might benefit from the country air. The house, with its intricate and elaborate internal panelling, survived intact until the morning of Sunday, 23 March 1862, when it was totally destroyed by fire.

The place to 'publish your clothes' in London was the middle aisle of St Paul's Cathedral, commonly called 'Powles Walk' or 'Duke Humphrey's Walk' (a reference to the tomb of Humphrey of Gloucester – which was, in fact, the tomb of Sir John Beauchamp). Every morning between 10 and 12 an impromptu fashion parade would take place as gallants strutted up and down the aisle showing off their clothes and accessories. It had become such an established ritual that it was the subject of at least two satirical pamphlets: 'The meeting of gallants at an ordinarie or the walkes in Powles' (1603) and Thomas Dekker's 'The Guls Horne-Booke' (1609). In the third chapter of the latter, 'How a Gallant should behaue himselfe in Powles Walkes', Dekker advises a newcomer to 'bend your course directly in the middle line, that the whole body of the

65 Edward Bower's portrayal of the costume of an unknown Cavalier is full of wonderful exaggeration. Panes on the sleeves extend from shoulder to elbow, ending in turned-back cuffs whose neat scalloped edges have been trimmed with black bobbin lace. The cloak is trimmed in a similar way. He wears Spanish hose – long-legged breeches closed below the knee with sash garters trimmed with hanging black bobbles. The deep lace edging of the boothose is carefully arranged to rest on the turned-down bucket tops of the fashionably-creased boots. Boots, once only worn by those engaged in military or country pursuits, have now replaced shoes as the most fashionable form of footwear.

His carefully co-ordinated outfit is completed by an embroidered sword-belt, plain leather gloves, a ribbon (probably a lady's favour) tied around the wrist, and a wide-brimmed, low-crowned hat, also adorned with a ribbon. (Edward Bower, 1638, Dunster Castle)

66 'Here's Jack in the Box', an anonymous engraving that forms the frontispiece of a penny book, 1657. The pedlar displays his goods for sale – a variety of patches, ribbons, a fringed sash, a feather fan and a mask.

church may appear to be yours; where, in view of all, you may publish your suit in what manner you affect most'. He further recommends that 'four turns' in the Walk are sufficient, as a fifth would mean that your suit 'would be stale to the whole spectators'.[74]

It was round Duke Humphrey's tomb that debtors and people seeking a free meal also gathered, so it was advisable to leave the Cathedral promptly in case it was thought you could not afford the cost of a meal. Visiting an 'ordinary' or eating-house was another highly effective way of showing off your clothes as they were graded according to cost, with the most expensive and fashionable charging two shillings for a meal. Slightly less fashionable people ate at the eighteen-pence ordinary, and below that there was the shilling ordinary, which was frequented by young knights and Justices of the Peace, and below that the ten-penny, the sixpenny and the threepenny, at which could be found the 'London Usurer, your stale Batchelor, and your thrifty Atturney'.[75] Servants would eat at the three-half-pence ordinary. After dinner (taken at midday) the gallant returned to St Paul's ostentatiously picking his teeth with a quill or a 'silver instrument', but he would not stay long, probably leaving to wander around the booksellers' stalls, tobacco shops and tailors' shops that were in the immediate vicinity of the Cathedral.

Arrangements for travelling around the country gradually improved during the first 50 years of the century. By 1637 a public coach service was running between St Albans and the Bell Inn in Aldersgate; by 1656 there was a service between London and York; and the next year one was running three days a week from the George Inn, Aldersgate, to Chester, a journey that took five days. By 1660 it was possible to travel by coach from London to Durham, Newcastle, Preston, Kendal, Exeter and Plymouth.

In London two new forms of transport, the hackney or hired coach and the sedan-chair, must have helped the weary shopper. Sir Edmund Verney was given the right to run the first stand for hackney coaches at the Maypole in the Strand in 1634, but these four-wheeled coaches drawn by two horses and seating six passengers were immediately named 'Hackney Hell-carts', due to their drivers' reckless style of driving. Despite this, they were extremely popular, and by 1669 there were already 800 hackney coachmen successfully plying for trade.

The sedan-chair was introduced to England from Italy in 1634 by Sir Sanders Duncombe, who obtained a patent from the King allowing him to provide 40 or 50 chairs for public use. There was immediate opposition to the scheme from the coach-drivers, who were worried about losing trade, and a pamphlet appeared which set out the cases of the opposing parties.[76] The two men who carried the sedan-chair would be preceded, at night, by linkboys, whose flaming torches provided lighting for the journey. Once the destination was reached the torches were thrust into trumpet-shaped extinguishers located by the front doors of the houses of the wealthy. The sedan-chair was not a popular mode of transport when it was first introduced, but by the end of the century there were some 300 licensed carriers as well as many privately-owned chairs, painted in the colours of the family's coat-of-arms and bearing the family crest. A number of eighteenth-century chairs, with their original and often elaborate upholstery, have survived in National Trust houses.[77]

The various different methods of transporting goods at this time are clearly set out in a letter written by Lady Sussex to Sir Edmund Verney in 1639. The item to be transported from London to Buckinghamshire was a copy of a portrait Van Dyck had painted of Lady Sussex. As it was a full-length portrait in a gilt frame it was bulky and heavy and could easily have been damaged. She suggests that it could either be sent with the coal waggon from London, or the waggon from St Albans, or that it could be carried by two porters or on horseback, laid across two panniers. The means of transport used is not revealed, but when the painting finally arrived the only damage was to the frame, which was 'a littell hurt, the gilt being robbede off'.[78]

It is rare to find detailed accounts of daily living expenses for people visiting London in the early seventeenth century, but the accounts of the Shuttleworth family of Gawthorpe Hall, Lancashire are a fascinating exception.[79] They give a vivid picture of what was entailed in organising an expedition to London, and of what shopping facilities were available in Lancashire. Richard Shuttleworth succeeded to the Gawthorpe estate on the death of his uncle, the Reverend Laurence Shuttleworth, in February 1608 and soon after married Fleetwood Barton (67). In July of that year Richard and Fleetwood and his two sisters, Anne and Eleanor, visited London. They appear to have stayed first in Gray's Inn, where his brother, Nicholas, was in chambers, and thence in lodgings in the Strand, a move which involved a four-pence payment to porters. Throughout August and September their steward endeavoured to find a suitable house for the family to rent. In October he went to see a house in Islington and in November a six-months' rental of £8 6s was paid to Mr Iremonger for a house there. Vital household items like a cooler, a great kettle, a grid iron, a washing tub, a frying pan and an iron pot, a truckle bed, six stools and three Venice glasses were purchased straight away, and workmen were called in to mend the gutters, resharpen the knives and deliver sea coal for heating. The family made sure that their neckwear was kept in pristine condition by purchasing an earthenware basin to put starch in and they paid 2s for 6lb of starch and 16d for 1lb of blue powder to whiten their linen.[80]

The family stayed in the house until May 1609. Their main expenditure was to Thomas Leaver, a confectioner and dealer in spices, with whom the family placed a substantial order each year. But sadly no mention is made of the clothes purchased by the family, save for one payment of 4d 'for the gentlewomen's gownes, to Mr Johnes' and the substantial payment of £7 to Mr Leigh, a tailor in the Strand, for making clothes for Richard. Amongst the items that they took back to Lancashire were 4lb of soap, 7lb of white starch, 1lb of blue starch and a quantity of pewter, which was delivered separately. They paid 2s 6d a day to hire a caroche in London – this was a lighter vehicle than a coach.[81] Leaving some of their luggage for collection by the carrier at the White Lion Inn in Islington[82] they made the journey back to Lancashire in a hired coach drawn by four horses. The journey took some nine days, with overnight stops in six towns and two nights spent at Warrington in Cheshire.

Richard and Fleetwood's first child and heir was born in 1610 with the assistance of a midwife who had to be fetched from Wigan. He was followed by another ten children, all of whose clothing requirements appear to have been met locally. Richard's clothes were occasionally bought in London. In September 1617, for example, 5 cloaks cost a total of £7 5s 6d, 20yds of grosgrain £9 17s, 10½oz of gold and silver lace 59s 5d and six dozen gold and silver buttons 9s. He also bought himself a hat for 14s 6d and a band and collar costing 26s for Fleetwood, together with a hat and 6yds of lace costing 12s 4d. In July 1620 a total of £8 19s 6d was spent on goods bought from a mercer, haberdasher

67 A portrait of Fleetwood Barton painted shortly after her marriage. She is shown wearing a somewhat restrained but fashionable outdoor costume, with a plain black bodice setting off the pristine whiteness of the circular ruff and its modest, but very decorative, edging of delicate bobbin lace. Pinned to her hair, its fullness created by padded rolls, is the tall-crowned, shallow-brimmed hat that was the popular form of headwear amongst the country gentry. Fleetwood has embellished hers with an embroidered hat-band.
(Unknown artist, *c.*1610, Gawthorpe Hall)

and silk man in London. Fleetwood had to pay 11s to change a cloak and 8d for a 'long button' to fasten it; also 12s 6d for a 'pair of Frenche bodies' and 15s for a ruff.[83] As the cost of transporting goods was high – it cost £3 to transport three trunks from London to Gawthorpe Hall in 1613 – shopping was usually done locally. Fleetwood frequently visited Manchester to buy material and the general store in Padiham, the local town, for small quantities of material like taffeta and fustian. Linen cloth and fustian were also purchased in nearby Colne and a substantial amount of material and trimmings were bought from Mr Towneley's shop in another local town, Hurstwood. All these towns were within a 30-mile radius of Gawthorpe Hall. A tailor called Henry Hopwood was often commissioned to make garments for Fleetwood and Richard, and at least two other tailors made clothes for the family and the servants on the premises. Liveries for the servants were made elsewhere, as a trunk containing them was collected from Bolton in 1612.

The Shuttleworths of Gawthorpe and the Verneys of Claydon were both families belonging to the five per cent of the population that formed the gentry. Above them were the nobility and directly below them were the plain country gentlemen and prosperous yeomen. There were about 500 of these politically-influential gentry families, whose members served as Members of Parliament and frequently held appointments as sheriffs or deputy lieutenants of the county. Richard Shuttleworth was MP for Preston from 1642 and at the outbreak of the Civil War in that year was appointed colonel of Parliamentary forces in defence of north-east Lancashire. An action in which he was involved precipitated the collapse of the Royalist cause in the county and certainly saved Gawthorpe Hall from destruction.

London was a Parliamentary stronghold during the Civil War so its citizens were required to contribute to the cost of the fortifications and the maintenance of the Parliamentary army. It must have been a gloomy and depressing time for the fashion trade, as nearly all building in the City and suburbs had been brought to a halt and many houses lay empty, deserted by the families of those who were fighting for the King. St James's Palace became a barracks for Cromwell's troops and weeds were growing in Whitehall.

CHAPTER THREE

Wigs & Drapery

1660–1720

{

I

In 1660 Samuel Pepys was a member of the deputation sent to The Hague to ask Charles II to return with them to England. He recorded in his diary on 16 May that the King was in 'a sad, poor condition for clothes and money' and that his clothes, and those worn by his attendants, were not 'worth 40s, the best of them'.[1] Later, on the journey back to England, Pepys was moved to tears hearing the King relate his experiences as a fugitive after the Battle of Worcester in 1651, when he was forced to wear 'nothing but a green coat and a pair of country breeches on and a pair of country shoes, that made him so sore all over his feet that he could scarce stir'.[2] Nine years of exile with dwindling, and at times non-existent, funds had forced Charles to move from one court of Europe to another, and in such reduced circumstances that he found it became increasingly difficult to maintain a suitably regal and impressive appearance.

It was not surprising then that Charles wanted to buy the most sumptuous and fashionable clothes possible for his triumphal ride into London and his Coronation the next year at Westminster Abbey. Five suits and cloaks for the latter were begun in Paris by the French tailor Claude Sorceau and finished in London by John Allen and William Watts at a cost of £2,271 19s 10d.[3] Lavishly embellished with gold and silver lace the clothes were, of course, in the French style.

> Everything new came from Paris, the Mecca of the civilised world, from sedan chairs, and dainty silver brushes for cleaning the teeth, to Châtelin's famous fricassées and râgouts. . . . Charles did achieve a change in English taste far greater than any transient turn of fashion. For it affected everything, our architecture, our dress, food and manners, our books, our whole attitude of life.[4]

Londoners who had been used to a relatively sombre uniformity of dress and absence of ceremonial costume during the Commonwealth must have been dazzled by the sight of Charles II and his retinue, dressed in the latest French fashions, riding across London Bridge to enter the City of London on the King's birthday, 29 May 1660. The anonymous author of a pamphlet entitled *England's Joy* (1660) described how the King 'found the windows and streets exceedingly thronged with people to behold him; and the walls adorned with hangings and carpets of tapestry and other costly stuff; and in many places sets of loud musick, and all the conduits, as he passed, running claret wine'.[5]

For many of the families that had been in exile with the King, the years had brought great hardship. Ralph and Mary Verney, who had spent the years in France, had lost five of their children, with only Edmund and John surviving. The Restoration heralded a change in their fortunes. John, a silk merchant trading in Italy, prospered in the Levant trade and was created Viscount Fermanagh in 1703. Edmund, or 'Mun' as his parents referred to him, was always in a rather precarious state of health for he had been born with a deformity of the spine which left one shoulder higher than the other and he had to wear a specially-made iron harness lined with leather, a treatment which was not successful.

On 13 July 1655 Edmund Verney, then living in Holland, had written to his father

68 (*previous pages*) Elizabeth Dysart with her second husband, John Maitland, 1st Duke of Lauderdale. The Duchess's nightgown has been left unfastened to reveal her smock – with the latest tiered sleeves – and most of her bosom. Dispensing with the conventional pearl necklace and ear-rings, her only accessory is a gauzy, gold-edged scarf.
The Duke's partially-buttoned coat has short sleeves buttoned back in a cuff, and there is a knot of ribbons on the right shoulder and bunches of ribbons at the waist and on the breeches. The Garter star is embroidered on his coat.
(Sir Peter Lely, *c.*1674, Ham House)

69 (*right*) Charles II wearing his sumptuous ermine-lined Parliament robes over his Garter costume, and the new St Edward's Crown, fashioned out of the old Imperial Crown. Anxious to restore the pomp and ceremony that had been such an essential accompaniment to the monarchy, Charles retained the traditional features of the Garter robes and regalia, but added lavish ribbon trimming to reflect fashionable taste. (See also p.104.)
(John Michael Wright, *c.*1676, Royal Collection)

88

Ralph asking for 150yds of black ribbon to trim a grey and black cloth doublet. His father had replied, rather unhelpfully, that he thought that this was an excessive amount, '. . . so a suite bee whole, cleane, and fashionable I care not how plaine it bee'.[6] However, Edmund eventually got his wish and soon after the Restoration two new suits were made for him, one was trimmed with 141 and the other with 216yds of ribbon. Both were padded so that his deformity was disguised. These unique silk suits, the only complete examples of their type in England, were kept by the family and are often on display at Claydon (see 70). They have been described in detail by Lesley Edwards in her article 'Dres't like a May-Pole'.[7]

It is thought that the suits were made between 1660, when Charles II introduced the fashion of petticoat breeches into England, and Edmund Verney's marriage to Mary Abell in July 1662. They have probably survived because the fashion for petticoat breeches only lasted another few years, when it was superseded by the new combination of vest, tunic and breeches. It would have been impossible to alter the doublets and difficult to alter the breeches and, in any case, Edmund had begun to put on an enormous amount of weight. A portrait of Edmund at Claydon painted in 1657–8 shows him to have been of modest build, a fact that is confirmed by the chest measurement of both suits, which is $36\frac{1}{2}$in. However, by 1673, when he weighed 20 stone, his complaint that his tailor made his coat 'too scanty in the circumference, a fault a man should not have committed that had ever seen me', suggests that his girth had become very noticeable.[8]

The first suit is in poor condition. It is made from black, finely-corded silk and consists of a padded doublet, with a stiff collar, that fastens down the front with 27 buttons (now missing) and matching breeches. Both doublet and breeches are trimmed with black Flemish silk bobbin lace, sadly now disintegrating because of the dye used, and ribbon loops made into bunches or knots. These knots of ribbons, or 'fancies' as they were called, were purely decorative. Earlier in the century points – ribbon ties that ended in a metal tag – were a vital accessory as they were attached to the waistband of the breeches and then threaded through matching eyelet holes in the doublet in order to unite both garments. When breeches were fastened to the inside waistband of the doublet by hooks and eyes the points lost their functional purpose but were retained as a decorative feature. As the desire for decoration increased, more and more yards of ribbon were required. The second suit (70) comprises a doublet, breeches and cloak all made from cream-coloured figured silk.

At the time of the Restoration some of the courtiers at Louis XIV's court in France were wearing these extraordinary petticoat breeches. They were immensely wide breeches, pleated into a waistband, and they reached to the knees, or even to mid-calf, and were edged at the waist and bottom edge with an enormous quantity of ribbon loops. Petticoat breeches found favour in England too: the circumference of each leg of the Verney suits is 62in. On 6 April 1661 Pepys records in his diary how his friend Mr Townsend put 'both his legs through one of his Knees of his breeches, and went so all day'.[9]

A matching doublet was cut short so that the shirt would show between doublet and breeches. To achieve a maximum exposure of the expensive linen shirt and its even more expensive lace trimming, the doublet was left partially unbuttoned. Sleeves were composed of narrow strips of brocade attached only at the armholes and the short cuff,

70 and 71 One of the silk suits made for Edmund Verney at the Restoration. The doublet is lined with white taffeta, visible as an edging on the panes of the doublet sleeves, which are joined to a band at the cuff. The spectacular breeches are joined together with a crutch seam and are fastened at the waist, front and back, with a single button, the only fastening. Identical buttons, but smaller in size, have been used to fasten the front of the doublet.

The lavish use of ribbon trimming cannot fail to impress: the colours before they faded must have been brilliant. Six types of ribbon in different colours were employed, combining deep salmon pink and plain yellow taffeta, double-sided satin of blue-green and plain cream, and figured ribbon in lilac, ivory and pink ivory. The 58yds of ribbon used to decorate the doublet are arranged in sixteen bunches of knots attached to each cuff. There are 158yds of ribbon on the breeches, used to make 36 knots, twelve of which have been stitched around the waist. Each knot was made up from a 22-in length of each of the six ribbons, worked into two loops of material.

thus allowing a display of lavishly-trimmed short sleeve. As much as 250yds of ribbon would be needed to decorate such an outfit and this, along with other trimmings and luxury fabrics, was produced in France. Louis XIV, acting on the advice of his minister Jean-Baptiste Colbert, had renewed a ban on imported embroideries, cloth of gold and silver, and Flemish and Venetian laces, creating instead a native industry by recruiting skilled Italian craftsmen and settling them in Alençon, Arras and Reims. These towns subsequently became flourishing centres supplying France and the rest of Europe with fashion textiles and accessories of the very highest quality.

Petticoat breeches were worn with canions. These were a decorative addition to the stockings and were displayed when the stocking was turned down over the garter under the knee, the voluminous folds of the deep fall of linen repeating the shape of the breeches, cravat and shirt cuff. They are mentioned by Pepys in his diary on 24 May 1660: 'Up, and made myself as fine as I could with the Linning [linen] stockings and wide Canons that I bought the other day at Hague.'[10]

This great enthusiasm for the French fashion was not shared by the diarist John Evelyn, who watched these sartorial displays with mounting dismay. In 1661 he published a pamphlet entitled *Gentle Satyr: Tyrannus or the Mode in a Discourse of Sumptuary Lawes* in which he wonders how the English, 'a nation so well conceited of themselves', should 'generally submit themselves to the French of whom they speake with so little kindness'.[11]

The Oxford antiquary Anthony à Wood felt that underneath their brightly-coloured clothes the courtiers of Charles's court were unprincipled and immoral men. He was able to observe them at first hand in 1665 when they sought refuge in Oxford from an outbreak of the plague in London. Although 'they were neat and gay in their apparell . . . they were rude, rough whoremongers; vain, empty, careless . . .'.[12] Pepys would have agreed with him for he felt that 'wicked men and women command the King . . . it is not in his nature to gainsay anything that relates to his pleasures'.[13] The fact that women were allowed on the stage in the 1660s meant that it was no longer possible or acceptable to see men dressed as women, so the adoption by men of feminine accessories was a matter of special censure. Wood wrote in December 1663 that it was 'a strange effeminate age when men strive to imitate women in their apparell, viz long periwigs, patches in their faces, painting, short wide breeches like petticoats'.[14]

In his pamphlet Evelyn had accepted the importance of clothes as a means of defining social position and wondered if the reintroduction of sumptuary legislation might encourage the fashion industry at home. The King could play a part in this process and Evelyn 'looked for the day when all the world shall receive their standard from our most illustrious Prince and from his Grandees'.[15] In fact, Charles did acknowledge that there were sound economic reasons for protecting the traditionally-important woollen industry. Pepys noted in his diary in late October 1665 that 'the King and Court, they say, have now finally resolved to spend nothing upon clothes but what is of the growth of England – which if observed, will be very pleasing to the people and very good for them'.[16] Charles's personal interest in fashion and his eagerness to experiment with new ideas also led him to promote changes in men's dress, a course of action which, he hoped, would have the threefold effect of encouraging native industries, establishing a standardised version of male dress and simplifying the dress worn at court.

On 13 October 1666 Pepys was present when the King's brother, James, Duke of York, tried on 'the King's new fashion'.[17] Two days later Charles wore it publicly for the first time. According to Pepys, the style was 'a long Cassocke close to the body, of black cloth, and pinked with white silk under it, and a coat over it, and the legs ruffled with black riband like a pigeon's leg'.[18] London tailors must have worked round the clock satisfying the demand for the new fashion, for when the Court gathered two days later, on 17 October, it was 'all full of Vests only, my Lord St Albans not pinked, but plain black – and they say the King says the pinking upon white makes them look too much like magpyes, and therefore hath bespoke one of plain velvet'.[19] The vest, or cassock as Pepys called it, was a collarless garment that fitted to the waist and fastened with a sash or girdle. It then hung in loose folds.

Evelyn regarded himself as one of the instigators of the style, for in his 1661 pamphlet, a copy of which he had presented to the King, he had praised the 'usefulness of Persian clothing'. He also recorded the new fashion in his diary: 'To Court. It being ye first time his Majesty put himself solemnly into the Eastern fashion of vest, changing doublet, stiff collar, bands and cloake into a comely dress, after ye Persian mode with girdle or sash . . . resolving never to alter it, and to leave the French mode, which had hitherto obtain'd to our great expence and reproach.'[20]

Charles's experiment was partially successful. Although the vest was largely abandoned in the 1670s, it was the prototype for the waistcoat, and the term 'vest' survived as the tailor's name for that garment. The new combination of a tunic, vest and breeches emerged, after a period of modification and experimentation, as the three-piece suit – that is, a coat, waistcoat and breeches – still the standard components of male dress. Although Pepys mistakenly reported that Louis XIV was so amused by the idea of the English King and his court wearing vests that he clad his footmen in an imitation of the style, the French King's obvious annoyance that Charles should create an independent style was enough to ensure the eventual success of the experiment in England. Discarding short doublet, voluminous petticoat breeches and cloak in favour of a loosely-cut coat with waistcoat of a similar length and narrow breeches, gave men the option of wearing garments made from wool or cloth for informal occasions and costly, imported materials for 'gala days'. This was a great advantage to those who had to attend court. Unlike their French counterparts, who were required actually to reside at court at Versailles, the English nobility only needed to dress up for special occasions, so a clear demarcation developed between formal court and everyday dress. By the early eighteenth century the comparative sobriety of male dress in England was apparent to visitors. In 1726 César de Saussure remarked that 'Englishmen are usually very plainly dressed, they scarcely ever wear gold on their clothes; they wear little coats called "frocks", without facings and without pleats. . . . You will see rich merchants and gentlemen thus dressed and sometimes even noblemen of high rank.'[21] Fashion was set at court and anyone who wished to purchase fine clothes would have done so in London. One member of the country gentry who occasionally visited London to buy a new suit and accompanying accessories was George Vernon of Sudbury Hall in Derbyshire. His plainer everyday clothes, meanwhile, would have been made by a local tailor in Derby.

When George Vernon succeeded to the estate of Sudbury in 1660, he immediately began to rebuild the old manor house and spent the next 42 years of his life either building or decorating it, laying out the gardens and improving the village. Vernon's detailed accounts have survived and they offer a fascinating insight into the progress of the building and decoration of the house and the expenditure on clothes bought for himself and his considerable family – of fifteen children by his three wives.

Vernon's expenditure on his own clothes is comparable with other country gentlemen in similar circumstances, but is modest when compared to Pepys's, for example. Pepys's elevation through the ranks of the Admiralty Board in London meant that he had an increasingly high-profile job which required him to mix with a select group of people who regularly attended court. Maintaining a fashionable and impressive appearance in such critical and sophisticated company was a matter of paramount importance to Pepys, and there are frequent references in his diary to anxiety attacks when he worries that he has misjudged or misinterpreted a new fashion. It is not surprising that he worried, for he spent a very high proportion of his limited salary (£324 16s in 1664) on his own clothes. In June 1665, for example, he spent £24 on a silk suit 'the best that ever I wore in my life' – almost exactly the same amount as James Cecil, heir to the Earl of Salisbury, spent the previous year on a similiar suit.[22] There was also a marked discrepancy between the amount that he spent on himself and on his wife Elizabeth's clothes – in 1663 the outlay was £55 on himself and £12 on his wife. In 1661 Lady Sandwich (the wife of his patron, Edward Montagu, 1st Earl of Sandwich) had noticed this situation and had told Pepys that he should spend more money on his wife, but eight years elapsed before he gave her a personal allowance of £30 a year, and this only happened after Elizabeth discovered him in a compromising situation with her maid.

George Vernon, on the other hand, was more generous to his three wives. In addition to their annual clothing allowance they often received supplementary gifts, like a gown for his first wife, Margaret Onley, that cost £8 7s, and £10-worth of lace for his second wife, Dorothy Shirley.[23] From 1660 onwards there are also regular payments in the Vernon accounts to 'ye Picture drawer Mr Wright'[24] (see p.99), and there is a particularly fine portrait of George Vernon by John Michael Wright which hangs in the Saloon at Sudbury, above the door to the Staircase (72). In the portrait Vernon wears his own dark, wavy hair, but from 1677, when he bought his first wig from a London supplier for £4 1s, wigs were purchased on a regular basis and were not limited to the adults in the Vernon household. Vernon's son Harry received his first wig when he was four years old, and the cost of a new wig and repairs to existing ones just seven months later totalled 17s 6d.[25]

The wig had to be worn over a shaven head and when Pepys was fitted for his first wig on 3 November 1663 he was filled with nervous anticipation: 'By and by comes Chapman the periwig-maker, and [upon] my liking it, without more ado I went up and there he cut off my haire; which went a little to my heart at present to part with it, but it being over and my periwig on, I paid him £3 for it; and away went he with my own hair to make up another of [wigs were made from human or animal hair].'[26] Feeling very self-conscious in his new wig he went to church the following Sunday, worried that everyone would look at him, but he 'found that my coming in a perriwig did not prove so strange to the world as I was afeared it would, for I thought that all the church would presently have cast their eye all upon me – but I found no such thing'.[27]

72 George Vernon in military dress, wearing a buff leather jerkin over matching doublet and breeches. A broad gold-fringed sash serves as a sword hanger, while a second sash, in black, is twisted around his waist.
(John Michael Wright, *c*.1660, Sudbury Hall)

Wigs became fashionable at the French court when Louis XIV lost his luxuriant head of hair and adopted one. Charles II introduced the wig (a shortened form of periwig, from the French *perruque*) to England in 1660 and it underwent a number of stylistic changes. The first style, which lasted until 1675, consisted of a mass of irregular curls which framed the face and fell around the shoulders. In the second style a mass of tight curls was evenly distributed over the entire surface to create a greater and more uniform volume of hair. The crown of the wig remained flat until the mid 1680s, but from then on it increased in height until it reached its maximum in the 1690s (a development which was paralleled by the female head-dress). These huge elaborate wigs were described as being 'full-bottomed' – a term in use from about 1680. In the last years of the century the hair was swept upwards from the forehead into two peaks at either side of a centre parting, the rest of the hair being arranged in loose curls that spread lower on one side than the other. The campaign or travelling wig appeared in the late seventeenth century. This was a more practical wig for the sportsman or soldier as it was shorter in length and divided into three locks, two of which hung over each shoulder, with a third, shorter, lock at the nape of the neck. Those men who had no pretension to fashion continued to wear their own hair, but it was usually arranged to resemble the wig style. Wigs became such an integral part of the fashionable man's wardrobe that it was completely acceptable to comb your wig ostentatiously in a public place, like the theatre or the coffee-house.

Needless to say, wigs were extremely expensive, so were an immediate and obvious indication of the wearer's social standing. When Pepys spent £4 10s on two new wigs in 1667 he decided that they were 'mighty fine; endeed too fine I thought for me'.[28] As wigs grew in volume and complexity prices soared. Commenting on such inflated prices a contemporary observed in 1694 that 'to speak plainly, Forty or Threescore pound a year for Periwigs, and Ten to a poor Chaplin to say Grace to him that adores Hair, is sufficient demonstration of the Weakness of the Brains they Keep Warm'.[29] A common street crime during this period was the theft of wigs: a child would be hidden in a basket balanced on the thief's shoulders and when an appropriate victim appeared the child would quickly pluck off the wig and hide it in the basket. It was such a well-known peril of walking the streets of London that John Gay mentioned it in his poem *Trivia, or the Art of Walking the Streets of London* (1716):

> Nor is the wig with safety worn;
> High on the shoulder, in a basket born
> Lurkes the small boy, whose hand to rapine bred,
> Plucks off the curling humours of thy head.[30]

In the Long Gallery at Sudbury there is a magnificent portrait by Wright, painted in the early 1670s, of George Vernon's second wife's brother, Sir Robert Shirley, created Viscount Tamworth and Earl Ferrers in 1711 (**73**). He was steward to the Royal Household from 1685 to 1705. The wig, composed of a mass of luxuriant curls arranged so that they are equally full at the sides of the head, has lengthened and is now on a level with the cravat. This has become even more exaggerated by the time Captain Thomas Lucy had his portrait painted by Godfrey Kneller in 1680 (**74**). The full-bottomed wig and the lace cravat have extended in length and now reach to the middle of the chest.

73 (*opposite left*) Sir Robert Shirley in court dress, a fashionable vest and tunic. The loose braid-trimmed vest tied with a striped sash is worn under a voluminous tunic arranged to disclose its white satin lining. The ribbon-trimmed sleeves of the vest have been turned back over the buttoned cuff of the tunic to create a wonderfully opulent mixture of decorative layers.

With the fashion for long hair, the lace collar was completely obscured, and so an attractive alternative was devised – a fall of linen or lace, or a cravat, mounted on a ribbon. (John Michael Wright, early 1670s, Sudbury Hall)

74 (*opposite right*) Captain Thomas Lucy's military buff leather coat has been cut like a fashionable formal coat, worn with a number of sashes fastened at hip level. It is decorated with a shoulder knot – an accessory worn always on the right shoulder – consisting of a ribbon or a looped cord. The coat fits the shoulders and thence hangs loosely, without a seam at the waist, to the knees or just below, fastening down the front with a closely-set row of buttons. Here, the elbow-length sleeves are finished with deep, turned-back cuffs enriched with embroidery. By now pockets consisted of either vertical or horizontal openings set so low that they were within a few inches of the hem of the garment and, typically, the coat worn by the servant has two low-set horizontal pockets decorated with gold buttons.

Lucy holds a tall-crowned hat with a wide brim of dark fur, gloves and a riding whip, and wears a lace cravat and full-bottomed wig. (Sir Godfrey Kneller, 1680, Charlecote Park)

Captain Lucy was the grandson of Sir Thomas Lucy III (and cousin of the picknicking George, see p.101). He inherited Charlecote in 1677, making extensive alterations to the house before his death in 1684. The portrait was painted in 1680 but records an incident in 1667 when Lucy, as a Captain in the Household Guards, was sent to Woolwich with his troop of horse as there were serious fears that the Dutch fleet would sail up the Thames and bombard London (they had already blockaded the river and burnt some of the Royal Fleet anchored at Chatham). The troops of cavalry can be seen in the background of the portrait, behind the figures of Captain Lucy and his black servant, who holds his horse.

Ostentatious display and self-indulgence in matters of personal pleasure were positively encouraged at Charles II's court, but women's formal attire still comprised a tightly-boned, stiffly-sleeved bodice and matching voluminous skirt, the hem of which enveloped the feet and swept along the ground. By 1660 the bodice had lengthened, reaching from beneath the arms to the waist, emphasising the more pointed and longer

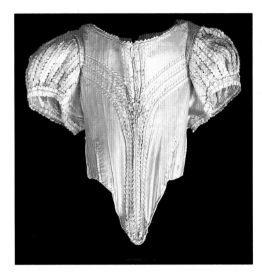

75 (*above*) This very rare lady's bodice, dating from 1660-5, is made of ivory silk, trimmed with pinked crossway strips of ivory satin. It is mounted on top of a stiff, boned corset made of two layers of linen, with quarter-inch-wide whalebone stitched between them. The bodice is cut in the long-waisted style that had come back into fashion in the previous decade, sloping to a deep rounded point in front, and finished with short tabs that flare out over the hips.

76 (*right*) An unknown lady in a costume that combines fashion and pseudo-classicism. The opulent fullness of her smock emerges from the restraint of a red satin bodice, with its emphasis on horizontal lines emphasised by the wide neckline and the sleeves caught togeher with jewelled clasps.The hair, no longer arranged in tight corkscrew curls, falls in wavy ringlets interlaced with pearls.
(Jacob Huysmans, *c*.1662-3, Polesden Lacey)

waistline which was once again the desired shape (**75**). Jacob Huysmans' portrait of an unknown woman was painted *c*.1662–3 before Peter Lely introduced the 'undress' style into his portraits, a style that was first seen in some of the 'pastoral' portraits of Van Dyck's late period (**76**). But the comfort offered by a loose nightgown after wearing bodices as tight as were then fashionable is easy to imagine. Worn over the smock, but without stays, the nightgown's only restriction would be a loosely-tied sash or girdle. In

77 (*above*) Barbara Villiers, later Duchess of Cleveland, wears a nightgown that opens down the front as far as the waist. The configuration of the creases, however, indicates a similar shape to the boned bodice of fashionable dress (see **78**). A swag of contrasting material and a rope of pearls draped asymmetrically across the bodice, flowing smock sleeves, a voluminous mantle and a pearl necklace and ear-rings were all essential accessories for both styles of nightgown.
(Sir Peter Lely, *c.*1662–5, Knole)

78 (*right*) Lady Cullen's nightgown is cut and boned like the fashionable long-waisted bodice. The clasps fastening the front of the bodice and the open sleeves cause the gold satin to be pulled into tight straining creases, in contrast to the soft billowing folds of the smock underneath. Further layers of drapery are provided by a black mantle and a draped sash, to which is pinned a loop of pearls.
(Sir Peter Lely, *c.*1662–5, Kingston Lacy)

Lely's portraits, Barbara Villiers and Lady Cullen wear variations of the nightgown (**77** and **78**), as does the Duchess of Lauderdale (**68**).[31]

On 18 June 1662 Pepys visited Peter Lely's studio in Covent Garden, hoping to see the portrait of the King's mistress, Barbara Villiers, that the artist was working on. Charles II's open liaisons with his mistresses were an acknowledged fact of life at court, though many loathed the women for accumulating wealth and favours for themselves and their illegitimate offspring. An experienced and discerning judge of female beauty, Pepys accepted that the King's mistresses were the undisputed leaders of fashion. Barbara Villiers, Countess of Castlemaine, later Duchess of Cleveland – from 1670, was Pepys's favourite, and his diary is full of details of his sightings of her, even keeping a record of those occasions on which he had seen her underwear laid out to dry in the Privy Garden at Whitehall Palace. He also approved of the actress Nell Gwyn, whom he saw one day standing at the door of her lodgings in Drury Lane, Covent Garden in her 'smock sleeves and bodice'. She was, Pepys decided, 'a mighty pretty creature'.[32]

Unfortunately when he visited Lely's studio, the portrait of Barbara Villiers was locked up, but Pepys did see a portrait of the King's sister-in-law, Anne Hyde, Duchess of York 'sitting in state in a chair in white sattin'.[33] According to the Comte de Gramont Lely had just been commissioned by the Duchess of York, who 'wished to have the portraits of all the most beautiful women at court. Lely painted them, devoted all his powers to the task and could not have worked on more lovely subjects.'[34] The set of eleven portraits was first hung at Whitehall Palace, moving to Windsor Castle when the Duke of York became King James II. They now hang at Hampton Court.

Lely portrayed the ladies in 'undress' – that is, they are clad not in their heavily-boned formal attire, but in a smock and a loosely-fastened nightgown in varying degrees of *déshabillé*.[35] Details like the clasps on the sleeve or bodice seams, the draped mantle and appropriate props satisfied the sitter's desire to be portrayed in a pseudo-classical and therefore timeless way. Eliminating the need to record the fussy details of fashionable dress also meant that the production of these portraits could be speeded up. Lely, appointed the King's Painter in 1661, and his successor, Sir Godfrey Kneller, both had an even larger clientele than Van Dyck, developing their studio practices to a fine art. They employed assistants who would specialise in painting the draperies, backgrounds, flowers or still-lives, and by 1670 Lely had arranged his available poses in numbered series so that the clients could choose their pose from a book. The painting of drapery was aided by the studio's collection of materials and garments, arranged on models or lay figures. This collection was sold, together with the rest of the contents of the studio, when Lely died in 1680, and many different types of silks in every imaginable colour are listed in the sale catalogue, from 'Isabella Cloth of Gold', a greyish-yellow colour, to 'Livered coloured saten', a dark reddish brown.[36]

The Duchess of Cleveland (Barbara Villiers) sat for Lely on many occasions and he used to say that 'it was beyond the compass of art to give this lady her due, as to her sweetness and exquisite beauty'.[37] Her heavy-lidded eyes, and sensuous mouth set in an expression of 'drowsy sweetness' may have been his ideal of feminine beauty, but one contemporary found that it adversely affected his depiction of all his other female sitters. 'Sir Peter Lilly when he had painted the Duchess of Cleveland's picture, he put something of Cleveland's face as her Languishing Eyes into every one Picture, so that all his pictures had an Air one of another, all the Eyes were Sleepy alike. So that Mr Walker ye Painter swore Lilly's Pictures was all Brothers and sisters.'[38]

Etiquette demanded that only someone of a superior rank could receive a person of lower rank when in a state of undress, and a person of inferior rank had to be fully and formally dressed when attending a person of superior rank. Wearing undress in a portrait therefore underlined the fact that the sitter belonged to an exclusive group, but the format was so successful and pervasive that within thirty years everyone, irrespective of rank, was depicted in a similar way. Undress was only worn in the privacy of one's own home, and Evelyn was rather shocked when he visited Charles II's mistress, Louise de Kéroualle, later Duchess of Portsmouth, in 1671 that she remained 'for the most part in her undresse all day and that there was fondnesse and toying with that young wanton'.[39] This comment implies that there might be some connection between this style of dressing and unconventional and permissive behaviour. It was certainly the connection made by nineteenth-century commentators. William Hazlitt's observation that Lely's Windsor Beauties were a 'set of kept-mistresses, painted, tawdry, showing off their theatrical or meretricious airs and graces, without one touch of real elegance or refinement' is a typical one.[40]

Even the Queen wore undress in her portraits. In 1662 Charles married the pious and gentle Portuguese princess, Catherine of Braganza, who arrived in England in formal court dress. Her 'monstrous fardingals' and stiffly-arranged hair-style were heavily criticised at the time, but in 1664 Jacob Huysmans painted a picturesque portrait of the Queen attired as a shepherdess, clad in a smock and loosely-draped nightgown that is falling off her shoulders, her hair cascading out from under a soft satin hat and a sheep, duck and ducklings at her feet. It is difficult to imagine a greater transformation.

Ladies appear to have relished the opportunity for role-playing in their portraits as, until the arrival of Van Dyck, it had been *de rigueur* to be depicted wearing one's best and most fashionable outfit, masque dress being an occasional exception. Later generations censured these ladies for posing as shepherdesses and classical goddesses in their scanty and provocative robes but, if challenged, the sitters would have replied that their only sartorial indiscretion was the omission of that essential accessory, a pearl necklace. Undress was also given the royal stamp of approval by Mary of Modena, the Duke of York's second wife, and by her stepdaughters, Mary and Anne, who chose to wear nightgowns for their portraits. A visit to any country house in England will show that the convention of wearing 'undress' continued into the early part of the eighteenth century, appealing as much to the middle classes as the aristocracy. Portrait painters offered sitters the choice of a full-length as well as a three-quarter-length portrait, but the convention for wearing informal dress remained. The painting of drapery was of great importance for it constituted the major part of the painting, and by the 1680s artists such as John Riley and John Closterman were dividing the work between them, with Closterman painting the drapery and Riley the rest.

Pepys had also visited the studio of John Michael Wright on 18 June 1662. Struck by the contrast between the styles of Wright and Lely, he recorded in his diary: 'Thence to Wrights, the painter's: but Lord, the difference that is between their two works.'[41] Wright could never have been accused, as Lely was, of making all his sitters look the same, being able to penetrate to the core of his sitter's character and, by his careful choice of background, clothes and accessories, to create an evocative atmosphere which complements it. In the 1650s Wright studied in Rome, where he became an impassioned antiquary. His interest in the antique also came into play when he painted portraits of ladies wearing pseudo-classical dress (see also p.98) as it gave him an opportunity to create a version that was based on his observation of the original. Wright painted a beautiful portrait of Mary, daughter of Sir Thomas Wilbraham, in 1671–3 (79).

79 Mary Wilbraham swathed in a gown which has a silk scarf draped across the neckline and threaded through jewelled buckles on the shoulders, to be tied in the middle like the male cravat. Her costume has been distanced from fashion by placing the pearl-studded girdle at the natural level of the waistline, rather than the lower position that had become the style of the early 1670s. The hair-style was introduced into England by Louise de Kéroualle, a member of the French retinue that accompanied Henrietta, Duchess of Orleans, on her visit to her brother, Charles II, in 1670. It parallels the bulkiness of the male wig, with the hair arranged in tight bunches of curls on either side of a flat central parting, with two or three long curls hanging over the shoulders.
(Copy, Chirk Castle, of John Michael Wright, 1671–3, Weston Park)

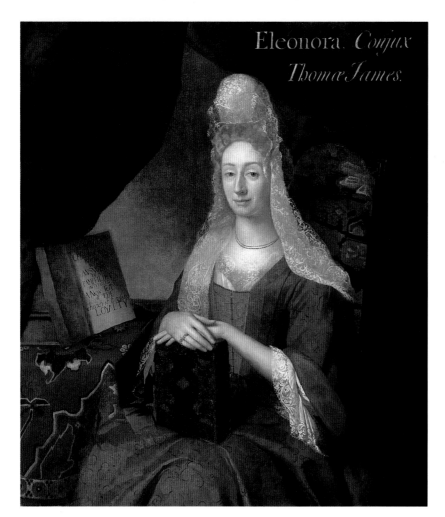

As a result of the vogue for undress, it is fairly rare to find portraits of ladies wearing fashionable dress in the second half of the seventeenth century. Information about it has to be sought in French fashion drawings and contemporary engravings and illustrations. Until the late 1670s it consisted of a tightly-boned bodice with stiff sleeves, petticoat and skirt worn over a smock, but then the one-piece mantua replaced the bodice and skirt as the garment to be worn on all occasions, save for royal weddings and formal court events. The mantua had evolved from the loose and informal nightgown and, unlike the bodice, which was made with a boning stitched into its lining, it was worn over a corset and petticoat and belted at the waist, the material pleated to fit smoothly over the torso. It was often made so that it was open in front and the square or round neckline was edged with a border which was brought forward over the shoulders to converge in a V-shape at the waist. This area could be filled either by an embroidered corset or by an embroidered stomacher that ended in a point at the waist. In the 1680s the mantua was worn over a bustle or small hoop to support the mantua skirts, which were looped back to reveal the decorative petticoat underneath. The swagged and layered effect created by this arrangement was echoed by the tall head-dress, called a *commode*, that first appeared in the early 1690s. It was a high-tiered head-dress of wired lace or linen frills attached to a small cap hat and worn with a slight forward tilt.

80 (*far left*) Eleanor James, portrayed in her widowhood when she ran the printing business in London established by her husband. She is wearing a stomacher of ochre-coloured satin, laced across the front under the V-shaped flat border of the bodice, and secured at the waist by a narrow belt tied in a bow. She proudly displays her fine collection of lace in the upright tucker attached to the neckline of her smock and as a frill under the cuff bodice.

Her spectacular head-dress consists of a wire frame formed into a high domed shape over which lace has been placed. It is gathered into ruffles at the sides of her face, then falls over the shoulders as two lappets. The cost of such delicate lace must have been considerable. (Unknown artist, *c.*1690, Gawthorpe Hall)

81 (*left*) A French lady dressed in the height of fashion for 1693. The narrower elongated lines of her elaborate costume are emphasised by the towering lace head-dress. The stiff stomacher front of the mantua is softened by a loop of material arranged like a Steinkirk cravat (see **243**), and by elbow-length sleeves with deep falls of lace. The tiered effect is complemented by the trained skirt, pulled back and bunched together to create a swagged effect – a style that was destined to reappear in the 1770s and again in the late 1870s. Underneath the mantua skirt there is a petticoat with a deep flounce and embroidered hem. Typically for this period, the lady wears black patches on her face and carries a fan.

82 (*above right*) In this detail from a bird's-eye view of Charlecote, the lady playing with the dog wears her mantua skirt draped up over a tiered petticoat edged with ruched ribbon. Although the hair is still brushed up from the forehead, the ladies are not wearing the tall and formal *commode* head-dress, preferring a simpler linen and lace cap or, in the case of the lady lying in the foreground, a low-crowned straw hat of the type widely worn in the eighteenth century, when it was known as the *bergère* or shepherdess hat.
(Unknown artist, 1696, Charlecote Park)

The portrait of Eleanor James by an unknown artist, *c.*1690, is a rare instance of an English lady wearing this style of dress, but undress would have been entirely unsuitable for a middle-aged widow (**80**). All Mrs James's energies were concentrated in running her husband's printing business in London and on producing a stream of political pamphlets on the state of the Church of England and giving advice to the King on how to run the country. The open books on the table refer to her most famous tract. Published in 1687 it was entitled *Vindication of the Church of England* and was written in response to a pamphlet critical of the Church.

Eleanor's costume is very sober and restrained when compared with that worn by a French lady, dressed in the height of fashion for 1693 (**81**). This is a fussily decorative look which required a variety of accessories, the most essential of which are enumerated in the poem *Mundus Muliebris; The Lady's Dressing-Room Unlocked*, attributed to John Evelyn's daughter, Mary:

> In pinup ruffles now she flaunts,
> About her sleeves are engageants [deep double ruffles, hanging down to the wrist]
> Of ribbons, various echelles [a stomacher laced with ribbons];
> Gloves trimmed and laced as fine as Nell's [Nell Gwynn].[42]

The Lucy ladies picnicking in front of Charlecote in 1696 (**82**) provide a fascinating record of the appearance of the mantua when the wearer was in a state of movement. A love of busy surface decoration, whether it be in the form of scarves, ruched ribbons, braids or bands of metal fringe, was typical of male and female fashion in the 1680s and 1690s, and it is apparent in this painting in which all the ladies sport fluttering scarves and looped-up mantua skirts. An early and rare depiction of the delights of country-house life, the Charlecote painting shows Colonel George Lucy and members of his family. This enthusiastic fondness of the English for the country becomes a dominant theme in eighteenth-century art and literature.

Pepys shared an enthusiasm for the 'picturesque' aspects of country life and was an admirer of the *bergère* hat – seen in the foreground of the Charlecote painting. A trip to

Hatfield, Hertfordshire, with his wife and some other ladies in August 1667 gave Pepys 'great delight' and 'as much pleasure as could be desired in the world for country pleasure and good ayre'. On the journey back to London the ladies put on 'some straw hats, which are much worn in this country and did become them mightily, but especially my wife'.[43]

Another development in female dress was the introduction of a distinctive riding costume. Made by tailors, the fitted jacket and skirt was often worn with a wig and a masculine-style hat. But this was not a combination that Pepys could approve of. On 12 June 1666, he saw the Queen's ladies of honour dressed 'in their riding garbs, with coats and doublets with deep skirts, just for all the world like men, and buttoned their doublets up the breast, with perriwigs and with hats; so that, only for a long petticoat dragging under their men's coats, nobody could take them for women in any point whatever – which was an odde sight, and a sight did not please me'.[44]

The acceptance and popularity of informal dress from 1660 onwards, even for men, meant that everyone chose to wear nightgowns in their portraits – or the artist decided on that ensemble. The best-documented such portrait is that of Pepys himself who, on 30 March 1666, went to the studio of John Hales and 'sat till almost quite dark upon working my gowne, which I hired to be drawn [in] it – an Indian gown, and I do see all the reason to expect a most excellent picture of it'.[45] The portrait of Pepys has survived (83). He was always acutely aware of the connection between dress and social status, so it would not have escaped his attention that being shown wearing a silk gown when working in his study or receiving visitors signified that he was a gentleman with a cultivated and leisurely lifestyle.

Although these gowns were called Indian, it seems that the word refers more to their oriental appearance than to their country of origin. The material for them may have been Indian silk or cotton, but they were made up, and remade if worn out, in London. We know from the accounts of William Russell, 5th Earl of Bedford (later 1st Duke) that a certain Henry Kirke sold new Indian gowns and remade old ones near St Clement Danes in the Strand in the 1680s,[46] and that the fashion had been given the royal seal of approval by 1684 when there were payments to an Indian Gownmaker to King Charles and his Queen. Henry Kirke was also paid £3 15s in 1688–9 for the 'gowne and Toylett, and a Capp Combcase, Sweetbags and Slippers' that he supplied to the Earl of Bedford. The 'toylett' mentioned in the bill was a piece of silk, usually made from the same material as the nightgown, that was used like a small table-cloth to protect the piece of furniture on which it was placed. All the brushes and combs required while the gentleman was dressing would be arranged on top of the cloth. These items later became more elaborate than the 'toylett' or 'toilette', and the word was transferred from the cloth to the objects – which usually comprised a mirror, a comb-case, boxes of different sizes, shaving brushes and brushes to remove powder from clothes.

The basic shape of the nightgown, or Indian gown, altered little during the seventeenth and eighteenth centuries – as seen in the portraits of Pepys (83) and Killigrew (58), and in Kneller's portrait of Charles Sackville, 6th Earl of Dorset, painted in 1706 (84).

Ham House in Richmond, Surrey, is perhaps the most complete seventeenth-century house to survive in Britain. It was extended and remodelled in the 1670s by Elizabeth Dysart and her second husband, John Maitland, Duke of Lauderdale, one of Charles II's

83 Samuel Pepys recorded sitting for his portrait in his diary entry for 30 March 1666, noting that he wore his Indian gown. This informal garment was of golden brown silk, cut rather like a kimono, with no collar or shoulder seams.
(John Hales, 1666, National Portrait Gallery)

84 Charles Sackville, 6th Earl of Dorset, wearing an opulent blue and gold damask gown casually arranged so that it discloses a pink satin lining. His turban is made of fur.
(Sir Godfrey Kneller, 1706, Knole)

ministers. A few years after their marriage in 1672 they had transformed Ham into one of the most luxurious and fashionable houses in England. Lauderdale was almost universally disliked. This opinion of him comes from Gilbert Burnet, later Bishop of Salisbury: 'He made a very ill appearance; he was very big; his hair red, hanging oddly about him; his tongue was too big for his mouth; which made him bedew all that he talked to; and his whole manner was rough and boisterous, and very unfit for a court. . . . He was haughty beyond expression, abject to those he saw he must stoop to, but imperious to others. . . . He was the coldest friend and the most violent enemy I ever knew.'[47] Elizabeth does not fare any better from Burnet's pen. Although she was deemed to be a great beauty and a very intelligent and learned woman, she was 'a violent friend' and a 'much more violent enemy' who 'would have stuck at nothing by which she might compass her ends'.[48]

Lely's portrait of this formidable couple was painted *c*.1674 (68). In the privacy of her own apartment the Duchess wears informal dress, and not the extravagant formal dress on which she spent so improvidently. (In the previous year, for example, bills from her tailor for herself and her daughters totalled £227, one of the items being a 'painted satin manteaux [gown] with diamond buttons'.[49]) The Duke has chosen to wear formal dress and proudly displays the fact that he is a member of the Order of the Garter.

Charles II was acutely aware of the need to reinstate and maintain the ceremonial, pageantry and 'trappings of royalty' that had been systematically destroyed during the years of the Commonwealth. One of his first actions was to rekindle interest in the Order of the Garter, to which only twenty-four Knights Companion could belong, and its ideals. He re-designed the robes (85) to retain the sixteenth-century fashion of 'trunk hose or round breeches, whereof the Stuff or Material shall be some such Cloth of Silver, as we shall chuse and appoint, wherein as we shall be to them an example, so do we expect they will follow us in using the same and no other'.[50]

Material for the full robes of the Order, at least 15yds of blue velvet for a mantle with white taffeta lining and a similar amount of crimson velvet for a surcoat, was supplied by the Royal Wardrobe. The Jewel House provided the collar of the Order, a chain of red and white enamelled roses separated by gold knots, on the understanding that it might not be 'sold, pledged or given away',[51] but both the collar and the robes were often retained by the family when the knight died and not returned to the Jewel House or the Wardrobe as they were supposed to be. The other insignia included the Great George, a gold and enamel pendant representing St George, which usually hung from the collar, but sometimes from a ribbon or chain, and the Lesser George, another smaller pendant, with an image of St George encompassed by a representation of the Garter. This was intended to fasten the riband, worn over the left shoulder, at the hip, but was sometimes hung round the neck. The Garter itself, blue velvet edged with gold, had the Order motto embroidered onto it, and the black velvet hat sported a large white ostrich feather.

Charles wore the Garter robes for his official portraits (69) and gave the old-fashioned style a fashionable twist by lavishly trimming the hose with ribbons and wearing the latest male fashion – a luxuriant black wig. The message was clear: the regalia of crown, orb and sceptre might be brand-new, it cost £30,000 to have them remade, but the traditions and values that they symbolised had not changed.

85 Prince Rupert, Charles I's nephew and his dashing cavalry commander during the Civil War. Samuel Pepys describes in his diary visiting Verelst's studio, shortly after the Dutch artist came to England in 1669, and admiring a still-life he saw there. The treatment of the Prince's Garter robes, and in particular the massive tassels of the blue velvet mantle, bears out Pepys's admiration for the rich, almost three-dimensional quality of Verelst's work. (Simon Verelst, 1669, Petworth)

PRINCE RUPERT

Full Garter robes were worn for the installation of a new knight and for the monarch's annual procession with the Knights on St George's Day for a service in the chapel at Windsor. The insignia, the George and the Garter, also had to be worn whenever a knight attended court, with the Greater George reserved for ceremonial occasions and the Lesser George for ordinary wear. Membership of the Order could also be displayed on everyday dress by having the star embroidered on the coat, as Lauderdale has chosen to do.

Although the monarch supplied a George and a Garter, the fact that they had to be worn all day and every day when at court meant that a variety of each insignia was necessary. When the 5th Earl of Bedford was installed as a Knight of the Garter on 3 June 1672 he bought two Georges: one was set with diamonds and cost £165; the other, simpler in design, was of onyx set with diamonds that cost £40. He also bought three Garters at a total cost of £85. An additional cost of £20, for the black heron feather to be placed in the middle of the white ostrich plume in the black velvet hat, shows how expensive the accessories could be. Fees for the installation at Windsor were also very high. The Earl paid £242 10s 0d to the Principal King of Arms and then found he had to borrow another £6 14s 0d from a friend as he had miscalculated the total sum and did not have enough money to pay the extra.[52]

On 11 April 1689 the Earl attended the coronation of William III and Mary II in Westminster Abbey, an event at which all peers of the realm had to wear the special robes reserved for a coronation. The Earl still owned the coronation robes he had worn when Charles II was crowned in 1661 and as they had previously belonged to his father, they were very old. He decided that they needed a complete overhaul. The cape and crimson velvet robe were edged with miniver, and this must have been in a sorry state for the furrier charged him £74 0s 6d to replace it. (Miniver came from the white under-belly of the grey squirrel, so it had to be imported.) The same robes were later passed on to his grandson, the 2nd Duke of Bedford, who wore them at the coronation of Queen Anne in 1702. By this time they were at least 70 years old and required a new cape made from 'extraordinary choice powdered ermines' purchased for £32 10s. These bulky robes, worn so infrequently, were not kept in the Duke's own wardrobe but in store at the furriers at a cost of one guinea a year.[53]

When Mary, daughter of James II, and William of Orange, were invited to take the throne of England in 1689, an event known to posterity as the 'Glorious Revolution', a more severe atmosphere was immediately apparent in the new court. William was at first criticised for his reticent manner and preference for the company of Dutch noblemen. His choice of accommodation also annoyed many courtiers, for William enjoyed living at the relatively modest palace Sir Christopher Wren designed for him at Kensington and at the extended and refurbished Hampton Court Palace, rather than the rambling but centrally-placed Palace of Whitehall (which burnt down in 1698). These problems were gradually resolved and a pattern emerged encompassing the business of government and administration and the festivities and ceremonies of court life. The social highlights of the year were the King and Queen's birthdays, when all who attended were expected to be lavishly dressed and bejewelled. But despite William's preoccupation with containing Louis XIV's power in Europe, France continued to exert the predominant influence on English fashion.

86 (*right*) A French fashion illustration, 1693, showing the evolution of the coat from its first loose and unstructured style into a more formalised and fitted garment with the skirts stiffened by lining and arranged into pleats at the sides and centre-back. Sleeves were very wide, with large cuffs, and pockets were set lower and adorned with pocket flaps.

87 (*far right*) This woven silk waistcoat, *c.*1700, buttons down the front with 50 small buttons (the last 12in of buttonholes are false) and it could have been worn under a coat of almost the same length. The material is drawloom woven and brocaded in a swirling pattern typical of the 1690s. Unfortunately, when the garment was washed and relined in 1926, the red dye ran, and the brocade lost its original brilliant colours and stiffness of texture.

Very few men's silk coats from the late seventeenth century have survived – a French fashion illustration of 1693 shows the full-length combination of coat and waistcoat as worn at the French court (**86**) – but there is a waistcoat, *c.*1700, which has done so (**87**). The grandiose feather-trimmed hat in the fashion illustration has the turned-up brim that is the prototype of the tricorne hat which remained in fashion for the whole of the next century. Large fur muffs, such as this nobleman was wearing, were also common accessories in London, as this advertisement placed in the *London Gazette* of 1695 makes plain: 'Lost . . . a large sable tip man's muff with a parting in the middle of it.'[54]

By the end of the seventeenth century men's and women's fashions had evolved into the more relaxed and elegant style that continued throughout the following century. This preference for an air of studied informality can be seen in a portrait of Ashe Windham of Felbrigg Hall, Norfolk (**88**), painted in 1696 by Sir Godfrey Kneller.

Kneller became the Principal Painter at the court of William and Mary and was the chosen painter of the dominant Whig faction – Members of Parliament, landowners, soldiers and writers, all of whom were united in their desire to uphold the Glorious Revolution and the Protestant Succession. Many of the King's ministers and supporters chose him to paint their portraits, and Whig supporters also feature in the finest of Kneller's later works, his portraits of members of the Kit-cat Club in London, painted between 1697 and 1721. Twenty of the paintings are displayed at Beningbrough Hall in Yorkshire and the same number can be seen at the National Portrait Gallery in London. The Club first met at the tavern kept by Christopher Cat near Temple Bar and took its name from his mutton pies, which were known as 'Kit-cats'. One of their number was Charles Mohun, 4th Baron Mohun, a soldier and a notorious duellist who was twice

88 Ashe Windham's plain linen cravat is simply arranged and his close-fitting blue satin coat has been cut like a waistcoat, but he has distanced himself from fashion by wearing it with decorative gold clasps. The deep swag of brown silk thrown across the lower half of his body may add another element of timelessness to the portrait, but the full-bottomed wig conforms to the contemporary fashionable ideal.
(Sir Godfrey Kneller, 1696, Felbrigg Hall)

89 Charles Mohun, Kit-cat Club member, soldier and duellist. The combination of shirt, waistcoat and coat is now fully established and the waistcoat, with its more evenly-spaced buttons, appears to be made from rich silver and gold brocade, whilst the loosely-fitting blue velvet coat is decorated with large silver buttons. His shirt has been left unbuttoned at the throat, and its fledgling ruffle is destined to become an exaggerated and highly decorative feature by the middle of the eighteenth century. (Sir Godfrey Kneller, *c.*1707, Beningbrough)

tried for murder by the House of Lords before he was twenty years old (89). He died in 1712 in a duel with James Douglas, 4th Duke of Hamilton, in which both were killed.

Queen Mary died, childless, in 1694, followed in 1702 by William. His stout, middle-aged sister-in-law Anne was proclaimed Queen. She had endured seventeen pregnancies, but just one child, the Duke of Gloucester, survived, only to die a few days after his eleventh birthday, in 1700. Anne was intensely patriotic and 'saw herself as a wholly English symbol of national aspiration and unity, upholder of Protestant ideals and the traditional "middle way" of her great predecessor Queen Elizabeth'.[55] Contemporary descriptions of Anne paint a picture of a lonely figure who was in constant pain from attacks of gout, so it is not surprising that her interest in clothes was somewhat desultory. On one occasion in 1706, when she was in great pain, she was 'much in the same disorder as about the meanest of her subjects. Her face, which was red and spotted, was rendered something frightful by her negligent dress.'

Although Anne had to be cajoled into wearing suitably fine attire for court occasions, she helped the London merchants and fashion traders when they asked her to support them – by buying new clothes on an annual basis for such events. Her old clothes were placed on the floor in six separate piles so that the Ladies of the Bedchamber could share them. Most fell into the hands of her Mistress of the Robes, a post held by her intimate friend and confidante Sarah Jennings, who married John Churchill, 1st Earl (and later 1st Duke) of Marlborough, the greatest soldier of his age. He was given the dukedom and the wherewithal to build Blenheim Palace in Oxfordshire, a reward for his historic victory over the French at the Battle of Blenheim in 1704. When Horace Walpole visited Blenheim Palace in 1760 he noted 'all the old flock chairs, wainscot tables, and gowns and petticoats of Queen Anne that old Sarah could crowd amongst blocks of marble'.[56]

Anne preferred to channel her energies into a meticulous observation of the correct procedures and etiquette for all ceremonial occasions, setting a precedent for court life for the next 200 years. Anne's own appearance might have been somewhat disordered, but she expected all at court to be properly dressed down to the tiniest detail. At the funeral of her husband in 1708 the order that everyone should wear black was imposed so rigidly that only black pins were supplied to the Palace and no one could use a coloured handkerchief.

Despite the twelve years of war with France there was a steady increase in Britain's trade and commercial prosperity as her economic competitors slowly declined, leaving unrivalled opportunities for expansion. Alexander Pope's patriotic poem *Windsor Forest* (1713) applauds the achievements of Anne's reign and prophetically imagines a time when the Royal Palace in London is the heart of a far-flung empire:

> Behold! Augusta's glitt'ring Spires increase,
> And Temples rise, the beauteous Works of Peace.
> I see, I see where two fair Cities bend
> Their ample Bow, a new White-Hall ascend!
> There mighty Nations shall inquire their Doom,
> The World's great Oracle in Times to come;
> There Kings shall sue, and suppliant States be seen
> Once more to bend before a British Queen.[57]

The restoration of the monarchy and the resumption of a royal court in 1660 had an immediate effect on the London fashion trade, for the courtiers who attended the festivities that accompanied the coronation required new suits of fashionable clothing as well as ceremonial robes, as these had not been worn since the outbreak of the Civil War. The 5th Earl of Bedford spent nearly £1000 on new liveries for the equipages and servants who accompanied him, and nearly £600 on his own outfit for the occasion, the most expensive item being the gold and silver lace, which cost £180.[58]

London retained and strengthened its position as the country's fashion capital after the Restoration. Commercial development of areas like Pall Mall and St James's ensured that there was a greater diversity and distribution of fashion outlets in the capital, a trend which was intensified with the rebuilding of London after the Great Fire of 1666. By the end of the century there was also a much greater variety of materials available for sale in England.

In the 1660s the East India Company had introduced the English to chintz, a painted or printed cotton cloth made in India which was used as a furnishing fabric and for the loose informal gowns worn at home. Its brilliant colours, the fastness of the dyes used and the adaptation of native designs to suit English taste ensured the popularity of the material. Attempts to found an English printed-cotton industry were made as early as 1676 when William Sherwin, a London engraver, took out a patent for 'printing and stayning such kind of goods'.[59] A calico printing factory was established near London and by 1700 calico printing was flourishing in many parts of the south west. Printing on cloth (calico was usually white or unbleached cotton) from a wood block was cheap (12d a yard in 1690), and it resulted in an attractive material that appealed to all classes of society: 'The calicoes now painted in England are so very cheap and so much the fashion that persons of all qualities and degrees clothes themselves and furnish their houses in great measure with them.'[60]

The foundations of the silk industry in England had been laid at the end of the sixteenth century when many Huguenot (French Protestant) and Flemish weavers, fleeing religious persecution in their own countries, had settled in Exeter in Devon, Spitalfields in east London and Norwich in Norfolk and their impact on the English textile trade was considerable. Louis XIV's Revocation of the Edict of Nantes in 1685 caused another wave of Huguenot weavers to flee to England and settle in Spitalfields, where they formed a tightly-knit community which maintained the culture and traditions of their homeland. However, in the 1690s there was a falling-off of trade as the influx of imported cottons reduced the demand for silks and the East India Company imported silks that sold at a cheaper price than home made ones. In 1697 5,000 weavers mobbed the House of Commons and in 1701 an act was passed that forbade the use or wearing of imported silks and 'calicoes painted, dyed, printed or stained' in China, the East Indies and the Middle East. This protectionist policy did not have complete success, and the wool merchants complained that people bought cheap calico instead of wool, but it did enable the native silk industry to continue. By 1730 the weavers were

90 Design for a fan, depicting the Chariot of the Virgin Queen, emblem of the Mercers' Company (see **92**), taking part in the Lord Mayor's Pageant, 1686. The barely completed Wren church of St Stephen Walbrook is visible in the background. The chariot is being pulled through the Stocks Market (the site of the present Mansion House), where the shops have been boarded up for the event.

The looped-up skirts of the ladies' short-sleeved mantuas reveal the fringed petticoats beneath. A comparison of the shape of the men's coats with that worn by Captain Lucy (**74**) shows that they now fit more closely the upper half of the body, and that the fullness of material is trained into pleats at the sides and back. Pockets appear in a variety of positions and shapes.

producing fine brocaded silks, plain silks and silk/worsted mixtures, but designs followed and copied French taste until the early 1740s. This deficiency in design was apparent to R. Campbell, who pointed out in *The London Tradesman* (1747) that 'The Spittlefield Weavers . . . ought to learn drawing to design their own Patterns; the Want of which gives the French Workmen the greatest Advantage over us.'[61]

Almost immediately after the coronation of Charles II plans for the transformation of the western suburbs of London into high-class residential and shopping areas were put into effect. Development of the bailiwick of St James's started soon after 1660. St James's Park, originally a meadow in which Queen Elizabeth had hunted, had been neglected and vandalised during Cromwell's time, but Charles took a personal interest in the park's reconstruction and built a new avenue along one side named Catherine Street after his Queen, Catherine of Braganza. However, it retained its popular name of Pall Mall, as the new street followed the line of an old alley where the game pall-mall (in which a ball was driven through an iron ring by a mallet) had been played. The fashionable reputation that Pall Mall enjoyed was ensured from the very beginning as the wealthy competed to buy or rent houses on the preferred south side, which bordered the gardens of St James's Palace.

Shops that fulfilled the needs of fashionable society, such as milliners, perfumers and peruke (wig) makers, soon filled up the north side.[62] Thus Pall Mall became the new southern boundary to an area of the Palace estate known as St James's Fields. In 1661 Henry Jermyn, 1st Earl of St Albans, the King's companion in exile, had been granted part of St James's Fields by Crown lease as a reward. By 1665 Jermyn had obtained the freehold of half of one field and he embarked on an extensive programme of development. St James's Square was the most prestigious scheme, as it involved the erection of 'thirteene or fourtene great and good houses' which were 'palaces fit for the dwelling of noblemen and persons of quality'.[63] The area's exclusivity was confirmed in 1698 when Whitehall Palace burnt down and the royal residence was transferred to the Palace of St James's. By 1716, when John Gay wrote *Trivia, or the Art of Walking the Streets of London*, Pall Mall had become synonymous with luxury:

O bear me to the paths of fair Pell-Mell . . .
Safe are thy pavements, grateful is thy smell! . . .
Shops breathe perfumes, thro' sashes ribbons glow,
The mutual arms of ladies, and the beau.[64]

In 1662 John Evelyn sat on a commission for the improvement of streets and buildings in London and he 'orderd the paving of the Way from St James North – which was a quagmire, and also of the Haymarket about Pigudillo'.[65] According to John Minsheu's dictionary of 1617, entitled *A Guide into the Tongues*, this area had acquired its name from 'that famous Ordinary near St James' called Pickadilly . . . that one Higgins a taylor, who built it, got most of his estate by Piccadillies, which in the last age were much in fashion [a pickadil was a wired support for a ruff or standing band].'[66]

The effects of the Great Plague and the Fire of London on the fashion trade in London are chronicled in vivid detail by that inveterate shopper Pepys. Earlier outbreaks of the plague had shown that the disease was so virulent that it could be caught by touching the clothes worn by a victim, so tailoring and the second-hand clothes business ceased to function during a plague outbreak, for, as someone had observed in 1536, it was 'better to be without a new coat than to abide the danger of the plague'.[67] In September 1665, a box of clothing arrived from London at the tailor's shop in the village of Eyam in Derbyshire. A fortnight later the tailor was dead and the sickness was spreading. It abated for a while, but when it returned in the spring the rector decided that a boundary line should be drawn around the village and nobody was to go beyond it. When the plague eventually ceased in October, fewer than 40 villagers were left out of an original population of 350.

From 7 June 1665, when Pepys first noticed red crosses painted on houses in Drury Lane, to the middle of September, approximately 100,000 Londoners died. London was deserted – an undergraduate visiting the city in July wrote to his tutor that 'thyr is hardly an house open in the Strand, nor the Exchange; the sickness is at Tottenham High Crosse'.[68] By 3 September Pepys felt that it was safe to put on 'my coloured silk suit, very fine and my new periwigg, bought a good while since, but darst not wear it because the plague was in Westminster when I bought it. And it is a wonder what will be the fashion after the plague is done as to periwigs, for nobody will dare to buy any haire for fear of the infection – that it had been cut off of the heads of people dead of the plague.'[69]

Pepys was the son of a tailor, and loved buying clothes and observing what fashionable society was wearing. His attractive wife, Elizabeth St Michel, wore the latest fashions and there are frequent references in his diary to their pleasurable trips to buy silk, lace, gloves and jewellery for her. However, there were heated arguments when he felt she had spent too much money or, even worse, bought something without his approval. Most of the women Pepys had affairs with were involved in the fashion business – perhaps not surprising, as it was standard practice to choose the most attractive girls to work on the seamstresses' stalls in the Exchange and for shopkeepers to use their wives to lure customers into their shops. When Count Lorenzo Magalotti visited the Exchange in 1669 he was struck by the 'well-dressed women, who are busily employed in work; although many are sewed by young men, called apprentices'.[70]

On 4 April 1665 Pepys went to the Exchange to buy a pair of cotton stockings at the

91 'Old Satten, Old Taffety or Velvet' from *The Cryes of London*, 1688 by Marcellus Lauron I. The flourishing trade in second-hand clothes and materials provided employment for many Londoners. This street seller wears a wide-brimmed, conical-crowned hat over a plain hood and a simplified version of the mantua – all typical of the dress of the lower classes. The bodice has been carefully pleated so that it closely fits the upper part of the body and the sleeves are set snugly into the shoulder seams. As there is little difference in length between the skirt and petticoat, the former hangs free and is not bunched up in the fashionable way.

shop 'of the most pretty woman there, who did also invite me to buy some linen of her; and I was glad of the occasion and bespoke some bands of her, entending to make her my seamstress – she being one of the prettiest and most modest-looked women that I ever did see'.[71] He visited the Exchange again on 26 July 1665, 'where I went up and sat talking with my beauty . . . a great while, who is indeed one of the finest women I ever saw in my life'.[72] This lady was Mary Batelier, whose brother Joseph held the tenancy of the linen draper's shop in the Exchange until 1671. The Bateliers lived opposite Pepys on the north side of Crutched Friars and they became great friends. A second brother, William, was a travelling salesman who went to Paris with commissions for buying books and engravings as well as clothes. On his return from a visit he would regale Pepys with all the news from the French court and on one occasion, in 1669, he delivered letters from Louis XIV to Charles II. Sometimes he would visit Mr and Mrs Pepys to show them the clothes and accessories that he had purchased in France, but these occasions usually 'vexed' Pepys as his wife always wanted to buy everything and he was forced to spend more money than he would have liked.

Pepys regularly bought gloves, stockings, lace and garters at the Exchange, and in 1662 he noted in his diary that ready-made petticoats were on sale there. His purchases were economical when compared to those of the aristocracy. The most expensive shop in the New Exchange belonged to Thomas Templar, who supplied the court with silk stockings. In November 1666 the Duke of Richmond and Lennox paid him £210 10s 6d for silks, ribbons and trimmings.[73]

Pepys was also susceptible to the charms of 'pretty Linen vendors' who sold linen items from stalls inside Westminster Hall. He bought linen for his neckwear from Betty Lane and her sister Doll and both ladies granted him sexual favours over a long period of time. There were also many street sellers in London selling a variety of items including hats, caps, pins and bone lace. Their appearance was recorded in a series of engravings by Marcellus Lauron the Elder which appeared between 1672 and 1688 with the title *The Cryes of London*. One shows a lady selling 'old satten, old taffety or velvet'. The high cost of new silk was so prohibitive that there was a flourishing market for second-hand materials and clothes. Pepys was quite happy to buy second-hand clothes and on one occasion in 1662 he 'walked to my brother Toms to see a velvet Cloake, which I buy of Mr Moore; it will cost me £8 10s – he bought it for £6 10s – but it is worth the money'.[74] Similarly, it was quite acceptable to sell one's clothes to raise money. When Sir Ralph Verney asked his friend in Paris to sell an old coat for him in 1650, Sir Henry Newton replied that he had some difficulty getting a good price as 'the moths have been very busie with it'.[75]

In the 1660s, when Pepys was writing his diary, the mercers, tailors, silkmen and lacemen were concentrated in Paternoster Row, a street behind St Paul's Cathedral, which was too narrow to cope with the density of wheeled and pedestrian traffic. A contemporary complained that the shops 'were so resorted unto by the nobility and gentry in ther coaches that oft times the street was so stop'd up that there was no passage for foot passengers'.[76] On 25 June 1663, when Pepys's wife wanted a new striped silk petticoat, he visited Paternoster Row and bought a 'very fine rich one, the best I did see there and much better than she desires or expects'.[77] On an earlier occasion he had gone to the street to buy 'greene watered Moyre for a morning wastcoate', and on 8 January

1666 he visited the shop of a mercer called Bennett for 'velvett for a coat, and Camelott [camlet] for a cloak for myself'.[78]

Pepys visited another mercer in Lombard Street in August 1666, but a month later the street was 'all in dust'. It had been consumed in the Fire of London, the conflagration which destroyed one third of the City during four days in September. Pepys was involved from the start and personally informed the King about the calamity. One of the most spectacular casualties was the Royal Exchange in Cornhill. An eyewitness was amazed at the speed of the fire as it ran 'round the galleries, filling them with flames; then descendeth the stairs compasseth the walks, giving forth flaming volleys, and filleth the court with sheets of fire . . . such noise as was dreadful and astonishing'.[79] Pepys visited the ruins a few days later and found it a 'sad sight', but was most impressed that the statue of its founder, Sir Thomas Gresham, had survived the inferno unscathed. Work on clearing the site began in April 1667 and on 23 October 1667 Pepys saw 'the King with his kettledrums and Trumpets, going to the Exchange to lay the first stone of the first Pillar of the new building of the Exchange'.[80] The shopkeepers were in their premises by March 1671, but it was never again as successful as the New Exchange in the Strand (see p.76).

Although the destruction wrought by the fire was great in terms of loss of stock and trading premises, the rebuilding programme initiated in 1667 had the effect of stimulating and expanding trade. Batelier found the rental in the New Exchange much lower than it had been in the Old and when Pepys visited it on 12 December 1666 Batelier told him that he 'sits here, but at £3 per annum, whereas he sat at the other at £100 – which he says he believes will prove of as good account to him now, as the other did at that rent'.[81] A linen draper who opened a shop near the New Exchange after the fire told Pepys that 'his and other tradesmen's retail trade is so great here, and better then it was in London, that they believe they shall not return nor the City be ever so great for retail as heretofore'.[82] In fact, this was not the case, and once the new brick houses and shops rose on the foundations and walls of the old wooden ones many of the merchants and shopkeepers returned to their former areas. Paternoster Row was rebuilt and continued to be the centre of trade for mercers, tailors and lacemen, and the drapers and booksellers returned to the yard of St Paul's Cathedral. Accessories and fashion goods could be found again in Cheapside and on London Bridge.

The rebuilding of London was carefully regulated. Important streets like Fleet Street, Cheapside and Cornhill had to conform to a designated width, and a Royal Proclamation of 13 September 1666 stated that all new buildings, whatever their size, were to be made from brick or stone, while the City was given new powers to establish regular street frontages and abolish 'bows and jetties' (92). The Commission for Paving was busy providing new pavements and paving those streets that had never had any. In a poem entitled *London's Resurrection*, written in 1669, the poet praises the efforts of the surveyors who 'fix the bounds . . . by the imperious line' thus ensuring that:

> Each house clasps with its neighbour; and the square
> Each front unto its fellow wall doth pair.[83]

As the Covent Garden development became more popular, new streets were built around the Piazza and many shopkeepers whose premises had been destroyed in the fire

Mercers Chappel.

92 The rebuilt Mercers' Hall in Cheapside, and the shops surrounding it with their elegant and regular new frontages. The façade of the Hall, designed by Edward Jarman in 1670 and erected a few years later, was rescued when the building was demolished in 1883 and now forms part of the Town Hall in Swanage, Dorset. The metal balcony still bears the date 1670 and the mercer's badge, the Virgin's head, can be seen with attendant cherubs above the doorway. The niches on either side of the central window are occupied by Faith and Hope, while in the pediment is Charity with her three children.

reopened in the area. One was Pepys's mercer, Bennett. When his shop was destroyed he found 'a fine house looking down upon the Exchange; and I perceive many Londoners every day come'.[84] Two streets were particularly renowned for their fashionable shops: Russell Street and King Street. Built in 1667, King Street was described as 'a broad thoroughfare with many fashionable shops and places of refreshment, constantly thronged with shoppers as well as pickpockets, prostitutes and other predators'.[85]

A rare embroidered waistcoat of the 1690s, in the collection of the Embroiderers' Guild, has an inscription on the lining that reads 'John Stilwell, Drawer at ye Flaming Sword in Russell Street'. In the late seventeenth and the eighteenth centuries the shops of the pattern drawers were located in Covent Garden, and designs were required not only for garments and furnishings, but also, in the earlier period, for pictures, looking-glass frames and coverings for work-boxes. These patterns were drawn in ink on thick white satin with distinctive green selvedges.

Thomas and Marie Cheret's 'French House' was also located in Covent Garden. Their highly successful establishment supplied the Duchess of Lauderdale with her millinery in the 1670s and the Cherets' name occurs every year in the accounts of Algernon Percy, 10th Earl of Northumberland, and of his son Joscelyn, the 11th Earl, as their milliners.[86] The Cherets supplied them with gloves, lace bands, cuffs, hatbands and ribbons, and Pepys noted in his diary that he bought a mask there in 1664.[87]

At the end of the seventeenth century many mercers had been tempted by the new wide thoroughfares of Covent Garden to trade in the area, but, as Daniel Defoe points out in his *Complete English Tradesman* (1726), within ten years 'the trade shifted again; Covent Garden began to decline and the mercers went back to the City'.[88]

By the end of the century the tailor's position as the only person who made male *and* female clothes had been challenged by the seamstresses. Consigned until then to sewing linen underwear and accessories, the seamstresses started making the unboned mantua and, when stiff-bodied gowns ceased to be fashionable, took over the making of all gowns. Known as mantua-makers, they opened up their own establishments leaving the tailors to make only women's riding habits while male stay-makers made the stays or

93 This apron, made between 1702 and 1714, shows the very high level of workmanship that would be employed on such an accessory. The ground of ivory ribbed silk has been embroidered with an attractive pattern of flowers, and its scalloped edges emphasised by the application of couched metal thread.

corsets, as these were now separate from the bodice. According to R. Campbell's *The London Tradesman* (1747), a guide for the prospective tradesperson, the mantua-maker was responsible for making 'Night-Gowns, Mantuas, and Petticoats, Rob de Chambres, etc. for the Ladies'. She 'must be a sister to the Tailor, and like him, must be a perfect Connoisseur of Dress and Fashion'.[89] When Lady Brownlow, of Belton House in Lincolnshire, rented a house in Hammersmith her accounts for 1690–1 show that she patronised three mantua-makers with decidedly French, and therefore fashionable, names: Mademoiselle de Neufville, Madame Fauvette, and Madame le Cerf.[90]

The fashionable tailors were situated in the Strand, the Temple and Covent Garden. When Pepys wanted something special made, he went to William Pym of the Strand, the tailor of his patron, the 1st Earl of Sandwich. When Pym left London because of the plague, Pepys was recommended to use Nicholas Penny 'against St Dunstan's Church' near the Temple, and it was Penny who made the suit of 'flowered tabby vest and coloured camelott tunic' which Pepys was worried about wearing in May 1669 because it was 'too fine with the gold lace'.[91] Mrs Pepys's clothes were made by John Unthank of Charing Cross. He must have been a fashionable tailor for, on 26 September 1666, when she was in his shop, the King's mistress, Lady Castlemaine came in and ordered a gown of flowered taffeta costing 15s a yard. Elizabeth Pepys immediately placed a similar order.

Travelling gradually improved throughout the kingdom during the second half of the century. Although the condition of the roads was still appalling, the means of conveyance and the rapid expansion of the public coach service greatly extended opportunities for travel. The design of private coaches improved: the unsprung wooden body of the earlier Stuart coach, which had been covered in black leather and studded with brass nails, was now brightly painted and gilded and suspended by leather straps from upright posts attached to the axle-trees. Further improvements were made to coaches when the Company of Coach and Coach-Harness Makers was founded by Charles II in 1677. Members of the Royal Society, founded in 1662, also made a contribution by investigating the use of springs.

In 1661 Lord Bedford wanted the most modern style of coach for his participation in the coronation procession to Westminster Hall, so he had one made in Paris at a cost of £170. It was fitted with the very latest innovation in comfort – glass panes in the windows instead of the usual leather flaps, but unfortunately three of these were damaged during the transportation of the coach to England and had to be replaced at a cost of 7s 6d.[92] By the 1670s it was estimated that there were some 6,000 private coaches in and around London alone. All these vehicles added to the 'loud medley of confusion' and

> . . . the brawls of coachmen, when they meet
> And stop in turnings of a narrow street.[93]

The public coach service was gradually expanded so that by 1681 there were 119 public coaches operating out of London, of which 60 to 70 were for long-distance journeys and the rest for journeys within a 20- to 25-mile radius of London, charging an average fare of 2d or 3d a mile. The 'Flying Machine' service between the Belle Sauvage Inn on Ludgate Hill and Bath was launched in 1667 with the accompanying advertisement:

All those desirous to pass from London to Bath, or any other place on the road, let them repair to the Belle Sauvage on Ludgate Hill in London, to the White Lion at Bath at both which places they may be received in a stage coach every Monday, Wednesday and Friday, which performs the whole journey in 3 days (if God permits) and sets forth at 5 o'clock in the morning. Passengers to pay one pound five shillings each, who are allowed to carry 24lbs. weight – for all above to pay three halfpence per pound.[94]

Coach services to Salisbury took two days, to Blandford and Dorchester two and a half, to Axminster and Exeter four days. There were also regular services to Newark, Doncaster, York, Wolverhampton and Shrewsbury and for £4 you could take a coach from London to Edinburgh.

By the beginning of the seventeenth century information about the layout of the road network could already be found in road books, and as early as 1625 itineraries were published giving information about the location and date of country fairs. A silk handkerchief, printed with a map, made *c.*1688 (94) illustrates the road system of England in great detail and in columns down each side lists the names of towns and the day of the week on which the local market was held. These maps would be used by the chapmen, who benefitted from the expanding demand for consumer goods from the lower ranks of society. A chap-book entitled *The Merchants's Ware-house laid open, or the Plain Dealing Linnen-Draper* was published in 1696.[95] It was an early version of a consumers' guide and was aimed at the customer and seamstress alike, who both wanted information about the huge variety of linen cloth available and which linen should be used to make specific garments. It was also intended to warn consumers against the hawkers and pedlars who were selling cloth of inferior quality.

A limited but efficient transportation system inevitably meant that information about the latest fashions could be circulated with greater speed, and this led to improved shopping facilities in towns throughout the country. The expansion of provincial shopping was observed by Celia Fiennes in her book *Through England on a Side Saddle in the Time of William and Mary*. This remarkable lady travelled on horseback throughout England during the late 1670s and 80s looking for evidence of progress and achievement in trade, intending to 'add much to its glory and esteem in our eyes'. Leeds particularly impressed her, for she discovered it was 'the wealthiest town of its bigness in the county, its manufacture is the woollen cloth the Yorkshire cloth in which they are all employ'd and are esteemed very rich and very proud'. In Liverpool she came upon an 'abundance of persons . . . very well dress'd and of good fashion'; and in Newcastle she found 'their shops are good and are of distinct trades, not selling many things in one shop, as is the custom in most country towns and cities'. The manufacture of gloves was 'the dominant trade' in Derby, whereas in Nottingham it was woven stockings. Norwich produced 'Crapes, Callimanco and Damaskes', which are 'fine and thinn and glossy', and in Colchester the 'whole town is employ'd in spinning weaveing washing drying and dressing their baize'.[96]

Fine shops could also be found in Edinburgh where, according to Rosalind Marshall's examination of the accounts of the 3rd Duke and Duchess of Hamilton, the Duchess 'could choose from grograms and silks from the Far East, and calico and muslins from

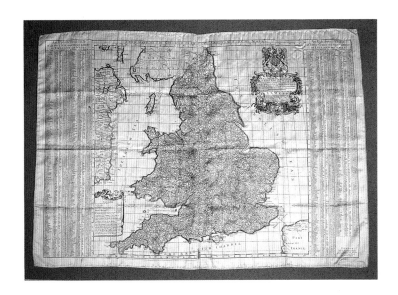

94 This silk handkerchief, *c.*1688, printed on a rolling press, would have been produced by one of the London map sellers who operated outside the restrictions of the Guild of Stationers and sold their own wares in fashionable shopping areas like Westminster Hall. One such, Charles Weston, at the sign of the Nag's Head, Bishopsgate Street, advertised that he sold handkerchiefs printed with *Ogilby's Roads*, a volume of maps first published by John Ogilby in 1675.

The combination here of a map of the English road system and details about market days provided the travelling trader and his customers with a surprisingly sophisticated pictorial aid.

the East Indies. In the winter her gowns were made of serge, stuff, curl cloth and mohair and for the summer there were silk mixtures – padasoy [paduasoy was a strong corded fabric], prunella [a worsted silk] and tabby, as well as pure silks and satins.'[97] The Duke and Duchess and their thirteen children lived in Hamilton Palace, a few miles south of Glasgow, and the shops of nearby Hamilton provided the Duke with his linen and the Duchess with a limited selection of 'dimity, serge and lace'. Her clothes were usually made for her by John Muirhead, a Hamilton tailor, but when a more spectacular outfit was required it would be made in London. From the 1670s onwards the Duke visited London once a year and he took with him details of his wife's measurements and a description of what she wanted, but this system was not always successful. In 1689, for example, he could not even identify the garment she wanted him to buy. He wrote: 'Your memorandum is so generall you put me to it . . . your "sallantine" I nether know what it is you mean by it, nor can I find any body that knowes what it is, so explain yourself by the next.'[98] The Duchess must have explained that she meant a pallatine, a tippet of sable which covered the shoulders, but she could not have provided her husband with the information he required, for he admitted in his next letter that 'I confess I like this trade of buying things worst of any, for I see I do not understand it'.[99] On another occasion the Duchess advised him to use a London tailor called Mr Renne to make her a black gown and a mantua and petticoat of 'verie grave cullers'. When the trunk arrived at Hamilton Palace she must have been most vexed to discover it contained 'a scarlet satin petticoat with silver and gold lace on it, a coloured, flowered silk gown, and a flowered gown trimmed all over with lace'.[100]

Another two hundred years were to pass before the illustrated mail order catalogue offered customers the convenience of ordering goods from home, avoiding such misunderstandings.

CHAPTER FOUR

Uniformly Elegant

1720–1780

I

In previous chapters, the tastes of the monarch have provided the opening theme. The accession of Henry VIII and the restoration of Charles II, for example, had a profound effect on fashionable dress, and although Sir Walter Raleigh might write bitterly of his banishment 'Say to the Court, it glows, and shines like rotten wood',[1] Elizabeth I's court acted as a magnet for ambitious men and women, who strove to be noticed by the costumes they wore, and where they led, the nation followed.

But matters were very different by the beginning of the eighteenth century, and the accession of the Hanoverian kings. The courts of George I (1714–27) and of his son, George II (1727–1760) were described by one German visitor – who one might expect to be sympathetic – as 'the residence of dullness'. By the 1730s, court dress had become stylised: George II's queen, Caroline of Anspach, wore stiff-bodied gowns, with heavily-boned bodices, separate petticoats and trains, all lavishly embellished with jewels. This was the style inherited by George III's queen, Charlotte of Mecklenburg-Strelitz, when she arrived in England in 1761, and which she continued to wear until her death in 1818, when it must have looked positively archaic, though the court continued to be the arena for spectacular and lavish display (see 121).

Changes to this formal style of dress were very slow. Hence the comment made by Frances, Countess of Hertford, in a letter written in 1740 about a Birthday Court: 'If I were to describe their [the royal family's] clothes to you, you would say you had seen them (or just such) at every Birthday that you can remember.'[2] So leaders of fashion looked to the French court for inspiration, despite ambivalent feelings that 'we take our fashions from the land we hate'.[3] The latest developments in Paris were conveyed across

95 (*previous pages*) Members of the Trevelyan family of Wallington, Northumberland, in a mid-eighteenth-century conversation piece. Sir George Trevelyan, 3rd Bart, wears his breeches in an old-fashioned style, with the stockings rolled up over the knee. His son, John, has a double fastening on his coat similar to William Windham's riding coat (**109**). The ladies' riding jackets are carefully shaped into the waist, where the skirt flares out from a vent on either side. Both wear flat-topped tricorne hats and have tied black bows around the frill-topped collars of their shifts, which have been cut like a man's shirt with a ruffle.
(English School, *c*.1745–50, Wallington)

96 *An Angling Party* portrays the natural world as being as organised and civilised as the human figures who inhabit it. They are shown in the grounds of their country house, which has an appropriately austere classical façade approached by a wide flight of steps lined by Roman statues. The angling takes place in an ornamental pond with some tastefully arranged broken pieces of masonry at one end. One lady is sitting on an elegant garden seat, another is sketching at a table that would look more at home in the drawing-room. All the ladies wear exquisite silk sack-back dresses and the two younger ones wear their *bergère* hats tilted at the extreme angle demanded by their elevated hair-styles. The manicured and rolling fields of the family's estate stretch away into the distance behind the perfectly-shaped trees, regularly disposed between the garden urns.
(Edward Smith, 1773, Wimpole Hall)

the Channel by means of fashion dolls. Many French milliners, mantua-makers and tailors operated in London, and even those who were not French adopted an appropriate name to attract trade. The successful mercer 'must have a deal of the French-man in his Manners, as well as a large Parcel of French Goods in his shop. . . . Nothing that is mere English goes down with our modern Ladies; from their Shift to their Topknots they must be equipped from Deare Paris.'[4]

The other major influence on eighteenth-century British dress was the concept of English Arcadia. Writing at the end of the Georgian era in 1818, Richard Rush, the American ambassador, describes:

> The enthusiastic fondness of the English for the country. . . . They have *houses* in London, in which they stay while Parliament sits, and occasionally visit at other seasons; but their *homes* are in the country. Their turreted mansions are there, with all that denotes perpetuity – heirlooms, family memorials, pictures, tombs. This spreads the ambition among other classes, and the taste for rural life, however diversified or graduated the scale, becomes widely diffused.[5]

The desire of the 'Cit' (London citizen) to have a country home of his own is derided by Robert Lloyd's poem, 1757:

> The wealthy Cit, grown old in trade,
> Now wishes for the rural shade . . .
> Scarce past the turnpike half a mile,
> How all the country seems to smile! . . .
> . . . And now from Hyde-Park Corner come
> The Gods of Athens, and of Rome.
> Here squashy Cupids take their places,
> With Venus, and the clumsy Graces.[6]

Nostalgia for a life of pastoral simplicity and felicity far away from the cares of court and city has existed in English literature from before the sixteenth century. Seen through its eyes, the English countryside becomes an idealised landscape wrapped in a golden classical haze. It is inhabited not by toiling workers, but by figures with Greek names who are enjoying a life of unsullied contentment (96).

Such yearning for the innocence of 'golden times' was perceived by the poet William Cowper to be a lost cause as he felt that the town had already 'ting'd the country'. In his poem *The Task* the desire of the 'rural lass' to be as fashionable as her counterpart in the town altered not only her appearance but also her character, and she:

> Whom once her virgin modesty and grace,
> Her artless manners, and her neat attire,
> So dignified, that she was hardly less
> Than the fair shepherdess of old romance,
> Is seen no more. The character is lost!
> Her head, adorn'd with lappets pinn'd aloft,
> And ribbands streaming gay, superbly rais'd,
> And magnified beyond all human size.[7]

Fashionable people were not, however, deterred by the reality. Clad in picturesque pseudo-rustic dress they enthusiastically created the Arcadia of classical Greece in the English countryside as they attended alfresco events like haymaking and *fêtes-champêtres*. Masquerades were also very popular entertainments, which offered the participants the opportunity to discard their fashionable clothes and dress up 'in what they have a mind to be' – whether an Arcadian nymph or shepherdess or in a style copied from past fashion. The work of the Old Masters, especially the portraits painted by Van Dyck, or Rubens's portrait of his wife Helena, inspired endless imitations that have been recorded in portraits (97).

The contrast between the artificiality of contemporary fashion and the simplicity of classical dress was pointed out by the philosopher Jean-Jacques Rousseau in *Emile* (1762): 'The Greek women were wholly unacquainted with those frames of whalebone in which our women distort rather than display their figures. It seems to me that this abuse, which is carried to an incredible degree of folly in England, must sooner or later lead to the production of a degenerate race. . . . Everything which cramps and confines nature is in bad taste; this is as true of the adornments of the person as of the ornaments of the mind.'[8] His equation of moral virtue with the 'flowing garments' of the ancients is one which would have been approved by Sir Joshua Reynolds, the artist and first President of the Royal Academy.

For those who wanted an approximation to classical dress, Sir Joshua offered his sitters a costume which had 'the general air of the antique for the sake of dignity and preserved something of the modern for the sake of likeness'.[9] This compromise was achieved by means of a loose, white cross-over gown far removed from the restrictive bodice and skirt of court fashion. Sir Joshua pointed out in a lecture given in 1776 that the dress of the inhabitants of ancient Greece and Rome had much to recommend it, for 'we may justly rank the simplicity of them consisting of little more than one single piece of drapery, without those whimsical capricious forms by which all other dresses are embarrassed'.[10] By the time he addressed his students in 1784, when he exhorted them never 'to lose sight of nature', the slow progression towards a simpler, classically-inspired dress for men and women was about to become reality.

Some of the lesser-known assets of the National Trust are its outstanding collections of eighteenth-century costume and accessories. The most extensive, made by Charles Paget Wade at Snowshill Manor, Gloucestershire, was the result of a lifetime spent scouring antique shops, 'dusty attics and narrow back alleys' in order to rescue an extraordinary variety and range of objects. Between 1911, when he inherited his father's West Indian estates, and 1951, when he gave Snowshill and its contents to the National Trust, Wade collected over 2,000 items of costume. These were kept in the Museum Room of the house until they were removed in 1982 for conservation and cataloguing by the Trust. At present they are kept in storage, but a selection of the most interesting garments and accessories have been photographed for this book. His collection encompasses over 300 years of costume history, from English Civil War armour and riding boots (4) to chiffon dresses of the 1920s, but it is the eighteenth-century costume, male and female, that constitutes the major and most important part of the collection. Wade's fascination with 'the things of every day' meant that he did not only limit

97 Jemima, Marchioness Grey, chose for her portrait to wear her version of a typical costume painted by Van Dyck a hundred years earlier. So widespread did this custom become that the term 'vandyke' came to mean any surface trimmed with cut edges, whether they were lace or not. She wears a gown of shimmering cream satin, the low, square neckline of which is veiled by a wide sloping lace collar (see also 55). References to the fashions of the late 1630s are also apparent in the full sleeves, closed by opulent lace cuffs, the delicate pearl jewellery and the distinctive ribbon rosette and trim on a tightly-laced stomacher. But the unbroken, fluid lines of the original style are modified by contemporary fashion, with a narrower and longer bodice, and a hoop under the skirt. (Allan Ramsay, 1741, Wimpole Hall)

himself to obtaining the most elaborate or finely-executed examples – although there are many of an exceptionally high standard – but he also bought working and everyday clothing. (See also p.9.)

A second major collection of costume is housed at Killerton House in Devon, where relevant exhibitions are mounted every year. The collection was built up by the actress Baroness Paulise de Bush and includes a number of extremely fine eighteenth-century gowns, and a variety of accessories, comprising ruffles, fans, aprons, two court suits and several embroidered waistcoats.

Another rich source of eighteenth-century embroidery is the Rachel Kay-Shuttleworth collection – which does not belong to the National Trust, but is housed at Gawthorpe Hall in Lancashire, which does. A permanent display is provided in one section of the house and a further study collection can be viewed on application. Sizergh Castle in Cumbria, the home of the Strickland family, also has an exceptional collection of eighteenth-century gowns and accessories, which have been treasured by succeeding generations of the family. A small but important collection of clothes is also kept at the Trust's Textile Conservation Workroom at Blickling Hall, Norfolk, including some very rare cloth riding jackets, a needlecord suit and a bright yellow silk domino – a hooded and enveloping garment that ladies wore to masquerades – all dating from the eighteenth century.

At Springhill, Co. Londonderry, the most splendid item in this important costume collection is an eighteenth-century court mantua (see 120). Made from silk that was woven in Spitalfields between 1759 and 1762, the mantua would have been worn for presentation at court. As such gowns were made from very expensive fabrics and were usually only worn once, they tended to be kept. This garment passed through successive generations of Lord Clanwilliam's family until 1979, when it was donated to Springhill.

Surviving garments yield information about the appearance, cut and construction of clothes, but they do not tell us how they were worn. Unlike portraits, they cannot carry the complex set of signals about the wearer's social status and aspirations. Fortunately, National Trust houses offer an *embarras de richesses* when it comes to eighteenth-century portraits, with examples by artists of the calibre of Thomas Gainsborough, Joshua Reynolds, Johann Zoffany and Allan Ramsay, as well as those painted by lesser known artists like Tilly Kettle.

The illustrations for this chapter, and the two that follow, can take advantage of this combination of sources. Enough clothes have survived to enable a choice to be made, and those that have been selected for photography are little altered, in excellent condition, and are representative of a particular style. They have been placed on dummies arranged with all the relevant accessories, and photographed in such a way that the finer details of the garment, as well as its overall appearance, can be appreciated. Alongside these pictures are dated portraits of people wearing similar garments, to show how the clothes were intended to be worn in a variety of situations.

The introduction of the conversation piece – a picture of a group of figures conversing or engaged in activity – into British portrait painting in the 1720s and 1730s is of importance in illustrating this point. A group of identifiable people is shown in an informal setting, giving the artist the opportunity to make a detailed depiction of dress on figures that are caught in different poses. One of the first pictures of this kind to be

98 (*left*) Philippe Mercier's conversation piece of the Tyrconnel family at Belton. Sir John Brownlow, Viscount Tyrconnel, wears the red sash of the Order of the Bath and its insignia. Mrs Francis Dayrell, Lady Tyrconnel's cousin, is on the swing: the invalid Lady Tyrconnel is seated in a wheeled chair pushed by a black page; Francis Dayrell stands next to her; Savile Cockayne Cust, a Brownlow cousin, pulls the string attached to the swing; and William Brownlow, Lord Tyrconnel's brother, leans against the tree trunk.

All the men wear discreetly trimmed three-piece suits. The fully-cut coat, with its wide side pleats, is either left unbottoned or fastened at the waist. The cuffs, deep, rounded and braid-trimmed, match the colour of the waistcoats.

Mrs Dayrell is informally dressed in a pale green satin closed gown with a muslin kerchief tied in front, a long apron and a neat lace cap. Lady Tyrconnel also wears a closed gown comprising a brown satin bodice and skirt, both decorated with gold military style frogging. (Philippe Mercier, 1724-6, Belton House)

99 (*right*) Sir John Cust is attired in a magnificent white and gold brocade waistcoat, brown coat and breeches. Captain William Cust's coat is decorated with the braid appropriate to his rank, and the profile view shows how it is fitted into the waist, from which it flares out.

Anne Cust wears a black widow's hood and lace trimmed kerchief, kept in place by a band attached to the robings of a closed blue damask gown. The gown has shallow pleated cuffs from which the smock sleeves emerge with a single matching lace frill. Anne and her daughter Dorothy, seated next to her, both wear long gauzy aprons. Dorothy's closed gown is made from the heavy, lustrous cream satin so popular in the 1740s. The frill on her smock forms a tucker, a white frilled edging that could either be the smock frill or sewn separately onto the bodice of the gown. (Enoch Seeman, 1741-5, Belton House)

painted in Britain hangs at Belton House, Lincolnshire (**98**). The masterpiece of the French artist Philippe Mercier, it was painted in 1724–6. The south front of Belton can be seen in the background and the figures are all members of the Brownlow and Cust families. Although they wear clothes that are not too ostentatious for taking a modicum of exercise in the garden, they still proclaim their fashionable taste and rank in society.

Ladies had three basic choices of dress during the eighteenth century. The first was a closed robe or gown. This was made as an entity and so did not require a petticoat. The second choice was an open robe – a gown that was open in front and so worn with a petticoat. It had a separate stomacher piece which was laced across, embroidered or covered in ribbons. The gown could be fitted into the waist at the back in a style that was known from the 1780s as the *robe à l'anglaise*, or it could fall in folds from the shoulders to the hem in a style known as a *sacque* or sack or *robe à la française* (see p.144). A bodice and skirt was the third option, and could take the form of a quilted jacket and matching petticoat, a *pet-en-l'air* – a loose-backed jacket – with matching or contrasting skirt, or a fitted riding jacket and skirt (see p.130).

Two examples of the closed gown can be seen in another portrait of the Cust family, a large conversation piece painted between 1741 and 1745 by Enoch Seeman (**99**). It depicts the widowed Anne Cust seated at the tea table, surrounded by members of her family. She had inherited Belton from her brother, Viscount Tyrconnel and passed it on to her eldest son, Sir John Cust, who is seated in the centre holding a miniature of his new wife. He wears the fashionable bag-wig, unlike the older man next to him, Savile Cockayne Cust, who wears the conservative full-bottomed wig. Introduced in the 1730s, the bag-wig arranged the hair at the sides into loosely-curling rolls to be caught at the back in a black silk bow. A clearer view of a bag-wig is afforded by Captain William Cust, Sir John's brother, who is pointing to a map of a naval engagement.

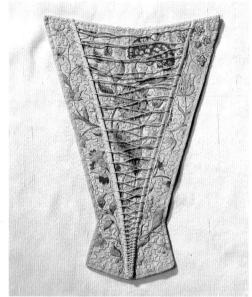

When a lady's open gown had a fitted bodice with a V-shape at the centre front the material folded back on either side of it formed flat sewn-down revers called robings. There is a rare set of silver lace robings, a matching stomacher and cuffs, made *c*.1750, in the Snowshill collection (100). The robings (see 99) would have been attached to the revers of the bodice and the stomacher would fill the unclosed area of the bodice. A stomacher (100, 101) was usually made with a series of projecting plain tabs pinned to the inside of the bodice so that there would be no gaps between it and the robings and, with its stiff, heavy bones, it kept the bosom absolutely flat, for 'no woman can be genteel, who is not entirely flat in front'.[11]

Eighteenth-century designs in embroidery and woven silks show an interest in the natural world (see 102 and 120). A gifted embroideress of the period, the intellectual socialite Mrs Mary Delany,[12] created images of flowers in many different media, but her exquisite flower pictures constructed out of tiny pieces of coloured paper, now in the British Museum, are botanical illustrations in their own right. This accuracy of depiction is also apparent in the floral brocades woven at Spitalfields in the 1730s and 1740s (102). The development in France of a weaving technique which dovetailed shades of colour so that a motif appeared almost three-dimensional in form allowed the shape and colour of flowers to be woven precisely and accurately. The pre-eminent English designer of the time, Anna Maria Garthwaite, daughter of a Lincolnshire parson, immediately utilised this technique but unlike the French, who used a coloured background, she arranged the flowers on a white ground, thus accentuating the individuality and freshness of each flower (see also p.154).

When George II's daughter Anne married Prince William of Orange in 1734 the newspapers reported that 'the newest-fashioned silks were white paduasoys with large flowers of tulips, peonies, emmonies, carnations & etc in their proper colours, some wove in the silk and some embroidered'.[13] The wide-hooped petticoats of the time allowed such large-scale patterns on both woven and embroidered materials a maximum area of display, but by the end of the 1730s this desire for naturalism had got out of hand. Mrs Delany wrote disapprovingly of a gown worn by Selina, Countess of

100 (*above left*) Part of a set of silver lace robings, stomacher and cuffs, *c*.1750. The cuffs are in the extended winged style of the 1740s and the stomacher shows the desire for a more decorative effect. The rows of raised loops of silver lace and a scattering of tiny silver sequins combine to create a glittering surface that would have looked very impressive when sewn onto the surface of a silk gown.

101 (*above right*) This beautiful stomacher, dating from the first half of the eighteenth century, is a triangular piece of ivory silk embroidered with a delicate coiling pattern in silver thread which imitates the pattern of quilting, and a variety of flowers worked in coloured silks. Unusually it has survived with its original fine white cord lacing across the front, and is bound round the edges with ivory silk ribbons. When seen from the back, it is apparent how the garment retained its rigidity, for a series of closely-set narrow whalebones are encased within two layers of fine linen.

102 (*right*) Part of an ensemble (see also **132**) made for the Strickland family at Sizergh Castle, Cumbria. This open robe has not been altered and the back view of the bodice shows how the pleats were arranged to curve from the shoulder straight into the skirt, the folds of which were disposed to maintain the continuity of the pattern. The Spitalfields silk was woven between 1740 and 1742, using an unusual and bold floral pattern. All the garments are lined with fine white silk.

Huntingdon, which had a pattern of 'a *large stone vase* filled with *ramping flowers* that spread almost over a breadth of the petticoat from the bottom to the top . . . it was a much laboured piece of finery, the pattern much properer for a stucco staircase than the apparel of a lady'.[14]

Both closed and open robes would have been worn over a hooped petticoat, a series of hoops made of whalebone encased in material, which could be bought ready-made in a hoop warehouse or made-to-measure from a hoop-maker. The full-length hoops that first appeared in about 1710 gave the skirt a conical shape and were followed in the 1730s by large circular ones. The side hoops introduced in the 1740s carried the skirt out horizontally from the waist on either side to hang vertically to the ground. They created a wide and squarish shape that Mrs Delany found particularly objectionable. She wrote to a friend in 1750, 'I am glad you *detest* the tubs of hoops, – I keep within bounds, endeavouring to avoid all particularities of being *too much* in or *out* of fashion.'[15] Despite their obvious inconvenience – perfectly summed up by Henry Fielding in *Tom Jones* (1749), 'The door of the room now flew open and, after pushing her hoop sideways before her, entered Lady Bellaston'[16] – they were universally worn until the 1760s and were retained for court dress until 1820. In a rather haunting 1749 portrait of Mrs Joshua Iremonger by Arthur Devis, a provincial artist who specialised in conversation pieces,[17] the shape of the side hoops is clearly discernible under the skirts of the closed sack (103).

The propensity of the English to develop informal styles of dress continued during the eighteenth century, influenced by the natural preference of many for country life and a passion for hunting and shooting. This inevitably had an effect on their wardrobes, making popular the various combinations of bodice and skirt or jacket and skirt. The plainer clothes worn in the country were also suitable for walking about town, and it was this simpler and more practical version of fashionable dress which was widely copied. When Pierre Jean Grosley saw some ladies walking in St James's Park in the 1760s he noted: 'The country life led by these ladies during a great part of the year and the freedom which accompanies that way of life make them continue an agreeable negligence in dress which never gives disgust.'[18]

Riding costume had already become an established part of the female wardrobe and although Pepys's disapproval of ladies attired in such a masculine costume (see p.102) was frequently repeated in periodicals, the functional nature of the costume meant that it was eminently suitable for travelling.[19] When the Duchess of Queensberry went to Europe in 1734 it is likely that she was wearing her riding habit, for her brother recalled with some amusement that 'she has been called *Sir* upon the road above twenty times'.[20] Two portraits of the period show what a sensible and functional outfit riding clothes could be for women (104 and 95). They incorporated practical elements from male fashion with femininity, a combination noticed as early as 1710 when a visitor to Epsom races found that there were 'vast crowds on horseback, both men and females; many of the latter wore men's clothes and feathered hats, which is quite usual in England'.[21] By the 1780s ladies' riding dress had become even more masculine in its cut, as in John Downman's 1783 drawing of Lady Mary Somerset, Duchess of Rutland (105).

Plain quilted petticoats first appeared in the late seventeenth century when they were worn as an undergarment for warmth, but by the 1740s, when skirts were open in front,

103 Mrs Joshua Iremonger in a sack-back gown borne out by large square hoops. The bodice, fitting tightly into the waist, is worn over the rigid elongated stomacher that ensured an entirely flat bosom. The heavy-weight silks worn by members of the Cust family (99) have given way to lighter varieties, and the shimmering surface of Mrs Iremonger's gown is enhanced by a very fine muslin or silk gauze kerchief and sleeve ruffles. The bodice has plain robings and winged cuffs.
(Arthur Devis, 1749, Uppark)

104 (*left*) In William Hoare's vivacious pastel portrait of Miss Vernon, the deep flat collar and double-buttoned revers of her riding jacket have been cut in exactly the same way as a man's frock-coat, and it is worn with a matching waistcoat. Her neckwear, a lace-trimmed collar turned down over a blue bow, is a very feminine interpretation of a man's stock and ruffle. There is, however, no hint of masculinity about her choice of hat: its distinctive shape, a shallow crown and wide brim decorated with a white ostrich feather, made it a popular alternative to the more severe lines of the tricorne hat. (William Hoare, 1760s, Attingham Park)

105 (*below*) A drawing of Lady Mary Somerset, Duchess of Rutland, shows her wearing a riding jacket cut tight into the waist, to slope away at the sides like a man's. It also incorporates the masculine feature of a high collar, revers and matching waistcoat. A practical ensemble, set off by an extravagantly-trimmed hat. (John Downman, 1783, Wimpole Hall)

106 (*left*) A quilted pink satin petticoat, with an attractive pattern of strawberries and strawberry leaves, has been photographed with a pair of shoes made in the 1720s from purple brocade. The shoes have straps that would have been buckled over a high tongue lined with red silk (the buckle marks are visible). Unusually, the shoes have survived with their original leather clogs – protective overshoes. All are in excellent condition.

Next to the shoes is an Italian fan dating from the 1740s. It has been painted with three figures in a landscape, the edges are decorated with embossed foil depicting putti, coronets and shells, and the ivory guards have been carved with figures from the *commedia dell'arte*.

107 (*right*) The lady's quilted white satin travelling petticoat, made between 1745 and 1760, would have been worn over another hooped petticoat. The bodice must have been uncomfortable on a journey of any length as it is stiffened with six bones at the back and two in front. It fastens down the front with hooks and eyes made from rounded tin wire.

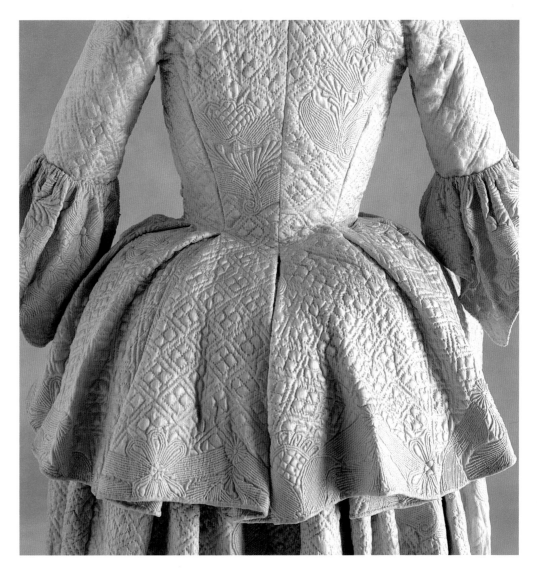

they had become a decorative garment in their own right. A gown with a quilted petticoat of a contrasting colour, a popular choice for informal dress, featured in many portraits of the period. As they were easily available – they could be bought ready-made in warehouses – their popularity and the relative longevity of the fashion meant that a large number have survived. To create a quilted petticoat the satin was backed with white silk and a layer of fine wool was placed between the two layers. Such padding could make it an uncomfortably heavy garment, as Mrs Purefoy found when she bought one in 1739. Henry Purefoy and his mother, Elizabeth, lived in Buckinghamshire, where Henry ran the family estate and was the county sheriff in 1748–9. In a letter written to their agent in London, Henry Purefoy explained that he had returned the 'quilt petticoat by Mr Eagles ye Carrier. It is so heavy my mother cannot wear it.'[22] During the 1740s the patterns embroidered onto the silk became increasingly complex and could be a combination of geometric and large-scale naturalistic motifs (106). In the Snowshill collection there is a rare and very beautiful hooded jacket and matching petticoat of quilted white satin that would have been worn for travelling (107).[23]

108 The unknown lady in this portrait is wearing a *pet-en-l'air*, confirming the impression that such a garment must have been a comfortable and elegant choice for informal occasions. She has trimmed her satin jacket with fur, and fur has also been used for the plain winged cuffs that were fashionable *c*.1745. The ends of her lace-edged kerchief have been tucked under one band of the stomacher. Plain muslin sleeve ruffles, a satin petticoat and a round-eared cap complete the outfit.
(Unknown artist, 1740s, Upton House)

Another popular choice for informal dress was to wear a petticoat with a *pet-en-l'air* jacket, made with a sack-back construction that fastened down the front (108). It could fasten with hooks and eyes sewn to tabs to form a stomacher or be pinned over a corset with decorative lacing. Either way, it was usual to arrange a muslin kerchief round the neck and hold its ends in position by tucking them under a tab or a band of the lacing.

Male dress was even more influenced by life in the country and its year-round activities of riding and shooting. In the 1730s gentlemen started wearing the frock-coat out of doors. These loosely-cut coats with flat round collars had previously only been worn by working men, a gentleman's coat, by contrast, being cut with side pleats and no collar. Gradually, the advantages of a collar for protection against the weather were realised and so it was incorporated in the informal frock-coat. An Englishman who visited Paris in 1752 longed to discard his formal coat, which made him 'so damned uneasy' and he 'frequently sighed for my little loose frock which I look upon as an emblem of our happy constitution: for it lays a man under no uneasy restraints but leaves it in his power to do as he pleases'.[24] Being such wearable and functional garments, very few cloth frock-coats have survived, but two that are thought to have belonged to William Windham II, son and heir of Ashe Windham (see p.107) of Felbrigg Hall, Norfolk, are now in the workroom at nearby Blickling Hall. One is part of a brown needlecord suit of 1735–40 and the other is a blue-grey napped cloth coat from the same period that was probably worn for riding.

These costumes came to light in 1969 when the contents and estate of Felbrigg Hall were bequeathed to the National Trust by Robert Wyndham Ketton-Cremer. He had carefully stored away a number of items that he had discovered in the 'immense rambling mansion' he had inherited in 1933.[25] These included a fascinating and unusual collection of eighteenth-century men's clothes, in excellent condition, that would have been worn on the estate for riding, shooting and other country pursuits (109).[26] They must have been put away in the spring of 1738 when William Windham II went on the Grand Tour. He returned to Felbrigg in October 1742 but after a brief stay he moved to London, and for country pursuits he rented a house in Warwickshire and he did not visit Felbrigg again until his father died in April 1749.

From the 1730s onwards men's coats began to curve towards the back and the waistcoat shortened slightly. The cut of the coat revealed more of the waistcoat, which, for formal occasions, was lavishly embellished with embroidery. The embroidery also followed the curving lines of the front of the coat, the hem and the centre panels of the back, ensuring that its back view was as impressive as the front. A particularly fine example of this elaborate and formal style of coat and waistcoat can be seen in a portrait of the much-travelled and cultivated George Lucy of Charlecote. It was painted by Pompeo Batoni in Rome in 1758 while Lucy was on the Grand Tour (110) and he paid 40 guineas for it. He is portrayed standing in his finery in the appropriate classical setting. Lucy was rather taken aback to discover that the sittings would last a month or five weeks, and that 'he [Batoni] would not undertake to do me in less time'. He also discovered that attitudes towards artists were somewhat different in Italy: 'These painters are great men, and must be flattered, for 'tis the custom here, not to think themselves obliged to you for employing them, but that they oblige you by being employed.'[27]

109 A jacket, *c*.1745, made for William Windham II of Felbrigg Hall, Norfolk. It is made from fine brown wool and fastens down the front with a double row of brass buttons. It was probably worn for riding.

110 George Lucy portrayed by Pompeo Batoni on the Grand Tour. The curve of his coat from mid-chest is very pronounced, allowing full display of the ornate waistcoat. The weight and luxury of his magnificent blue velvet coat is increased by rich gold embroidery trimming the front edges, deep cuffs and pocket flaps. The waistcoat is white satin, embroidered all over with sprigs of tiny flowers and gold wire laid in a scrolling pattern. Waistcoats and coats as elaborate as these would have been reserved for formal occasions, and when they went out of fashion the gold and silver wire would be removed and resold to the laceman, costed according to weight. When the blue velvet of this suit eventually wore out, Lucy's house-keeper, Philippa Hayes, cut it up and made it into cushions.
(Pompeo Batoni, 1758, Charlecote Park)

Lucy enjoyed acquiring and wearing splendidly embroidered velvet suits, but when he visited Naples in 1755 he found that fashionable society there 'dress much and I have been obliged to daub myself all over silver, accompanied with a sword and a bag wig'.[28] Wearing a sword was more commonplace on the Continent than in Britain, where the practice was restricted to formal occasions only. Feeling a little under-dressed, perhaps, he wrote to his housekeeper Mrs Hayes requesting her to send a box from Charlecote

111 (*above left*) Eighteenth-century suits of silk, velvet or brocade have survived in some numbers, but those made of cloth, highly susceptible to the ravages of moth, have not. Fortunately George Lucy decided to protect this plum-coloured suit, perhaps because he wore it to the Shakespeare Jubilee celebrations in Stratford-on-Avon in 1769. As a result, the rich silver decoration and elegant buttons, seen here on the pocket, sparkle as brightly now as they did on that memorable summer's evening.

112 (*above right*) This man's suit, dating from the 1760s, is made from a rose-brown uncut silk velvet with a pattern of green flowers on a ground of cream stems and stripes. The coat, rather more worn than the waistcoat, has deep cuffs buttoned across the top. The breeches are made with a front flap opening and buckle closely to a point just below the knee.

packed with his 'best embroidered suit, the light-coloured suit of uniformity laced with gold, the white Dresden waistcoat with the 2 pairs of velvet breeches, one red, the other black, and half a dozen more shirts with the Dresden ruffles tacked to them'. (Dresden was a fine white embroidery in openwork patterns which gave it the delicacy of lace.) His stipulation that she should not send the 'lace'd ones' as he was sure they would never reach him in 'these dangerous times' proved prophetic. The ship carrying the clothes was boarded by Moorish pirates and the box was carried off to Algiers.[29]

Fortunately one of Lucy's suits has survived (111). Of plum-coloured cloth, trimmed with silver lace and buttons, it is believed to be the suit he wore to the Shakespeare Jubilee Celebrations held in Stratford-on-Avon in 1769. Charlecote is situated not far from Stratford, and tradition has it that the young Shakespeare was caught poaching in the park in the 1580s and brought before Sir Thomas Lucy, resident magistrate. The playwright may have wreaked his revenge for his subsequent fine, and possible flogging, by modelling the snobbish, pompous Justice Shallow in *II Henry IV* and *The Merry Wives of Windsor* on Sir Thomas.

To celebrate the two-hundredth anniversary of Shakespeare's birth, the great actor David Garrick master-minded festivities that took place over several days in a wooden rotunda specially constructed in the middle of a field. A midnight masquerade was 'hysterically gay' as the guests, some dressed in Shakespearean costume, consumed vast quantities of hot turtle soup, brandy and madeira. Despite the rain, 'dancing did not end until 5, and by then the coaches were too deep in mud to be moved and the guests had to

113 (*left*) A magnificent portrait of William Colyear, Viscount Milsington. The roll of curls on his bag-wig is now set much lower and is worn with a solitaire – the black ribbon from the bag of a wig which was brought round from the back and tied in front over the stock and lace ruffle. Colyear holds a tricorne hat similar in shape to the braid-trimmed one on the chair shown in **112**.
(Allan Ramsay, 1764, Penrhyn Castle)

114 (*right*) Detail from a court coat of the 1770s of velvet with a striped design of checks and diamonds. The surface, already rich, has been further decorated with what appears to be panels of lace, but is in fact embroidery imitating a lace pattern. Executed in coloured silk and chenille thread with a design incorporating sprays of flowers, leaves and buds, it follows the edges of the coat, back vents and cuffs. Inside the right sleeve 'J. Munden INV & DEL' has been written in ink, but whether this refers to the embroiderer or the person who drew the design it is impossible to say.

walk to their lodgings through the wet dawn'.[30] It is wonderful, therefore, that George Lucy's costume has survived.

Men's clothing from the period 1740 to 1800 is very well represented in the Snowshill collection, including a complete suit (**112**) made in the 1760s from rose-brown uncut silk velvet. The fashion for surface embellishment continued, but Allan Ramsay's portrait of William Colyear, Viscount Milsington, painted in 1764, shows how the deep pile of a plain velvet suit lined with white satin could look as rich and sumptuous as one decorated with embroidery (**113**).

The use of velvet in cut or uncut patterns is more often found in men's suits than in women's gowns, and the inclusion of light-catching elements like glass, foil and

spangles amongst the embroidery ensured a richness and brilliance of effect when worn
in candlelight (119). Mrs Delany, always critical of excess, found that the embroidery on
Lord Villiers' coat at a court event in 1773 was somewhat over the top. He wore 'pale
purple velvet coat, turned up with lemon-colour, and embroidered all over with S.S.'s of
pearl as big as pease, and in all the spaces little medallions in beaten gold, *real solid*, in
various figures of *Cupids* "and *the like*". . . . At best it was only a fool's coat.'[31] Two of
the court coats in the Snowshill collection show the fashion for this and are embroidered
with designs of great complexity, variety and beauty (114 and 5).

In female dress, too, the 1760s onwards saw a period of maximum surface decoration,
though the volume of the skirt had reduced with the discarding of the massive hoops, as
in a portrait of Lady Frances Harpur and her son Henry, painted by Tilly Kettle, *c.*1766
(116). 'Mother and son are dressed handsomely but not grandly in the clothes of their
time, with no allusion to the antique, a fashion that was being revived at the hands of
Reynolds and others. The antique is however strongly evoked by the urn and the circular relief beneath it. . . . [This] natural ease in great surroundings or even a studied
indifference to the pomp of wealth and power'[32] is a characteristic of English portrait
painting of this time, and there are few portraits in which the sitters have chosen to wear
the grand and formal clothes required at a court function.

Court costume developed at a much faster pace in the late eighteenth century as
fashionable society sought to emulate the complex sequence of styles that flowed out of
the court of Louis XVI and Marie-Antoinette. Despite military, political and commercial decline in France, French court dress reached new heights of extravagant excess
(122). The coloured fashion plates printed in Paris and London from the early 1770s
recorded these rapid changes in fashion, creating a bewildering variety of new gowns,
including styles *à la circassienne, à la levantine, à la sultane, à la polonaise* and *à la*

116 Lady Frances Harpur with her son Henry. The buttoned front of her bodice and skirt is almost hidden behind her patterned muslin mantle, which is trimmed with lace and casually knotted at waist level. A veritable cascade of lace ruffles covers her arms from elbow to wrist. A slight puffed effect has been created in the skirt – now without the massive hoops of the previous decade – by gathering the silk into a deep, furbelow-trimmed border around the hem, typical of the surface decoration fashionable in the 1760s.
(Tilly Kettle, *c*.1766, Calke Abbey)

créole. However, the traffic in fashion ideas was often a two-way one with the British adopting gowns like the *polonaise* in the 1770s and the French adopting the *robe à l'anglaise*. The *polonaise* was an attractive and useful garment that could be made in silk or cotton and consisted of a short open gown, reaching well above the ankle, and a draped overskirt, which was pulled up by drawstrings to form puffed swags (**117** and **118**). The back of the gown fitted into the waist in the same way as the *robe à l'anglaise*. This was a gown with a fitted bodice that had been worn as an informal garment in Britain before it was introduced into France in about 1775. The central section of the back bodice was pleated and sewn down to the fitted lining, the lines of the pleats following the shape of the corset underneath. These pleats extended without a waist

117 A cotton *polonaise* from the 1770s, with a yellow-spotted background and flower sprays in red and green alternating with a meandering pattern of tiny white leaves outlined in red. Inside the skirt are two tapes and a loop of cotton: when these are fastened together an attractive bunched-up effect is created at the back. The *polonaise* is worn over a cotton skirt of contrasting colour – this one is modern, as are the straw hat and muslin kerchief, both essential accessories with this style of garment. Unlike many silk gowns in the Snowshill collection, this cotton dress has exceptionally fine stitching, seen at its best at the back of the bodice where the seams taper elegantly into the waistline.

The red leather shoes lying in front were also made in the 1770s. The two flaps crossing over at the front would have been secured there by a buckle. Unlike the 1740s shoes (**132**), with very pointed toes, acutely curved heels and a substantial sole, these have slender heels, a deep curve under the instep and a much lighter sole.

118 Lady Henrietta Herbert wearing what contemporaries would have described as 'fashionable undress', an informal style worn without hoops. Her skirt is caught up in the casually elegant *polonaise* style. In the 1770s, when this portrait was painted, a very high coiffure topped by a fanciful hat would have been the acme of fashion, but in the next decade, when the hat was added to update the picture, hats had totally changed in shape, becoming very large with sweeping brims and wide crowns.
(Sir Joshua Reynolds, *c*.1777, Powis Castle)

seam into the skirt. In the 1770s and 80s the pleats so reduced in size that they eventually became seams. The technique of cutting the back bodice piece in one with the skirt was called 'en fourreau'.

There are a number of silk *polonaises* from the 1770s in the Snowshill collection but the one illustrated here has been made from a very fresh-looking cotton (117). Another *polonaise* can be seen in the 1777 portrait of Lady Henrietta Antonia Herbert, Lady Clive (later Countess of Powis), painted by Sir Joshua Reynolds (118), but unlike the Snowshill *polonaise*, where the skirt is pulled up from inside, hers is looped up by a band of material on the outside. The portrait hangs at Powis Castle, Powys, near a 1778 engraving derived from it, which shows her wearing neither the large hat nor the muslin mantle draped across the upper half of the body in the portrait. These items must have been added in the 1780s when large picture hats, worn with dresses of light floating muslin, were in vogue. Adding a softly-draped mantle and a fashionable hat tilted at the appropriate angle brought the costume up to date and thus avoided the necessity of repainting the portrait.

119 (*left*) A sack-back gown and petticoat of French silk, early 1770s. Wide stripes of cherry-red rib alternate with a brocaded pattern of flowers on a cream satin weave. (A detail of the back of the dress is shown in 128.) Unusually the material has been cut so that the stripes run down the arm instead of around it. The sleeves are finished with a treble-falling fan-shaped cuff trimmed with a narrow red silk braid, which is also used on all the ruched or pleated trimmings. These trimmings, furbelows, are typical of the fashion for a curving serpentine line that breaks up the even surface of the silk, and they follow the gown from neck to hem and across the hem of the petticoat. The deep cuffs are complemented by lace engageantes.

The gentleman is wearing a 1770s court suit – coat, waistcoat and breeches – in striped purple velvet with a small yellow spot. The coat and waistcoat have been embroidered with white leaves and flowers set around cut-glass lozenges and circles. The coat curves sharply away to disclose a short waistcoat.

120 (*opposite*) This court mantua was made from a cream tabby silk brocade woven in Spitalfields between 1759 and 1762. Its formalised design of poppies, forget-me-nots and ears of corn, woven in brilliantly-coloured silks and silver gilt on a cream ground, would have been seen to best advantage in the candlelit splendour of the reception rooms at St James's Palace.

The most typical dress of the eighteenth century was the *robe à la française* or sack, whose elegant lines are exemplified in a splendid unaltered example from the Snowshill collection (119 and 128). This style was perfected in France by Madame de Pompadour, mistress of Louis XV and queen of French fashion until her death in 1764. Derived from a loose negligée gown that could only be worn in the privacy of the home, it developed into a loose dress worn over a tight bodice and a full underskirt or petticoat. Its main feature was double box pleats, which were set in on a straight-back neckline to fall unbelted to the ground in a train. In front, the pleats converged to a point low on the waistline with the opening either sewn or caught together with bows. By 1755 the sack had become a formal dress and the back pleats were sewn down from the shoulder, thus giving the bodice a closer and tighter fit. It was usually worn open in front to show the petticoat and this was often cut from the same material.

As court dress became more stylised, the train of the skirt was designed to be fastened up at the back, and this resulted in the formal style known as a 'court mantua'. The one on display at Springhill (120) is a beautiful example of the formal costume required when one was presented at court in the 1760s and 70s. Folding back the draped skirt of

121 (*far left*) Thomas Gainsborough painted a portrait of Queen Charlotte in full court dress in 1781, and this provided the original for several copies. The Queen had insisted on the retention of hoops at court, even though they had disappeared from fashionable dress. Decorative interest had now moved to the trimmings on the gown, selected and arranged by the milliner, and these items could cost more than the plain silk ground they adorned. Spangles and silver and gold foil were used to add glitter and lustre to rows of gauzy flounces, ruchings and frills. (Gainsborough Dupont, 1790, Wimpole Hall)

122 (*left*) Engraving from the *Cahier de costumes français*, 1779. The lady wears a full court dress of 'Pekin', a type of silk, in the latest colour 'prune de Monsieur'. She is accompanied by an 'écuyer', an equerry, who wears 'Demi-Gala' dress – unlike full court dress, which was embroidered all over with gold and silver, only the edges of his suit are decorated.

French and English female court dress retained the features of the late seventeenth-century mantua, but the French left the train to trail on the ground, while the English arranged the trained skirt in a series of carefully pleated folds. A new group in French fashion, the *marchands des modes*, were responsible for devising ideas for ornamentation (their association was recognised in 1776). The milliner was the English counterpart.

123 (*above right*) This attractive print of a lady of fashion of the early 1780s was created by pricking the paper with pins so that the resultant series of minute holes merged into a discernible pattern. The lady is dressed for the outdoors and wears a calash – a folding hood made of silk and built up over expandable arches of cane or whalebone to keep the hair uncrushed – and carries a delicate beribboned parasol. Her bunched-up *polonaise* skirt is worn over a matching underskirt.

124 (*below right*) This engraving depicts a 'St. James Macaroni', one of the young aristocrats of the Court (St James) circle. Their exaggerated manners and mode of dress, which included a huge wig, a short and close-fitting frock coat and waistcoat, a small round hat, a sword that was a decorative accessory, and a mincing gait, led to charges of effeminacy.

the mantua meant that the petticoat underneath was fully exposed and the full impact of the brocade or the embroidery could be appreciated. The Springhill mantua passed through successive generations of the Clanwilliam family and it was worn again in 1845 by Lady Ernest Bruce, a family friend, when Queen Victoria and Prince Albert held a fancy dress ball at Buckingham Palace and invited the guests to wear the court costume of a hundred years before. It was a splendid and appropriate choice, described by James Robinson Planché, the costume historian, who saw it there, as 'silver tissue, brocaded with bouquets of variegated flowers'.[33]

In 1761, the year after his accession, George III married Charlotte, a young princess from the minor German duchy of Mecklenburg-Strelitz. Thereafter, year after year, Charlotte presided at assemblies in the Drawing Room at St James's Palace on Thursdays, after chapel on Sundays and, of course, at the annual Birthday Balls and other festivities. Her insistence on the wearing of hoops at court, even after they had gone out of fashion, and on a formalised and increasingly archaic style of dress meant that the court became steadily isolated from the mainstream of fashionable life. Although everyone was still expected to dress very grandly, it was possible to wear the same gown every year and just rearrange or revive the trimmings. Thomas Gainsborough's nephew, Gainsborough Dupont, made a number of copies of his uncle's original portrait of the Queen wearing court dress, which has been described as 'an exercise in formal grandeur, taking a fashionable silk gauze dotted with spangles and arranging it over a more substantial silk and contradicting its natural simplicity with ruched robings, scalloped and serpentine tiers of decoration, glittering tassels and large satin bows'.[34] The 1781 original is in the Royal Collection and one of the copies, *c*.1790, can be seen at Wimpole Hall (121). The royal family and nobility 'formed the society of

the court, and the core of fashionable society. Within it the isolated majesty of the crown was emphasised in a dress of high ceremony, at coronations and royal weddings, a dress set apart by its archaic element and a display of precious metals and jewels of an assessable magnificence.'[35]

When the French/American Louis Simond visited London in 1810–11, he was amazed to observe ladies carried to court in sedan-chairs 'in the fashion of fifty years ago, as more suitable, I suppose, to the age of their majesties, with their immense hoops . . . folded like wings, pointing forward on each side'.[36]

One of George IV's first actions on his accession in 1820 was to announce that 'His Majesty is graciously pleased to dispense with Ladies wearing Hoops', but this admittance of contemporary fashion was not extended to men, who still had to wear the late eighteenth-century uniform of dark cloth suit, embroidered waistcoat, silk stockings and flat pumps.

French court dress of the 1770s, with its extraordinary festoons and swags of fringe, ruffles, tassels, ribbons, plumes and frills, was completed by fantastic hair-styles, in which the hair was brushed up over a wired structure, covered with powder and then decorated with fanciful objects – sometimes arranged to create miniature *tableaux* (122). The impractical vogue was adopted with great enthusiasm by British fashionable society, but ladies had to seek out ways to protect their massive *coiffures* from damage (123). Mrs Delany, attending an event at court in 1780, wrote disapprovingly of 'rows above rows of fine ladies with *towering tops* . . . I must own I could not help considering them with some astonishment, and lamenting that so absurd, inconvenient, and unbecoming a fashion should last so long, for though every year has produced some alteration, the *enormity* continues, and one of the most beautiful ornaments of nature, fine hair, is entirely disguised.'[37]

The Englishman's preference for a plainer and simpler style of costume than his European counterparts was challenged in the 1770s by the 'macaronis'. These young English noblemen had adopted Continental manners and fashions as a result of their experiences on the Grand Tour. Originally the name 'macaroni' – first used in 1764 and derived from the Italian dish which they introduced to England – was applied to anything that was chic and stylish, but the term soon became a derogatory one as their single-minded pursuit of 'extravagances of dress'[38] led them into flights of sartorial fantasy (124). They wore very tight and short waistcoats and coats, elaborate wigs that could be 'nine inches above the Head'[39] and carried nosegays of flowers and other feminine accessories. Their individual approach to fashion marked them out as style victims and they were mercilessly lampooned by satirists and caricaturists.

These attacks on the macaronis might have had a deeper motivation, for it was felt to be unpatriotic to copy foreign fashions in the face of a 'growing sense of cultural nationalism'.[40] In a society in which 'Britishness and foreignness were viewed in moral terms' and John Bull epitomised all the patriotic and manly virtues of the Englishman, the effeminate macaronis were seen as a threat to the country's security for, as one contemporary grimly observed, 'in the most perilous of times' England could not hope to be defended 'by such *things as these*'.[41] With hindsight it can be seen that the macaronis' high-profile promotion of 'continental and Courtly styles and values' was ill-timed, for events were taking an ominous turn in France.

II

The economy of Britain flourished and prospered to an extraordinary degree during the eighteenth century, as merchants expanded their horizons and consolidated their interests in all parts of the world. The pursuit of profit and the creation of a high-production, high-wage economy, acclaimed by Adam Smith in his book *The Wealth of Nations* (1776), met with such success that Dr Johnson was prompted to observe: 'There was never from the earliest ages a time in which trade so much engaged the attention of mankind, or commercial gain was sought with such general emulation.'[42] Overseas trade was powered by a fast-growing empire, described by Daniel Defoe as 'The great British Empire, the most flourishing and opulent country in the world . . .',[43] which included major primary producers such as the West Indies, Canada and India. As imports and exports doubled between the beginning of the century and 1770, a similar expansion took place in the merchant marine, which almost trebled in size during the same period, from about 3,600 to 9,400 vessels.

Dull though they may have been, the first two Hanoverian kings, George I and George II, nevertheless provided a period of stability after the constitutional upheavals of the previous century. A settled and fast-growing economy and the opportunity to make money meant a rapid rise in standards of living and an increase in consumerism, encouraging the growth of the middle class. A new group also joined the ranks of the *nouveaux riches*: those who had made money in India or the colonies of the East or West Indies and America, and were anxious to spend it when they returned to England. The Scottish novelist, Tobias Smollett, observed this new breed when he visited Bath: 'Clerks and factors from the East Indies [India], loaded with the spoil of plundered provinces; planters, negro-drivers, and hucksters, from our American plantations, enriched they know not how . . . men of low birth, and no breeding, have found themselves suddenly translated into a state of affluence, unknown to former ages.'[44]

A certain degree of affluence also filtered down to those classes who, in other countries, would have been disadvantaged. Their desire to copy the manners and fashions of social superiors is a theme that constantly recurs in foreigners' observations of English society, whether it be the German writer, Karl Philip Moritz, who wrote about his journey round England in about 1782, and who noticed that the countrymen of Oxfordshire were dressed 'not as ours are in coarse frocks, but with some taste, in fine good cloth',[45] or the French poet, Madame Boccage, who also travelled in England and whose views were reported in letters to her sister. She was surprised that 'the poorest country girls drink tea, have bodices of chintz, straw hats on their heads and scarlet cloaks upon their shoulders'.[46]

The Italian adventurer Casanova observed: 'In London, everything is easy to him who has money and is not afraid of spending it.'[47] It was estimated that there were 200 different types of shops in the capital by the end of the century. Visitors were particularly impressed by the elegant and sophisticated shops of the mercers, milliners and haberdashers which were distributed between Covent Garden, the City, Pall Mall and the Strand. Writing in 1772, another outsider in London found that:

The finest shops are scattered up and down in these courts and passages. The grand company which they draw together, the elegant arrangement and parade made by the shops, whether stuffs exposed to sale, fine furniture, and things of taste, or the girls belonging to them, would be motives sufficient to determine those that walk, to make their way in preference to any other, even if they had not neatness and security to recommend them.[48]

The inexorable movement westward had, by the 1780s, created the new shopping streets of Oxford Street and Bond Street. However, Paternoster Row and the area around St Paul's Cathedral was still populated by lace merchants, haberdashers and milliners and remained the centre of the wholesale drapery business until the twentieth century. Ludgate Hill, next to the Cathedral, was 'entirely occupied by merchants' wares, silken tissues of beautiful and costly kinds being sold there'.[49] As mercers could also be found in Cheapside and in Covent Garden, visiting all the shops for a particular material was a time-consuming business. When Mrs Jonathan Russel wanted to find a particular material in 1771 she had to visit 'every Mercer and peace [piece] broker [who bought the tailor's remnants and sold them on for mending etc.] from Charing Cross, all round Covent Garden, Strand, behind St. Clements, Fleet Street, up to Cheapside to match the green Lutestring [a glossy silk fabric] I am to make up . . . I got better than I expected in Pall Mall.'[50]

125 In 1753 William Windham II of Felbrigg Hall bought this view of London Bridge from St Olave's Stairs on the Surrey bank. Looking upstream the northern bank can be seen, where the dyers dipped their cloth in the water, and the Great Stone Gateway, such a prominent feature in Visscher's engraving of 1616 (see **35**), is clearly silhouetted against the sky. (Samuel Scott, 1746, Felbrigg)

London Bridge was still an important thoroughfare into the City of London, but it had become very dilapidated and extremely congested. Thomas Pennant, writing before the buildings were demolished, described it as 'narrow, darksome, and dangerous to passengers from the multitude of carriages: frequent arches of strong timber crossed the street, from the tops of the houses, to keep them together, and from falling into the water'.[51] Between 1758 and 1762 all the buildings on the Bridge were pulled down, thus increasing the width of the thoroughfare from 20 to 46 feet. The Bridge was finally replaced by a new one in 1831.

London's population doubled during the eighteenth century, reaching just under one million by the time of the 1801 census. This unparalleled expansion meant that by that date ten per cent of the British population was living in the capital, whereas only two per cent of the French population lived in Paris. Manufacturers, faced with an unprecedented demand for goods, soon realised that advertising could direct and harness the spending power of these potential consumers. Relying solely on a sign hanging over a shop to attract customers inside was no longer feasible or effective, and it was found that printed trade cards, advertisements in newspapers and news-sheets and even sandwich-men, employed to carry larger advertisements through the streets, produced the desired result. Advertising became an integral part of retailing.

John Gay's poem, *Trivia: or the Art of Walking the Streets of London* (1716), had urged the visitor to London to:

> . . . observe the signs, for signs remain,
> Like faithful Land-marks to the walking train.[52]

The view down any London shopping street would have been obscured by these low-hanging shop signs creaking noisily on their heavy iron frames on a windy day.[53] In 1742 Joseph Trigge displayed a sign with Queen Elizabeth's head on it outside his mercer's shop in Ludgate Street, which caused passers-by to stop and stare. According to *The Spectator* periodical, they were so impressed by the artist's 'masterly judgement' and the 'pomp and splendour' lavished on it by 'the gilder and carver' that it was felt to be more 'like a capital picture in a gallery than a sign in a street'.[54] When the Swiss César de Saussure visited London in 1725 he found that 'every shop, has a sign of copper, pewter, or wood painted with gilt, some of these are really magnificent and have cost as much as one hundred pounds sterling'.[55] But the old signs were no longer a reliable source of information as the pictorial symbols on them usually had a very tenuous or non-existent connection with the goods sold beneath them, though some shopkeepers tried to remedy this situation by tying examples of their merchandise to the pole.

The proliferation of signs also created a hazard for the pedestrian and there were many instances of injuries when a sign, and sometimes the wall it was attached to, fell down on top of a passer-by. When London was rebuilt after the Great Fire it had been the intention to replace these signs with carved stone panels let into the face of the buildings, but this regulation had not been universally observed or enforced and so in 1762 an Act was passed which stated that all hanging signs had to be removed. A shopkeeper could replace it with another sign above his doorway as long as it was flat against the wall. Once the hanging signs were removed, the systematic process of naming and numbering streets commenced and picturesque addresses, like that of the

NICHOLE'S,
FRENCH & ENGLISH STAY MAKER,
Nᵒ.349, Oxford Street;
Begs leave to inform the Ladies in general,
he has now ready made by the best town
Workmen, a large & elegant assortment of
Stays of all patterns, which he is determined
to sell from 10 to 15 per Cent under what is generally
by charged, which from the excellence of the
Manufacture renders it an object of
considerable importance.

126 The stays, or corset, illustrated in this 1788 trade card, were designed not only to elevate and push out the bosom, but also to make the torso fit the extremely narrow shape of the bodice. Such a corset, with its closely-set rows of boning, must have been very uncomfortable.

mercer Rebecca English 'at the Old White Swan and Rowl [Roll], over against the Iron Gates on the south-side of St. Paul's Church-yard', were no more.

Distribution of printed trade cards (**126**), giving the name of the shop and its owner, and information about the goods and services that were for sale, was an effective and cheap means of advertising which reached its peak between 1730 and 1770. The design usually incorporated the sign hanging above the premises and brought it up to date by placing it within a fashionable cartouche. One of William Hogarth's first commissions was to design a trade card for his sisters' ready-to-wear clothes shop which had moved in 1730 to 'ye King's Arms, joyning to ye Little Britain Gate near Long Walk'.[56]

Tradesmen who specialised in clothing were the first to use cards as advertisements and to ornament their bills with a simplified version of the engraved picture on the card. As these bills were precisely dated and a number have survived in family papers and museum collections, they are an invaluable source of information about the charges for particular goods and services.

London shops were judged to be the finest in Europe. Their design was carefully considered and the incorporation of classical features like columns, pilasters and pediments was so widespread that a visiting Frenchman felt it made them look more like temples.[57] The splendour of one establishment, that of the mercers Thomas, William and Robert King at the sign of the Wheatsheaf and Sun in King Street, Covent Garden, can be judged from an engraving of its frontage on a bill dated 1781 (see **127**). As shopping became a leisure activity as well as a necessity, the London shopkeepers also soon realised that improving the presentation of goods and perfecting sales techniques would increase trade, and the mercers were particularly successful at this. As early as 1709, when Mrs Mary Manley, the author and journalist, visited the mercers' shops on Ludgate Hill, she found that they employed smartly-dressed shop assistants who could flatter and cajole the customer into making a purchase. In an article for *The Female Tatler* she wrote:

> [they were] perfect gilded theatres, the variety of wrought Silks so many Changes of fine Scenes, and the Mercers are the Performers in the Opera. . . . They are the sweetest, fairest, nicest, dished-out Creatures; and, by their elegant Address and soft Speeches, you would guess them to be Italians. . . . We went into a shop which had three Partners: two of them were to flourish out their Silks . . . and the other's sole Business was to be Gentleman Usher of the shops, to stand completely dressed at the Door, bow to all the Coaches that pass by, and hand Ladies out and in.[58]

From the end of the seventeenth century the more expensive shops had paned-glass windows, but these were usually very small and any display in them was usually limited to one item. By the 1750s shops were constructed with double-bowed frontages, thus allowing a greater display area and the possibility of internal window lighting. This was needed because, until 1761, lighting in the streets was the responsibility of private citizens. It was fairly limited as it consisted, in the better class areas, of a lamp burning whale-oil on a cotton wick occasionally suspended from a pole outside each citizen's property. An Act in 1761 provided for levying a special rate from all householders in London so that streets could be properly paved and lit, and by 1780 the lighting in Oxford Street was believed to be superior to anything in Paris.[59]

The glittering appearance of the fashionable shops at night is something that frequently occurs in contemporary correspondence. One of the most enthusiastic observers was Sophie von la Roche, who visited Oxford Street in 1786 and was very impressed by the lighting and the sophisticated display techniques:

> We strolled up and down lively Oxford Street this evening, for some goods look more attractive by artificial light. Just imagine, dear children, a street taking half an hour to cover from end to end, with double rows of brightly shining lamps . . . and the pavement inlaid with flagstones can stand 6 people deep and allows one to gaze at the splendidly lit shops in comfort. . . . It is almost impossible to express how well everything is organised in London. Every article is made more attractive to the eye than in Paris or any other town. We especially noticed a cunning device for showing women's materials whether they are silks, chintzes, or muslins, they hang down in folds behind the fine high windows so that the effect of this or that material, as it would be in the ordinary folds of a woman's dress, can be studied.[60]

As purchase was still by negotiation and prices were only disclosed when the customer enquired, Londoners were amazed when Flint and Palmer opened a shop on London Bridge in 1750 with price tags attached to every item. Robert Owen, who worked at Flint and Palmer at the end of the century, also believed that they were the first to sell their goods for ready money, though their customers were 'of an inferior class'.[61] The staff were instructed to point out to the customers, politely, that they had to accept the price on the tag and not enter into any form of negotiation. This novel system had earlier been used by the silk merchants Peter and James Ferry, who announced their autumn sale in 1744 with the blunt statement: 'N.B. The Lowest Price will be fix'd on each Piece, without any Abatement.' Establishments like the warehouses (see p.165), which had a large turnover of reasonably priced goods, had adopted the system as it had the obvious advantage of speeding up transactions.

In *Observations on England*, published in 1772, Pierre Jean Grosley remarked: 'A mode begins to be out of date at Paris, just when it has been introduced at London by some English noblemen. The court and the first-rate nobility immediately take it up: it is next introduced about St. James's, by those that ape the manners of the court; and by the time it has reached the city, a contrary mode already prevails at Paris.'[62] Information about the latest French styles was circulated by means of dressed dolls, sent from Paris to the most fashionable mantua-makers and their clients. The excitement engendered amongst ladies when they rushed to examine these French 'babies' or 'wooden mademoiselles', dressed in a perfect replica of fashionable dress with the relevant accessories, was made fun of in *The Spectator*. An imaginary correspondent wrote that she 'was almost in despair of ever seeing a Model, when last Sunday I heard a Lady in the next Pew to me, whisper to another, that at the Seven Stars in King-street, Covent Garden, there was a Mademoiselle completely dressed just come from Paris'.[63]

In 1748 Lady Anson of Shugborough (sister-in-law of the Marchioness Grey, see below) was sent a dress that had been made in France, but she was waiting for a doll to arrive so that she would know how to arrange her hair in the correct style. Unfortunately, the doll 'dressed exactly like Madame de Pompadour did not arrive in time enough for me to be able to adjust my coiffure quite in the Taste it ought to have been in, which indeed was the only thing defective in my appearance'. When it finally arrived with three complete dresses it was accompanied by 'all sorts of Coiffures, Agréments [decorations] suited to them all, and written explanations and directions to every part of her Attire.'[64]

In the early 1770s an English publication, *The Lady's Magazine*, was the first to include a fashion plate within its pages. Compilers of ladies' pocket books and almanacks soon copied the idea and regularly inserted an illustration of the latest dresses and accessories in their publications. These were used as a source of information by many, including Barbara Johnson, daughter of the vicar of Olney in Buckinghamshire, when she compiled a collection of samples of material recording all the clothes she bought between 1751, when she was thirteen, and 1823 (see also p.170).

Much information about the buying of silks and the making-up of clothes can be found in the letters of Jemima, Marchioness Grey (see **97**), written to her daughters and her sister-in-law, Lady Anson. Jemima married Philip Yorke, later 2nd Earl of Hardwicke, in 1740, the year that his father purchased Wimpole Hall in Cambridgeshire. Philip and Jemima resided at Wimpole and began a series of alterations and improvements to the house. The letters describe the search for suitable silks for gowns for Jemima and her two daughters, Amabel, who married Lord Polwarth in 1771, and Mary, who married Lord Grantham in 1780.

In 1753, when Lady Anson was looking for a silk for herself and Jemima for the Birthday Court of that year she 'turned over all Carr's and Swann's shops two or three times'. Eventually she found what she wanted from Mr Hinchcliffe, who 'says he must have three guineas pr. yard, I say 3£'.[65] The two mercers mentioned by Lady Anson in her letter were Carr and Co, whose shop was at the sign of the Queen's Head on Ludgate Hill, and Swann and Co, at the sign of the Wheatsheaf in King Street, Covent Garden, directly opposite the end of Bedford Street. In the 1760s the shop was renamed the 'Wheatsheaf and Sun' and was run by Thomas King and Joseph and John Harris. In 1781 Thomas was joined by William and Robert King (see p.151). Carr's, King's and Hinchcliffe and Croft at the sign of the Hen and Chickens in Henrietta Street (see p.155), also in Covent Garden, were the most fashionable mercers in London.

Twenty-one years later Jemima was looking for silk to make a gown for Amabel, who was going to attend a Court Birthday:

> I have been at two Mercers this week and can give you little satisfaction on the subject. . . . The Flowered Silks at Carrs I cannot recommend, at Kings there are much greater variety and prettier, but then the best of them and these not looking Rich are from 30s and 38s a yard, an enormous price, some very neat, but in appearance slight styles there are at 14s and 16s. The Flowered Tabbies from Carrs I thought pretty but fitter for sacks than gowns and petticoats.[66]

She also complained that the price of 30s was unduly high as it was twice the price of the silks she has been considering for *her* court appearance in the 1750s and the silks were not such good quality.

Prices fluctuated throughout the century, but a length of the finest woven silk fabric, whether it came from France or Italy or was made in Spitalfields, remained high. There were a number of factors that governed the price. The raw silk imported into England

127 The 'Wheatsheaf and Sun', King Street, Covent Garden was one of the most fashionable mercer's shops in London. This 1781 bill shows its elegantly impressive façade, with four classical columns. The large multi-paned windows and doors would have ensured good lighting for the interior. By this date hanging signs had been abolished, replaced by flat boards above the door, inscribed with the owner's name. The original sign on the hanging board, a wheatsheaf and shining sun, has been retained on the bill as a logo.

from Italy or the East Indies was first sent to the 'silk-thrower', who would use 'a great Number of Female Hands' to spin and wind it. It would next be passed to the weavers, who would first have to prepare their looms. This could take from 3 to 6 weeks, during which time the weaver had to pay for the upkeep of his drawboy (who pulled the cords of the harness during weaving). The master weaver was also restricted – by the mercer – to weaving only a small number of pieces from each pattern in order to ensure its exclusivity. A length of silk, usually $\frac{1}{2}$ ell wide ($19\frac{1}{2}$–21in), would take a 'long time to weave perhaps $3\frac{1}{2}$ days for a dress length of 14 yards of plain material while patterned fabrics might take twice as long or even longer'.[67]

One mercer, Vansommer, was a designer as well as a partner in his weaving firm, but usually the mercer either purchased designs which would then be executed for his exclusive use, or purchased finished silks directly from the weavers. Silks could also be bespoke – woven to order from a pattern chosen by the customer. This service was provided for Lady Mary Coke in 1766 when she wanted a gown for a Birthday Court. She sent for King from Covent Garden. 'At half an hour after two the Mercer sent me word the silk would not be out of the loom till the next day . . . [on Tuesday] the mercer brought my silk. I paid him seventy pounds.' She does not mention who the mantua-maker was, but when she tried the gown on the following Friday morning she decided it was 'extremely pretty'. It was delivered to her, completed, the following day and when she wore it at court she was delighted when a friend 'took my gown for imbrodery, 'twas indeed a beautiful silk'.[68]

Marchioness Grey visited King's in 1780 when she wanted a gown for her daughter Mary's marriage. They found the right design but were informed that it could not be woven in under a fortnight. They proceeded to Mr Vansommer's shop, which was 'ransacked with no better success and at last after a 2nd jaunt to Kings he promised to try if a slight white and gold could be ready for the beginning of next week'.[69]

R. Campbell's complaint in *The London Tradesman* (1747), that the English weavers merely copied French designs was remedied in the 1740s when Spitalfields produced a range of silks of which the most typical, a brocaded design on a white ground, was uniquely English. Floral motifs predominated but these were not purely conventional and a genuine attempt was made at botanical naturalism as sprigs of brilliantly-coloured flowers were scattered across an open silk ground. The leading designer was Anna-Maria Garthwaite. Her surviving dated designs show that she was working in London from the 1720s to 1756. Between 1742 and 1749 she sold thirty designs commissioned by Carr and Co, and Thomas Hinchcliffe's name appears on three designs. It is possible that she designed the Spitalfields silk illustrated in 102 as it shares distinctive stylistic similarities with her other designs of this period, many of which also feature unusual plants and flowers.

To protect the English silk industry a heavy duty was exacted on imported French and Italian silks and many were smuggled in to avoid paying it. The embargo on French silk in 1766 was occasioned by a crisis in the industry as there was so much competition from printed materials and imported silks (though a ready-made silk dress could be imported without contravening the legislation). The circulation of illicitly-purchased silks was rife in fashionable society and an instance of this practice can be found in Samuel Richardson's novel, *Clarissa*. Clarissa receives a letter informing her Mrs

128 Detail of the back view of a sack gown of the early 1770s (for a full view, see 119). The pleats falling from the wide neckline show off the French silk with wide red stripes alternating with a brocaded pattern of flowers on cream satin. This kind of rich fabric would be offered for sale at silk mercers like Carr's, King's and Hinchcliffe and Croft in London's Covent Garden.

Townsend of Deptford is in London selling duty-free goods: 'She has her days of being in town, and then is at a chamber she rents in an inn in Southwark, where she has patterns of all her silks and much of her portable goods, for the conveniency of her London customers.'[70] Mercers would charge from 8s a yard for a plain taffeta, to just under 20s for a worked silk and 70s a yard for a rich flowered silk brocaded with gold. The sack gowns that were popular in the middle of the century required 20 to 22yds of material, making the price of a silk gown anything between about £10 and £70.

Patterns on the luxury silks changed regularly and the discerning eye would recognise whether a silk was the latest design or a couple of years old. If the latter was the case, the wearer would be marked out as being *démodé* in a fashionable assembly. The high investment in a wardrobe required for regular attendance at court and appearance in the capital can be estimated by a remark made by Lady Louisa Stuart, whose *Memoirs* and *Letters* provide a lively commentary on eighteenth-century society, that '15 or 16 hundred a year, would not do much for people, who must live in London and appear in fine clothes at St. James twice a week'.[71] This calculation can be compared with one made by the *London Advertiser* of 1786 for the amount of money needed to support a comfortable lifestyle in London for a man (defined as a respectable citizen renting a house), his wife, four children and two maids. Out of an annual income of £400 the husband and wife could expect to pay £40 on their own clothes and £24 on their children's. Food, heating and other domestic necessities were costed at £3 13s 5½d a week – the same amount as a yard of the most expensive silk.[72] The high cost of a silk garment, and the use of uncut lengths of material in it, meant that it was a fairly simple matter to unpick and remake the dress when fashion changed. It is apparent from the large number of surviving garments that gowns of the 1740s and 50s were remade in the 70s and 80s.[73]

Changes in the way clothes were cut were, by comparison with the changing silk patterns, relatively slow. It apparently took the mantua-makers some time to acquire the considerable sewing skills required to fashion the stiff silks, as the stitching employed on the seams and pleats of early gowns is clumsier than that of the 1770s and 80s. They would have had to learn different techniques from those for plain sewing – stitching straightforward seams on linen garments. Mastering the skills of cutting and fitting, matching the large designs of the silks and setting the sleeves in neatly would have offered a challenge to the most experienced needlewoman.

By the end of the century there was a marked improvement in the skill and finish in sewing, but this was not reflected in the prices charged. The discrepancy between the amount the dressmaker was paid and the cost of material had always been huge. When Marchioness Grey's aunt, Lady Jemima Grey, married Lord Ashburnham in 1724, silks costing £90 11s 5d were purchased from the mercer John Vickers. The most expensive item was 18yds of white and silver silk, made into a mantua by Elizabeth Ackers. The silk cost £45 and Elizabeth received 16s for making it up. Spending so much on a fabric that would need to last for many years meant that the purchaser was bound to look at the quality, design, colour and price of the silk with a highly-critical eye, and all the mercers would be visited and pestered until they came up with something suitable.

Thomas Hinchcliffe, who originally had a shop in Ludgate Hill, moved to Covent Garden in the 1740s in partnership with his brother William. They were joined by James Croft in 1750. Their shop, on the south side of Henrietta Street, was visited by Elizabeth

Parker in 1751 when she was looking for silk for her wedding dress. She chose a beautiful white brocade woven with a pattern of flowers twisted round a column that cost £18 18s 0d for 18yds (130). Another customer there was John Russell, 4th Duke of Bedford, who bought brocade for his coats and waistcoats at 25s a yard. His accounts for 1752–4 also show that he paid them 10s 6d a yard for a 'flowered tabby' – a silk that was available in many different varieties and would have been used for everyday wear – and 27s a yard for the 'richest crimson Genoa velvet'.[74]

The development of Covent Garden as an important retailing area was inevitable once Francis Russell, the 4th Earl of Bedford had been granted permission in 1631 to construct 'stately houses for Persons of Quality' around the Piazza and the 5th Earl (later 1st Duke) had secured the right to hold a permanent market 'for the buying and selling of all manner of fruit flowers roots and herbs whatsoever' (see pp.79–80). This gave the rural market-gardeners, who had been forbidden to enter the City, the opportunity and venue for the sale of their produce and the market area gradually expanded, particularly after the Fire of London. Twenty-two shops with cellars were built against the garden wall of Bedford House and when the house was demolished in 1704 a further row of 48 shops was built nearer the middle of the Piazza.

Across one end of the Piazza in Covent Garden a series of wooden shacks housed Tom King's Coffee-House, renowned as a 'fashionable Rendezvous for all Rakes, Spendthrifts and Strumpets'.[75] It is depicted as such in William Hogarth's painting *Morning* from the series 'The Four Times of the Day', in which dishevelled bleary-eyed rakes are seen leaving the premises in the morning (131). Hogarth was a regular patron of the coffee-house, whose boisterous and licentious customers gave him an endless sequence of models for his paintings. Tom and Molly King's policy of serving anyone and everyone meant that people from all walks of life and classes mixed together, and class distinctions disappeared as all became uproariously drunk with the prostitutes who were touting for trade. Taverns like the Rose (the location of the orgy scene in Hogarth's *The Rake's Progress*, 1733–5) and the Shakespeare's Head may have acted as social levellers, too, but many contemporaries were offended that they were 'the Haunt of every kind of Intemperance, Idleness and the Eccentric and Notorious in every Walk of Life. . . . Noblemen would go in full Court Dress with Swords and Bags in rich brocaded Coats and walk in and talk . . . with Chimney-sweeps, Gardeners and Market People.'[76]

The 'astonishing medley of people' which thronged the streets of Covent Garden was matched by the mixture of shops and dubious trades that operated there. The area was choked by the coaches and sedans belonging to the fashionable as they did their shopping leisurely, but Covent Garden had acquired a highly unsavoury reputation which meant that it was no longer the place where the beau monde chose to live. The Turkish baths in the Little Piazza, which became popularly known as the Humumms, were originally well-conducted and highly respectable, but they deteriorated and became bagnios or brothels in which there were frequent outbreaks of rowdy vandalism. The bagnios soon spread beyond the area of the Little Piazza, and even by the beginning of the eighteenth century the *Tatler* had reported: 'Every house from Cellar to Garret is inhabited by *Nymphs* of different orders, so that Persons of every Rank can be accommodated.'[77]

129 and **130** Hinchliffe and Croft of Covent Garden were fashionable silk mercers in the mid-eighteenth century, patronised by the royal family and members of the aristocracy.

(*above*) A bill issued in 1769 to Mrs Blaithwaite for 22½ yards of silk would have been sufficient to make a sack-back gown (see **119**).

(*right*) A sample of the silk purchased by Elizabeth Parker for her wedding dress in 1751 from Hinchcliffe and Croft at a cost of 18 guineas. The silk has a striking and very unusual design, and is described on her bill as being 'New flowered gro'd Gros detour Broc'd Column'. The coloured floral figures were swivel woven, a complex mechanical process which wove each block of pattern separately, thus saving yarn.

A number of stalls in the Piazza catered for the customers of the bagnios and brothels by selling contraceptives, quack medicines and obscene prints. In Half Moon Alley (now Bedford Street) a shop originally opened in about 1738 by Constantia Theresa Phillips was run by her niece in the 1770s, purveying 'all sorts of fine *Machines* called *cundums*' as well as a range of 'Perfumes, Wash-balls, Soaps, Waters . . . Ladies' Black Sticking-plaisters'.[78]

During the 1660s Thomas Wriothesley, the 4th Earl of Southampton, had also developed the area around Southampton House in Bloomsbury as another fashionable and sought-after suburb. His house, described as 'the handsomest, the most agreeable and the Best turned out', and the Bloomsbury estate, were both inherited by the 2nd Duke of Bedford through his mother, Lady Rachel Wriothesley, in 1723. Southampton House became the home of both the 3rd and 4th Dukes, and the latter renamed it Bedford House in 1734. At this time Bloomsbury was still very close to the countryside and when the poet Thomas Gray moved into Southampton Row in 1759 he found it 'so rus-in-urbish I believe I shall stay here'.[79]

The accounts of the 3rd Duke of Bedford, and those of preceding generations, show that they had bought their clothes and accessories from shops in the area around St Paul's Cathedral. With the establishment of the 4th Duke at Bedford House however, all the family's clothing requirements, with one or two exceptions, were met by shops in Covent Garden. The Duke's steward, Mr Butcher, would meet all the tradesmen in Tom's Coffee-House, and as he kept all their bills, headed with the name of the supplier, they give a detailed picture of what was sold and by whom.

It is indicative that the Duke paid as much for 'superfine' cloth as he did for the brocade he bought from Hinchcliffe and Croft. By the 1770s the woollen drapers were rivalling the mercers as gentlemen chose to wear fine cloth coats and breeches instead of the silks, brocades and satins worn previously. These fabrics were now only used for the waistcoat, the richness of the material being highlighted by the contrast with the plain-coloured wool of the coat. However, a silk or brocade coat, waistcoat and breeches would still be worn on 'gala days', as at weddings or court balls, after which they would be carefully stored away – hence the survival of so many of them. The Duke's hectic public and private life (he was Lord Lieutenant of Ireland and Ambassador to France), meant that he required a high proportion of silk garments in his wardrobe and also patronised several woollen merchants. Gabriel Fouace at the Pearl and Crown in Bedford Street supplied him with cloth in a variety of colours – claret, deep blue and 'blossom' (a peach colour) – that cost between 17s and 25s a yard. James Morris at the Black Spread Eagle and King's Arms in Russell Street was another supplier of high-quality cloth, and he also sold less expensive material that was used to make liveries for the Duke's servants. Ready-made coats and jackets for the male servants were bought from Charles Torkington at the sign of the Turk's Head on the corner of York Street and Charles Street, Covent Garden.[80]

Haberdashers sold a wide range of trimmings, accessories and some ready-made items like quilted petticoats, but they did not make up caps and head-dresses as this was done by the milliners (see p.160). Francis Flower and Francis Bishop were rival Covent Garden haberdashers who could be found in King Street at the Rose and Woolpack and the Sun and Dove respectively. Francis Flower's 1759 trade card is interesting as it states

131 *Morning* from Hogarth's 'Four Times of the Day'. Using artistic licence, the artist has repositioned Tom King's Coffee-House so that it is in front of St Paul's Church rather than along one side of the square. An elderly lady, accompanied by her page, makes her way to early morning prayers. Her only concessions to the freezing weather are a fur muff and a pair of mittens. Her stomacher is decorated with a series or ribbon bows, *échelles*, and is worn with a wide skirt and short apron. It is possible that she has come from Lord Archer's house, the last nobleman's house in the once-grand square.

Outside the coffee house there is a mêlée of drunken customers caressing the market girls who wear the distinctive headgear of the lower classes – a wide-brimmed, flat-crowned hat of straw or chip.
(William Hogarth, 1738, Upton House)

that he 'draws all sorts of patterns, sells shades of silk and worsted and canvas for Working'.[81] This meant that he was continuing the practice of drawing a pattern for the customer to embroider. The Duke bought small items like pins and ribbons from Bishop and leather gloves from Flower.

Men bought their headwear from hatters, who also supplied ladies with the fashionable tricorne beaver hat. The Duke's first supplier was William Finch at the corner of Tavistock Street and opposite Long's Warehouse, but in 1759 the Duke forsook him for Mr James Lock's shop in St James's Street (which still survives).

The bills for the materials for clothes for the Duchess and their daughter Caroline have not survived, but they would have come from the same shops that the Duke used. However, bills have survived from those who did the work – a mantua-maker, a male sack-maker, a hoop-petticoat-maker and a tailor, who made the Duchess a riding costume. Elizabeth and Jane Munday, mantua-makers, did ordinary dress-making work for the Duchess, including mending and repairing of all kinds, and they charged her 14s for making a 'pink and silver gown and coat', whereas the male sack-maker charged £1 1s 0d to make a black silk sack and petticoat. But no London mantua-maker or milliner exerted so much power and influence over court fashion as Rose Bertin at the court of Marie-Antoinette (see p.176) and there appears to have been an unwritten law that the mantua-maker should not disclose the name of her clients. One mantua-maker was immortalised by Henry Fielding in his novel *Tom Jones* (1749), in which he likens the charms of the heroine Sophia Western to those of Mrs Hussey, and a footnote explains to the reader that she was: 'A celebrated mantua-maker in the Strand, famous for setting off the shapes of women.'[82] Mrs Hussey, who purportedly lived to be 105, opened a shop in the Strand, a few doors away from the Half Moon Tavern on the corner of Half Moon Passage and the Strand.[83]

During the second half of the century interest passed from the fabric to the trimming, and this development meant that milliners had a more important and creative role in fashion as they were the suppliers of trimmings. They also made aprons, handkerchiefs, ruffles, caps and head-dresses 'with as many Etceteras as would reach from Charing Cross to the Royal Exchange'.[84] When Marchioness Grey was ordering her daughter Mary's wedding clothes in 1780, she found a white and gold silk at Mr King's shop which was then sent to the milliner, Mrs Beauvais. The milliner assured her that it would be ready in time,

> ... but [they] did not keep their word in shewing me any trimmings put together; so all I could do this morning was to fix in a general on a Crape with Gold Spangells and intermixed here and there with Green and Pink Foils in the shape of very small Roses and some of that Silver Chain you saw to be introduced also with some light Gold and Silver Tassels but I limited the price to 20 and 30£. I fixed on the Suit of Point for 56£ thinking it on the whole rather finer looking than the other with the Ruffles in an intire piece.[85]

These extremely high prices suggest that the trimmings were now more costly than the material onto which they were stitched. The price Lady Grey paid for the 'Suit of Point', a set of lace to be worn at Court, was usual for lace of this high quality. It would have been fashioned into caps, ruffles and neck handkerchiefs.

132 The shoes have been made from the same silk as the open robe illustrated 102. They have very pointed, slightly upcurved toes, and are bound with green silk taffeta.

Flat-crowned, wide-brimmed straw hats tied with ribbon had been a feature of rural dress since the seventeenth century. In the mid-eighteenth century they became fashionable and were made from a fine straw-plaiting imported from Leghorn in Italy (the plait produced by English wheat straw was considered coarse). Chip, fine shavings of willow or poplar, was sometimes used instead of straw. This hat has been made from stiffened figured grosgrain bound with silk taffeta and has its original taffeta ribbon ties still pinned in place.

133 An early eighteenth-century letter from the Verney Collection noting: 'The broad gold and silver weighs about 1oz in a yd & comes to 4s 6d a yd. . . . The narrow gold & silver allmost 3 yds in an ounce wch will come to 20d a yd. The Br[oa]d gold 3/4 oz in a yard & comes to about 4s a yard. The nar[row] gold 2 yds in 1 oz comes to 3s 4d a yard'. Still pinned to the letter is a sample of early eighteenth-century gold braid in pristine condition. Gold and silver braid was sold by weight; any left over could be taken back to the supplier, who would also refashion it for the customer.

Lace trimming and accessories could also be bought from the lace shops or chambers, where one could find expensive imported Brussels and Mechlin lace, as well as English-made laces. Originally found near St Paul's, the lacemen had also moved to the Covent Garden area and the Strand. In the 1760s and 70s Mrs Chancellor ran a famous establishment in Duke Street, and in 1775 the writer James Boswell was so charmed by her sales talk about her fashionable customers that he found he was trapped 'in her Mechlin toils' and bought a suit of lace for his wife for 30 guineas, a far higher price than he had originally intended to pay.[86]

In the latter part of the century Turnpike Trusts began to improve and maintain the major routes out of London. Finance for the schemes was obtained by collecting tolls at turnpike gates at the principal exit points out of the capital. Destinations just outside London were serviced by short-stage coaches, and regular stage-coach services provided the long-haul travellers with an efficient transport system that noticeably reduced the journey time as the century progressed. A journey from Bath to London, for example, which had taken 50 hours in 1700, took 40 in 1750 and only 16 in 1780. The introduction of the new light-weight mail-coach service in 1784 further benefitted the passenger and those awaiting delivery of parcels. This rapid but expensive service kept to a very strict timetable and departed from the General Post Office in Lombard Street. A much cheaper but slower alternative was still provided by the carriers' waggons, which continued to carry goods and passengers from all the larger provincial towns to appointed London inns and back again.

Some proprietors of London coaching inns would act as shopping agents for families who lived in the country and did not want to travel to London to do their shopping personally. The Purefoys (see p.133) used the proprietor of the King's Head Inn in Islington, Mr Robotham, throughout the 1730s and 40s.[87] Mr Robotham bought all sorts of material, trimmings and accessories for Mrs Purefoy and Mrs Robotham sent her information about the latest designs. On one occasion in 1741 Mrs Purefoy wanted a 'very good whalebone hoop petticoat of the newest fashion'. It was to be purchased at a shop in Covent Garden, Long's Warehouse in Tavistock Street, and given to Mrs Eagles, who operated a carrier service from the George Inn, Smithfield. Mrs Eagles left the inn at 4 in the morning on a Tuesday and delivered the petticoat to Shalstone in Buckinghamshire on Wednesday evening.[88] The Purefoys seldom left home and relied on others for fashion information.

The improvement in communications and the increased mobility of the population meant that new designs could reach the provinces quite quickly and all but the very poorest were aware of fashion. A somewhat patronising article in the *Connoisseur* of 1756 describes the scene in a provincial town:

Where the newest fashions are brought down weekly by the stagecoach; all the wives and daughters of the most topping tradesmen vie with each other every Sunday in the elegance of their apparel. The same genteel ceremonies are practised there as at the most fashionable churches in town. The ladies immediately on their entrance, breathe a pious ejaculation through their fansticks and the beaux very gravely address themselves to the Haberdashers bills [advertisements] glued upon the linings of their hats.[89]

The lack of a distinctive regional dress and the integrated nature of British society also helped this instant spread of fashion and broke down the barriers between town and country dress. Sir John Hawkins, who wrote a *Life of Samuel Johnson* (1787), felt that this development was one of the most dramatic in English social life during the previous fifty years.

> The convenience of turnpike roads has destroyed the distinction between town and country manners and the maid of honour and the farmer's wife put on a cap of the latest form almost at the same instant. I mention this, because it may have escaped the observations of many that a new fashion pervades the whole of our island almost as instantaneously as a spark of fire illuminates a mass of gunpowder.[90]

Demand for the latest fashions in the provinces was intense and this growth in consumerism throughout the country meant that cities like Bath, Birmingham and Norwich boasted shops as sophisticated as any in London. London shopkeepers were quick to see that opening a branch in Bath for the season could be a profitable move, and a well-known London dealer in English and imported lace, Elizabeth Chancellor and Co, and a firm of mercers and milliners, Thomas Paulin, the mercer at the 'Statue of Queen Elizabeth' in Tavistock Street, both opened branches there.

Visitors had been coming to Bath since Roman times to take the mineral waters. At the beginning of the eighteenth century it was a modest town with a population of about 2,000, but by 1800 it had become a pleasure resort with an international reputation and a population of 34,000. This transformation was achieved by Richard, 'Beau' Nash, who arrived in Bath in 1703 aged 28. Through his determination and forceful personality he created an elegant and decorous environment for all 'polite society' to enjoy. In 1706, when he had become Master of Ceremonies, he laid down a code of behaviour known as 'Rules', which encouraged sociability between the growing gentry class and the aristocratic elite, who had traditionally kept themselves apart. The 'Rules' comprised a clearly stated dress code: no lady, for example, could 'dance country-dances in a hoop of any kind and those who chuse to pull their hoops off, will be assisted

134 *The Circus*, by Thomas Malton, 1784. The well-paved and spacious streets of Bath meant that a journey in a sedan-chair would be relatively smooth.

by proper servants in an apartment for that purpose'.[91] They also contained strictures about etiquette and behaviour. The imposition of these 'Rules' and Nash's dislike of snobbish behaviour meant that the less fashionably-minded visitors found that they were on an equal footing with their social superiors.

An impressive building scheme was also implemented. Elegant terraces and crescents provide plenty of apartments for visitors to rent during the season (October to early June) and the streets were very well lit and paved. Then there were the splendid public facilities of the Theatre, Pump Room and Assembly Rooms to enjoy, as well as shops as fashionable as any in London.

A delightful book entitled *Lady Luxborough goes to Bath* describes that lady's visit to Bath in 1752. Henrietta was the wife of Lord Luxborough, afterwards Earl of Catherton. She hoped that drinking the waters and bathing would cure her of her nervous disorder, and she stayed at the boarding house of Mrs Hodgkinson in Orange Grove, close to the Abbey, an establishment renowned for its comfort and good food. Her first visitor was Beau Nash, then in his eightieth year. In a letter to the poet William Shenstone, Lady Luxborough wrote:

> [Bath can] offer you friendly conversation, friendly springs, friendly rides and walks, friendly pastimes to dissipate gloomy thoughts; friendly booksellers, who for five shillings for the season will furnish you with all the new books; friendly chairmen, who will carry you through storms and tempests for sixpence. . . . Would you see our law-giver, Mr Nash, whose white hat commands more respect and non-resistance than the Crowns of some Kings. . . . To promote society, good manners, and a coalition of parties and ranks; to suppress scandal and late hours, are his views; and he succeeds rather better than his brother-monarchs generally do.[92]

As well as taking the waters in the Pump Room and being immersed in the King's Bath Lady Luxborough made sure that she enjoyed all the other 'Pleasures of the place'. To this end she regularly visited Mr Brown's Theatre, the rival establishment in Orchard Street, attended numerous concerts and, on 3 March, the King's birthday, was present at a grand ball presided over by Beau Nash. In the mornings she particularly enjoyed walking round the town relishing its architectural splendours and elegant well-stocked shops. She patronised the mercers Peter and James Ferry (see p.152), who showed their goods at 'the last house on the North-Parade, near the Grand-Parade' and professed to have 'Fresh Parcels and New Patterns . . . every Week . . . from their own Loombs in London', and the shop of James Graham in Green Street, which sold 'Lawns, Cambricks, Velvets' and 'a good choice of Lace'. She purchased seals from James Beresford, a jeweller and goldsmith in Market Place, and, during the course of her morning perambulations, would seek out antique coins, rings of hair and other 'elegant presents' for her friends. By the beginning of April her health was restored and she returned to her home, Barrels, in Henley-in-Arden, Warwickshire.[93]

To maintain a successful provincial business a milliner had to keep in constant touch with fashion developments in London. Elizabeth and Susannah Towsey, who ran a milliner's shop in Chester, took the stage-coach to London twice a year in the 1780s to select the new season's models from the City wholesalers. When the new stock arrived in Chester they would place an advertisement in the local paper inviting the public to come to view it. The shop run by these enterprising ladies, one of whom married a Mr Brown, eventually became the famous Brown's department store of Chester.

One of the most interesting and lively sources for details of middle-class shopping in the eighteenth century can be found in the diary kept by Parson Woodforde. He lived in the parsonage of Weston Longeville in Norfolk where, in 1779, he was joined by his twenty-two-year-old niece, Nancy. She never married, living with him until his death in 1803, and his diary is full of information about their shopping expeditions to Bath and London. These occurred every three or four years when they visited their relatives in Somerset and broke the journey by spending a few days in the two cities. Nancy must have looked forward to these trips as she found life in the parsonage extremely dull, and it was only enlivened by her friendship with Mrs Custance, who lived nearby. Mrs Custance was the wife of the local squire, a minor court official, and the two ladies delighted in their entertaining conversations about fashion and in exchanging news. Occasionally Mrs Custance gave Nancy presents – in 1781 it was a 'fine India fan, another for common use but all the Fashion at London'.[94]

Norwich was the nearest large town and when Nancy and the Parson visited it from the parsonage they did business with a mantua-maker, Mr Clarke, the Parson's tailor, who made Nancy's first riding habit in 1782, and they patronised two mercers, a hatter, a linen dealer, a haberdasher, a hairdresser, a shoemaker, a staymaker and, most importantly, Mrs Browne the milliner. Mrs Browne's establishment at No. 1 Bethel (also called Bedlam Street) was only a few yards from the inn where Nancy and the Parson stayed, and it was a prime source of information about the latest fashions and, of course, which hats, trimmings and accessories were in vogue. The Parson noted in his diary in 1794 that he 'walked out with Nancy to Mrs Browne's to see the fashions',[95] but in June 1802 Nancy was in the forefront of fashion when she wore a 'Pick-Nick' bonnet sent by her London mantua-maker and milliner, Miss Ryder of Southampton Buildings, Chancery Lane. Mrs Custance said 'it was very handsome and had seen nothing like it at Norwich as yet'.[96]

However, disarrangement of clothing, whether intentional or accidental, was a cause of great social embarrassment in the eighteenth century, and when it happened to Nancy Parson Woodforde recorded the incident in his diary: 'Poor Nancy was greatly chagrined and mortified going up to Portland Place [in Bath] which stands very high and the Wind much power . . . the wind took Nancy's riding Hat and feathers with a green vail entirely off and was blown some little way, and her hair tho' but just dressed, quite destroyed.'[97] Her discomfiture was made worse by the fact that the cousins she was about to visit and impress with her new clothes had witnessed the entire incident.

Travelling salesmen supplied Nancy and the maids at the Parsonage with printed cottons, linens and muslins as well as accessories like hats, stockings, shawls, aprons and gloves. These pedlars or petty chapmen operated in the same way as their predecessors had in the previous century. In 1781 the Parson noted that Mr Aldridge, 'who goes about with a cart with Linen, Cottons, Laces, etc called at the House this morning to know if we wanted anything in his way'. The Parson bought cotton for a morning gown and 5½yds of chintz (costing £1 14s) to make a gown for Nancy. From then on Aldridge called regularly 'once in ten weeks' and from 1788 supplied the Parson, Nancy and the maids with materials, trimmings and accessories up to three and four times a

135 *The Unlucky Glance*, an engraving of 1777, shows the interior of Exeter Change, built *c*.1676 on the site of Exeter House in the Strand. Designed as a series of small shops for hosiers, milliners, booksellers and drapers, the Change was not a successful venture, and not long after this engraving was published, it was turned into a menagerie with the stalls transformed into cages for wild animals. The building was demolished in 1829.

year.[98] Stock came from Aldridge's shop in Norwich and was replenished by buying trips in London.

In February 1792, Mr and Mrs Burdon, based in London, called at the Parsonage and left Nancy with 'a very handsome Chintz Gown which I liked very well and which they are to call again for in May if I do not chuse to keep it. I am to give two Guineas and a half for it, as that they declared is the lowest price. I shall buy it as it is a very handsome good Gown.'[99] When the couple returned in May Nancy paid them £2 10s. This incident illustrates not only how easy it had become to obtain some ready-made garments directly from the capital, but also the fact that these goods were sold at a fixed price for 'ready money'.

The advantages of this system were recognised by warehouses, retail or wholesale establishments selling goods that were not necessarily made on the premises. They had existed in London from the end of the seventeenth century, when Bourne and Harper's warehouse in Covent Garden sold riding habits, cloaks and nightgowns. Warehouses 'depended on quick turnover of stock, which in turn meant regular replenishment, moderate pricing (and usually a refusal to allow customers credit), active sales promotion, and a standard rather than exclusive range of goods'.[100]

Warehouses in the eighteenth century sold a wide variety of goods, including stockings, shirts and waistcoats, but some were more specialised. Hogarth designed a trade card for an Italian warehouse in the Strand, listing all the stock from Genoa velvet to olive oil,[101] while Paulins Warehouse in Tavistock Street sold and hired out masquerade outfits. Drapery warehouses flourished in the 1780s and 90s, reacting to the popular demand for cotton. One such entrepreneur was Richard Prynn, whose aggressive advertising policy ensured success for his drapery warehouse in the market-place in Bath. In 1796 he added cheap ready-made and made-to-measure footwear to the 'infinite variety' of his warehouse, assuring his customers that his shoes were 'astonishingly cheap' and that 'Ladies may be fitted exact by sending a Pattern Shoe'.[102]

Such warehouses, with their unique combination of value and variety, 'ushered in a brasher style of salesmanship, yet offered consumers a wide choice of merchandise at reasonable prices. They helped to clothe the Georgian middle class and looked forward to a further consumer revolution, the arrival of the high-street chain store.'[103]

CHAPTER FIVE

Perfect Cut & Fit

1780–1850

I

When Samuel Greg set off on horseback in 1783 to explore the potential for a water-powered mill to spin cotton in the vicinity of Manchester, he had chosen a propitious moment, 'at that time Manchester was intoxicated with the idea of cotton spinning'.[1] Greg found the perfect site in a valley ten miles south of Manchester, where the fifteen-foot fall in the River Bollin could be harnessed to provide power.

Quarry Bank Mill was begun in 1784, and by 1790 Greg had become one of the pioneers of the factory system by recruiting and training local people and employing children from the local workhouse as apprentices. The latter, forming one-third of his workforce, were housed in an Apprentice House close to the mill. This has recently been restored to show how the children lived there in the 1830s. His adult workers were provided houses in the neighbouring village of Styal, where he also built a school and a general shop.

Finding that he needed to expand his spinning capacity, Greg took one of the ablest millwrights of his time, Peter Ewart, as his partner, and by 1801 they had almost doubled the length of the mill, adding a second water-wheel. Their cotton empire expanded rapidly. In 1844 it occupied the 'first rank among the manufacturers. It consumes annually nearly 4 million pounds weight in cotton, possesses five factories, four thousand looms and employs more than 2,000 people.'[2]

Greg's rapid success was due to the fact he was the right man in the right place at the right time. 'Intoxicated' Manchester had become the centre of the cotton industry by the

136 (*previous pages*) The four sons of the Reverend George William Lukin, Dean of Wells and step-brother of William Windham III, in front of the parsonage at Felbrigg with their pack of excited spaniels. William – who later inherited Felbrigg and took the Windham name – stands in the middle, ramming down the charge of the gun, while the keeper kneels to fasten one of his gaiters. Robert and George are both dressed in frock-coats and white breeches. The youngest brother, John, on horseback at the back of the group, wears a black coat, his more sombre choice reflecting his choice of career – he was destined to become a curate at Felbrigg.
(William Redmore Bigg, 1802, Felbrigg)

137 (*left*) Crammed into the machine room at Quarry Bank Mill in Cheshire are rows of bobbin winders used in spinning the yarn. Once it had been treated with starch to prevent it from fraying, the yarn would be dispatched to the weaving sheds.

138 (*right*) Cotton dress from 1795-1800, with a woven stripe, block printed and pencilled with stems, flowers and leaves. Drawstrings pull the narrow frill around the neck and the hem of the bodice, which has a front opening and separate linen underpieces that are joined to the back lining. As there are no signs of fastening at the front, the bodice was probably pinned into place once the dress had been put on. There was a choice of sleeves: fashionably long ones finished with one small button; and a pair of elbow-length ones.

The skirt falls from the waist over a tiny bustle or pad that would have been tied or pinned to the bodice under the skirt gathers.

end of the eighteenth century. Its predominant position as a producer of dress fabrics and household linen meant that the word 'Manchester' became synonymous with cotton or linen goods. When a retail and wholesale establishment opened in London in 1843, the owners described themselves as 'silk, Woollen and Manchester Ware-housemen', meaning that they also dealt in cotton and linen. Travelling salesmen who specialised in selling cotton materials were known as 'Manchester Men' and later in the century, stores with a department that sold household linen like towels and sheets would call it 'Manchester Goods'.

The late eighteenth century was a critical moment in British industrial history – new cotton spinning technology was available to those with enough capital to invest in it. John Kay's invention of the Flying Shuttle in 1733 had speeded up the weaving process, but a machine was needed which would also accelerate the spinning of the yarn. Richard Arkwright's invention of the spinning frame, patented in 1767, operated by means of a pair of rollers, was succeeded by James Hargreaves's Spinning Jenny, patented in 1770. That allowed 120 spindles to be wound evenly at one time. Nine years later, Samuel Crompton came up with the idea of combining Arkwright's rollers with the spinning action of Hargreaves's Jenny. Called a mule, because Arkwright's first rollers had been worked by two asses, Crompton's machine was a breakthrough, for yarn of a fine quality could be produced in enough quantity to satisfy the requirements of the weavers.

Quarry Bank Mill is now owned by the National Trust and leased to the Quarry Bank Trust. It has been restored as a working mill, filled with the type of machinery that turned raw cotton into cloth in Lancashire in the nineteenth century. These machines can still be seen in their full working order, operated by skilled textile workers who produced medium-weight calico intended for domestic use.

Not only was the technology for turning raw cotton into finished cloth improving by leaps and bounds in the late eighteenth century, but methods of printing on material were also developing. The ban imposed on the production of British printed cottons in order to protect the silk industry was lifted in 1774 in the Imported Cottons Act. Demand for cotton as a dress fabric was inevitable, as it had two outstanding qualities – it was cheap and it was washable.

Printed cottons of the 1770s and 80s usually have a light ground with a block-printed trailing flower motif, emulating contemporary woven silks. Block-printing was a slow and laborious process, using a separate wooden block for each colour. The main pattern was printed as a dark brown outline, then yellow, madder and indigo were added. Four metal pins fixed one in each corner of the block made tiny dots on the fabric, to act as guides for positioning the next block. Blues and yellows were 'pencilled' in on the colour prints, that is, they were painted by hand. Green was produced when yellow was overpainted with blue. A number of informal gowns printed by these means are in the Snowshill collection (see 138). There are also examples of printed cottons with elaborate 'pin grounds' – finely-outlined patterns achieved by means of metal strips and pins inserted into the wood blocks.

A new method of printing, first developed in Ireland in the 1750s, involved engraving the design on copper plates instead of blocks. The plate was 36in square, so a yard could be printed in one movement, enabling the production of a larger design with a more detailed and finer line. However, copper printing could only be done in one colour,

139 Detail of an unusual copper-plate-printed cotton dress, made between 1795 and 1800. The closed bodice has a deep square neckline, elbow-length sleeves, and an open skirt. It would have been worn with a plain petticoat, a bustle pad tied at the centre back of the waist to give the skirt a lift, and a muslin kerchief loosely knotted in the front.

whether red, blue, purple or sepia – there is an exceptionally fine example of copper-plate printing in sepia on an informal gown in the Snowshill collection (139). The scenes depicted were taken from *The Adventures of Telemachus, the Son of Ulysses* by Fénelon, first published in France in 1699.[3] The selvedges of this gown have the three blue threads that show it was manufactured wholly of cotton woven in Great Britain. This mark was adopted to distinguish home-produced cottons from imported ones, particularly Indian, which were banned, following the passing of the Imported Cottons Act of 1774 – a measure intended to protect the Lancashire and Scottish industries.

Barbara Johnson, only daughter of Reverend Woolsey Johnson, kept a record of all the clothes she purchased between 1746 and 1823 (see p.153). Her clothes budget was £60 a year. (Jane Austen (1775–1817) had one of £20.) In 1778 Barbara recorded that she needed 7 yards of a 'purple and white copper-plate linnen' to make a gown at a cost of 3s 2d a yard. Such a gown would have been worn as a morning dress when doing light housework or needlework. In Sheridan's *School for Scandal* (1777) Sir Peter Teazle reminds his wife that before he married her and introduced her into smart London society she was '. . . the daughter of a plain country squire. Recollect, Lady Teazle, when

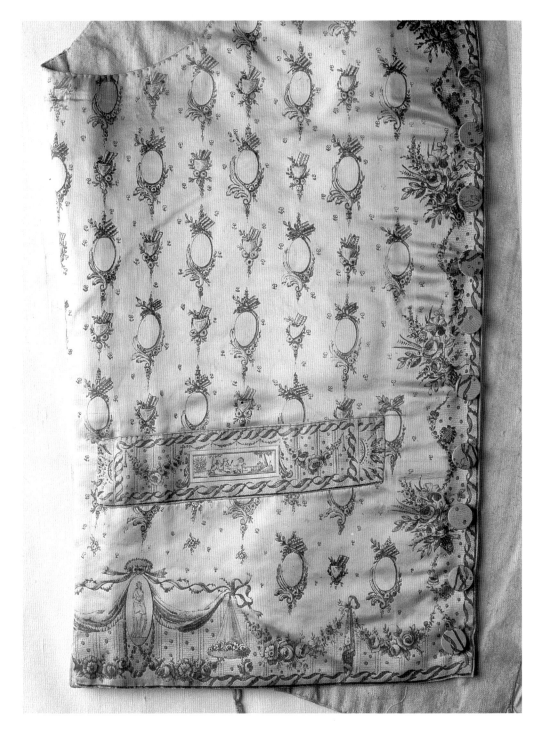

140 Copper-plate printing could also be employed on silk, and examples of its use can be found on this waistcoat from the Snowshill collection, and in a print entitled *The Woodman c.*1800 (see **171**) engraved in a needlework box. The waistcoat, dating from 1810 to 1820, has a minute vignette of three putti printed in brown ink on the pocket flap.

I first saw you sitting at your tambour, in a pretty figured linen gown with a bunch of keys at your side.'⁴ The snippet of material that Barbara Johnson has pinned into her scrap-book shows that it had a simple trailing floral motif printed in purple on a white ground, but the Telemachus print and other examples of copper-plate printed linen and cotton demonstrate that extraordinarily precise and very complex patterns could be produced by this technique (**140** and **171**).

141 Detail of a day dress of *c*.1815, with the typical combination of a fall-front bodice and apron skirt. It is made from a very pretty pale yellow and white striped cotton, roller printed and patterned with alternate sprigs and trailing flowers in red. It has the air of youthful freshness conveyed in fashion illustrations of the time.

In 1783 Thomas Bell patented a method of printing from engraved metal rollers and this was adopted by Lancashire mills to produce dress fabrics. The machine consisted of a cylinder engraved with the design, which was revolved through a bath of dye onto the cloth. At first roller printing was used for cheap prints in small monochrome patterns, often with a stripe, but as the process expanded, so larger and more elaborate designs could be produced (141). In the 1820s new bright, clear colours like chrome yellow, Prussian blue, green and the somewhat strident 'Turkey red' were popular (see 162). The last was a clear red dye, created from the roots of the madder plant by means of a process that involved soaking the cloth in oil and soda. In the 1840s, as printing became a more exact process and colours easier to produce, a wide variety of naturalistic motifs could be executed in a free-flowing and fluent way.

These technological developments increased the output of cotton materials, and improved the range that could be produced. For the first time ordinary people were given the opportunity to choose from a wide variety of fabrics, often beautifully coloured and attractively patterned, at affordable prices. The demand created required an inexhaustible supply of that raw component, cotton, and this was ensured by the 'three-way trade'. British merchants sailed to Africa with manufactured goods such as clothes, furniture, watches, cutlery and jewels to exchange for negroes, who were then transported to the West Indies as slave-labour on the sugar and cotton plantations. For example, British exports to Guinea, on the west coast of Africa, included 'some Woollen and Linnen goods, Cutlery Ware, Fire-Arms, Swords, Cutlasses, Toys of Glass and Metal, etc. and receive in return Negroes for the Use of our Plantations, Gold Dust, and Elephants' Teeth'.[5] This human cargo was exchanged for supplies of rum, sugar, indigo and logwood (both dyes), and the all-important cotton. The rapid growth of cotton imported can be judged by the fact that in 1791, when Britain transported 38,000 negroes from Africa to America, that figure represented more than half the entire European slave trade for the year.

Technological revolution resulted in social revolution. Craftsmen working from home or with other artisans in a nearby workshop, were superseded by a large workforce in a factory, with accommodation close by, as at Quarry Bank Mill. A wholesale redistribution of the population was taking place. In the early nineteenth century, towns in the north of England were doubling in size every ten years. London in 1801 had a population of just under 1 million, by 1851 this had doubled to 2.5 million, and by 1911 it had reached 4.5 million. In 1801 only 20 per cent of Britain's population lived in urban areas, but by 1851 the figure was 38 per cent, and by 1911 a staggering 75 per cent.

Dress, too, was being affected by social revolution. Men and women of fashion had always worn equally flamboyant and elaborate clothes. But by the middle of the nineteenth century, men were universally garbed in discreet, sober clothes in dark muted colours (see 181). Women, on the other hand, had become decorative accessories, proclaiming the family's wealth and status by their display of fashionable dress.

Politics had something to do with this shift. The Englishman who sighed for his frock-coat in Paris in 1752 and described it as 'an emblem of our happy constitution' (see p.135), had been very perceptive. When the American loyalist Samuel Curwen visited the House of Lords in 1783, he was surprised to see that Lord Effingham 'had the appearance both in his person and dress of a Common Country Farmer, a great coat with brass buttons, frock fashion, his hair short, straight, and to appearance uncombed, his face rough, vulgar and brown, as also his hands. In short he had the look of a labouring farmer or grazier.'[6] In common with other peers who were enthusiastic farmers as well as great landowners, Lord Effingham chose his clothes according to the practical activity in which he was engaged. Presumably he did not feel any need to proclaim his superior social status by wearing elaborate clothes.

Writing in the 1760s, Rousseau had drawn an equation between the informality of British dress, embracing the virtues and simplicity of country life, and the relative liberty of the British constitution. He hoped by his formulation of 'a state of Nature' philosophy to change the traditional attitude of the French aristocrats, who eschewed life on their country estates in preference to the glittering artifice of court. He believed that man could only discover true happiness by being in close contact with the earth, adopting a simplicity of manners and modesty in dress. This equation became a reality twenty years later: as France advanced towards revolution, so the French began to adopt the British fashion for dark blue frock-coat, buff waistcoat and breeches, riding boots and unpowdered hair, while the ladies sported the redingote, an open robe derived from

142 Elizabeth Foster wearing an elegant muslin dress with a broad sash, the romantic style of which is complemented by a wide-brimmed straw hat with ostrich feather plumes. Her lightly-powdered hair has been arranged in a relaxed way, with loose curls framing her face and soft tendrils falling over the shoulders. (Angelica Kauffman, 1784, Ickworth)

the Englishman's riding coat, and woollen jackets and skirts based on the English-woman's riding coat (see 105).

The shift towards more informal dress for women, paradoxically, came in the opposite direction – from France to England. Although the French Queen, Marie-Antoinette, and her ladies wore clothes of extreme artificiality on state occasions, away from court they often wore *robes à la créole*, thought to have originated in the French West Indies, or 'chemise dresses'. This dress was 'revolutionary in its simplicity, for, in its early form, it was merely a tube of white muslin with a drawstring at the neck and a sash at the waist'.[7] The eventual popularity of the chemise gown meant that the lighter and cheaper fabrics like printed cotton, silk gauze and fine muslin, a delicately woven cotton fabric, originally from Musul in Iraq, displaced the woven floral silks that could not be adapted to the new style.

Although the fashion soon spread to England, the chemise dress remained an informal garment, worn in the privacy of the home. This situation changed in August 1784 when Georgiana, wife of the 5th Duke of Devonshire, attended a concert 'in one of the muslin chemises with fine lace that the Queen of France gave me'.[8] Georgiana and her close friend, Lady Elizabeth (Betty) Foster, daughter of Frederick Hervey, 4th Earl of Bristol, Bishop of Derry and builder of Ickworth in Suffolk, were the acknowledged leaders of fashion in Britain. Early in 1784 Lady Elizabeth Foster visited Naples and took the opportunity of having her portrait painted by Angelica Kauffman (142). The head, with its huge hat, was completed at this sitting. The figure, clad in a white muslin chemise dress with an opulently layered collar, was finished later in Rome. Her next visit to Italy, at the end of 1784, was conducted in somewhat different circumstances, as she had become pregnant by the Duke of Devonshire, and she gave birth to a girl in August the following year. The *ménage à trois* managed to retain complete affection for one another. Indeed, when Elizabeth was about to give birth she became extremely upset when she had to relinquish her 'beloved medallion', a miniature of Georgiana that she always wore around her neck, and which is prominently displayed in the Kauffman portrait.

London society had been quick to follow Georgiana's and Elizabeth's example. When Madame Roland visited St James's Park in 1785, she noticed that 'many of the women wear beautiful white muslin dresses . . . they all wear curls under their hats, some large, some small. The hat is also very varied in form and loaded with ribbons, very few are so light and elegant as ours.'[9]

The large-brimmed, ribbon-trimmed hats were complemented by hair-styles of soft, lightly-powdered billows of curls and thick ringlets which replaced height with extreme width. Attention was drawn to the waist and hips by placing hip-pads called rumps underneath the skirt of the *robe à l'anglaise*. The fullness at the back was counterbalanced by the puffed-out appearance of the bodice. This was achieved by means of a buffon – a large, often starched muslin kerchief which was bunched up in front of the bosom. The end result was an artfully contrived one that had little to do with 'natural' simplicity.

In 1789, the Duke, Duchess and Lady Elizabeth Foster were visiting Paris and became witnesses of the tumultuous events taking place there. In May, the elected representatives of the people of France, the Estates General, had met for the first time since 1614. Even on this momentous occasion, dress was a political issue, for Louis XVI had decreed that the First Estate, the clergy, should wear appropriate clerical dress; the Second Estate, the nobility, could wear their luxurious silks and lace; whereas the Third Estate, comprising the 'people', should be clad in black woollen suits devoid of any trimming. In June the Third Estate declared itself a National Assembly and prepared to enact legislation without the participation of the first two Estates. France was moving towards revolution.

Despite the political upheavals, the Devonshires and Lady Elizabeth were visited at Chantilly by Rose Bertin, Marie Antoinette's '*marchande de modes*', whose lavish and spectacularly expensive creations for the Queen had helped to bankrupt the Crown. Two days after Rose Bertin's attendance, on 27 June 1789, the *ménage à trois* was present at 'a curiously silent and thoughtful dinner' at Versailles, where the two ladies wore their white gowns. Less than a fortnight later the Paris mob stormed the famous state prison, the Bastille, on 14 July. Elizabeth was concerned to note that ladies walking in the Palais Royal that day were surrounded by hostile crowds who sniffed at their scented powder and muttered 'that smells of the *noblesse*'.[10]

Revolutionary dress became high fashion overnight, worn enthusiastically by everyone, whatever their political allegiance. The Bastille itself became a fashion statement: stones from the rubble were placed in gold settings and worn as necklaces and bracelets; and Bastille bonnets and buckles appeared alongside Revolutionary motifs on gloves and fans. The tricoloured cockade, adding revolutionary red and blue to the white of the *ancien régime*, led to a predominance of this colour scheme. Even Marie-Antoinette sported tricoloured ribbon on Bastille Day in 1790. Lady Elizabeth Foster and the Duchess of Devonshire had returned to Paris in May that year, and noticed that anyone not wearing cockades was threatened by the crowd. On 19 June, when the aristocracy were ordered to abolish their armorial blazons, Elizabeth wrote in her journal: 'It is really affecting and distressing to be with some of the great families – to hear them giving orders for effacing the arms on their carriages, relinquishing the respected names they have borne.'[11]

In 1793, following the execution of Louis XVI and Marie Antoinette, and the institution of the Reign of Terror, it was not safe to wear anything that might suggest support of the *ancien régime*. Fashion as an organised industry ceased to exist. No fashion magazines were published from the spring of that year until 1797. Many fashionable tailors, hairdressers and modistes, realising what was afoot, sold up and escaped with their capital and skills to open new businesses in other European cities. Rose Bertin, for instance, fled to London. Luxury fabrics disappeared, ruining the silk-weaving industry in Lyons. Instead dress with overt working-class affiliations was adopted. Jackets and skirts from printed cotton, the basic costume of working women, were popular. Flat, heelless shoes completed the outfit, for walking now replaced travel in carriages.

The Revolution began to disintegrate in 1794 with the fall of Robespierre. Now street battles broke out between the radical Jacobins and the counter-revolutionaries, the *Incroyables*, brought under control by the moderate republicanism of the Directoire (1795–9). The Incroyables wore what was essentially the costume of an English country gentleman, but with all the details of colour, cut and ornament carried to an extreme to create a calculatedly sloppy and careless appearance. Their female counterparts, the *Merveilleuses*, wore clinging muslin dresses that fully revealed the female figure (see 146). Their exaggerated version of classical dress gave rise to the apocryphal story that the ultra-fashionable dampened their gowns with water to achieve the desired effect.

These developments in style in France were adopted in a more peaceful and restrained

143 The unknown subject in this portrait wears a turban of blue satin material shot through with silver, crossed with bands of white- and gold-striped gauze and trimmed with a large bunch of ostrich feathers. The low-cut bodice of the dress is edged with delicate layers of lace, and is worn under a white satin coat with narrow, buttoned revers. The diminutive heels on her elegant shoes show how far these had decreased in size from the 1770s when the French traditional style attained its maximum height. (A.W. Devis, late 1780s, Wimpole Hall)

144 (*right*) Anne North, daughter of the Prime Minister, Lord North, and third wife of Lord Sheffield. The elegant, uncluttered lines of Anne's white muslin chemise dress confirm the arrival of a 'classical' silhouette. Although padding and corsetry have been dispensed with, the newly-fashionable slender line still retains some soft fullness at the back. The waistline has risen from its natural level to a position just below the bust.
(Henry Edridge, 1798, National Portrait Gallery)

145 (*far right*) The three ladies in von Heideloff's 1796 fashion-plate engraving wear open robes of silk over muslin petticoats, and elaborately plumed and bandeauxed hair-styles. These are more formal versions of the cotton dresses from Snowshill (**138** and **139**).

manner by the leaders of English fashion. English ladies had worn muslin dresses with sashes from the mid-1780s, but as the new fashions filtered out of France necklines dropped and waistlines rose. When Arthur William Devis's portrait of an unknown girl (**143**) was painted in the late 1780s, the waistline had moved slightly above its natural position, and was defined by a twisted pink sash, with a matching satin stole flowing out behind. It is likely that this portrait was painted during Devis's sojourn in India, from 1785 to 1795.

This high-waisted style, with its slender elegance of line can be seen in a portrait of Anne North (**144**) and in a printed cotton dress, 1795–1800, from the Snowshill collection (see **138**). It has a woven stripe, block-printed and pencilled with trailing stems, flowers and leaves in red, blue and yellow and green. The neckline is high, with a drawstring to pull a narrow frill round the neck. The lady who wore this dress must have welcomed a practical and comfortable fashion that allowed her to move with ease, enhanced by the flat, heelless shoes that appeared in the late 1790s.

An engraving by Niklaus von Heideloff in his *Gallery of Fashion* for May 1796 (**145**) illustrates the more formal version of this style. Heideloff was a German engraver who fled from Paris to London during the Revolution and first worked for Ackermann, the print seller and later publisher (see p.203). The *Gallery of Fashion* was published in monthly parts, each consisting of two aquatints, beautifully coloured by hand and enriched with gold, silver and other metallic tints. The magazine, published from 1794 to 1803, was available on yearly subscription at the very high price of three guineas, or 7s 6d per copy. Its circulation was relatively small – there were probably never more than 450 copies printed in any one year. Heideloff wrote in the editorial that the dresses illustrated were 'not imaginary but really existing ones', and were intended to be a 'Repository of English National Dresses of Ladies'.[12]

Although the soft and flowing fabrics of these dresses were supposed to suggest classical drapery, they are not as revealing or as provocative as those worn in France at that time. Sophie von la Roche, visiting England in 1786, expressed disappointment not to find Englishwomen 'like the originals of Reynolds' pictures, nobly and simply attired with Greek coiffures'.[13] Ten years later, Lord Glanville told Lady Elizabeth Foster on his return from Paris that he found it 'very extraordinary' that women should be dressed 'in imitation of statues of the antique – sandals on their feet – and flesh-coloured stockings, gloves – crop wigs imitating antique busts'.[14] But the radical fashions emanating from post-revolutionary Paris (146) finally prevailed upon the more cautious English. The new antique style did require boldness, for wearing a simple muslin dress based on the drapery depicted on Greek vases and statuary meant dispensing with corsets and reducing underclothing to a simple shift. The wearer had to bare her arms, draw attention to her bosom by raising the waistline and lowering the neckline of her dress, and have her hair cut 'in the manner adopted by the most eminent Greek sculptors'.[15]

For the first decade of the nineteenth century, white was the most fashionable colour, though often offset by natural colours such as stone and terracotta, or brilliant ones – lapis blue and malachite green – for contrasting accessories like bags and stoles. Edmund in Jane Austen's *Mansfield Park* (1814) says to Fanny, 'A woman can never be too fine while she is all in white.'[16] Figure-hugging muslin was the most fashionable material – 'now sheer undressing is the general rage' exclaimed one contemporary. In a letter to her sister Cassandra dated 8 January 1801, Jane Austen reported: 'Martha and I dined yesterday at Deane to meet the Powletts. . . . Mrs Powlett was at once expensively and nakedly dressed; we have had the satisfaction of estimating her Lace and Muslin.'[17] Wearing muslin in the middle of winter in rural Hampshire demanded a degree of devotion to fashion that we might find difficult to share, but in order to create the desired effect of allowing the figure to appear through 'snow-white draperies in that fascinating manner which excludes the least thought of impropriety',[18] it was essential.

This widespread desire to look like an antique statue did not please everyone. In March 1803 the *Ladies Monthly Magazine* criticised the style:

> . . . a party of high-bred young ladies, who were dressed or rather undressed in all the nakedness of the mode; and could either their limbs or their tongues have been keep quiet, and had they been placed on pedestals or niched in recesses, they might have passed for so many statues very lightly shaded with drapery . . . it really was as much of hazard of health as it was trespass against modesty, to come into public en chemise, as if they were just out of their beds.[19]

Luckily there were garments that offered some protection against the cold. One was a 'bosom friend', a kind of tippet that protected the bare throat and chest; another was a spencer, a short-waisted, long-sleeved jacket that first appeared in the 1790s. It was supposedly named after George John Spencer, 2nd Earl Spencer, who first wore such a tailored jacket. That these garments were needed even on summer days is evident from two entries in Parson Woodforde's diary. In June 1799 he wrote: 'Though June, it was very cold indeed today, so cold that Mrs Custance came walking in her Spencer with a Bosom-friend.'[20] A July day in 1802 must have been even colder, for on that occasion she arrived 'in a fur tippet, a bosom friend and a Muff and a Winter Cloke'.[21] Ladies' outer garments followed the line of the dress very closely, be they a fitted spencer or a pelisse.

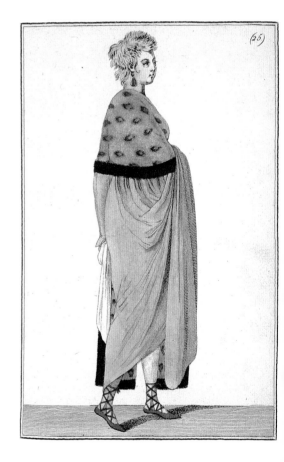

146 According to the text that accompanies this fashion plate from the *Journal des Dames et des Modes*, 4 March 1798, this ultra-fashionable Parisian lady was seen on the Boulevard des Capuchines. Endeavouring to create an impeccably 'antique' appearance, she has disposed the bulk of her trained dress to maximise its figure-hugging potential, and revealed flat shoes tied with red ankle ribbons, copies of classical Greek 'cothurnes'. An orange shawl spotted with red and edged with black velvet provides a brilliant and dramatic contrast to the flowing folds of the dress. Her short spiky hairstyle was known as *chevelure à la Titus*.

147 Gillray's cartoon about the back-stage preparations for an evening entertainment makes the point that the low-necked, high-waisted, flimsy gowns then in fashion were not suitable for ladies with substantial figures. Other participants appear in a variety of costumes including Harlequin (the dancing figure on the right) and Alexander the Great (on the left in medieval armour and a 'vandyke' lace collar). The seated lady in the foreground is pulling on a pair of tightly laced boots over her stockings – the garter can be seen just above the knee. Her costume, presumably including the breeches on the ground, is an incongruous mixture of male and female garments. (J. Gillray, 1803, Wimpole Hall)

During the first five years of the nineteenth century the pelisse was half-way between an over-tunic and a coat. It was usually made with long sleeves and a high waist, and was knee-length, extending to the ankles only after 1810. Added draperies in the form of loose mantles, cloaks, stoles and shawls could be employed to break up the severity of this figure-hugging style.

Such draperies were essential additions to these flimsy fashions, and could take the form of an exquisitely embroidered muslin or a more substantial shawl. Cashmere shawls were originally produced in the Kashmir region of India, where they were laboriously hand-woven from the wool of Tibetan mountain goats. When it was discovered that copies using sheep's wool could be made in Britain, shawls with a plain field and borders of large floral cones in brilliant colours were produced by the weavers of Norwich, Edinburgh and Paisley. The *buta* (pinecone) pattern was originally small and simple, but in time became larger and more complicated. From the early nineteenth century Paisley became synonymous with the shawl and the pattern.

The longevity of the fashion for white muslin dresses and the impossibility of altering them to suit subsequent fashions in the 1820s meant that many have survived. The examples at Killerton and Snowshill illustrate the different styles that were available and the ways in which they could be decorated (**148** and **149**). The finest muslins were imported from India – Madras muslin, for example, had a woven pattern in a thick soft thread on a transparent ground. Organdy was a soft opaque muslin with a raised-spot pattern and leno was a very light, open fabric, originally a silk from Gaza. A gown embroidered all over with a sprig or spot was known as 'sewed muslin' and tambouring was a very popular technique for achieving this. The muslin would be stretched over a tambour or frame, a hook was held beneath the frame and the loops of thread were pulled through to the top of the fabric creating a fine chain stitch. An exquisite example

148 The neckline, sleeves and waistline of this 1812–15 muslin evening dress have been embroidered with single, very fine strands of coloured silks for the flowers, buds and fern, while the leaves and stalks have been worked in silver-gilt thread.

of embroidery worked with a needle can be seen on an 1812–15 evening dress in the Snowshill collection (148). Other methods of enlivening the surface of the muslin included the insertion of panels of drawn-thread-work and whitework embroidery. A finely-sewn muslin dress in the collection at Killerton (149) has a bodice decorated with three vertical rows of tucking and very fine white twisted cord.

Between 1800 and 1820 bodices were usually cut with the 'fall-front'. This involved cutting the back of the bodice with a centre panel and two side panels to which, inside at the side seams, were joined two pieces of lining material. These were fastened in front under the bosom to push it up. When these underpieces were in place the front of the bodice, which was attached to the skirt at the waist, would be pulled across and fastened in place with pins, buttons or tapes at the shoulders. Skirts were made with an apron-front. This meant that the top section of the skirt was slit at the sides and the front lifted up to be fastened with long tape ties that were tied around the waist. From 1806 the neckline was wide and square for both day and evening dresses, but for less formal day wear the dress would be worn over a chemisette. This was a high-necked, sleeveless muslin half-shirt worn as a fill-in for low-necked dresses.[22] In the Killerton collection there is an attractive example of a typical day dress in soft muted colours c.1815 (see 141) – in contrast to another dress, c.1810, from the collection (150).

149 The almost transparent quality of the material in this muslin dress, *c.*1800, is enhanced by the tiny lines of drawn-thread that run through it. The bodice has a drawstring around the neckline so that it could be adjusted to fit. It is decorated with three vertical rows of tucking and very fine white twisted cord.

At the back the skirt has been gathered into the seam at the 'waist', and a small bustle pad would have been inserted underneath to hold out these back gathers to prevent the straight skirt from falling into the small of the back, spoiling the hang.

The attractive cream satin cap, made between 1800 and 1810, has been cut exactly like a standard jockey cap, with a plain projecting brim stiffened with wire. But the crown is decorated with panels of tight ruching outlined with twisted cord braid and an exquisitely worked tassel that hangs from the back of it.

150 (*left*) Detail of a dress *c.*1810 made from an intensely vivid pink silk, almost the same shade as Schiaparelli's 'shocking pink' of the 1930s. The front of the bodice has been altered, but the back, seen here, is in its original state. It has a deep curved collar and a central, vertical seam fastened with three yellow buttons. The yellow thread used to stitch the buttonholes has also been employed on the waistline and darts, providing a discreet but unexpected dash of colour.

151 Lydia, wife of Sir Thomas Acland, 10th Bart, with two of her children. She holds a fashionable jockey-style cap with a feather trimming. Her higher and narrower bodice is accentuated by an embroidered stole, placed under the bust and twisted over short puff sleeves. Another yellow stole, with a vaguely classical border, is draped behind her. (Sir Thomas Lawrence, 1817–8, Killerton)

Soon simplicity and restraint gave way to a more exuberant taste which expressed itself in complex surface decoration on stiff, printed cottons and light-coloured silks, and an extraordinary array of bonnets and hats bristling with ribbons and trimmings. One of these was the jockey-style cap, adapted from the racing fraternity, which had become fashionable wear for men in the middle of the eighteenth century for sporting and country pursuits. The fashion crossed the Channel at the end of the 1780s and evolved into a chic style of headwear, worn by both sexes in France. The fashion then returned to Britain and ladies sported their own versions – as in this lively portrait by Sir Thomas Lawrence of Lady Acland with her two sons, 1817–18 (**151**). There is also a cream satin cap made in this style between 1800 and 1810 in the collection at Killerton (see **149**).

The period from 1815 to 1825 was a transitional one for women, as skirts became fuller, with gored panels, and hemlines rose above the ankle. Waists rose higher, too,

152 (*left*) Detail of a blue silk evening dress of the early 1820s, with padded decoration on the neckline and swirling rouleaux of silk on the bodice that are typical of the period. So, too, are the historical references in the sleeves, cut in panes so that the fabric can be pulled through, recalling the distinctive puffs of the Elizabethan era. Drawn into a tight band, this short sleeve is finished by a 'vandyked' cuff under which can be glimpsed the original trimming of lace.

153 (*above*) The production of an 1820s evening dress such as this would have demanded a high degree of time and labour. Every swag of the appliqué silk flowers and flounces would first have been stiffened with muslin. Further stiffness was provided by rouleaux, each of which was carefully padded before being attached.

Hairstyles were usually finished in a top-knot, with the Apollo knot being particularly favoured. These very high arrangements were supported by a wire frame, and were held in place by ornamental pins and decorations of feathers, ribbons or flowers.

and width across the bust was emphasised by puff sleeves (152). Decoration, increasingly lavish, was concentrated especially on the hem, where deep bands of ruching, puffs, rouleaux and padded ribbons were applied in an increasingly heavy-handed way. Sleeves widened, the neckline gradually filled in and the waist began to drop, stopping in 1827 at its natural level. In the late 1820s ever-widening sleeves and skirts focused attention on the waist, which had to be as tiny as possible. This look of youthful, fragile prettiness was complemented in the daytime by lavishly-trimmed picture hats, and for the evening a hairstyle called the Apollo knot (153). This involved piling loops of rigid, plaited hair onto the top of the head and then decorating them with feathers and jewellery and piercing this edifice with over-size pins.

A wedding dress worn by Mary Elizabeth Williams when she married George Hammond Lucy of Charlecote in December 1823 survives (8). She recalled the event in her *Memoirs* many years later:

. . . Though more than sixty years have passed . . . I fancy I see that dear old Nurse . . . dressing me . . . in my Bridal robe of snow white silk, which she entreated she might do, and then standing by to watch my lady's maid, Turner, arrange my hair, and the wreath of orange blossoms, with the lace veil of texture fine as a spider's web falling over all.[23]

When the ceremony was over:

Nurse wrapped me in a large swan's down tippet which reached to my feet, with my hands in a muff of swan's down large enough for a Harlequin to jump through. The bridesmaids prepared to throw old satin shoes for good luck and dearest Papa put me into my husband's new chariot which, with four horses and postilions decked out with large white favours, was waiting at the door of the cathedral to take us 12 miles to Cerig Llwydion, my uncle Williams' seat, lent to us for our honeymoon.[24]

The male equivalent of the lady's clinging draperies was the perfectly-tailored, figure-revealing style devised by Beau Brummell and his circle, who were the first generation of 'dandies'. It has been said that Beau Brummell 'dictated the main lines of male fashion to the whole of Europe for the next hundred years'.[25] His profound influence was quite extraordinary as it was achieved without any of the aristocratic advantages normally thought essential for fashionable society. His father, Frederick Brummell, was private secretary to Lord North (Prime Minister from 1770 to 1782), but Beau Brummell achieved success and approbation by the sheer force of his personality and a total and unwavering commitment to what he considered to be good taste. His good looks, style and wit made a strong impression on the eldest son of George III, George, Prince of Wales, when they first met in the late 1790s and their subsequent friendship gave the entrée to the exclusive circles which welcomed him until 1816, when he fled to France to escape his debtors.

Brummell's style was based on the conservative precepts of perfect fit, faultless construction and exquisite attention to detail, as exemplified by a coat in the Snowshill collection (**154**), at a moment when interest in male dress switched from cut to fit:

By the end of the eighteenth century English tailors became the leaders of men's fashions, because their long experience of the subtleties of cloth had developed their skill and they gave style and elegance to the practical country coats and so made them acceptable for fashionable wear. Beau Brummell, not an innovator but a perfectionist, set the seal on the new fashion by removing the odour of the stables. He had the floppy cravat starched, the muddy boots polished and, above all, he demanded perfect cut and fit.[26]

Brummell turned the double-breasted riding coat into an elegant garment by giving it a curved front and tailoring it to fit the body closely. Under it was worn a short waistcoat and a fine white linen shirt with a carefully-arranged cravat. The time and trouble that Brummell devoted to this part of his toilette became legendary: a famous story tells of a morning visitor, who enquired about the large heap of crumpled cravats on the floor. Brummell's valet answered, 'Those Sir, are our failures.'

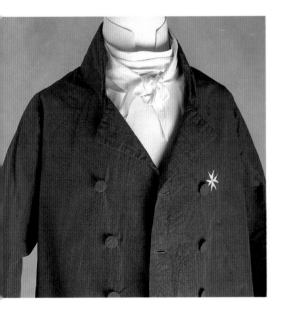

154 A double-breasted amethyst-coloured coat made in the first decade of the nineteenth century from a ribbed silk and wool mixture. It has a high stand-up collar and a square cut-away front sloping gently to wide tails. The cotton Maltese cross applied to the left-hand breast appears to be contemporary with the coat, but as it is not thought to be a reference to court or uniform dress (a Knight of Malta, for example), the reason for it is a mystery.

155 (*left*) The gentleman sitting on the right in this drawing wears cream breeches or pantaloons, which could have been cut on the bias of the fabric to ensure such a tight fit – a close-fitting line that is continued by the V-fronted tasselled boots, or Hessians. His double-breasted coat curves above the straight-cut waistcoat, to which is attached that vital accessory, a seal. The older man is dressed rather more conservatively, in breeches buckled at the knee, and a formal coat.
(Henry Edridge, 1818, Saltram)

156 (*right*) Major Vincent Hawkins Gilbert, portrayed in the centre wearing a pink coat and holding a fox's mask, is evidently the Master of Foxhounds. On the right, Sir William Heathcote, also wearing pink; on horseback, his son, the Rev. William Heathcote, is in a dark colour. Their frock-coats are cut in the fashionable style, with high shirt collars. All three men wear the round hat with a tall crown that was the precursor of the top hat of the nineteenth century.
(Daniel Gardner, *c.*1790, Montacute)

Breeches were replaced by light-coloured pantaloons which were tighter fitting and extended to the mid-calf or below. V-fronted Hessians, named after the boots worn by the Hessian mercenary troops from Germany, needed constant polishing if they were to pass muster in fashionable society. For George Augustus Sala, writing in 1859, the resultant 'refulgent lustre' was their chief glory and he bemoaned their passing: 'The Hessians of our youth are gone. The mirror-polished, gracefully-outlined, silken-tasselled Hessians exist no more.'[27] Short gloves of cotton or leather completed this look of studied simplicity. Beau Brummell's strictures about perfect cut and fit would have been satisfied by the outfit worn by the gentleman seated on the right in a drawing of two chess players by Henry Edridge, 1818 (155). Between 1807 and 1825 trousers, originally only worn by working men, appeared as an alternative to the tight-fitting pantaloons. They were skin-tight to the knees and below the knee they were somewhat looser and anchored in place by straps that buckled under the instep, a device possibly introduced by Brummell to ensure that the trousers' unwrinkled perfection could be maintained. By 1850 trousers were fastened with a central-buttoned front fly instead of the side-buttoned rectangular panel, although this last continued for another hundred years in sailors' uniforms. A stylish alternative to breeches and pantaloons or the fashionable trousers could be the flamboyant 'cossacks'. These were inspired by the Czar of Russia's visit to London in 1814 when the allies met to discuss the consequences of Napoleon's defeat. These voluminous trousers were pleated to the waist and gathered at the ankle.

By the end of the eighteenth century, when the established attire for town wear had

157 The Cust brothers wearing casually elegant 'natural' clothing fashionable in the 1790s. Under his sharply-cut black frock coat, Henry wears a white waistcoat with narrow sloping revers and double row of buttons, whereas John's coat is worn over a black square-cut waistcoat and a white under-waistcoat. Both boys' breeches fit the leg so closely that there is scarcely the hint of a wrinkle. With the artificial device of wig and powder out of fashion, hair was worn in this romantic, casual style. (John Hoppner, 1795, Belton)

become a dark cloth suit and a frock coat, and that for the country a buff waistcoat, breeches and boots (see 136), changes in male fashion were concerned with cut, fabric, decoration and accessories rather than form. This situation ensured that Britain was once again a fashion leader, for British tailors had an unsurpassed reputation throughout Europe and America as being the finest cutters of woollen fabrics, the material now almost exclusively used for male clothing. Looking back at developments in male dress during the eighteenth century, the social commentator James Peller Malcolm, writing in 1807, felt that it had 'changed almost insensibly from formality to ease',[28] a situation that was destined to be reversed within a few decades.

During the eighteenth century hunt meets had become increasingly public events and some hunts evolved their own distinguishing uniform. Motifs like foxheads could also be incorporated in the uniform, whether embroidered on or in the shape of buttons.[29] Fox-hunting men wore red coats – called 'pink' – whereas hare-hunting men wore green. But whatever colour was worn in the field, the frock-coat was always cut in the fashionable style, sloping away at the waist with a high velvet collar, and, if unbuttoned, disclosing a waistcoat with wide, sloping revers, as in a vigorous portrait of Sir William Heathcote, the Rev. William Heathcote and Major Vincent Hawkins Gilbert out hunting, *c*.1790 (156).

A portrait of the Honourable John Cust (later 1st Earl Brownlow) and the Honourable Henry Cust, of Belton, painted by John Hoppner in 1795 when they were aged 15 and 14 respectively, shows the casually elegant 'natural' clothing that was fashionable in the 1790s (157). The stylishly-dressed participants in William Redmore Bigg's painting *The Shooting Party* (1802) (see 136) perfectly illustrate the attire of the English country gentleman at the beginning of the nineteenth century.

Acquiescence to an accepted uniformity of taste gave way to a desire for self-expression and individuality. The Romantic movement stressed the creative power of the 'shaping spirit of Imagination' and was motivated by a desire to escape from the chilly neo-classicism of the turn of the century and the harsh realities of the Industrial Revolution. It manifested itself in dress by an enthusiasm for extrovert personal display and theatrical fashions which, in the 1820s and early 1830s, led to men wearing their clothes with a swaggering bravado and panache. This desire for dramatic effect is apparent in Ramsay Richard Reinagle's 1828 portrait of Sir George Crewe (158).

In the 1830 and 40s came a second generation of dandies, amongst whom Benjamin Disraeli was a leading figure. At Hughenden Manor in Buckinghamshire there is a drawing of the young Disraeli by Daniel Maclise, recording his appearance in 1833 when he was back from the Grand Tour but was not yet an MP (159). As the emphasis in male dress was still on impeccable cut and fit rather than unusual design, the waistcoat was the one garment which could proclaim individual taste and satisfy a need for colour and pattern (see 173). A description of an outfit worn by Disraeli in 1835 gives another vivid picture of the impact that his clothes made on his more soberly-dressed contemporaries: 'He was very showily attired in a dark bottle-green frock-coat, a waistcoat of the most extravagant pattern, the front of which was almost covered with glittering chains. . . . He wore a plain black stock, but no collar was visible. Altogether he was the most intellectual-looking exquisite I had ever seen.'[30]

Disraeli's predilection for colourful, patterned waistcoats was shared by the novelist

158 (*left*) Sir George Crewe with his son John. The 8th Bart's interest in fashion is apparent in his choice of a short, shawl-collared waistcoat, a high-collared coat with a slight puff on the shoulders, and a very decorative and elaborate cravat studded with a jewelled pin. He is also wearing the fashionably high, pointed shirt collar with neat tucks in the shirt front and, typically for this date, his hair is brushed forwards and he sports the fashionable side whiskers introduced in the mid-1820s.

John Crewe, aged 4, wears a dress with puff sleeves, spreading white collar and ruched decoration – all features of fashionable female dress adapted for children. It would have been worn over trousers of the type illustrated **246**. (Ramsay Richard Reinagle, 1828, Calke Abbey)

and journalist Charles Dickens. Criticised on his lecture tour to America in the 1840s for wearing waistcoats that were 'somewhat in the flash order', Dickens was often referred to as a 'gent' rather than a gentleman because of his penchant for such showy clothes.[31] Whatever the final judgement on his sartorial status, Dickens's writing contains many descriptions of 'gents', a new social class who were a 'product of the modern world',[32] and have been described thus: 'He earned his living in shops and offices, warehouses and counting-houses. He was one of the new breed of wage-earners, whose small salaries

159 (*above*) Benjamin Disraeli's shawl-collared waistcoat has been cut very tightly across the chest, and his watch and chain are tucked into its pocket. His morning coat has been cut with the fashionable M-notch lapels and has a roll collar cut high at the back. Trouser-straps ensure the trousers retain their tapered line. (Daniel Maclise, 1833, Hughenden Manor)

160 Cruickshank's caricature fastens upon the most notable features of female dress of the time, namely minute waists created by excessive tight-lacing, and the massive size of hats and sleeves. He also points up the fussy styles of decoration – hats swamped by overblown ribbon flowers, bows and plumes of feathers. Muffs, stoles, parasols, lace-trimmed handkerchiefs, drop ear-rings and bags of unusual shape and design were all essential accessories for the lady of fashion.

Turning to men, Cruickshank lampoons the revival of the fashion for facial hair, and the way the female shape is mimicked by wearing tight-waisted coats with huge sleeves.
(George Cruickshank, 1827, Killerton)

were yet sufficient to provide some luxuries in life. . . . Modern trade needed the Gent, and others like him to work for it and to buy its products. So the Gent continued to flourish and does so to this day.'[33] The journalist George Augustus Sala, who observed them in London spending their income on fashionable, ready-made clothes, decided that they were the 'dashing young parties' who are 'the glasses of city fashion, and the mould of city form, for whom the legions of fourteen, of fifteen, of sixteen and of seventeen shilling trousers . . . are made'.[34]

Female dress in the 1820s had also been characterised by an exuberance of decoration, reaching a pitch of feverish activity in the early 1830s when hats, sleeves and skirts attained their greatest width. The hour-glass figure that was the subject of exaggeration in Cruickshank's cartoon (**160**) became reality as the waistline reached its natural level in 1827. A tiny waist, created by tight, boned stays, was then given even greater emphasis by increasingly padded sleeves and widened and stiffened skirts. Cottons with figured prints and stripes and silks in muted colours were popular for daytime, and in the evening the sheen of lustrous satins could be veiled by over-dresses of soft net. Large hats were perfect for indulging the desire for decoration and trimmings and they appear in a seemingly inexhaustible sequence of colours and shapes. But their size, and the difficulty of storing them, has meant that they have not survived in great numbers.

Although the desire for fanciful surface ornamentation had subsided by the 1830s, sleeves and skirts continued to inflate and shoulder width was further accentuated by the addition of very wide pelerines and capes (**161**). This strong horizontal emphasis in the upper half of the body was complemented by a bell-shaped skirt supported by a number of stiff, cotton petticoats. In 1837 a mill in Lancashire produced a roller-printed cotton with a dark brown background on which were scattered vivid blue leaves on white stalks. It was used to make a day dress (**162**) and although the material must have been a relatively inexpensive one, the sewing on the dress is exceptionally fine. During

161 (*far left*) This lady's morning dress, in an 1830–5 silhouette, has sleeves that are extremely full to the elbow and tapered to the wrist. Width across the shoulders, emphasised by the gently curved lines of a lace-edged pelerine and a tightly pulled-in waist, is balanced by a full gathered skirt. The muslin cap, tied under the chin, is drawn into a high, full crown.

162 (*left*) A cotton day dress of the late 1830s, with very fine sewing particularly noticeable on the bodice, where the softly-draped pleats emanate from tiny gathers. The dropped shoulder line leads to the full but gathered sleeve that is broken at the elbow by a narrow band piped with white. This more rounded line is complemented by a muslin pelerine embroidered with delicate whitework.

163 (*right*) Lady Katherine Manners has been treated in this portrait as if she were a model for a fashion illustration, with miniscule waist and hands, an impossibly swan-like neck and dainty rosebud mouth. Sleeves continued to be an exaggerated feature in the 1830s, here billowing dramatically from shoulder to elbow, then narrowing into tightly-fitting lace-trimmed cuffs. The deep, gauze-covered flounce on the skirt is a variation of the fashion of the previous decade, which sought to create a shimmering pastel effect by veiling the coloured silk of the skirt by adding an overdress in a lighter tone. (Alfred Chalon, 1831, Ickworth)

164 (*far right*) This pelisse-robe, a day dress derived from the outer garment called a pelisse, was made between 1837 and 1840 from a wool and silk mixture. It has a matching cape that fastens at the throat with a button. Typically for this type of dress, it has been trimmed to suggest it has an opening down the front. In this example, the front of the skirt has been given a layered effect by the application of two scalloped panels outlined with wavy blue braid and a vertical line of buttons. Braid also defines the pointed waistline that came into fashion at the end of the 1830s.

the second half of the decade the bodice became more pointed (see **164**), the sleeves deflated and the shoulder line was dropped so that the sleeve was set much lower on the arm. Emphasis on the slope of the shoulder and a general concern with roundness of contour also affected the design of bonnets and hair, both of which were carefully arranged so they did not detract from the perfect oval of the face.

There can be few combinations as luxurious and flattering as silk and lace, and blonde lace was particularly valued for veils and trimming because of its distinctive sheen of silk. (It was a very fine silk bobbin lace, originally made with cream-coloured China silk thread.) Extensive use has been made of the lace in the dress and pelerine worn by Lady Katherine Manners in an engaging portrait of 1831 by Alfred Chalon (**163**). His Huguenot family had settled in England at the time of the French Revolution and his watercolour portraits are of particular interest as they capture vividly the manners and fashions of the day.

In complete contrast to the strong colour scheme and bold pattern of the 1837 day dress, a pelisse-robe made between 1837 and 1840 (**164**) has a pretty print of sprigs of pink roses on blue and cream stripes. This design reflects a revival of interest in eighteenth-century silks brocaded with flowers, a trend that led many ladies to unpick dresses made some eighty years before and remake them in the current style.

When Victoria was crowned Queen in 1837 the full-blown look of the early 1830s, with its extraordinarily exaggerated sleeves, had already subsided and a more subdued look emerged. Fashion illustrators no longer depicted the fashionable lady as a spirited and animated being, but rather as a timid, reticent and self-effacing person sheltering behind the ever-encroaching brim of her bonnet. The fashionable silhouette attained a somewhat drooping air as the hemline dropped, skirts gradually widened and the bodice extended into a long curved waistline and even hair-styles drooped as the hair was arranged flat against the head in loops and ringlets (see **172**). The lower and more pointed waistline, emphasised with lines of pleated bands, and the wider domed-shaped skirts of the 1840s, can be seen in a day dress of 1841–3 (**165**).

By 1845 two features had appeared that were to be dominant ones in female fashion in the next decade. The first was the introduction of the jacket bodice with a basque, the other was the flounced skirt. Christopher Talbot's photograph of the Rev. and Mrs Calvert R. Jones and their daughter, taken *c*.1845, shows Mrs Jones wearing this new basqued jacket with a frilly trimming, anticipating the softer styles of the 1850s (**166**).

165 (*left*) The lady wears a day dress of 1841–3 made from fine cream wool, with a silk stripe, printed with nasturtium-like flowers in red and green. The green has also been picked out in a fringe of silk and rosettes and bands of satin. A separate pelerine matching the dress is fastened with cord and elaborate tassels. Layers of heavy cotton petticoats would have given the skirts a wide, dome-like shape.

The gentleman is wearing a *paletot*, a short informal coat usually cut without a waist seam. This example has been made from a fine satin-weave wool with a rather dashing velvet short cape. To maintain a crisp line, trousers continued to be made with a strap passing under the instep, and the straps, fastened with a button, are still in place here. The top hat is made from glossy straw woven round radiating spokes of split cane. We know that the owner of this hat was Mr Baillie as there is a photograph of him, taken by Disden et Cie of Paris, in the hat-box together with a note that the hat was made by Bastide, a Parisian hat-maker.

166 (*above*) The matching skirt and basqued jacket in this photograph of Mrs Calvert R. Jones, taken *c*.1845, are worn under a satin dress apron and are made of a small geometric pattern. The Rev. Jones wears a straight-cut, double-breasted waistcoat and dark frock-coat, but his light-coloured trousers do not conform to the ideal of straight-cut perfection – as depicted in a fashion illustration of 1841 from *Modes de Paris* (see **173**). By the 1840s the frock-coat had become the usual garment for formal wear and was thus a safe choice for the conservative middle classes.

A 1803 guide book to London informs the visitor:

> There are 2 sets of streets, running nearly parallel, almost from the Eastern extremity of the town to the Western, forming (with the exception of a very few houses), a line of shops. One, lying to the South, nearer the river, extends from Mile End to Parliament Street [through the City and along Fleet Street and the Strand]. . . . The other to the North, reaches from Shoreditch Church almost to the end of Oxford Street, including Shoreditch, Bishopsgate Street, Threadneedle Street, Cheapside, Newgate Street, Snow-hill, Holborn, Broad Street, St. Giles, Oxford Street. The Southern line, which is the most splendid, is more than 3 miles in length, the other is about four miles. There are several large streets also occupied by retail trade, that run parallel to parts of the 2 grand lines, or intersect them, among the most remarkable of which are Fenchurch Street . . . Pall Mall, St James's Street, Piccadilly, King Street, Covent Garden, and New Bond Street at the West end of the town.[35]

This description shows that by the early nineteenth century retailers, expanding beyond the confines of the City in both westerly and northerly directions, had created a concentration of shops that was roughly square in shape. The western boundary was formed by Edgware Road, Park Lane and Grosvenor Place and the northern boundary by the New Road from Paddington to the City. Shops within this area operated in the same way as they had done previously: goods were sold by individual shopkeepers who owned the shops, lived on the premises and were often the craftsmen who made the goods. The exceptions were the warehouses: a term which was applied to any retail or wholesale establishment selling goods that were not necessarily made on the premises (see also p.165). Customers usually lived in the same locality as the shops and would decide which to patronise by word-of-mouth recommendation. There was no clear demarcation between retailers and wholesalers, but during this period the cosy relationship between the shopkeeper and customer began to change.

Louis Simond, a Frenchman who had settled in America, was struck by the mobility of the population and the frequency with which people made trips to the capital. He wrote: 'You meet nowhere with those persons who never were out of their native place, and whose habits are wholly local – nobody above poverty who has not visited London once in his life; and most of those who can, visit it once a year.'[36] This situation, caused by improved communications, the diffusion of information about fashion through illustrated magazines, and technical developments in clothing production meant that a greater variety of styles and more rapid changes in fashion became possible.

Advances in the spinning, weaving and printing of cotton in the eighteenth century had already brought attractively-patterned, washable fabrics within the purchasing power of the majority of the population and this process was furthered by the introduction of machines which could produce essential dress accessories. Embroidery and lace had previously been manufactured on a small and limited scale by craftsmen

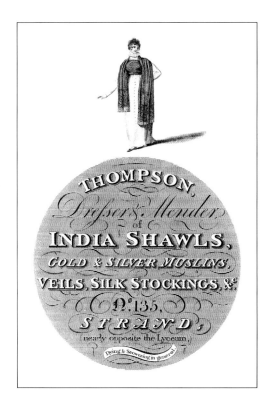

167 Shawls and fine muslins from India were very fashionable and extremely expensive. Thompson's in the Strand specialised in comprehensive mending, dyeing and cleaning services, as this 1809 trade card shows. Mark Wade, who operated a dyeing and cleaning business in London from 1788 until 1802, charged 10s 6d to clean a silver muslin dress, whereas a cotton one cost only 1s 6d.

and sold locally, but making the same products in a factory meant that they could be dispatched to haberdashers' shops throughout the country. Although some garments, like wrapping gowns, masquerade outfits and cloaks, had been available ready-made in the eighteenth century, and an embryonic ready-to-wear industry existed by the end of that century, a new gown was still a length of material which would have to be cut out and made into the appropriate style. In December 1798 Jane Austen wrote, 'I cannot determine what to do about my new gown: I wish such things were to be bought ready-made.'[37] Half a century later the wish had become reality. Mass-production of clothes in factories became possible when the sewing machine appeared in the 1840s.

In London and ports like Bristol, Portsmouth and Liverpool all kinds of simple working clothes and complete outfits intended for emigrants to the colonies were available in 'slop shops'. These shops originally sold 'slopwork' which was, according to Campbell's *The London Tradesman* of 1747, 'all kind of Shirts, Jackets, Trousers and other wearing Apparel belonging to Sailors, ready made'.[38] Slop shops were also known as show shops, because the goods in them could be seen before purchase. These shops, catering for the lower end of the market, were centred on Rosemary Lane in London. (Now called Royal Mint Street, it was also the site of an infamous street market for old clothes familiarly known as Rag Fair.) By the 1840s the garment-making firms who supplied these shops had become well established: the two best known were E. Moses & Son Ltd of Aldgate and Minories, and H. J. & D. Nicholl's of Regent Street. Both firms used middlemen contractors who farmed out the work to outworkers. By working in unregulated conditions they were able to do the work for less money than the piecework journeymen, who would originally have been employed to work on the premises at a set rate per garment. Conditions in the trade worsened and women, so limited in their choice of employment, were soon being exploited.[39]

The conditions endured by seamstresses were appalling. Henry Mayhew's investigative journalism for the *Morning Chronicle* (1849–50) revealed the desperate poverty in which these women lived. He quoted the example of one woman who told him:

> I am a shirt-maker, and make about three shirts a day, at 2½d a piece, every one of them having seven buttonholes. I have to get up at six in the morning, and work till twelve at night to do that. I buy threads out of the price; and I cannot always get work. I am now living with a young man. I am compelled to do so, because I could not support myself. . . . Sometimes we have been for two days with a bit of dry bread and cold water.[40]

Using such cheap labour enabled Moses to sell men's shirts, jackets, coats and trousers at extremely low prices in a shop which was an early version of a department store. Customers from all walks of life were attracted by the novelty of the set prices, of being able to browse without any obligation to buy, and of a money-back guarantee. The shop was very successful and soon expanded, despite *Punch* magazine's crusading campaign against Moses's methods of production and the appalling misery it created. In 1842 *Punch* wrote derisively about the shop:

> For mourning suits this is the fittest mart
> For every garment helps to break a heart[41]

168 According to the accompanying text, this 1824 plate 'represents the Dress-Maker taking the pattern off from a lady, by means of a piece of paper or cloth; the pattern if taken in cloth, becomes afterwards the lining of the dress'. Dressmaking had not become any easier since Campbell wrote his career guide, *The London Tradesman*, in 1747. He had pointed out that a successful dressmaker would have to be as skilled as her male counterpart at cutting and sewing, be fully conversant with all the latest fashions and have the right temperament for dealing with customers.

The campaign gained much publicity the next year when *Punch*'s Christmas issue featured Thomas Hood's *The Song of the Shirt*, which had been inspired by the plight of shirtmakers working for Moses.

When E. Moses & Son expanded and upgraded during the 1840s they could cater for a much wider clientele, which enabled them to make the transition from being a 'slop-seller' to a 'clothier and outfitter'. Alongside their working men's department there was one which made fashionable coats, trousers, waistcoats and overgarments and, in keeping with the practice of the smartest London tailors, ladies' riding habits. They also sold all manner of undergarments and accessories and operated a scheme for 'self-measured' bespoke suits.

A tailor would start as an apprentice at the age of twelve to fourteen and spend two years doing a variety of menial jobs in the workroom. He spent the next five years working towards his journeyman status, learning all the relevant stitches and processes. He would then be allowed to sew linings and cover buttons before progressing to the final stage of putting the suit together and pressing it properly. There was a great variety in the size of tailoring establishments throughout Britain, ranging from a small room or shop in town or country operated by a single man, to those with one or two apprentices or journeymen, to a smart London establishment which would employ as many as 50 or 60 journeymen.

Another development which changed the production of clothes was the introduction into tailoring of the sectional system. This meant that instead of each tailor making a whole suit, the work would be divided between several tailors each making a separate part – a system that was already in use in at least one tailoring establishment at the beginning of the nineteenth century. Francis Place had been trained in the 1780s as a leather breeches-maker (a separate trade from that of the tailor) and he became an expert cutter, but when he found that the demand for leather breeches was declining he decided to open his own shop selling ready-made and made-to-measure cloth breeches. The shop, at 29 Charing Cross, opened in April 1799 with a window display of 'very fashionable waistcoats'. His choice of location, as is often the case in the history of shopping in London, ensured the success of the venture, for there was 'no shop at the West-end of the Town which exposed first rate fashionable articles of dress for men in the windows'.[42]

A disagreement with his partner led to the closure of this shop but on 8 April 1801, Place opened a bigger and better one at 16 Charing Cross. The premises had undergone an expensive and extensive programme of renovation, for Place had found that the sale of goods displayed in the windows had been enough to pay for the rent of his first shop. 'I put in a new front as elegant, as the place would permit, each of the panes of glass in the shop front cost me 3 pounds, and 2 in the door, 4 pounds each. The whole of the work as well as the fitting up inside was done in 14 days, the painting etc. were finished in 2 days more . . . such shop fronts were then uncommon, I think mine were the largest plate glass windows in London if indeed they were not the first.'[43] Publicity for the opening was ensured by a window display of silk-braided pantaloons, so novel in appearance that few of his customers would have dared to wear them, but they excited curiosity about what else was in the shop.

Operating on the principle that a generously remunerated work force would be an

169 There would appear to be little difference in working methods between this tailor, *c.*1824, and his sixteenth-century counterpart (**39**), but the increased use and importance of tailored woollen garments meant that cutting and fitting had become an exacting and competitive art. Many guides to cutting, often written by London tailors, were published, endeavouring to establish a scientific approach.

efficient and loyal one the staff were paid well over the going rate. From their crowded workrooms at the back of the shop they produced ready-made and made-to-measure breeches for customers who were never 'neglected or disappointed'. It was a winning formula and Place's profits soared. He had opened his first shop with just 1s 10d cash in hand, by 1816 his profits were in excess of £3,000 per annum.

Place's name was painted in large gilt letters over the doorway, for the disappearance of sign boards meant that this distinguishing information had to be clear and distinctive. The cumulative effect of the London shop fronts was described by Wordsworth in the 1805 version of *The Prelude*:

> the string of dazzling wares . . .
> Shop after shop, with symbols, blazon'd names,
> And all the tradesman's honours overhead;
> Here, fronts of houses, like a title-page
> With letters huge inscribed, from top to toe;
> Station'd above the door, like guardian saints.[44]

The 'tradesman's honours' were given to those who had 'the good fortune to serve any branch of the Royal Family' and consisted of 'large sculptures of their several arms and supporters over their doors, and their own names and business in golden characters'.[45]

James Peller Malcolm's account of London shops in 1807 found that 'the great windows of large panes exhibit the richest manufactures and the doors of the Linen Drapers are closed by draperies of new muslins and calicoes'. This refers to the linen drapers who drew attention to their shops by draping the doorway with huge swags of material – a custom thought to have an ulterior motive, as the darkness caused inside the shop prevented 'keen eyes from discovering coarse threads'.[46]

Napoleon may have dismissed the English as being 'a nation of shopkeepers', but when General Blücher visited London in 1814 he is said to have exclaimed 'What a place to plunder.' London shops were considered to be amongst the finest in Europe and much care went into the design of the façade, the arrangement of goods in the window and the provision of a comfortable and elegant environment for the customer.[47] Some London shops were even using canvas awnings to protect customers from the elements, as is apparent from a poem called 'London's Summer Morning' written *c*.1794 by Mary Robinson:

> . . . Now the sun
> Darts burning splendour on the glittering pane,
> Save where the canvas awning throws a shade
> On the gay merchandise . . .[48]

Although gas-lighting was invented in 1792 it was not in general use until the beginning of the nineteenth century. Rudolph Ackermann, who ran a highly-successful print shop at 101 Strand and published the fashion journal *Repository of Arts* (see p.203), boasted that he was the first shopkeeper to have his premises illuminated by gas when it was installed there in 1810. The first London street to be lit by gas was Pall Mall in 1807 and by 1824 virtually all the main streets were gas-lit. Lighting in the streets of London was provided formerly by parish lamps, which burnt an inferior type of oil and cast a

170 Schomberg House in London's Pall Mall was the prototype of the modern department store. The owners' boasts that there was 'scarcely a manufacturing town in the kingdom' that had not supplied the shop, and that they also imported the finest foreign goods, was indicative of a new trend in retailing.

pretty feeble light. Those shop-keepers who could afford it would have outside lights called 'patent lights' trained on their windows, and the resulting improvement in the level of street lighting in the winter months was much appreciated by passers-by.

Space inside drapers' and silk mercers' shops was limited by the practice of arranging lengths of material around the walls so that customers could appreciate fully the effect of the patterns and the quality of the material. This method of display can be seen in a delightful illustration which appeared in the *Repository of Arts* (1809) (170). It shows the interior of a shop owned by Harding, Howell and Co., opened in 1796 in the splendid premises of Schomberg House, 80–82 Pall Mall. The house, constructed in 1698 for the 3rd Duke of Schomberg, had been divided in 1769 into retailing premises below and apartments above. Unlike the exchanges, where small units were rented to outside retailers, the company owned and ran all the departments, which were stocked with goods exclusive to Harding, Howell and Co.

It was a unique experiment in retailing. The spacious and elegant ground floor, 150ft in length, was divided into four departments separated by glazed mahogany partitions and columns. Each department had an upper storage section, which accommodated the huge bolts of material, a middle section, filled with smaller bolts and boxes, and a lower section where goods were stored in drawers. A ring was attached to each column to facilitate further display of material. The advertising text explained that 'immediately at the entrance is the first department which is exclusively appropriated to the sale of furs and fans. The second contains articles of haberdashery of every description, silks, muslins, lace, gloves etc.' In the third shop on the right 'you meet with a rich assortment of jewellery, ornamental articles in ormulu, French clocks etc, and so on, and on the left, with all the different kinds of perfumery necessary for the toilette. The fourth is set apart for millinery and dresses; so that there is no article of female attire or decoration, but what may be here procured in the first style of elegance and fashion.' Small items of furniture could be found in the west wing, whilst the east wing housed 'Every article of foreign manufacture which there is any possibility of obtaining'.[49]

A fine staircase led to a room on the first floor where customers were served with wine, tea and sweetmeats. Offering extensive views over St James's Park, it soon became a fashionable rendezvous from which the refreshed customers could peruse the extensive display of furnishing fabrics situated on the same floor. In the workrooms on the floor above, 'Forty persons are regularly employed on the premises in making up the various articles offered for sale, and in attendance on the different departments.' Harding, Howell and Co. shrewdly realised the benefits of gaining royal patronage, and were commissioned by George III to design and print the hangings for his bedroom at Kew Palace. The King also allowed them to sell the Anglo-merino cloth that was woven from the fleeces of the royal merino flock at Windsor Park. It was marketed as being: 'Nearly as fine as muslin in its texture and highly elegant for evening wear . . . the closest imitation to the real Indian shawl fabric ever produced in this country.'[50] They also obtained the rights to sell a number of printed dress silks woven exclusively at Spitalfields for Queen Charlotte and her daughters. However, the company's success at marketing luxury goods could not be maintained when the Napoleonic Wars (1803–15) made it impossible to obtain supplies of merchandise from the Continent and there was a general depression in trade. Another blow was the loss of two partners, Howell and James, who set up a similar establishment at 5, 7 and 9 Regent Street, and their shop retained its status as one of the most fashionable shops in London throughout the nineteenth century.

In the eighteenth century St James's Street was already catering for the needs of the fashionable gentleman and two of the original shops from that period have survived. One is No.6, occupied by James Lock's Hat Shop, and the other is No.3, the premises of Berry Bros. and Rudd the wine merchants. From 1765 the latter offered its customers a unique service as a publicity stunt: they could be weighed on the Great Scales, used for weighing tea, sugar and spices, and have their weight recorded in a book, which was confirmation of one's social status, and many famous names can be seen in its pages. Beau Brummell was one of their regular customers and the records of his weight, beginning in 1798, note whether he was wearing 'half-boots, boots or boots and great-coats'.

With the style-setter Brummell and the Prince of Wales and his circle patronising the shops in St James's Street, many other purveyors of high-class fashion goods opened shops there and the street developed a reputation for exclusivity and quality that rivalled that of Old Bond Street. One of the shops in the latter, hitherto the unchallenged province of the man of fashion, was owned by Mr Weston, a tailor of 'superior genius'. He was the man whom Brummell entrusted to turn the outfits created in his 'sublime imagination' into reality.[51]

Another fashionable place to walk and shop in London was the Burlington Arcade. Opened in 1819, it was described by its architect as 'a Piazza for all Hardware, Wearing Apparel and Articles not offensive in appearance and smell',[52] and it comprised a number of small, bow-fronted shops which stocked high-quality fashion goods. The practice of employing beadles to enforce the rules of the Arcade – some of which are that no one is to sing, run, carry open umbrellas or large parcels – is observed to this day.

These innovations in retailing, however, had very little effect on those who lived in country towns and villages. The village store still stocked everything one could possibly need, and the local dressmaker or tailor would run up whatever garment was required.

171 This well-stocked needlework box, covered in red leather, has a lid lined with a print, *The Woodman*, engraved on satin by Francis Eginton (see also 140). The contents of the box, of ivory, include a tape measure, reel holders, thread winders, an emery pad, a bodkin case, a pot containing wax, a silver-plated thimble, scissors and a leather needlecase. There are also bobbins, and shuttles for tatting.

Jane Austen's letters to her sister Cassandra clearly detail the difficulties involved in interpreting a new fashion, whether it be achieved by adapting an existing garment or by entrusting a dressmaker with the appropriate material and trimmings to make a new one. Despite the occasional frustrations and setbacks Jane obviously enjoyed her shopping expeditions to Bath and London from Hampshire and set about renewing a depleted wardrobe, of which she was 'so tired and ashamed', with great enthusiasm. In *Northanger Abbey*, published in 1818, Jane described her heroine, Catherine Morland, wondering what to wear for her next ball, 'debating between her spotted and her tamboured muslin, and nothing but the shortness of the time prevented her buying a new one for the evening'. She goes on to add that 'it would be mortifying to the feelings of many ladies could they be made to understand how little the heart of a man is affected by what is costly or new in their attire; how little it is biased by the texture of their muslin, and how unsusceptible of peculiar tenderness towards the spotted, the sprig, the mull [muslin] or the jackonet ['jacconet' was a thin cotton textile]'.[53]

However, in her correspondence Jane reveals that she is just as discerning and knowledgeable about the subtle differences in quality and design of muslin as her heroine, and she certainly spent a lot of time scouring the London shops to find the perfect purchase. When Jane's brother Henry married she was able to stay in the couple's house at 64 Sloane Street, which was then a long tree-lined road leading from the village of Chelsea to the main thoroughfare into the City of London. On 18 April 1811 Jane wrote from there to Cassandra to explain that she had visited a linen draper's shop and 'I am sorry to tell you that I am getting very extravagant and spending all my money; and what is worse for *you*, I have been spending yours too'.[54] She had been looking for a checked muslin but had been 'tempted by a pretty coloured muslin' with a 'small red spot' pattern, and had bought 10yds at a cost of 3s 6d a yard. In a letter written in January 1801 she enjoys estimating the cost of the muslin and lace worn by a fellow guest at a dinner party. In the same month, on the 25th, Jane wrote that she wanted two types of muslin: one was to be 'plain brown cambric muslin for morning wear the other which is to be a very pretty yellow and white cloud I mean to buy in Bath. Buy 2 brown ones if you please and both of a length but one longer than the other – it is for a tall woman. 7 yards for my mother, 7½ yards for me.'[55]

Grafton House is frequently mentioned in Jane's letters. Owned by Kent and Wilding and situated at 164 New Bond Street, it sold linen drapery and hosiery, and appears to have been a very popular shop. When Jane visited it in April 1811 she 'set off immediately after breakfast and must have reached Grafton House by ½ past 11, but when we entered the Shop, the whole counter was thronged, and we waited *full* an half-Hour before we could be attended to'.[56] On this occasion Jane bought bugle (bead) trimming at 2s 4d and 3 pairs of silk stockings for a little less than 12s a pair. In 1813, on 16 September, when staying with her brother, who had moved to a house in Henrietta Street in Covent Garden, Jane decided to make an early start: 'At nine we are to set off for Grafton House, and get that over before Breakfast.' This obviously did the trick for 'we got immediate Attendance and went on very comfortably'.[57] But service was not as speedy or efficient in November 1815 when Jane had to endure 'the miseries of Grafton House'.[58]

Another favourite shop was Bedford House. Owned by Layton and Shears, this silk mercer's shop was conveniently situated at 21 Henrietta Street. In September 1813 Jane visited Bedford House 'before breakfast' and was delighted to find 'Very pretty English poplins at 4/3; Irish, ditto at 6s; more than pretty, certainly – beautiful'.[59] Later that year Jane wrote from Godmersham Park, Kent, the home of her brother Edward Knight Austen, to find out on behalf of Harriet 'Whether they sell Cloths for Pelisses at Bedford House and if they do will be very much obliged to you to desire them to send her down patterns with the width and prices – they may go from Charing Cross almost any day in the week.'[60] In an earlier letter we learn that 'pelisses are 17 shillings each' the cost of making them being 8s but 'the buttons are expensive'.[61] (Harriet was Jane's brother Charles's sister-in-law. When Charles's wife Frances died in 1814 Harriet looked after her sister's children and she and Charles later married.)

Jane also seems to have encountered problems with her dressmakers – her longing to buy ready-made gowns in 1798 was occasioned by 'a dreadful epoch of mantua-making'. In 1801 she had to alter a gown by Mrs Mussell of Bath as it was not quite right. 'She does not always succeed with lighter colours. My white one I was obliged to alter a great deal.'[62]

By 1800 fashion illustrations and magazines were providing reliable and detailed

172 Fashion plates in the magazine, *Modes de Paris*, illustrated specific garments, fabrics and accessories that could be purchased in the French capital. In this issue, dated March 1841, the drooping silhouette that was to be such a feature of the decade is already apparent. Hair was parted in the centre and the front section was either sleeked down to be looped over the ears, or draped in long ringlets and wound into a knot or chignon.

As the lady on the right is wearing the more revealing evening dress, the artist has emphasised the fashionable sloping line by ignoring the natural shape of the shoulders and merging them into the uncomfortably low-set sleeves. Evening dress was somewhat restrained in this decade, relying for effect on the contrast between the plain silk, liberal trimmings of lace and a scattering of artificial flowers. Both ladies have the tighter and stiffer bodice which extended into a curved point.

173 A plate from *Modes de Paris*, January 1841, shows the frock-coat, waistcoat and trousers combining to present a more unified and integrated silhouette. Flamboyance is now expressed in patterned waistcoats and exaggerated styles of neckwear. Waistcoats have a pointed front echoing the development in women's bodices. Trousers are narrow, their sharpness of line enhanced by a vertical seam and instep straps. Elongated, square-toed shoes, shiny, flat-brimmed top hats and thin black canes topped with gold knobs were essential accessories.

information about the latest styles. This meant that the customer no longer had to rely on verbal directions to the dressmaker about the appearance of a finished garment, but could give her a hand-coloured fashion plate instead, often accompanied by an explanatory caption. Fashion illustrations were an invaluable source of information during the Napoleonic Wars when it became impossible to visit France and observe developments at first-hand, and many plates from French magazines like *Costume Parisien* continued to appear in English journals during the hostilities. In 1814, when peace seemed imminent, English tourists flocked to Paris to observe and purchase the latest fashions.

The early nineteenth century was a difficult time for the fashion trade as the importation of raw materials was uncertain and foreign markets were in a state of flux. Napoleon's decree of 1806, proclaiming his intention to go to war with any European country which traded with England, cut off supplies of raw silk and made things difficult for the English silk weavers. An unexpected bonus arose from this situation. The Clark brothers of Paisley in Scotland developed a smooth cotton yarn as a substitute for the silk that had previously been used in the cotton weaving looms. Hitherto all sewing thread had been made of silk but soon the advantages of this new cheaper thread for hand sewing became apparent. James Coats started a small factory at Paisley in 1826 to produce his own thread, and soon his and the Clarks' thread were available in haberdashers' shops throughout England.

The enterprising print seller Ackermann launched an entirely new type of publication in 1806. Appearing in monthly parts the *Repository of Arts, Literature, Commerce, Manufactures, Fashion and the Politics* covered a wide range of topics and in every issue included two or more hand-coloured fashion plates, specifically intended to be a guide to ladies and their dressmakers. The *Repository* produced about 450 fashion plates before it ceased publishing in 1829. In the 1811 issue Ackermann asked all 'Manufacturers, Factors and Wholesale Dealers in Fancy Goods to submit 3 or 4 samples of their latest dress and furnishing fabrics'. Small samples of those materials that fulfilled 'the requisites of Novelty, Fashion and Elegance' were then pasted onto an appropriate setting, enabling the reader to see and feel the quality of the latest materials and find out where to buy them.[63] Ackermann maintained a very high standard of design in his magazine and any issue or individual fashion plate provides a unique insight into the taste of that time.

Another innovative idea in the presentation and sale of fashion appeared in the magazine *La Belle Assemblée*. It was published by Mr Bell with the sub-title 'Bell's Court and Fashionable Magazine' and remained an arbiter of taste from 1806 until 1832, when it became *The Court Magazine and Belle Assemblée*. It cost 2s 6d an issue if you purchased with monochrome plates and 3s 6d with colour plates. The standard of illustration was extremely high. The first fashion illustrator to work for the magazine was the portrait painter Arthur William Devis and he was succeeded by Thomas Stothard. Originally a pattern-maker for Spitalfields brocades and known as an illustrator of historical works, Stothard was elected to the Royal Academy in 1794.

The toilettes depicted on the pages of the magazine were frequently described as being 'Invented [designed] by Mrs Bell'. Mr Bell's wife was a leading London dressmaker with premises called 'The Fashionable Millinery and Dress Rooms' at 22 Upper

King Street in Covent Garden, where a display of costumes was 'produced on the first day of every month' and she designed and made every conceivable type of gown from wedding dress to riding habit.

At some point before 1830 Mrs Bell moved to 3 Cleveland Road, a prestigious address opposite St James's Palace. These premises, called the 'Magazin des Modes', offered the customer a 'novel and splendid display of Millinery, Dresses, and Head-dresses, just prepared in Paris exclusively for Mrs Bell', and were supplemented by agents in other European countries who provided her 'exclusively twice a week with every foreign novelty'.[64]

Mrs Bell had gained fame in 1820 for her invention of the 'Chapeau Bras', a hooped hood that could be folded up and placed in a bag, and the 'Bandage Corset', specifically designed to reduce 'protuberance' and to support the stomach before and after pregnancy.[65] The Duchess of Kent wore one when she was expecting the future Queen Victoria in 1819, so Mrs Bell was able to call herself 'Corset Maker to her Royal Highness, the Duchess of Kent'.

The indefatigable Mrs Bell received further publicity in 1824, when she became director of a monthly fashion magazine entitled *The World of Fashion and Continental Feuilletons*. Published by her husband, it was an elegant and stylish magazine which contained extensive advertising for Mrs Bell's shop thinly disguised as editorial comment. Colour engravings of Paris fashions were featured prominently on its pages and this led to a rather tricky situation in 1830 when Queen Adelaide, the wife of William IV, announced her intention to ban French fashions from the court to encourage British-made ones. At first Mrs Bell declared her full support for the scheme, emphasising that 'the talents of the English dress-maker and milliner cannot be surpassed'.[66] However, she did not want to dispense with the services of her European agents and lose her lucrative sales of imported fashions. She also perceived that a 'Buy British' campaign was destined to be a failure because it could not compete with the more sophisticated and innovative French fashions. An anonymous letter was published in the magazine criticising the Queen for wearing foreign fashions and employing foreign dressmakers, and it was followed a few months later by an editorial praising the Queen for wearing Spitalfields silk and castigating those who dared to appear at court in 'exotic finery, upon which has been executed all the *un-English* skill of some dress-decorator with an *outlandish name*'.[67] The Bells obviously intended to profit whatever the outcome of the campaign, and their journalistic skirmishings demonstrated their clever manipulation of the printed word in order to maintain their position as arbiters of taste and highly-successful fashion retailers.

In 1850 *The World of Fashion* was the first fashion magazine to include paper patterns for the benefit of its customers, a development which brought fashion within the reach of the home, albeit for the skilled dressmaker – though it had been possible, some twenty years earlier, to buy paper patterns from an enterprising tailor, Mr B. Read of 12 Hart Street, near Bloomsbury Square. He sold striking colour prints of men's and women's fashions, together with paper patterns and his patent method of measuring clothes. The set cost 8s and was available from booksellers throughout England. In the 1830s Read opened a branch of his tailoring establishment on Broadway, New York, so he must be considered one of the first exporters of British fashion to the USA.

174 A fashion plate from a series published by Benjamin Read, an enterprising tailor with premises in Bloomsbury Square, London, shows winter fashions of 1833-4 in the Pantheon, Oxford Street. Read used these lavish plates, featuring fashionable locations, as publicity for his business.

One of his prints (174) shows men, women and children wearing the winter fashions for 1834–5 inside the Pantheon Bazaar in Oxford Street. This neo-classical building had been built for masquerades and other evening entertainments by James Wyatt in 1772, but its popularity declined and after spells as a theatre and an opera house it was stripped and left empty in 1814. In 1834 it was turned into a bazaar – a retail establishment which sold fashion accessories of all types. The print shows the elegant arcades of the Pantheon Bazaar furnished with stalls selling millinery, linen accessories and toiletries. A series of mirrors hung above the stalls, angled so that the customers could see their reflection when trying on the goods on display. It was stated in the deeds of the Pantheon that whoever bought the premises had to retain a black frontage and display the words 'The Pantheon' on it. This stipulation has been observed to the present day and, although the site is now occupied by Marks & Spencers, bright-green neon lighting spells out the name of the original eighteenth-century building at night.

A bazaar opened in Manchester in 1821 operated on the same principle, namely that of the proprietors hiring out counters to outside tradespeople. According to the original advertisement for the Manchester Bazaar it was open from 9.30am until 8pm, except on Saturdays when it was open till 9pm. All items were marked with prices 'from which no abatement shall be made' and stall-holders were not to gossip, eat or drink behind their counters. The Bazaar was really an early version of the department store as it intended to 'secure to the Public the choicest and most fashionable articles in every branch of Art and Manufacture, at a reasonable rate'. Interestingly, in 1836 three men who originally worked in the Bazaar, James Milne, Adam Faulkner and Thomas Kendal, opened a

175 (*left*) A shoe shop in the mid-1820s, with the stock neatly housed in shelving across the walls. The shoes are arranged heels facing out, and their ribbon ties are left to hang free. The lady trying on shoes is wearing a fashionable mantle over a lightweight silk dress with very full gigot sleeves and a striped belt that defines a waistline now back to its normal level. Her accessories have been carefully chosen to match her mantle, from her elegant parasol to the pink roses adorning the sweeping curves of her wide-brimmed hat. Her companion's yellow shawl is trimmed with a Paisley pattern.

The young man who is serving wears a long apron and his shoe horn is positioned close at hand. On the other side of the shop, a smartly-dressed boy is trying on a pair of shoes and there appears to be a pile of boot-shapers on the floor.
(Unknown artist, *c*.1830, Wimpole Hall)

176 (*below*) A pair of yellow- and white-striped silk shoes from the mid-1820s. Their canary-yellow ribbon ties are a reminder of the clear, bright colours that were so fashionable in this decade. *The Ladies Pocket Magazine*, 1829, is open at an illustration of 'Rural Ball Dress'.

store called 'Kendal, Milne and Faulkner' which was destined to become the premier department store in Manchester.[68]

In 1813 an Act was passed allowing a new street to be built in London – the first to be planned from the very beginning as a shopping street, unlike earlier developments which had gradually evolved into commercial centres. It was called Regent Street in deference to the Prince Regent, the originator of the scheme. (The Prince of Wales became Prince Regent for nine years during his father's final illness, from 1811 until George III's death in 1820.) Regent Street was intended to form part of a new thoroughfare that would link the Prince's residence of Carlton House in Pall Mall with Marylebone Park (now called Regent's Park), where the Prince intended to build a villa. The Prince chose John Nash to design this prestigious and ambitious undertaking, avoiding the fashionable area of St James's Square, which remained intact. Circuses (open spaces where streets converged) were constructed at the junctions with Piccadilly and Oxford Street to make the intersections less awkward and to provide continuity. The section between Regent Circus South (now Piccadilly Circus) and Regent Circus North (Oxford Circus) was called the Quadrant and was intended to be the shopping section, whereas the remainder of the road, which ended at Portland Place, was residential.

It was Nash's intention that the street should be as impressive as any in Europe by providing 'room for all the fashionable shops to be assembled in one street'.[69] When the project was completed in 1820 the 'noble street', with its elegantly-colonnaded façade housed 'palace-like shops, in whose broad shewy windows are displayed articles of the most splendid description, such as the neighbouring world of wealth and fashion are daily in want of'.[70] Building a pavement 15-ft wide instead of the customary 7ft, and a roadway double the width of Bond Street, meant that the street 'had an air of grandeur and space' and 'affords facilities to carriages and horsemen in turning from one street to the other'.[71]

When Sophie von la Roche visited Oxford Street in 1786 she had been struck by the elegance of its shops and the sophistication of the goods on display (see p.152), but by the time building began on Regent Street, Oxford Street was no longer patronised by fashionable society and Nash had actually promised that Regent Circus would avoid 'the sensation of crossing Oxford Street'.[72] However, it was still a busy and prosperous street devoted to selling fashion goods of every conceivable variety to the middle classes. According to Johnstone's *Commercial Guide and Trade Directory* of 1817 there were 153 shops in Oxford Street selling fashion goods, amongst which were 33 linen drapers, 17 hosiers and glovers, 10 straw hat manufacturers, 1 ribbon warehouse and 24 boot and shoemakers.[73]

One of these shoe shops was owned by Mr Pattison, and the interior of his shop at 129 Oxford Street is the subject of an unusual painting at Wimpole Hall in Cambridgeshire, painted in the mid-1820s by an unknown artist (175). The fashionably-dressed lady is trying on the flat pumps with ribbon ties that were so popular at that time (176). The shop is simply but smartly furnished, with wooden panelling and a glass-partitioned door with the owner's name written on it in gilt letters.[74]

The area around Piccadilly was already generating a lot of trade at the end of the eighteenth century as it was the terminus for mail coaches arriving from the West Country, Portsmouth and Brighton. In a letter dated 8 June 1791 Horace Walpole

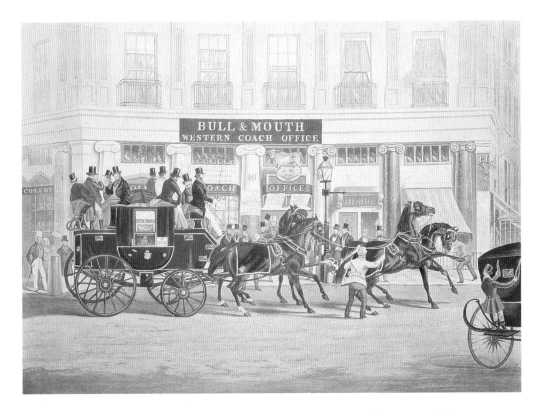

177 This 1841 print depicts the Beaufort coach leaving the Bull and Mouth Inn at 10 Piccadilly, premises of the Western Mail Coach Office. Regular mail coach services, introduced in 1784, altered the character of Piccadilly as a number of inns acted as termini for coaches from Bath and the West Country.

wrote: 'I have twice this spring been going to stop my coach in Piccadilly, to inquire what was the matter, thinking there was a mob – not at all, it was only passengers.'[75]

In 1812 the Bull and Mouth Inn at 10 Piccadilly, the premises of the Western Mail Coach Office, was purchased by William Edgar and George Swan, who turned it into a haberdashery shop that was destined to remain on the same site until Swan & Edgar closed in 1982. Edgar began his retailing career by selling men's haberdashery on a market stall in St James's Market, where he met his partner Swan. Although Swan died prematurely in 1821 his name remained. A new shop front was constructed in 1841 and by 1848 the shop occupied 45–51 the Quadrant and nearly all the corner site of Piccadilly Circus. This development was typical of many other shops that opened in Regent Street as the movement towards larger retailing units led to the integration of three or more shops operating as one store.

The 1830s were a boom time for 'retail adventurers', many of whose premises in Regent Street had expanded into highly-successful department stores by the end of the nineteenth century. One such was Dickins and Smith, who moved their haberdashery shop from premises at the Golden Lion, 54 Oxford Street, to 232 and 234 Regent Street in 1835. Acquiring a partner called Jones, they set up their sign of the Golden Lion above the entrance to their new shop and it remained there until Regent Street was rebuilt in the 1920s, the last eighteenth-century sign to be displayed in the West End. The shop, Dickins and Jones, is still on the site.

Peter Robinson, the son of a Yorkshire haberdasher, opened a linen draper's shop in the cheaper premises of 103 Oxford Street in 1833. It was extremely successful and by

1860 he had acquired a block of six shops. In 1856 he was selling ready-made garments such as skirts and mantles and mourning dress as well as a dressmaking service. Robinson realised that selling ready-made goods at a fixed and reasonable price would generate a high volume of trade, so he advertised his stock in the newspaper with set prices and displayed it in the shops with price tags attached. The mourning side of the business did so well that he opened a large shop devoted entirely to the 'apparel and apparatus of grief' in 1865. His Court and General Mourning House at 262–265 Regent Street was in direct competition with Mr W.C. Jay's The London General Mourning Warehouse which had had the monopoly on the lucrative mourning clothing trade. Jay had opened his splendid premises at 247, 248 and 249 Regent Street amid a blaze of publicity in 1841.

Another type of specialist shop found in Regent Street was the shawl shop. One of the first was J. & J. Holmes Shawl Emporium at 171–5 Regent Street, which opened *c.*1825. According to *The World of Fashion* this was the 'most splendid establishment even in that vicinage, deserving the flattering encomiums bestowed on it by the fashionable who visit it'.[76] The stylish shawls on sale there ranged in price from 1 guinea to 100 guineas and, according to the shop's trade card, it supplied the Queen and other members of the Royal Family. It also stocked 'An immense variety of India Shawls and Oriental Curiosities'. This sideline was expanded when the store was taken over by Farmer and Roger, who opened it in 1850 as 'The Great Shawl and Cloak Emporium'. India supplied them with 'the largest and most magnificent collection in England, comprising the latest designs of India, Gold, Delhi, Benares, Decca and Lahore'. In 1862, when the store was also selling ready-made cloaks, dresses and jackets, it took on an 18-year-old apprentice. His name was Arthur Lazenby Liberty.

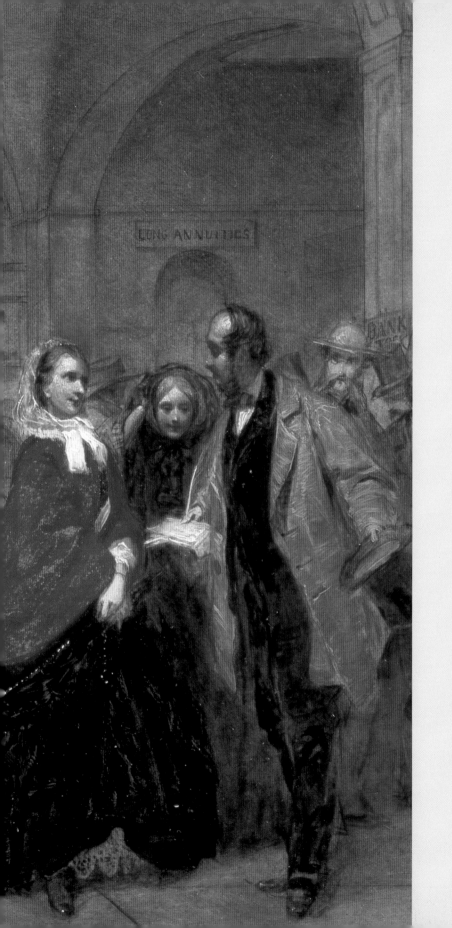

CHAPTER SIX

Tyranny of Fashion

1850–1914

I

When the Great Exhibition at the Crystal Palace in Hyde Park closed on 15 October 1851, it had been visited by over 6 million people. Three of those visitors, Mary Elizabeth Lucy of Charlecote and her two sons, William and Henry, had been 'enchanted, delighted and bewildered with excitement' when they 'entered the great hall of Sir Joseph Paxton's building' on 3 July. Mary recorded in her *Memoirs*: 'One general effect of beauty had been produced by the infinitely varied work of the thousands who had separately co-operated towards this marvellous display, and the structure in which it was set, by its graceful lines and the free play of light which it admitted, seemed to fulfil every condition that could be desired for the setting of the treasures thus brought together.'[1]

The public was not only dazzled by the exhibits, which showed the results of nearly a century of industrial expansion, and impressed by the range and diversity of goods brought from the far-flung shores of Britain's colonies, but was also amazed by the massive glass and iron edifice, soaring to such a dizzying height that it easily encompassed fully-grown trees. Its total floor space was nearly 1 million square feet and the materials employed included about 300,000 panes of glass, 330 standardised iron columns and 24 miles of guttering, so the scale of the Exhibition was as awe-inspiring as the extraordinary range of exhibits. Machine-made objects from all over the world were displayed there, arranged in five major divisions, each with a number of sub-groups. Amongst the latter was Class XX, entitled: 'Hats, Caps and Bonnets; Hosiery; Gloves; Boots, Shoes and Lasts; and Under Clothing and Upper Clothing'. Some of the marvels of science that could be seen in this group were 'a life-preserving elastic cork jacket capable of being worn unobserved under a coat' and a 'bachelor's shirt of peculiar construction without buttons'.[2]

The Great Exhibition was conceived by Prince Albert, Queen Victoria's consort, to celebrate the achievements of the Industrial Revolution. It marked a turning point in British industrial and commercial life, with unprecedented prosperity for many people. It was the middle classes, marvelling at the products of the new technology, who were most keen to exercise their spending power on acquiring its products for their homes and personal adornment. The growing wealth and influence of this group, and their powerful position as consumers, meant that increasingly they became the predominant arbiters of taste and, therefore, of fashion.

The range of visual information and the enormous number of garments and accessories that have survived from the late Victorian and the Edwardian periods give a wide choice of illustrative material, and in the sixty-four years between 1850 and 1914 the pace of change in fashions accelerated to an extraordinary and bewildering degree. Glancing at any fashion illustration and its accompanying text one is also struck by the multiplicity of terms used to define every part of the costume and its general style, from the shape of a sleeve to the type of trimming. There is also more information available about the dress of the lower middle-class and working classes, hitherto somewhat sketchy. This is largely a result of the repeal of paper tax in 1861, which led to a

178 (*previous pages*) *Dividend Day at the Bank of England* celebrates quarterly day when dividends on Bank Stock were paid to personal callers. This event gave the artist the opportunity to depict a wide range of classes and types. On the extreme left is an elderly Jewish man seated in an invalid carriage. Behind are two ladies: one in a pale coloured cloak over a crinoline, the hem of which has been looped for greater ease in an early walking version, the other in a blue bonnet and skirt, almost enveloped by a voluminous Paisley shawl. The girl surrounded by her luggage is dressed in a skirt and shawl of modest dimensions; her companion, an elderly man, in an old-fashioned caped coat. The foreground is dominated by a lady in a lace-trimmed bonnet and a dark skirt of the exaggerated size demanded by fashion, over which is draped a bright red shawl. The sad-looking lady behind appears to be in mourning dress.
(George Elgar Hicks, 1859, Wimpole Hall)

179 On 1 May 1851, 'the happiest, proudest day of my life', Queen Victoria opened the Great Exhibition at the Crystal Palace in Hyde Park. She wore a dress of pink watered silk embroidered with silver and diamonds, and a head-dress of feathers and jewels, while Prince Albert was in full uniform, and their eldest son, Bertie, wore Highland dress. The silhouette of the female spectators can be seen to be pyramidal, an inevitable consequence of a fashion that encased the head in a rounded bonnet and the body in a draped shawl and excessively wide skirt.

flood of cheap newspapers and journals containing illustrations of ordinary people from all classes in a variety of situations.

The new and developing art of photography is also revealing of costume and fashion in this period. The daguerreotype photographic process used in the 1840s gave surprisingly clear details of contemporary dress, but it was a slow, laborious and expensive business. When glass negatives and multi-lensed cameras were invented in 1851 it was possible to produce more than one print, and to obtain eight small likenesses, from one negative. These were cut out and mounted on thick, gilt-edged pieces of card the size of a visiting card – hence a 'carte-de-visite'. Here was a relatively cheap way of recording one's appearance, ranging from a guinea for a dozen prints and a choice of poses in a good professional studio, to half a guinea in one of the provincial studios that immediately sprang up all over the country. Cartes-de-visite were also an inexpensive source of information about the fashions worn by members of the Royal Family and society beauties, as they were available in shops, where black-and-white prints sold for one or two pence and hand-coloured prints for four or six pence. In 1863, when Albert Edward, Prince of Wales married Princess Alexandra of Denmark, black-and-white prints of the couple were available by post for 1s 6d and coloured prints for 3s. Millions of cartes-de-visite have survived in public and private collections and even today it is possible to purchase one for under 50p.

By the middle of the nineteenth century a desire to be fashionable had penetrated right down the social scale to such an extent that in 1858 it was observed that it is 'almost impossible to recognise working people when in their Sunday best',[3] although this may have been a sweeping statement, for the English have always had a fine nose for nuances of class. It is also difficult to determine the social status of some of the sitters in carte-de-visite photographs (180), though a close look at the quality of the clothes might reveal it.

But the gradual 'democratization' of fashion was not universally applauded. When the horticulturalist and garden designer Gertrude Jekyll looked at a photograph of a 'wedding party of the labouring class' at the turn of the century she exclaimed:

> The bridegroom wore one of those cheap suits aforesaid and had a billy-cock [bowler] hat pushed back from his poor, anxious, excited face that glistened with sweat. In his button hole was a large bouquet and on his hands white cotton gloves. No more pitiful exhibition would well be imagined. Have these people so utterly lost the sense of their position that they can derive satisfaction from the performance of such an absurd burlesque?[4]

A quick glance at a group of Victorian men at a location like a race meeting or a railway station suggests that they were clad in indistinguishable and interchangeable clothes, but within this seeming uniformity there was a clear demarcation between the classes. Mass production of clothes might have brought respectability within everyone's grasp, but class divisions were still clearly expressed by the quality of clothing. A factory-made suit worn by a working-class man would have been a cheap and shoddy imitation of the latest fashion, badly cut and made from inferior materials. The middle and upper classes would have worn a version made from good quality cloth that was noticeably better cut and finished. But an upper-class gentleman would be wearing a made-to-measure suit that demonstrated his tailor's attention to immaculate cut and fit.

180 A photograph from the early 1860s showing a lady in a splendid skirt of moiré (a stiff silk with a subtle watered pattern) and a velvet jacket with pagoda sleeves. The subject is in fact Sarah Davies, previously photographed in a daguerreotype taken of the staff at Erddig, Clwyd in 1852 when she appeared in her uniform as under-housemaid. By the time this later photograph was taken, she had become nurse to the Yorke children, who affectionately called her 'Lalla'.

181 A group photograph of the Douglas-Pennant family and visitors at Penrhyn Castle in Wales in 1866, showing two men in lounge suits. The man seated on the left wears the suit with an early version of the bow tie, and has his hair cut in the fashionably short, side-parted way. In front of Colonel Douglas-Pennant, formally clad in dark frock-coat, cravat and top hat, is the Hon. Edward, wearing a very stylish version of the suit with a soft, round-crowned hat. Other members of the group include the Archbishop of Canterbury, at the back in the centre, to his right Henry George Liddell (father of *Alice in Wonderland*), with Mrs Liddell, wearing a smart, feather-trimmed hat, seated in front of him. Herbert, son of William Gladstone – who became Liberal Prime Minister in 1868 – sits on the ground, and Mrs William Gladstone is seated centre right.

There was very little colour in the male wardrobe: suits were generally in black or dark muted shades – light-coloured trousers were usually only worn by the flashier 'gent'. In the evening, a black tailcoat with matching trousers and a white satin waistcoat were *de rigueur* for the upper classes, although the anonymous author of *Complete Etiquette for Gentleman* (*c.*1880) leaves it to the discretion of the wearer as to whether he should wear a black or white necktie, having a decided preference for the white himself as it is 'considered unexceptional at any season or hour, in any rank, profession, or capacity'.[5]

There was some variety in informal dress as there were a number of different short coats available and, in the 1860s, the aptly-named loose lounging jacket which, when worn with matching trousers and waistcoat, evolved into the lounge suit, popularly called a 'suit of dittos' (181). Braid was used to trim the edgings of the jacket and in the 1860s it had narrow cuffs and a high-set button fastening. Trousers were cut straight but did not have a central crease or a turn-up until the 1890s, and although the fashion illustrations depict trousers as being uncreased and hanging in a sharp line, this is not borne out by photographs of the 1850s and 60s, which show that the heavy wool fabrics then in fashion sagged very badly.

A lounge suit could not be worn in town or when making a social call. The appropriate attire for both these occasions was a frock-coat and top hat. Sonia Keppel, born in 1900, remembered her father wearing 'a dark blue, skin-tight frock-coat . . . over his shirt and, when paying afternoon calls, he could not take if off. In his lapel he wore a carnation. In those days, if calling on a lady at tea time, implicitly he had to give the impression that he was merely "looking in". Into her drawing room he carried all the paraphernalia of his walk: his top hat, his walking stick, his gloves.'[6] Although frock-coats were in sombre colours – black, dark grey or dark blue – the style was capable of slight variations. The coat could have a velvet collar and deep lapels and the really stylish would wear it with trousers that had a broad dark band down each outer seam.

The frock-coat had 'the hallmark of Victorian respectability'[7] (**182**) and was worn by the upper, middle and professional classes, but there was an alternative – the morning coat. This garment, when worn with striped trousers and a top hat, became the conventional costume for the professional classes and offered the wearer the possibility of being 'dressy without being formal; stylish without being stiff'.[8] Like the lounge jacket, the edges of the morning coat were bound with a lighter-coloured braid and could be worn with either a matching or a contrasting waistcoat and light-coloured trousers. This combination (**183**) was the choice of the architect Richard Norman Shaw who was photographed, *c*.1873, with his friend, William Eden Nesfield, a fellow-pioneer of the Old English Movement, which set a trend away from the Victorian style back to traditional Georgian design.[9]

The move towards a greater informality in men's clothing at the turn of the century eventually led to the acceptance of the lounge suit for all informal occasions, and for town wear, when it could be teamed with a bowler hat (see **220**). A reporter for *The Tailor and Cutter* magazine sitting in Charing Cross Station in 1897 noted that the ratio between formal and informal dress was 'nearly two lounge suits to one morning coat and quite three lounges to one frock-coat'.[10] However, the demarcation between the social classes was maintained as the black lounge suit became Sunday best for workers in town, and the working uniform for 'superior artisans'. The rules of dress were applied as rigidly to men's clothes as to women's, and those who did not belong to the aristocratic élite would not have dared to challenge them: 'The top of society could break rules of dress, but those just below dare not. Thus the Mayfair set could go as they pleased, but in bourgeois Belgravia and South Kensington formality was oppressive – hence the saying "it is always Sunday afternoon" on Cromwell Road, with black frock-coats and black toppers obligatory.'[11]

Crisp fine white linen continued to be a status symbol and the pristine appearance of shirt collar (a separate accessory from the 1840s), shirt front and cuffs was maintained by a judicious use of starch, which became widely available in 1849 when Reckitt & Sons developed a soluble rice starch. It was essential (in the upper and middle classes) to change one's linen every day as dirty linen was a sign of social inferiority. According to a book entitled *Etiquette for Ladies and Gentlemen*, *c*.1850, 'Cleanliness is a prominent feature in the appearance of a gentleman . . . a disregard of cleanliness is a direct insult to society, and is a certain indication of filthy habits and a vulgar education.'[12] It went on to advise that choice of dress should be governed by what is 'good taste', and that no gentleman should be seen wearing 'shabby gloves or a bad hat, nor will he be seen in the drawing room in a surtout [a short informal coat, so quite unsuitable for the formal setting of the drawing-room].'

The top hat was ubiquitously worn, but the quality of the hat could reveal the social status of its owner. A London hatter, Mr Willis, recalled at the turn of the century: '[I] could tell the social standing of a customer by the way he asked for it. If he described it as a silk hat we knew he belonged to suburbia and respectability, if he asked for a top hat

182 (*left*) An unknown gentleman photographed in the 1860s in the studio of Camille Silvy, Porchester Terrace, Bayswater, one of the most prolific and prestigious studios in London. He wears formal dress, a well-cut frock-coat, light trousers and a bow-tie, and he carries a silk top hat and a furled umbrella.

183 (*left*) Richard Norman Shaw was photographed with fellow architect, William Eden Nesfield, *c.*1873. Shaw's typically single-breasted morning coat jacket trimmed with braid is worn over a turn-down shirt collar and narrow necktie. Nesfield sports full side whiskers and an informal wool jacket, with rather badly-cut trousers of another colour and fabric – an ensemble designed for comfort rather than style.

184 (*right*) This illustration of men's and boys' garments from the *Gazette of Fashion*, January 1857, includes a very smart dressing-gown with the latest accessory, a smoking cap.

he belonged to the City (Stock Exchange or Mincing Lane) but if he demanded a topper he was out of the top drawer.'[13] The headgear of the working class, the cap, was adopted by the fashionable for sporting events like cricket and boating. At informal events men also wore a straw sailor's hat, later called a boater, which became an essential part of the Edwardian man's summer costume of striped blazer and flannels (flannel trousers, usually cream coloured).

Dressing-gowns were a popular choice for informal dress in the nineteenth century as they allowed the wearer to enjoy a degree of flamboyance, colour and comfort that normal day and evening wear did not. Those illustrated in fashion magazines for men (184) have contrasting shawl collars and cuffs and cord ties and edgings and are distinctly more stylish than the one worn by Thomas Carlyle in a portrait painted by Frederick Tait in 1857 (see 187). Thomas Carlyle was a renowned writer, philosopher and historian whose reputation rests chiefly on his epic works the *History of the French Revolution* (1837) and *Frederick the Great* (1858–65). In 1834 Thomas and Jane Carlyle moved into 5 (now 24) Cheyne Row in Chelsea and it remained their home until they died (Jane in 1866 and Thomas in 1881). The portrait is painted in their sitting-room there. Carlyle's dressing-gown, smoking cap and two waistcoats have survived and are in a chest-of-drawers in Jane's bedroom with one of her shawls.

Cigarette smoking had become popular for men during the Crimean War (1854–6), as tobacco was cheap in Turkey, and ladies encouraged men to adopt special caps and jackets to wear for the purpose because they objected to the smell of tobacco on their clothes. These caps (see 184), made from silk, wool or velvet, were usually in the shape of

a pillbox with a hanging tassel, and would be embroidered in a variety of colourful patterns, often Turkish. Smoking jackets were loose-fitting with a quilted silk collar and decorated with braid or frogging, and they remained in fashion until at least the end of the century. By then, according to the novelist Elinor Glyn, they had become rather opulent garments:

> When the ladies exchanged their afternoon dresses to appear at 5 o'clock in exquisite tea-gowns that were terribly expensive and very luxurious the men had also changed into equally attractive velvet smoking-suits. I remember Lord Cairns had an emerald green one, and Clayton's was sapphire blue, while Seymour Wynne Finch had one made out of a thick silk Paisley shawl with black facings. The most regal of all was that of the Grand Duke Michael [of Russia], whose suit was of rich crimson velvet.[14]

At the end of the 1840s the emphasis for women was on the increasing volume of the bell-shaped skirt, supported by multiple, starched petticoats. This arrangement had become cumbersome and uncomfortable, but it was a necessary inconvenience as the fashionable silhouette was one that combined a closely-fitting bodice with a long pointed waist, low-set sleeves and a very full skirt. By the 1850s the increased width in the skirt, achieved by wearing as many as five stiffened petticoats, including one made of horsehair, and a slight rise in the waistline had created a look that was essentially a wide-based triangle. Flounces, pinked edges, fringe decoration and a preference for lightly-patterned fabrics like roller-printed cottons and silks gave a blurred effect.

The horizontal emphasis that was demanded by fashion in the 1850s did not favour those who were short in stature. Queen Victoria's lack of height – she was 4ft 10in – and a tendency to put on weight, were not helped by her preference for fussy, tiered skirts, flounces of lace, ribbon and bows, oversized accessories and a liberal distribution of jewellery (see **179**). In 1847 Mary Elizabeth Lucy was invited to 'the ball of the Season' at the Duchess of Sutherland's house. When the Queen arrived Mary took the opportunity of observing her closely. She decided that she 'dances beautifully and is very graceful, though short and a bad figure. Her dress was white tarlatan [a stiff muslin] embroidered in colours round double skirts, with a wreath of flowers mixed with many diamonds on her head, and in her hand she carried a bouquet nearly as large as herself.'[15] Queen Victoria, with her harmonious marriage to Prince Albert and her large family, might represent a moral ideal for the nation to emulate, but her matronly short figure and her whimsical taste in clothes excluded her as a leader of fashion.

The invention in 1856 of the light-weight steel crinoline, whose bands could be sewn into a single petticoat, replaced the stiffened layers and reduced the weight of women's clothes. The 1850s and 60s were a time of economic expansion, reflected in the ever-increasing volume and solidity of female dress. Crinolines enabled the hems of ladies' skirts to attain the imposing width of some 6ft by the mid-1860s, and as they could be produced quickly and cheaply they became the first fashion to be adopted universally by all ages and classes. They were worn under every type of dress from a maid's uniform to a duchess's ball gown.

Despite the obvious fact that a crinoline made simple movements – like passing through a door, sitting on a sofa or getting in and out of a carriage – very difficult, and

185 Detail of faded green silk taffeta dress, *c.*1855, with flounces. As skirts grew wider and wider in the 1850s, their surface was enlivened by layers of flounces, often with pinked or, as in this example, scalloped edges, and they were printed *à disposition*. This flounce has a particularly elaborate pattern that combines classical cartouches and swags with Paisley patterns derived from Indian shawls.

that it could blow inside out like an umbrella in a high wind, it remained in fashion for nearly a decade. Women were impervious to *Punch*'s sustained campaign against them. When the crinoline finally went out of fashion in 1868 servants were still expected to wear one. *Punch* published the following ironic verse about the domestic hazards that the crinoline wearer could expect to encounter:

> No more ladies death will find,
> In their frames of steel calcined,
> Set on blazes by a grate without a screen;
> Though some cookmaids yet may flare,
> Who dress out, and don't take care,
> For the servants still will wear, Crinoline.[16]

The introduction of the crinoline, and the layered and multi-flounced skirt which was worn over it, influenced the style of printed fabrics in the late 1850s. Often they were printed *à disposition*, which meant that they had specially-designed border prints, one intended for the skirt flounces (185) and the other, narrower, border for the bodice. One of the most popular motifs was the Paisley pattern (see p.179) that had originally been derived from imported Indian shawls. Dress fabrics and shawls were also printed with floral and coral patterns on a light ground. Heavier-weight cottons used the discharge and resist dye process to create a shaded background on which strong geometric patterns were superimposed. The collection at Killerton contains a number of dresses from this period, including one (186) made between 1858 and 1860.

By the mid-1850s some low-crowned, wide-brimmed hats were available as an alternative to the bonnet, giving a horizontal emphasis to the head that served to balance the immense width of the skirt. Hair continued to be neatly parted in the centre and arranged either in ringlets or draped over the ears and then pulled back into a knot behind the head. This is the style favoured by Jane Carlyle in the portrait of the Carlyles painted by Robert Tait in 1857 (**187**).

Other portraits and photographs of Jane confirm that her taste in clothes was modest. She was also ill for most of her life, suffering from neuralgia and frequent states of very deep depression, which certainly affected her attitude to her appearance. Another reason for her distressed state of mind was her jealousy of her husband's intense admiration for a leading society hostess, the clever and witty Lady Harriet Ashburton, eldest daughter of the Earl of Sandwich. Jane was determined to accompany her husband to the social functions that this friendship involved them in despite the fact that she disliked them and felt uncomfortable in fashionable evening wear.

Victorian evening dress was very revealing when compared to daytime wear as the décolletage clearly showed the shoulders and its shorter sleeve length the arms. Jane had an evening dress made for a grand ball at Bath House, Lady Ashburton's residence in Piccadilly, in 1850, and she was most concerned at the thought of:

> being bare – at my age after being muffled up so many years! . . . So I got a white silk dress – which first was made high and long sleeved – and then on the very day of the ball was sent back to be cut down to the due pitch of indecency – I could have gone into fits of crying when I put it on – but I looked so astonishing well in it in the candle light, and when I got into the fine rooms amongst the universally bare people I felt so much in keeping that I forgot my neck and arms almost immediately.[17]

Fashions in the 1860s favoured the matronly figure of the older woman (**188**), and the combination of exaggerated crinolines, brash colours and shapeless mantles was too much for one French visitor, the philosopher, historian and critic Hippolyte Taine, who found that 'colours are outrageously crude and the figure ungraceful. Crinolines too hooped and badly hooped, in lumps or in geometrical cones the mantle falls shapelessly over the hips, the skirt is absurdly puffed out and the whole effect is badly chosen, badly made, badly arranged, badly put on and the loud colouring simply shrieks out . . . the glare is terrible.'[18] The Victorians' love of novelty in dress and their delight in the latest inventions resulted in widespread adoption of the vivid and often garish colours produced by chemically-made dyes – emerald green, Magenta, Solferino and 'Azuline' (see **191**). Sir William Perkin's accidental discovery of a brilliant mauve dye in 1856 had led to a whole new industry in which dyes were produced from coal tar. They were particularly effective when used on silk, and many surviving garments are a harsh colour that makes one sympathise with Taine's complaints.

During the 1860s the fashion rules for women allowed the crinoline to change its shape, becoming flatter at the front and then shrinking to a half-crinoline with half hoops at the back. The fullness of the skirt was thus concentrated behind, a shift in emphasis which can clearly be seen in a carte-de-visite of *c.*1864 (**189**) and in a very similar moiré dress of *c.*1869 (**190**). During the late 1860s tunic-dresses or double skirts

186 The brilliant striped shot silk in pale and dark blue used for this dress, made between 1858 and 1860, is indicative of the taste for brighter and harsher colour schemes prevalent at the end of the decade. The sleeves have been cut in the very popular pagoda style, which gradually flared out from the shoulder, here accentuated by contrasting bands of black velvet. A softly-pleated bodice is caught into a series of tightly-sewn horizontal gathers at the waist. The full skirt, when supported by a crinoline, would have assumed a distinctive bell shape.

187 (*left*) Jane and Thomas Carlyle in their sitting-room at Cheyne Row, Chelsea. Jane is wearing informal dress and her hair, severely parted in the centre, is looped over her ears and worn with a small lace cap. A narrow length of black lace is crossed at her throat and secured with a small silver brooch; under it is a white blouse with lace-trimmed cuffs turned back over the plain black bodice and matching skirt.

Thomas Carlyle is also in informal morning dress – in this case a dressing-gown with a red and black tartan pattern, the standing collar and necktie of formal day dress, straight-cut black trousers and soft black leather shoes. (Robert Tait, 1857, Carlyle's House)

188 (*above left*) From 1856 the crinoline had given skirts a distinctive, bell-like shape, but by the time this unknown lady was photographed, *c*.1860, it had become fan-shaped, and during the next few years attained its greatest dimensions. Trimmings on the skirt – in this example, rows of pinked flounces – continued to emphasise the strong horizontal line. Her draped bodice, decorated with three vertical tassels, has open three-quarter-length sleeves worn with white undersleeves closed at the wrist. She holds an elegant, low-crowned hat trimmed with a feather. The photograph was taken at Camille Silvy's studio (see also **182**).

189 (*above right*) In December 1864 this stylish couple were photographed in Chapple's studio in Ilminster, Somerset. He wears a velvet jacket, dark waistcoat, striped tie, checked trousers, and holds a cane. The lady's crinoline, worn under a moiré skirt, causes it to slope steeply to a rising waistline. It is worn with a very chic velvet mantle and elaborate bonnet.

190 (*below right*) A dress of brown moiré, similar to that worn by the lady in the 1864 carte-de-visite (**189**), but later in date, *c*.1869. The arrangement of complex drapery at the back of the skirt, such a feature of fashion in the 1870s, is anticipated here with a separate, but matching, apron-shaped basque, tied at the back. Muslin undersleeves throw into relief the delicate trellis-work of narrow velvet ribbon that decorates the fullish sleeves. The dress has been photographed with a man's lightweight, fine quality wool frock-coat, with the very full sleeves and lower, less defined waistline, typical of the 1860s period.

further heightened this interest in the back, and the lower skirt was often extended as a train (191).

The introduction of the walking crinoline in the 1860s (see 178 for an earlier version) must have made that particular activity a little easier. Although it still distended the skirt, the overskirt could be bunched up around the hem to reveal a shorter-length decorative petticoat, thus avoiding the necessity of trailing one's hem in the dirt and mud. As it could be worn with a loose three-quarter-length jacket it was a far more practical and useful combination than the enveloping mantle or shawl.

Technology endeavoured to keep up with all these developments and in an advertisement of 1863 the latest crinoline, the 'ondina', was described as being made from 'wave-like bands' that did away 'with the unsightly results of ordinary hoops' and so 'allow a lady to occupy a fourth seat in a carriage without inconvenience to herself or to others'.[19] Whatever type of crinoline was worn, Taine found that the motion adopted by the ladies wearing them was quite objectionable: 'their dress follows and precedes them like the ticking of a clock . . . energetic, discordant, jerking, like a piece of mechanism'.[20]

The pace of change in fashion was accelerated by the use of paper patterns. Although these had been in use in Britain from the 1830s it was an American company that realised the extent of their commercial potential. The Butterick Company opened a branch in Regent Street in 1876 when Farmer and Roger's Great Shawl and Cloak Emporium closed down and it took over their premises. The company produced 40 to 60 designs a month costing from 3d to 2s for each pattern and proving enormously successful. Fashion magazines also included paper patterns, as well as patterns for beadwork (192), woolwork, lace, knitting and crochet, for making items that could be used as fashion accessories.

The plethora of fashion magazines that appeared from the 1850s gave extremely detailed visual and written information about costumes suitable for specific times in the day and for different occasions. In the first half of the nineteenth century Mr and Mrs Bell (see pp.203–4) were the most successful husband-and-wife team publishing fashion magazines but in the second half that honour went to Mr and Mrs Beeton. Mr Beeton founded two of the most popular fashion magazines of the period, *The Englishwoman's Domestic Magazine* in 1852, and *The Queen* in 1861. A consistently high quality of fashion plates appeared in the magazines as they were purchased from the French magazine *Le Moniteur des Modes* whose chief artist, Jules David, was an outstanding illustrator (see 203). Isabella Beeton wrote the famous *Book of Household Management* – without which any Victorian home would have been incomplete. It was published in book form in 1861 but had appeared in parts in *The Englishwoman's Domestic Magazine* between 1859 and 1860. Unlike the Bells, who were aiming at the very wealthy upper class, the Beetons were catering for the requirements of the middle classes.

Once the crinoline finally disappeared in 1868 the vast skirts of the early 1860s became overskirts. These were flat in the front and looped up at the sides with the fullness drawn back over a bustle. This was originally a variant of the half-crinoline but soon became a large pad of horsehair tied around the waist with tapes. This emphasis on draping material at hip-level can be seen clearly in James Tissot's 1869 painting *The Rifle Range* (193).

Skirts with trains were overlaid with increasingly complicated arrangements of swags

191 (*left above*) By 1865 the crinoline had begun to shrink, and in December 1867, when this illustration of outdoor dress appeared in *Journal des Demoiselles*, the skirt is flat in front, with all the fullness taken to the back where it has lengthened into a train. The brilliant colours of the skirts show the improved quality and popularity of chemical dyes. Boldness of colour was matched by aggressive styles of trimming. The black velvet mantle, with its segmented sections, has bands of brown fur. Black geometric patterns draw attention to the rather angular lines of the other woman's vivid blue jacket and skirt.

192 (*left below*) A drawstring bag, called a reticule, was a practical alternative to separate hanging pockets or pockets built into the garment. Women's magazines issued embroidery patterns for bags which, when completed, could be sewn onto a ready-made frame. Patterns composed of tiny glass or metal beads were particularly popular, and sumptuous effects could be created when full-blown flowers, depicted in naturalistic tones, were set against a dark background. This bag dates from the 1850s.

193 (*right*) The stylish young lady depicted in *The Rifle Range* wears her tiny hat perched at a rather precarious angle on her chignon. The crinoline has been replaced with a looped *polonaise* overskirt and bustle, with which she wears a grey jacket printed with a dramatic black Paisley pattern and trimmed with a border of black fur. The skirts of the jacket have been pulled out and arranged in bulky folds around the hips. Under these she wears a black trained skirt, a style indicating the importance that this back section of the skirt achieved in the 1870s. (James Tissot, 1869, Wimpole Hall)

and two or three different materials trimmed with an extraordinary variety of folds, frills and pleats. From 1872 tapes were also attached inside the back of the skirt, so that they pulled the upper part into a puff in the style of the *polonaise* of the 1770s (**194**). A similar effect was created by wearing a separate overskirt draped like an apron at the front, as seen in a photograph of the Lemann family, taken in 1875 (**195**). The family left the French part of Switzerland in 1780 and settled in England, where they changed their name from Le Man to Lemann and pursued their occupation of clock-making. They were a prosperous middle-class family living in Somerfield House, near Ashford in Kent, where John Chester Earle, who was married to one of the daughters, took photographs of them over a period of years.

Fur-trimmed velvet jackets and mantles were a popular choice for outdoor dress in the late 1860s and 70s. An illustration from *The Englishwoman's Domestic Magazine*, 1870–5, features one model wearing a matching jacket and skirt of velvet trimmed with heavy fringing, whereas her companion wears a mantle cut with a box pleat centre back to accommodate the bustle-supported skirt (**196**). (See also **189** and **193**.) The mantle was a versatile garment either taking the form of a cloak or a loose-fitting wrap half-way between a coat and a cloak, with wide sleeves or armhole slits.

Such complex and fussy styles would have been inconceivable without the aid of the sewing-machine and the production of machine-made trimmings like lace, braids, fringes and ribbons, all of which were an essential part of the ultra-feminine, curvaceous silhouette of the 1870s. By the mid-1860s the mechanical sewing-machine had almost

194 (*above left*) A photograph from Elliott and Fry's studio, 1873, showing a lady in a fashionable day dress, with a square-necked jacket bodice with slightly pagoda-shaped sleeves edged with satin piping, a bow and a lace frill. Lace also forms a decorative border to the bodice and basque section on the skirt, arranged in the *polonaise* style.

195 (*above right*) The Lemann family, photographed in 1875 by John Chester Earle. The tightness of the ladies' boned bodices is so pronounced that it produces rigid creases across the waistline. Mrs Lemann is wearing mourning dress, her daughter next to her a double-apron overskirt and a matching underskirt trimmed with bands of flat ruching and pleating. This trimming is also employed on the square neckline of the bodice. Typically for this date, it is worn with a high-collared white blouse closed with a bow, over which are arranged two bead necklaces.

196 (*above*) Outdoor costume as depicted in *The English Woman's Domestic Magazine*, 1870-5, with the fringed curve of the tartan mantle echoed by the curve of the skirt underneath. The rest of the skirt has been arranged into a series of extravagant swags and points outlined with fringe. This fussiness is echoed in the hair, dressed high on the head in coils, plaits and ringlets arranged at the back, causing the hat, a concoction of ribbons, feathers and flowers, to be set at an acute angle.

197 (*right*) Detail of a matching jacket, bodice and skirt, made between 1875 and 1880 from a finely-striped taffeta, giving a relatively plain but interesting example of how a variety of trimmings were used to enhance and exaggerate the tight-fitting lines of the bodice. The jacket bodice has been seamed so that it curves into a large bow set at the centre of the back waistline. From this focal point full, box-pleated basques, trimmed with ribbon and fringe, flare out over the hips. The long sleeves narrow at the elbow, where a stiff triangle of fabric juts out, its angular shape defined by a fringe, satin ribbon and a bow.

completely replaced hand-sewing in the commercial production of clothes. It was invented in 1845 in the United States of America by Elias Howe, but it was a fellow American, Isaac Merritt Singer, who realised its enormous marketing potential. In 1851 Singer patented a version that could be readily mass-produced and in 1856 he opened the first of a series of shops throughout Britain, making his machine easily available to professional and amateur dressmakers. Customers were given the option of either buying one outright or hiring it on a weekly basis. The cost was relatively low – in 1889, for example, the latest Singer sewing-machine model cost from £4 4s 0d with ten per cent discount for cash, or it could be hired from 2s 6d a week.

A narrower silhouette appeared in 1874, introducing a sheath-like bodice which fitted over the waist and hips, thus necessitating a new style of corset. The flat effect down the front of the skirt was further enhanced by tapes inside the skirt which pulled it closer to the body. In conjunction with this tightening of the silhouette, the bustle grew smaller and was positioned lower down, where the fullness of the skirt extended into

198 A typical formal day dress of the 1870s, of pastel-coloured silk overlaid with all manner of pleating, frilling, flouncing and fringing. (Cabaillot Lassall, 1874, Hinton Ampner)

a long train. *The Ladies Treasury* commented in 1876 that the 'long trains, even for ordinary walking purposes, are universally worn, these must be held up with one hand, or thrown *à l'Amazone* over one arm'.[21] The arrangement of this veritable cascade of drapery at the back of the skirt is depicted in all its undulating extravagance in a painting, dated 1874, by the French artist Cabaillot Lassall (**198**).

The combining of contrasting materials and trimmings drew attention to the narrow vertical line that was fashionable at the end of the 1870s and in early 1880s. The new Princess style, which did not have a waist seam, further served to emphasise this effect. A delightful version of the Princess dress is worn by the three daughters of the Prince and Princess of Wales in a watercolour by H.H. Emmerson (250), painted in 1884 as part of a series to commemorate the royal visit to Cragside, Northumberland, that year. The Princess style was probably named after Princess Alexandra. She was blessed not only with beauty and an elegant figure but also with a faultless and imaginative dress sense, and once Queen Victoria had withdrawn from public life and court functions after the death of her beloved Prince Albert in 1861, the spotlight focused more and more on the Princess of Wales.

A Victorian woman was expected to be a decorative accessory whose energies should be concentrated on the running of an efficient and harmonious household, so it is not surprising that a large part of her life should be devoted to her appearance – for, as *Punch* observed in 1869, 'the typical and average woman can no more deviate from the dress of the day than an animal can choose to change its skin or its spots'.[22]

Conforming to the fashionable ideal meant that the Victorian woman had to have a tiny waist and the ideal measurement of 19in was only possible, in an age when dieting and exercise were not considered, by wearing a rigid corset laced tightly to create the desired effect. The medical profession's wholesale denunciation of tight-lacing was occasioned not only by a desire to release women from discomfort and pain but also by concern that it might impair their child-bearing potential. They also criticised the new silhouette of the 1870s, in which a pinched-in waist, a bunched-up skirt in the *polonaise* style, high-heeled shoes and boots and a piled-up *coiffure*, combined to pitch the body forward into 'The Grecian Bend' (see 198). An article in *The Lancet* in 1878 complained about 'the absurd and ungainly practice of mounting the hinder part of the feet on stilts whilst the toes press the ground and bear the weight, is one against which it is not easy to write with temper. The device of strangling the waist with tightly-laced corsets was contemptible for its ignorance; that to which we now allude is outrageous in its defiance of the laws of gravity.'[23]

There were women who refused to conform and who dared not to wear corsets or replaced them with lightly boned under-bodices – in the full knowledge that loose clothing was often equated with loose morals. This alternative mode of dress can be seen in the paintings of the Pre-Raphaelite Brotherhood, of whom Dante Gabriel Rossetti, John Everett Millais and William Holman Hunt were among the founding members (in 1848). They were inspired by the art of the Early Renaissance and its ideal natural way of life, as they perceived it, in contrast to the crass materialism and ugliness of their own industrial age. They created a style of costume with medieval influences for their female sitters, who echoed it in their daily clothes, rejecting modern fashion in favour of the 'simple and elegant' lines of the past.

Women who braved this style of dress wore loose-waisted gowns cut with wide armholes and a dropped shoulder line, so removing the discomfort caused by setting a sleeve in a fashionably low position. Dispensing with the corset, the crinoline and the fussy and elaborate trimming demanded by fashion gave them freedom of movement, but involved a rejection of high fashion that few women dared to contemplate. The ladies who later wore 'aesthetic dress', from the mid-1870s, were also a tiny and isolated

199 In common with the style adopted by Pre-Raphaelite ladies, Mrs Nassau Senior's hair is not fashionably arranged into sleek loops and ringlets, but is allowed to fall free. Her naturally-waisted, vivid violet-blue dress with its flared sleeves flows over the body, with decorative effect limited to a line of braid on the sleeves and a rich Indian cashmere cloak draped over a chair.
(George Frederic Watts, 1857–8, Wightwick Manor)

200 Lady Adelaide Talbot, Countess of Brownlow in a square-necked overdress edged with black velvet worn over a muslin chemisette threaded with narrow black ribbon. Confined at the waist only by a band of matching material, the skirt falls in voluminous folds to a darker band at the hem. An underskirt that matches this band is slightly trained. The bunched-up effect of the folds at the side of the skirt certainly suggest the fashionable *polonaise* style, but the gathering of the sleeves into a series of puffs is indicative not of high fashion, but of 'aesthetic dress'. (See also 208.)
(Frederic, Lord Leighton, 1879, Belton House)

group. They tended to be from artistic or intellectual circles and were given a critical and unsympathetic reception, accused of wearing natural-waisted dresses of 'indescribable tints'.[24] A contemporary account of an artistic 'at home' noted that 'two sad-eyed damsels' were wearing 'lank garments of white muslin, crumpled in a million creases', with two puffs on the shoulders which 'gave the impression of being dilated by an immense sigh'.[25]

An early example of these looser styles can be seen in a portrait by George Frederic Watts, painted in 1857–8, of Mrs Nassau Senior (199), a great friend of both Watts and Rossetti, and the sister of Thomas Hughes, author of *Tom Brown's Schooldays*. In 1874 she became an Inspector of Workhouses and was closely associated with the movement for women's rights. This side of her character must already have been apparent when Watts painted her portrait, as he observed that he had painted her watering flowers as an allusion to her gracious and beneficent nature. Lady Adelaide Talbot, who married

Adelbert Cust, 3rd Earl Brownlow, in 1868, was another lady who used a simple and dramatic costume to be fashionable in her own way. One of the daughters of the 18th Earl of Shrewsbury, she was thought to be the most beautiful of the three sisters, who were described in 1893 as 'the salt of the earth . . . they looked like the Three Fates'.[26] (The other two were the Marchioness of Lothian and the Countess of Pembroke.) Mary Gladstone, the Liberal leader's daughter, was enchanted in 1875 when Adelaide appeared 'at teatime today in white embroidered with gold regular toga sort of thing, and tonight with red beads, white handkerchief on head. Oh lovely!'[27] Her portrait was painted by Frederic, Lord Leighton in 1879 (200), and comparing the elegant ensemble depicted, which relies for effect on the way the lustrous silk is draped and gathered into folds, with the rigid and over-decorated styles then in vogue, it is not surprising that Mary Gladstone's immediate reaction was that it had been inspired by classical dress.

A very different fashion influence first appeared in 1876. When Madame Nicolle of 29 New Street, St Helier, Jersey, made a simple black evening gown for one of her regular customers, she could not have foreseen that all fashionable society in London would admire it, and admit the lady wearing it into their hallowed circle. When the actress Lillie Langtry made her triumphant entry into Lady Sebright's drawing room she was 'in deep mourning' for her beloved brother Reggie, who had died some months before. Wearing her modest gown with 'no jewels . . . and with my hair twisted carelessly on the nape of my neck in a knot'[28] was a matter of necessity, as it was her only evening dress. But the 'meagreness of my wardrobe' did not stop everyone from wanting to copy her clothes and the way she wore them. As a contemporary poem put it:

> She's a lovely lady in a plain black gown
> She isn't very rich but she's taken all the Town:
> London Society has gone quite silly
> Fallen at the feet of the Jersey Lily.
> There's the Langtry this and the Langtry that,
> The Langtry bonnet and the Langtry hat
> The Langtry slipper and the Langtry shoes
> Langtry purple and Langtry blue.[29]

Lillie was an astute businesswoman, and when she became a Professional Beauty she made sure that she profited from the huge demand for photographs showing her wearing the latest fashions.[30] Her 'exquisite purity of complexion' was another asset, and she was used by Pears to promote their soap and endorse their product, with the slogan 'for years I have used your soap, and no other'. Frances (Daisy), Countess of Warwick, said of her: 'She had dewy violet eyes, a complexion like a peach. How can words convey the vitality, the glow, the amazing charm that made this fascinating woman the centre of any group she entered.'[31] She met the Prince of Wales at a dinner party in 1877 and became his mistress.

Lillie's pursuit of an independent and intensely active life marks her out from her contemporaries and, as the poem implies, she initiated many fashions, the most important being the 'Jersey Costume'. This was a close-fitting, long-sleeved garment of knitted silk or wool that swathed the figure from a high round neck to well below the hips and was worn over a tight tie-back skirt pleated all round from the knee (201).

201 *Punch*'s version of the 'Jersey Costume', popularised by Lillie Langtry, exaggerates its figure-hugging tightness.

202 (*right*) Unlike many less formal garments, this wedding dress has survived in excellent condition because it was so carefully stored away. It was made in 1880 by a skilful dressmaker who used the cream grosgrain to create a beautifully-shaped bodice and matching skirt with a spectacular train, worn over a bustle, decorated with serrated ruching. The bodice has been boned so that it is shaped into the waist to curve into a deep point at the centre. Typically for the 1880s, the bodice is closely buttoned up the front to the throat and is finished with a small standing collar edged with a frill, while a Honiton lace frill finished the narrow sleeves. It has been photographed with a bridal veil also of Honiton lace, delicately and exquisitely patterned with roses, and a typical head-dress of the period – a circlet of apple blossom and leaves made from wax.

203 (*left*) This 1887 fashion-plate of walking dress is by Jules David. He worked for *Le Moniteur de la Mode* from 1843 until his death fifty years later, and was one of the first illustrators to place figures in a highly detailed rather than an impressionistic setting. The silhouette produced by the bustle could only be fully appreciated when the figure was seen in profile, presenting the artist with the problem of how to show the front view of the ensemble. David and other illustrators endeavoured to solve this by twisting the body at an unnatural and awkward angle.

204 (*right*) Detail of a short mantle dating from the 1880s. The edges of the border have been left unbound so that the threads create a brilliantly coloured fringe. The total effect is a gorgeous kaleidoscope of colour, pattern and texture. It is also an interesting example of fashion recycling – turning an accessory that was no longer fashionable, in this case an 1860s shawl, into a useful and eye-catching garment.

The tight, narrow silhouette of the late 1870s continued into the 1880s, but the trained, tie-back skirt was eventually dispensed with, although a train was retained for evening and formal wear (202). With hems rising slightly, this left the skirt as a straight tube of material, often encrusted with horizontal bands of ruching and pleating. Variations were created by draping the skirt and the underskirt and by wearing bodices with an attached overskirt almost as long as the underskirt. As almost every dress had some drapery across the skirt none was perfectly symmetrical, and each side presented a quite different aspect. The overall effect of all this draping and swathing was a somewhat severe one, due to the fact that the fabrics were much firmer and the pleated edgings attached to them – including collars – much stiffer than the soft ruffles and flounces of the 1870s.

In the 1880s an even more artificial shape was made possible by the reintroduction of the bustle which dominated the silhouette of that decade. It was a narrow angular construction often made of small steel hoops which could project the back of the skirt for as much as two feet behind the wearer. An advertisement for an American 'braided wire' bustle boasted that it was recommended by leading doctors because it placed less stress on the spine than another model. But whatever model was chosen, it must have been an extremely cumbersome thing to wear. Formal day and trained evening dresses had elaborately frilled skirts that were draped over the bustle, and complex and sturdy corsetry was required to make the tight-fitting bodices look as if they were moulded to the upper half of the body (see 203).

Lord Ernest William Hamilton, son of the 1st Duke of Abercorn, did not approve of the bustle and wrote: 'A more extraordinary distortion of the human form is not easy to conceive. As though in protest against Nature's niggardly dole, large wicker panniers were pinned on where, to the ordinary eye, any such addition would seem to have been least called for.'[32]

The mantle retained its popularity as a garment for outdoor wear throughout this period. It could be made from a variety of materials in a number of styles. One made in the early 1880s (204) is particularly beautiful and unusual as it has been made from a fine woollen shawl that was probably originally from Kashmir. It has also been designed to accommodate the bustle.

Despite the artificiality of the bustle, the general trend during the 1880s was towards simpler styles, with the most important fashion innovation being the tailor-made suit. Although women had worn close-fitting plain suits for riding since the eighteenth century, the demand for women's emancipation was gathering momentum and the new activities that women were able to take part in demanded less restrictive clothing.

In the 1880s the Rational Dress Society, founded by Viscountess Harberton, endeavoured to promote a style of dress for women based on 'considerations of health, comfort and beauty'. Contemporary fashion was rejected because it 'impedes the movement of the body' and made 'healthy exercise almost impossible'.[33] Viscountess Harberton believed that a divided skirt would be the perfect garment for a woman who wanted to enjoy sports like tennis and yachting, but when this idea was announced to the public it was greeted with universal mirth. A poem printed in *Punch* in 1883 entitled *The Rational Dress Show* was derisive:

> See gowns hygienic, and frocks calisthenic,
> And dresses quite worthy a modern burlesque;
> With garments for walking, and tennis, and talking,
> All terribly manful and too trouseresque.[34]

205 Gertrude Hussey in a photograph taken at Scotney Castle, *c*.1890–5. She is wearing a 'tailor-made' to walk her dogs. She also sports a rather flamboyant tie and a tweed cap – another accessory from the male wardrobe.

By 1889, however, the 'tailor-made', originally informal outdoor dress, had become fashionable morning wear. It consisted of an untrimmed matching fitted jacket and gored A-line skirt and was usually made from wool. It must have seemed wonderfully comfortable after the bustles, trains and swags of drapery of the previous decade. Often it was worn over a blouse with an uncomfortably high stiff collar and could be combined with masculine accessories such as waistcoats, neckties and straw sailor hats, making it popular for outdoor activities (205). (See also 220 and 228.) A smart and efficient-looking ensemble, it perfectly suited the 'New Woman', a term coined by *Punch* to describe women who worked for their living (mostly teaching and office work) and were determined to have a more active physical and intellectual life. The 'New Woman' of the 1890s was also keen to show that she was the equal of any man and during this decade the first international ladies' hockey match took place (1897) and the Original Ladies' Cricketer Club (1890) and the Ladies' Golf Union (1893) were formed. In 1894 the bicycle gave women mobility, an important and crucial asset in their pursuit of independence.

There had been a number of attempts by women throughout the nineteenth century to devise a form of trousered dress, in the belief that they could only attain equal status with men if both sexes wore similar clothes. But when the American Amelia Jenks Bloomer attempted to promote a radical costume of dress and pantaloons in Britain in 1851 it was greeted with such universal derision by the press and the general public that it actually harmed the cause of women's political and social emancipation. However, as the bicycling craze swept the country in the 1890s, a few daring ladies wore divided skirts in the form of voluminous knickerbockers – described by George G. Harper in 1895 as 'Bloomerism with a difference'. They too appear to have been an American invention as the name is the same as that given to New Yorkers descended from the original Dutch settlers, who were perceived to have worn something similar. The *Lady Cyclist* magazine endeavoured to campaign for dress reform, pointing out that 'conditions of a living death will never be removed until the corsets, banded skirts and petticoats, irrational footgear and other errors in clothing are abandoned'.[35]

Although the liberated 'New Woman' of the 1890s was able to indulge in more sporting activities, the fashionable female silhouette tightened up in the 1890s. In 1889 Miss Florence Woolward, 'a talented painter of flowers and birds', went to Peter Robinson's Mourning Warehouse in Oxford Street where she bought a formal afternoon dress in the colours of half-mourning (206). By this date the bustle had disappeared and although the dress still had a train, attention was now focused on the shoulders and sleeves, which had a distinct puff where they were fitted into the armhole. During the 1890s that puff grew steadily until it attained the hugely swollen shape so similar to the gigot sleeves of the 1830s.

The etiquette of mourning was an incredibly complicated issue throughout the Victorian period, and many women turned to the magazine editors for advice about what they should be wearing and for how long. On the occasion of the death of a member of the Royal Family an announcement of court and national mourning would be made, and those who could afford them would rush off to the mourning warehouses to buy new outfits. (A dress of the quality and style of Miss Woolward's would have cost between four and five guineas.) The length of time that mourning was observed would be determined by the closeness of the deceased to the sovereign. In December 1861, when it looked certain that the Prince Consort's illness would prove fatal, Mr Jay worked the staff of his Mourning Warehouse, the biggest and most stylish in London, round the clock in readiness for the publication of the order for court and general mourning. *The Illustrated London News* of 28 December 1861 commented that the 'late melancholy event which has plunged the nation into so deep and lasting regret has, as may be imagined, created an almost incalculable demand for mourning', and it advised its readers that suitable materials for outdoor mourning dress are 'cashmere, paramatta [a dress fabric of wool and cotton or silk] and merino. . . . For ball costumes, dresses of black tulle, or crape over black silk. . . . Mourning pocket handkerchiefs are frequently embroidered in black or violet, and have no trimming of lace.'[36]

The death of Queen Victoria, in 1901, occurred at a particularly inopportune time for the drapery industry – the first day of household linen sales. This meant that the shop windows were full of white linen, and an employee of Dickins & Jones remembers that 'by the next morning everything was turned to black – it was one of the biggest transformations in the history of the trade. Everything that could be dyed was used to meet the colossal demand.'[37]

The last widespread display of court and general mourning occurred on the death of Edward VII in 1910, when the London shops 'were literally besieged from morning to night' as ladies chose the appropriate black dresses and hats.[38] Fashion was so affected by this widespread adoption of mourning dress that Ascot, an important event in the social calendar, was immediately dubbed 'Black Ascot'. Two ten-year-old girls, Victoria Dane, a goddaughter of Queen Victoria, and Sonia Keppel, whose mother Alice had been the King's mistress, found that his death had an immediate impact on their daily routine. Sonia recalled that: 'A pall of darkness hung over the house. Blinds were drawn, lights were dimmed, and black clothes appeared, even for me, with black ribbons threaded through my underclothes.'[39] Victoria was 'put into full mourning, a black coat and skirt, until the Court mourning was over, Aged ten! If you were anything official, which Father was, you had to go into full mourning, black lines round the writing paper and all that sort of thing, and the children had to too.'[40]

The contents of a widow's wardrobe were carefully regulated according to three periods of mourning. The first, and most intense, period, also called 'deep mourning', lasted twelve months and a day, when the widow wore a dull black bombazine (a twilled material of worsted mixed with cotton or silk) dress entirely covered with black crape, a stiff fabric with a crinkly surface which quickly lost its intense black lustre. When indoors the widow wore a white crape cap with streamers down the back, and outdoors she wore a black crape bonnet trimmed with long crape veils. No part of mourning dress should shine or gleam, nor could one wear a white collar and cuffs, white gloves or underwear, or even white fur.

The quality and extent of someone's mourning wardrobe proclaimed their social status, so buying a new outfit was an expensive business. In 1887, for example, the most 'economical' widow's dress at Peter Robinson's Mourning Warehouse cost £2 19s 6d, and this was made from Borada crape, a cheap mourning fabric. According to the magazines, a complete wardrobe for first mourning would have to include two dresses, one mantle, one jacket and a wide range of accessories from a summer parasol to a winter muff, both covered with crape. So it is not surprising that widows would place advertisements in magazines like *Exchange and Mart* (first published in 1868) in the hope that they could sell their old mourning clothes to other newly-widowed women who, in turn, would want to sell their coloured clothes. A lady from Gloucestershire, for example, placed an advertisement in *Exchange and Mart* in 1889 offering: 'New rich soft black silk dress trimmed deep lace flouncing handsome jet embroidery etc. Suit tall stout lady, Court dressmaker worth 11 guineas take half cash. Deep mourning.'[41] A lady from Sussex put an advertisement in a 1905 edition of the magazine for what must have been a cape worn during the second period of mourning: 'Widow's smart new three-quarter corded silk cape, lined silk, trimmed deep crape, storm collar. Cost 5 guineas, will accept 50 shillings.'[42] This period lasted a further nine months, and although the widow was no longer entirely encased in crape it was still applied to the surface of her black dress and her headwear in a variety of decorative ways. Surfaces could also be enlivened by the addition of jet trimmings, and black silk fabrics were permitted, though these should not be too shiny.

After two years a widow could wear half-mourning and the length of this third period lasted from six months to a lifetime depending on the choice of the individual. She could

206 A formal afternoon dress (see also 233) in the colours of half-mourning, bought in 1889. The matching bodice and skirt are of black figured silk patterned with a silver cream/grey willow-leaf design that gleams as it catches the light. The cuirasse-style bodice is buttoned down the front and has a short stand-up collar, a pointed waistline and four weighted basque tabs at the back. The elegant train is padded and has a machine-made lace frill.

now wear the fashions of the day, but made up in special half-mourning colours which included shades of grey and soft mauves. The journalist Henry Mayhew, describing some half-mourning fabrics he had seen in Jay's Mourning Warehouse, shows that these could comprise some very subtle shades and combinations of colour: 'Delicate shades of slate-colour, grey mauve and purple, and a certain delicate robe of the palest violet tint fairly frosted with crystal spots.'[43]

The severity of mourning dress worn by men, on the other hand, diminished in the nineteenth century. In the previous century chief male mourners at a funeral would have worn enveloping black cloth mourning cloaks and black hatbands with 'weepers' of material that fell down the back. But by 1860 these cloaks were only worn by the undertaker and his men and 'weepers' were gradually discarded. Male mourners wore black, sometimes white, sashes across their left shoulders and black crape hatbands. By 1900 the only distinctive sign that a man had been bereaved was a black armband.

Trends in male fashion in general were echoing those in female fashion towards the end of the nineteenth century. Men too were benefitting from a move to greater informality in daytime wear:

> The tweed-suit fashion was probably the greatest break-away from established tradition in the history of dress. . . . Before the 1850s, country dress was no more than a mild modification of town dress, formal and absurdly unsuited to the negotiation of 'moor and fen or crag and torrent'. . . . It was quickly recognised that tweeds – or at any rate, something weatherproof and serviceable – were an almost necessary corollary to the new sporting ardour which, at that time, swept over Society. . . . The new sporting tweeds were worn, not only for shooting, but in a modified form for ordinary country house purposes.[44]

The Prince of Wales was a prime mover behind the rationalisation of the male wardrobe. He informed male guests on his country estate at Sandringham in Norfolk that they no longer needed to change four times a day, but to limit their clothes to shooting tweeds in the morning and evening dress at night, He also devised a new shooting suit, asking his tailors to create a fuller style of jacket that would not impede his arms when aiming a gun. They came up with the Norfolk jacket. Made of a heavy wool tweed, it had a distinctive box pleat at the centre back and large patch pockets on each front, concealed vertical breast pockets and a matching belt. The Prince wore it with tweed knickerbockers and the ensemble then became a Norfolk suit, a comfortable, warm and hard-wearing outfit for country and sporting wear. Knickerbockers were a fuller version of knee-breeches and both garments could also be teamed with a jacket in the lounge suit style, giving a suit in checked woollen material or tweed. These variations can be seen in a photograph of a shooting party taken on the Saltram estate in Devon in 1894 (207). A day's shooting was normally part of a country house weekend. The men in the party would start out at 10.30am, breaking for an alfresco lunch, when they would be joined by the ladies, who would either remain for the afternoon, as spectators, or return to the relative warmth of the house. The greatest coup for the host and hostess of a country house party was the presence of the Prince and Princess of Wales, which would be recorded for posterity by a photograph of all the guests stiffly posed on the front steps of the house.

207 The men enjoying a shooting party at Saltram in 1894 are all wearing tweed, either breeches or knickerbockers, with heavy stockings and gaiters – garments that have been 'borrowed' from the working-man's wardrobe. The ladies are sporting stout walking shoes and ankle-length tweed skirts – with fitted jackets, as worn by the lady on the left of the group, or with a looser, longer-length jacket like the one on the right.

Sir William Armstrong, a leading industrialist, decided to commemorate the visit of the Prince and Princess of Wales to his house, Cragside, in Northumberland, in August 1884 by commissioning the artist H.H. Emmerson to paint a series of watercolours, including a portrait of the Prince sitting on the terrace against the dramatic scenery of the landscaped hillside (2). (See also 250.) The Prince expected those in his circle to observe every detail of dress etiquette and he was quick to admonish those who did not. But his love of food meant that he put on a great deal of weight over the years and this led to two sartorial innovations. In 1895 he modified the frock-coat by leaving it to hang open, or to be held by two linked buttons, and later he left the bottom button of his waistcoat undone. This seemingly minor detail of dress was copied and it 'became an all-important social message', implying that one was a member of his inner circle.[45]

The importance of being correctly dressed was not new, but during the Victorian era it was socially disastrous to be inappropriately dressed. It was essential, therefore, to be conversant with the minutiae of the etiquette of dress to gain access to the right social set. Applications to the Lord Chamberlain's Office for presentation at court were carefully scrutinised. Divorcees and the 'wives and daughters of general practitioners . . . solicitors . . . merchants . . . men in business (excepting bankers)' were excluded. Those who belonged to 'aristocratic professions' – that is, the clergy, military and naval officers, physicians and barristers – would be considered, together with the country gentry and, of course, the nobility. The social cachet of presentation was such that the number of applications steadily increased through Queen Victoria's reign. By the end of the century it has been estimated that some 4,000 families were actively involved in the London 'season' and sometimes as many as 3,000 people would be crammed into the Drawing Rooms of Buckingham Palace. For a girl of 17 or 18 presentation at court marked the beginning of her adult life, as it allowed her to enter into fashionable society and take part in a hectic social calendar in the hope of finding a suitable husband. If she was successful, a second presentation would occur after marriage.

Those who had acquired wealth by being 'in trade' were denied the ultimate social triumph and affirmation of status – presentation at court and admittance to court circles – so they compensated by formulating their own version of court etiquette in the hope of acquiring an added social distinction and privileged status. Thus, the wives of the *nouveaux riches* would organise 'a social round hopefully based on the aristocratic practice. Every nuance of Court etiquette was endlessly probed in the new middle-class women's magazines. Every fad and fashion of the aristocratic world was produced as carefully as possible in middle-class homes. The women, in order to be ladies, had to be kept in a state of obvious idleness – they could not possibly be allowed to work.'[46]

This enforced idleness for Victorian women was only enlivened by frequent changes of dress, a complex procedure occurring at least three or four times in the day. Morning was the time for household and domestic duties, so a fashionable but fairly plain outfit would be worn. Afternoon visiting required a more formal dress. To make a 'morning call', one would visit between three and four o'clock and stay for precisely a quarter of an hour. This was an entirely formal visit, signifying the desire of the visitor to pursue the acquaintance of the lady of the house and to be put onto her guest list. A call made between four and five o'clock was of a slightly less formal nature, and a call made after five o'clock was altogether more friendly, though even then it was not the equivalent of an invitation to a tea party (which started at 5pm and where formal clothes would be worn), as this required greater intimacy before it was offered or accepted.

On returning home the fashionable lady changed again for dinner, a meal taken in the evening. Further distinctions were made between an evening dress that could be worn to a dinner party or to the theatre, and a ball dress, which would have had a far more revealing neckline. Add to these outfits the separate costumes required for walking in town and country and at the seaside and, later in the century, for activities such as tennis, bicycling, skating and boating, and it is apparent that fashion magazines and illustrations must have been an invaluable source of information. The magazines also contained articles on deportment, etiquette and the right and wrong way to wear certain garments.

Ladies on a four-day visit to a country house could not wear the same dress twice and so would have required at least twelve to sixteen complete ensembles. When they returned from the shooting party, the next highlight of the day would be the five o'clock tea party, for which they would change into a tea-gown. First introduced in the late 1870s, this was an informal, unboned garment that gave relief from the restrictive daytime fashions. One variation of the style was in the form of an overdress with a loose under tunic which, because it was unwaisted, did not need to be worn over a corset. It became more elaborate in the 1880s and by the end of the decade could be worn as an informal dinner dress. Lavish creations of silk and lace selling at between four and six guineas were available in shops like Harrods and Liberty's, where Alice Fane, the wife of the 4th Marquess of Bristol, bought one in 1897 (208). Its unusual 'greenery-yallery' colours and soft, clinging materials are typical of aesthetic taste, in complete contrast to the harsh colours and strident patterned fabrics then in fashion. ('Greenery-yallery' is a quote from the Gilbert and Sullivan opera *Patience* (1881), a deliberate satire on the

208 The bodice of this 1897 Liberty tea-gown has been made from green satin, its hanging sleeves, yoke and girdle are moss-green velvet. The typically puffed inner sleeves, neck ruching and hem are sky-green chiffon. The velvet has been trimmed with marguerite-style flowers, composed of topaz and beads.

Aesthetic Movement. The term came to mean the gentle, muted colours favoured by the movement.) The relative simplicity of the line and shape of aesthetic dress and its soft muted shades had a beneficial effect on the production of textiles, as the style required pure fabrics that would drape well. (See also pp.229–31.)

After tea everyone changed into formal evening dress, which for men was a tail coat, black waistcoat and white tie. Dinner jackets became common in the 1880s and were, according to Lord Hamilton, 'a mushroom product of Manchester and Birmingham, at first despised but, afterwards, universally blessed'. They first appeared on the 'provincial scene' before making their way into the wardrobes 'of the illustrious'.[47] Ladies' evening dresses in the late 1880s and early 90s were characterised by a V-shaped or heart-shaped décolletage and minimal sleeves, a swathed bodice and trained skirts. Hair was arranged in a small curly fringe and a knot on the top of the head and could be decorated with a flower or feather trimming. The style is illustrated in a portrait painted in 1891 by the French painter Carolus-Duran of the Hon. Mrs Ronnie Greville (**209**), a renowned London Society hostess who became the chatelaine of Polesden Lacey in Surrey in 1905. She was described by her goddaughter Sonia Keppel as resembling 'a small Chinese idol with eyes that blinked'.[48]

The new fashion magazine *Vogue*, first published in America in 1892, was particularly interested in the wardrobes of Society women, the most newsworthy being those American heiresses who had married into the British aristocracy. One of these was the great beauty and fashion leader, Mary Leiter, who married George Curzon, later Marquess Curzon of Kedleston, in 1895. Three years later she accompanied him to India when he became Viceroy. Mary was one of the Society beauties sketched by the American illustrator and cartoonist Charles Dana Gibson to celebrate the ideal of the well-bred American woman. Mary had arrived in England in 1890 wearing the stylish 'Gibson Girl' look, which comprised a crisp 'tailor-made', a blouse with a stiff-collared shirt and tie and a boater perched at a jaunty angle on top of carelessly swept-up hair. The archetypal 'Gibson Girl' had a great influence on American fashion as she 'was the first great American glamour girl long before there were movie stars' and 'personified the spirit of the new century',[49] being an intelligent and independent female who could play golf and tennis and cycle with equal skill and enthusiastic *joie de vivre*.

When Mary visited London in 1890 she was introduced to a very different social set. At her first dinner party she met some of 'The Souls', a close circle of aristocratic friends – brilliant and serious – sharing mutual interests in literature and art and entertaining each other at their famous country-house weekend parties. The group included, amongst others: A. J. Balfour, the future Conservative Prime Minister; Margot Tennant, later wife of the Liberal Prime Minister, Herbert Asquith; Lord Curzon; the beautiful Violet Granby, later Duchess of Rutland; the Earl and Countess of Brownlow (see p.231); the Earl's cousin Harry Cust; and Lord and Lady Desborough. When Mary Leiter first met the Countess of Brownlow she wrote that she was 'one of the most noble women. . . . She has the beauty of an Empress.'[50]

The ladies, clad in 'long draperies and pleated dresses',[51] signalled membership of their exclusive group by wearing 'bay leaves fastened by paste brooches'.[52] This very feminine, lacy style of dress retained all the romantic and picturesque features of aesthetic dress and it was clearly distanced from what had become middle-class fashion.

209 The Hon. Mrs Ronnie Greville wearing a sumptuous deep pink velvet coat with a deep brown fur border and cape over her black velvet evening bodice and skirt, which is heavily boned and pointed. The décolletage is masked by a draped white fichu. The arrangement of the drapery, and her slightly twisted pose, are suggestive of the sweeping curves and contrapposto that were to become such a pronounced feature in the Edwardian period. (Emile-Augustus Carolus-Duran, 1891, Polesden Lacey)

Mary Leiter and George Curzon met at one of the Brownlows' country house week-ends at Ashridge Park in Hertfordshire, and married at Curzon's family home, Kedleston Hall in Derbyshire in 1895. After they were married Mary changed her style of dress to please her husband and her perky 'Gibson Girl' look was replaced by one that was more suitable to her elevated status in society. The ladies in Mary's wedding photograph are all wearing the fashion of the early 1890s (210). Skirts were plain – drapery and ornamentation having disappeared with the bustle – and they were pulled tightly to a small waist, flaring over the hips. Any fullness in the skirt was taken to the back. The innovatory technique of building a skirt from segments of a circle gave it a flared shape and this made it much easier to wear than the narrow, restrictive styles of previous years. Attention was directed to the top half of the body: huge jacket sleeves – called 'leg of mutton' – were hard and formal and, when worn with massive revers, obliterated the lines of the body. Elaborate dress blouses and bodices were worn under the tailored jackets, and bodices were often cut and draped to look like jackets. Dresses and blouses were made with a high standing collar that tightly encased the neck and was topped with a small frill, often fastened with a brooch, and a lace jabot was a popular accessory with a blouse (see 216 and 227). The width of the upper half of the body was balanced by wide-brimmed hats, encrusted with all manner of artificial flowers, feathers, ruchings and ribbons. Hair-styles were severe, with no fringe and the hair scraped back into a bun.

Towards the end of the 1890s this angular and masculine style of female fashion, with its wide sleeves, narrow waists and heavily-boned, high-collared blouses, began to relax. A more fluid silhouette emerged: hair was softened by being swept up over pads, bodices were padded and pouched at the front to give a new dimension and the sleeve subsided, leaving a residual puff at the shoulder. This style is illustrated by the clothes worn by the younger ladies in a photograph taken in August 1898 at the coming-of-age of Viscount Boringdon, later 4th Earl of Morley, of Saltram in Devon (211).

210 (*left*) The wedding of George Curzon and Mary Leiter at Kedleston Hall in 1895. All the ladies in the photograph wear the fashionable 'leg of mutton' sleeve and wide-brimmed, heavily decorated hats. The three standing to the left of the bride show how elaborate the dress blouses and bodices worn under tailored jackets could be.

211 (*right*) In comparison, the young ladies in this 1898 photograph taken at Saltram are wearing the softer lines of the draped and tucked bodices and skirts, cut to fit more closely over the hips to flare out from below the knees.

212 A black velvet evening dress, *c*.1899, with swags of black net decorated with a myriad of diamanté and spangles. Such dresses must have looked beautiful in candlelight.

Like day dresses, evening skirts were also flared and were made with a train which had to be held up when dancing. The ladies must have looked magnificent in their low-cut and opulent gowns, such as a black velvet evening dress made *c*.1899 (**212**). But the novelist Elinor Glyn, who was to become George Curzon's mistress, recalled that as one did not wear coats or scarves over them, 'you became absolutely frozen by draughts in passages, even when the rooms themselves were not horribly cold', when moving around in an unheated country house, though a guest fortunate enough to be staying at Easton Hall, Essex, the home of Frances (Daisy), Countess of Warwick, would be provided with a corsage to pin onto her evening gown, a 'magnificent spray of gardenias, stephanotis or orchids, as it was the fashion to wear these long sprays in those day'.[53] Display of rank in costume and jewellery was expected, and it would have been considered an insult to the hostess if one was not arrayed with a suitably impressive selection of the family's jewels. An ostrich-feather fan and long gloves were other essential accessories, the latter would be taken off during the course of the meal and replaced at the end of it. At a country-house weekend, when everyone had assembled for dinner the 'guests went in to dinner arm in arm, according to rank the first night, but less formally afterwards'.[54]

When Queen Victoria died in 1901 Edward VII came to the throne at the age of 59 and reigned for only nine years. In the brief but opulent Edwardian age, ladies' dress attained new heights of sheer femininity. Cecil Beaton's earliest memory – he was born in 1904 – was of ladies 'laced into corsets that gave them pouter-pigeon bosoms and protruding posteriors. Perched on their heads, and elevated by a little roll just inside the crown, were hats which had grown as frivolous as the milliner's trade could make them – enormous galleons of grey velvet with vast grey plumes of ostrich feathers sweeping upwards and outwards, or they would be trimmed with artificial flowers and fruit.'[55]

The curves of Art Nouveau, a late-nineteenth-century movement typified by orna- mented and flowing naturalistic designs, insinuated themselves into women's fashion and the female form was trained into a distinct S-shape (see **217**). This shape is apparent in the pose adopted in portraits, such as John Singer Sargent's painting of the American Nancy Astor (**213**). Exhibited at the Royal Academy in 1909, it portrays Nancy as a 'tall and willowy beauty – whereas in fact she was very short. Despite her size though, Nancy was extremely beautiful.'[56] Women needed to be fairly tall and statuesque if they were not going to be swamped by a fashion which emphasised height by means of swept-up hair worn over artificial pads, plumed hats, puffed shoulders and narrow costumes composed of a series of undulating curves.

Rigorous corsetry was required to create this curvaceous look, achieved by means of an extra-long flat-fronted corset, boned so that it threw the hips back and bust forward. This was an elaborate process which is described in Vita Sackville-West's novel, *The Edwardians* (1930), set at Knole, her ancestral home in Kent. The maid Buttons is dressing her mother:

> Buttons knelt before her, carefully drawing the silk stockings on to her feet and smoothing them nicely up the leg. Then [her mother] would rise, and, standing in her chemise, would allow the maid to fit the long stays of pink coutil [a strong cotton fabric], heavily boned, round her hips and slender figure, fastening the busk down the front, after many adjustments; then the suspenders would be clipped to the stockings; then the lacing would follow, beginning at the waist and travelling gradually up and down, until the necessary proportions had been achieved. The silk laces and their tags would fly out, under the maid's deft fingers with the flick of the skilled worker mending a net. Then the pads of pink satin would be brought, and fastened into place on the hips and under the arms still further to accentuate the smallness of the waist.[57]

Day dress was a delicious concoction of delicate silk chiffons and crêpes in soft pastel shades overlaid with yards of fine lace, embellished with embroidery and trimmings, and fashioned into frothy high-necked gowns, as in a 1902 portrait of Mrs Julius Drewe by Charles Hardie (**214**). Hair was swept up and piled on top of the head in a series of luxuriant waves and worn with 'enormous over-trimmed hats which were fixed to the armature of one's puffed-out hair by long and murderous pins'.[58]

213 Lady Astor's evening dress, with billowing sleeves of soft gauzy chiffon and a floating pink stole, appears to be of a relatively simple construction. The bodice, however, would have been heavily boned and worn over a corset of complicated design that pulled in the waist and forced it to slope further in front, so that the bust appeared to overhang the stomach. An extremely low neckline front and back revealed the shoulders and bosom in all their opulent glory.
(John Singer Sargent, 1909, Cliveden)

214 Mrs Julius Drewe wearing a suitably picturesque day dress. It has a striped, transparent gauze overskirt with a deep flounce at the hem, and both it and the underskirt have been cut with additional fullness at the back to form a short train. The high-necked bodice has a V-shaped flounce which falls in soft folds over the shoulders and chest. A black sash draws attention to her tiny waist.
(Charles Hardie, 1902, Castle Drogo)

215 This photograph was taken at Montacute House in 1905, when the house was leased to the Ponsonby family, and records Cricket Week in August. Apart from Molly Ponsonby, who holds a camera, the ladies wear wide-brimmed straw hats with blouses and skirts. The men, all bare-headed, look relaxed in their informal clothes, easy-fitting lounge jackets with narrow lapels and single-breasted fastening, light-coloured trousers and shirts with a knotted tie.

The Edwardian age, described by Vita Sackville-West's son, Nigel Nicolson, as being one of 'fevered luxury', was also one in which society's strict dress code was still rigorously maintained and there was a clear division between the way the classes dressed. Even when enjoying a 'cricket week', a very popular country-house entertainment during the summer season, the male participants had to wear their clothes in a particular way (**215**). On the day of the game the men who were playing would change from their 'country clothes' into 'flannels in a tent erected on the cricket ground. Every player had to wear flannel trousers and a flannel shirt, buttoned at the neck and finished off with a small bow tie. Round the waist there had to be either a belt or a sash. A player appearing in a shirt open at the throat would have caused widespread consternation among the ladies.'[59]

The figure of the substantial, well-corseted Edwardian lady was assembled, rather than dressed, with jewels, lace and embroidery. Everything she wore was fragile and of the highest possible quality – purchased, if her husband could afford it, from Paris. Paris was incontestably the centre of fashion again and the elegant salons of the French couture houses were a Mecca for fashionable women all over the world (see also p.265). Of the ten leading couture houses in Paris in 1900 four were run by women, one of whom, Madame Paquin, was president of the fashion section of the Great Universal Exhibition of 1900, while the 'Callot Soeurs' offered their customers unashamed

FASHIONS DE LUXE
AUTUMN 1907

A BOOK OF INTEREST TO LADIES.
Price 6⁰

216 (*left*) The Baroness de Bush, mother of Paulise (see **6**), wearing an elaborate afternoon toilette, *c*.1901. This comprised a fur-lined mantle and bolero-style jacket over a lace-trimmed, high-necked blouse, and a dramatically-trimmed skirt that fitted smoothly over the hips but became fuller at the back, where it extended into a train. Complex decorative effects were created by the application of boldly-patterned lace, embroidery and *passementerie* – a handmade trimming purchased by the yard or by the motif.

217 (*right*) It was inevitable that fashion illustrators would want to exaggerate the S-bend silhouette that resulted when corsetry pushed the bosom forward whilst the hips were thrust back. The evening dress featured in the Autumn 1907 edition of *Fashions de Luxe* has a deep V-shaped bodice disclosing a lace under-bodice and corsage. From a miniscule waist, the profuse folds of the trained skirt sweep smoothly over the hips and bottom. The ruche-encrusted edges of the skirt frame an underskirt patterned with a delicate trailing motif.

femininity and luxury, as their creations were made out of old fabrics and lace. Of the others Jacques Doucet was renowned for the exquisite delicacy and subtlety of its designs, which were executed primarily in the soft pastel tints of the eighteenth century. Opulence was the keynote of the house of Worth, described by a contemporary as a 'veritable Temple of Fashion', which passed on the death of its founder, the Englishman, Charles Frederick Worth, in 1895 to his son Jean-Paul, who made 'clothes which were marvels of art and purity'. Only the very wealthy, such as Lady Curzon, could afford to visit Worth's luxuriously-appointed salon and fitting rooms, where an evening gown could cost many hundreds, even thousands, of pounds. A concoction of delicate tulle, silk flowers, spangles and fine gauze might only be worn once or twice, as 'one damp journey home and its pristine freshness would have been transformed into a limp rag'.[60]

Voluptuousness was the keynote for evening, and the sensuous effect of a satin evening dress worn with pearl jewellery is described by Vita Sackville-West in *The Edwardians*: 'Oyster satin flowing out at her feet, pearls vanishing into the valley between her breasts, pearls looped round her wrists, a rosy scarf tossed round her shoulders.'[61] Edwardian evening dress was made from 'spangled chiffon, filigree-embroidered tulle, veils, billowing ostrich-feather boas',[62] but the frail and delicate nature of these fabrics has meant that many of the gowns have not survived in good condition. A magnificent exception is the dress that Worth made for Lady Curzon to wear at the Coronation Durbar in Delhi, India, in 1903 (**218**). A guest at the ball remarked: 'You cannot conceive what a dream she looked.'[63] Her appearance that day was recorded in a portrait by William Logsdail (**219**). In 1904, when Lady Curzon was

218 and **219** Lady Curzon's dress for the Coronation Durbar in Delhi, 1903. Designed to be seen in a room lit by electricity, it was made from shining cloth of gold embroidered by Indian craftsmen with a pattern of overlapping peacock feathers in metal thread, each one studded with a jewel. The spectacular trained skirt was trimmed with white roses. Full evening dress that year was expected to 'literally fall away from the shoulders' and was cut so that it was either off the shoulders, with straps, or held up by a band of lace enclosing the point of the shoulder. The Peacock Dress has brief, epaulette-style sleeves that fall from a shoulder strap and a pouched bodice veiled by what would have been described as a 'vandyked lace bertha'. This was a revival of an 1830s–40s fashion, a deep falling collar attached to a low neckline.
(William Logsdail, 1903, Kedleston)

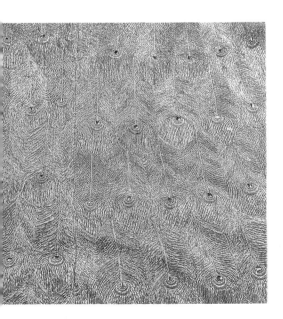

220 A fashion plate showing the exterior of Harrod's department store in Knightsbridge, 1909. The ladies' silhouettes emphasise the vertical, with the waistline raised and the skirt width reduced. The lady in the foreground, who wears a cream military-style coat over her pinky-grey chiffon dress, holds a drawstring bag called a 'Dorothy'. Handbags became essential accessories once narrowing skirts precluded the use of pockets. Applied decoration in the form of braid, tassels, beading and embroidery remained an essential feature of fashion.

The ladies' hats, deep-crowned, wide-brimmed and swathed with feathers and ribbons, have reached gargantuan proportions. Hats are also very much in evidence amongst the men in this scene: the doormen and the men in morning coat and formal frock coat (in front of the entrance and on the extreme right, respectively) wear top hats; the man in the less formal brown lounge suit wears a black bowler.

seriously ill and thought to be near death, she asked her husband to 'keep the feathers picture of me – that is the best'.[64] She never made the mistake of overloading her outfits with too much fussy and distracting decoration, preferring to leave her exquisitely embroidered gowns to make their own dramatic, yet suitably regal, impact.[65] Even Queen Alexandra was so impressed by Lady Curzon's unique style of dress that she asked her to design a number of costumes for her own Coronation, which took place on 9 August 1902.

The last decade of the nineteenth century saw the demand for women's emancipation gathering considerable momentum, and the Women's Social and Political Union began its militant agitation in the autumn of 1905. At this time the whole concept of women's clothing began to change imperceptibly. There were signs that the S-bend was about to be replaced by a more vertical silhouette, as the waistline was raised above its natural level, the skirt was narrowed and the longer and straighter-fitting corset, introduced in 1908, produced a much smoother and more elongated shape. Despite this narrower, tailored style (220), day dresses and coats were still trimmed with embroidery, braid, tassels and large decorative buttons, and dwarfed by their massive hats adorned with varied plumage. The wholesale slaughter of birds to provide the decoration for this 'murderous millinery' was railed against by the newspapers and the Church, but to no immediate avail. A group of ladies from Manchester formed the Fur, Fin and Feather Group in 1889 in an attempt to stop the killing for fashion, and this organisation later became the Royal Society for the Protection of Birds.

Tailor-mades continued to be an indispensable item in ladies' wardrobes (see 252) offering those ladies who wanted to walk rather than promenade a smart and practical alternative to the flimsy day dress. Ease of movement was further helped in 1908 when the skirts of tailor-mades were cut with less fullness. According to a fashion magazine of that year: 'Modern skirts don't rustle, and cling closely to the figure, swirl as we walk, and are absolutely free from the loose fullness which has been their characteristic in the past few years.'[66]

Lady Diana Manners (later Cooper) became aware of a new and revolutionary force in fashion at about this time, when Princess Murat was a guest of her parents. Diana, then eleven years old, was very impressed by the unusual evening gowns the Princess had brought with her from Paris and the information that they were made by 'the rising star Poiret, an eccentricity, a new word and a new mania'.[67] Paul Poiret began his career apprenticed to Doucet and in 1901 he joined Worth, where he felt he 'represented a new spirit, in which there was a force (he felt it) which was to destroy and sweep away all his dreams'.[68] In 1903 he opened his own fashion house at 5 rue Auber, Paris, and in 1906 he moved to 37 rue Pasquier, where he was determined to dispense with the basic structured fashion of a bodice and skirt then in vogue, replacing it with a simple, high-waisted garment inspired by the fashions of the French Directoire period of 1795–9 (see p.176).

In 1908 he promoted his redefined neo-classical look in *Les Robes de Paul Poiret*, a *de luxe* book of his designs, illustrated with great wit and style by the artist Paul Iribe (221). The dresses were very simple and severe in shape with a straight, tubular skirt, devoid of any fussy decoration or rigid corsetry. Rejecting the 'sweet-pea colourings' currently in fashion, Poiret brought in an entirely new and vivid palette of bright colours. He wrote in his *Autobiography* that he threw out 'lilacs, swooning mauves, tender blue hortensias, nile greens, maizes, straws, all that was soft, washed-out, insipid', and replaced them with 'reds, greens, violets, royal blues. . . . I carried with me the colourists when I took each tone at its most vivid, and I restored to health all the exhausted nuances.'[69] As one fashion magazine observed in 1910, it was 'assuredly the young folks' hour',[70] and by 1915 this trend was even more apparent, leading a magazine to comment: 'In the matter of dress history teaches that the modes of Fashion have ever reflected the moods of the people . . . it is for the young that we want fashions nowadays.'[71]

In Paris in 1909 and London in 1911 theatre-goers were thrilled and mesmerised by Sergei Diaghilev's Ballet Russe, whose sets and costume designs by Leon Bakst revealed an exotic orientalism and vividness of colour and pattern that seemed almost barbaric. The Ballet Russe's influence was so pervasive that it affected not only fashion but also interior design, and an 'exotically Eastern element began to percolate into typically English homes as walls were painted midnight blue, or black, or garish ochreous yellow. Carpets were taken up, and floors, too, were painted and highly polished. Leopard skins and Oriental rugs replaced the carpets.'[72]

Poiret, who had always been fascinated by oriental costume, devised an exotic evening outfit in 1910 comprising a turban with a tall feather plume and an overtunic, shaped like a lampshade, over a skirt that was worn swathed around the legs. He boasted that he had freed the bust but 'shackled the legs', as the long slim skirt was cut straight to the ankle without the relief of a vent or opening, thus making it impossible to take more than the shortest of steps. When it reached its extreme form in 1911–12 it was

221 Poiret's uncorseted fashions embraced a brilliant new palette of colours. The natural lines of the body were enhanced by simple tubular dresses, inspired by the fashions of the Directoire period but drawing on elements from oriental dress, such as turbans, harem pants and wide kimono sleeves. By grouping the figures together against a stark white background, devoid of any distracting detail, and filling the precise outlines with large blocks of unshaded colour, the artist Paul Iribe has exploited the dramatic potential in *Les Robes de Paul Poiret*, 1908.

222 (*left*) In 1914 Madame Louisette of Manchester employed her considerable dressmaking skills to create an elegant beaded evening dress with a hobble skirt. It is made from a pale sea-green silk with a floral pattern brocaded in a silver thread. The crossover panel at the front of the bodice has been made from blue georgette with white paste stones on silver thread, rows of cream beads on net and a pattern of darker silver beads with pearls around the edge. The waist is lightly-boned and finished with a rose, its centre composed of white paste stones, and its wired edges outlined with pearls.

This dress is something of a rarity, for many evening dresses of the period were damaged by the application of heavy decoration to delicate backing materials.

223 (*right above*) The caption for 'Modèle 6' in a 1914 edition of *Paris Fashions* explains that the 'jacket is kimono cut, with the front being on the straight with a tab – recalling the skirt – to finish it over the smart piqué or moiré waistcoat'. It is a practical ensemble, combining simplicity of line with a witty interpretation of that most masculine of garments, the waistcoat. A last vestige of the hobble skirt, a buttoned tab on the hem of the skirt, remains.

224 (*right below*) This photograph of an unknown woman was taken at the outbreak of the First World War, August 1914. The hobble skirt has been replaced by full skirts with a belted overdress in this simple cotton garment. The hairstyle reflects the move to simplicity – gone is the top-heavy Edwardian coiffure, instead the hair is brushed low over the forehead and ears, decorated with a velvet bandeau.

called a hobble skirt and was worn with a hat of enormous dimensions. Daytime and evening dresses (**222**) were both cut in the new tight-fitting style.

In retrospect it seems ironic that just when the struggle for female emancipation had reached a new peak of militancy, women should choose to wear skirts that restricted movement and hats that required constant attention if they were to remain on their heads. But the 'chains of fashion's tyranny'[73] were strong and few women dared to break them. The Suffragettes themselves wore fashionable clothes and when Sylvia Pankhurst described the impression made by a fellow suffragette at her court appearance in 1906, she was at pains to stress how feminine her appearance was. 'You must not picture her as being either big-boned, plain-looking and aggressive and wearing "mannish" clothes. . . . She is always dressed in low-toned greys and lilacs, and her

clothes are gracefully and delicately wrought, with all sorts of tiny tuckings and finishings which give a suggestion of daintiest detail without any loss of simplicity or breadth.'[74] Women who wanted to support the campaign for votes for women could purchase sashes and accessories in the movement's striking colours of purple, white and green, representing dignity, purity, fertility and hope.

Experimentation with the straight skirt took the form of overtunics and bodices, lengthened into jackets, creating a layered look – which suggested that there was indecision about the length of the skirt – such as the suit featured in the 9 May 1914 edition of *Paris Fashions* (223). This was a monthly magazine, published in London, which could be dispatched 'to any part of the world' at 16s for a year's subscription. It was aimed at the amateur and professional dressmakers who wanted reliable information about the very latest Paris fashions – a pattern for the latest creation from a French fashion house like Jenny could be purchased for 3s 9d, post free. All the designs were accompanied with an explanatory text in both French and English.

With the outbreak of the First World War in 1914 the Directoire revival was over and the narrow hobble skirt was abandoned in favour of a shorter, fuller one which flared towards the hem (224). Freed from the burden of figure-distorting corsetry and the restrictive hobble skirt, women in 1915 were, according to a contemporary fashion magazine, 'learning to walk with an ease, grace, and a certain abandon that betokens a direct unimpeded movement from the hips, and are realising the exceeding ugliness of the erstwhile waddle. . . . Waists are normal in the truest sense; and there follows a neatness and trimness of outline that is restful and pleasing to the eye.'[75] This emphasis on practicality and comfort meant that a far sharper contrast began to develop between day wear and evening clothes, with luxury and glamour being reserved increasingly for the latter.

The simplification of the female silhouette was a necessary one as more and more women were employed in factories and industry to replace the men who had gone to the front to fight. Although they were paid less than the men and it was assumed that their employment was only 'for the duration' they were able to enjoy a higher standard of living, and single, younger women had a disposable income to spend on clothes and accessories. Active jobs, especially for those involved in agriculture, meant that functional garments like boiler suits or jodhpurs were essential. Those who wore them helped to accustom people to the once shocking idea that women could wear trousers.

Daytime clothes, whether they were tailored dresses or tailor-made suits, were in serviceable materials, cut so that they provided the wearer with complete freedom of movement. But though women were no longer restricted and oppressed by their clothing, and were seeking social independence, they still strove to conform to the fashionable ideal. Lillie Langtry wrote:

Every woman is entitled to her independence. It is her right to dress conspicuously or modestly as she chooses. It is her right to ignore the dictates of fashion and dress in a manner that is most becoming to her own character and personality. In these days when women are being granted the vote everywhere, we hear she is at last man's equal but she will not achieve true equality until she breaks the chains of fashion's tyranny and strides out on her own.[76]

II

Writing in 1934 about his childhood in Bromley, Kent, in the 1870s and 80s, the writer H.G. Wells observed:

> The germinating forces of the Modern World-State which is now struggling into ordered being, were already thrusting destructively amidst the comparative stabilities of the old eighteenth century order before I was born [1866]. There was already a railway station on the Dover line and this was supplemented, when I was about twelve years old, by a second line branching off from the Chislehurst line at Grove Park. The place which had been hardly more than a few big houses, a little old market place and a straggling High Street upon the high road, with two coaching inns and a superabundance of small 'pull-up' beerhouses, was stimulated to a vigorous growth in population. Steadily London drew it closer and suburbanized it.[77]

Two simultaneous revolutions were taking place which entirely changed the way people lived, worked and shopped. One was the rapid expansion of London and other conurbations, such as Manchester and Birmingham, as developers began to obliterate surrounding fields and woods and build thousands of cheap houses, and the other was the creation of a rail network offering an increasingly fast and efficient method of transport throughout the country. London's population grew at an extraordinary rate during the nineteenth century, rising from 865,000 to 1½ million in its first thirty years. The railways made it possible for London to expand outwards still further. About half a million people were added to the population living in and around the capital each decade after 1841. The advent of the railways also meant that the great days of the stage-coach and stage-waggon were over. Although some towns which had been coaching centres flourished as railway junctions, many others did not, and were destined to suffer the fate of a town described by Charles Dickens in *The Uncommercial Traveller* (1860): 'It had been a great stage-coaching town in the great stage-coaching times, and the ruthless railways had killed and buried it.'[78] Improved railway services also brought shoppers into the large towns from suburban and country districts, and the ease of access to them and the wider choice found there inevitably affected the small country shopkeeper.

The building of the great London terminus stations, such as London Bridge in 1836, Euston in 1838, Waterloo in 1844, Kings Cross in 1850, Paddington in 1854 and St Pancras in 1867 was accompanied by a marked improvement in the public transport system, thus enabling the shopper to target precisely which street or shop he or she wanted to visit. The Great Exhibition of 1851 brought about a boom in the omnibus trade as London was flooded with new middle-class consumers anxious to spend their considerable purchasing power on the latest fashions, furniture, furnishings and the other trappings of affluence. In London by 1853 there were 3,000 horse omnibuses, run by many individual enterprises, each carrying 300 people daily and, when these small companies were absorbed by the French General Omnibus Company of London

225 This 1884 photograph shows the extensive and impressive frontage of Whiteley's, West-bourne Grove, one of the first department stores to be opened in London. William Whiteley started with one shop selling drapery, opened in 1863, and gradually expanded his premises. By the time of this photograph clothes, jewellery, groceries, ironmongery, and books could be purchased from the 'Universal Provider' and services such as dry-cleaning, hairdressing, laundry and even house agency were on offer.

(founded by two Frenchmen, but taken over by a British company in 1859), services were reorganised and regularised.

As the speed and frequency of trains improved and day-return tickets became available it was possible to visit London from further away than the suburbs for a day's shopping and still return home in the evening. This was a great advantage, according to the *Lady's World*, if you happened to live in Bath and had 'a day's shopping to get through, or winter gowns and mantles to be tried on at your favourite London Modiste's'.[79] When Gwen Raverat, the granddaughter of Charles Darwin, recalled her childhood in Cambridge in the 1880s, a day's shopping in London was a regular occurrence. 'One of the important duties which ladies had to perform was going to London for the day to shop. They had to catch the 8.30 Great Northern Train to Kings Cross. In those days no one ever went to St Pancras by the Great Eastern Railway if they could help it; and Liverpool Street was unknown to the genteel.'[80] The large stores with their restaurants and cloakrooms were an obvious attraction for the out-of-town customer, and the establishment of the ABC tea-shops in 1880 was another important milestone for, until that time, there was nowhere where young, unmarried ladies could meet outside the home and enjoy a meal.

The novel idea of building an underground rail system in London also benefitted the shopper, and opened up a new area for retailing. The Metropolitan Railway was the first. It was opened in the summer of 1863 and ran from Farringdon Street Station on the edge of the City to Bishop's Bridge Road, next to the Great Western terminus at Paddington. The open area around Paddington had been developed during the 1840s and filled with smart residential developments, but retailing there had been so disastrous that Westbourne Grove was known in the drapery world as Bankruptcy Row. This fact did not deter William Whiteley, an ambitious haberdasher from Wakefield, in Yorkshire, who perceived the potential of an area that was served by a railway and a frequent omnibus service.

A few weeks after the Bishop's Bridge Road station opened he purchased a small shop in Westbourne Grove and sold ribbons, lace, trimmings and fancy goods. By 1867 he had added a number of other lines including dresses, millinery, jewellery, furs and silks. The business continued to expand and in 1870 he offered John Barker, one of his assistants, the job of department manager at the huge salary of £1,000 per year. Barker declined the post and left to open a similar establishment of his own in another up-and-coming area, Kensington High Street. Whiteley continued to enlarge his premises by buying adjoining properties, and he had the novel idea of providing services as well as goods for his customers. These included a hairdressing department, a dry-cleaning and dyeing service, a house agency service and a refreshment room. Called the 'Universal Provider', Whiteley's store, much to the annoyance of local traders, sold not just drapery and fashion items but also groceries and meat, ironmongery and books. The concept of selling a diverse range of goods and providing a number of useful services under one roof was very successful, and was copied immediately by other stores.

Profits from the Great Exhibition of 1851, together with funds granted by Parliament, enabled the Royal Commissioners to buy the land between Kensington Gardens and the Cromwell Road on which to build a number of museums and premises for learned societies. To the west of this area the developers had created a smart residential district

226 In 1873 William, John and Sydney Ponting opened a drapery and millinery shop at 125 Kensington High Street. By the end of the century they had acquired four adjoining properties, including Scarsdale House, the London mansion of the Curzons of Kedleston. Unable to convert the house into a retailing unit, they pulled it down and a new store was built on the site. When Pontings went into liquidation in 1906, the store was bought by its Kensington High Street neighbour, John Barker & Co., who retained the name.

This part of the ground floor of Pontings in 1913 was devoted to trimmings, presumably for hats, offering its customers a bewildering choice of opulent feathers and sprays of flowers and fruit. On the floors above are evening wraps, coats and summer dresses.

and they decided to turn Kensington High Street, then a narrow twisting road full of public houses, into 'A handsome range of shop property' to provide services for the residents. Three drapers' shops there, Derry & Toms (1862), John Barker (1870) and Ponting Brothers (1873), were destined to become highly-successful department stores, retaining their original premises until the 1960s.

Another area which was developed after the Great Exhibition was the market-garden land between the Cromwell Road and Brompton Road, which was filled with housing for the wealthy, thus giving the existing shops in Brompton Village and Brompton Road a new set of customers. However, when Charles Digby Harrod bought his father's small grocer's shop in Brompton Road in 1861 few could have envisaged its expansion. Harrod's success was due to the fact that he decided to run the business on a strictly cash basis. Maintaining the standard practice of allowing the aristocracy and the upper classes to buy on credit meant that prices had to be kept artificially high because cash flow was so unpredictable. Harrod decided to provide goods that were equal in quality to those of his competitors but, because he was selling them for cash only, he could charge a lower price for them. In 1884 he installed cash desks in the store and a 'Pay at the Desk' note was displayed on every counter. Once the public had accepted this novelty without complaint, limited credit was given to approved customers – social celebrities, for example, like the actress Ellen Terry, and Lillie Langtry.

A little way up the road from Harrod's there was a linen-draper's shop which had been opened by Benjamin Harvey in 1813. When he died in 1850 his daughter carried on the business and married a silk buyer called Colonel Nichols, hence the name of the famous department store that is still operating there today. The great department stores, Harvey Nichols, Whiteley's, Peter Robinson, Dickins & Jones, Debenham & Freebody, Bourne & Hollingsworth and Swan & Edgar, had all started as small shops selling either drapery or haberdashery and certain ready-made articles of clothing. As their premises expanded and there was a demand for more varied merchandise, provision of a greater range of competitively-priced ready-made garments became an essential part of the retailing trade.

Advertising these goods to a wide section of the general public was essential, and in this area Peter Robinson was a trail-blazer. From 1866 on he was placing advertisements every week in *The Illustrated London News*, of which the following is a typical example: 'An endless variety of ready-made suits in Navy Blue Tweed, Serge, Diagonal Cloth . . . Fancy Summer Cloth, and Beach Linseys [mixed wool and cotton]. Yachting, Seaside, and Summer Jackets in endless variety. The Inverness with cape; the Sea-coast with hood and sleeves, Circular Waterproof Mantles in Shrewsbury Waterproof Tweeds, A., B., C., sizes.'[81]

When he opened a separate Mourning Warehouse in Regent Street in 1865 he publicised it with what must have been the first ever photographically-illustrated catalogue, and it predates the earliest foreign example, which appeared in *L'Art et la Mode* of 1881. The photographs of models wearing the mourning clothes and the bonnets are 'prints of very high quality, amazingly clear and successful in imparting charm to all-black gowns hardly designed to enhance'.[82] In 1876 he came up with another innovative idea, a photographic catalogue called a *Book of Styles*, which launched a mail-order, ready-to-wear department. The photographs were of carte-de-visite format, with all the details, prices and descriptions of the clothes written on the back.

This idea of sending garments through the post was taken up by some of the other department stores by the end of the century. They perceived that the production of illustrated catalogues and a mail-order purchasing scheme could be a lucrative sideline. Separate departments had to be created to deal with this side of the business, and they became highly-organised and labour-intensive operations. In 1888, for example, Marshall & Snelgrove's Country Rooms received over 1,000 letters a day and employed more than 100 clerks and accountants to process and dispatch the orders. The proliferation of newspaper and magazine advertising in the 1890s and the first decade of the twentieth century encouraged such business and enabled the general public to enjoy a wide choice of ready-made and affordable garments.

Those working women with a more limited budget could buy cheaper versions

227 William Straw had this calendar printed in 1893 to advertise his grocery shop in the Market Place, Worksop in Nottinghamshire. The fashionable lady wears a hat with a shallow, turned-up brim trimmed with velvet orchid-type flowers in a matching colour. Frizzy hair was popular at this time, brushed into a neat fringe and twisted into a bun. The lady's blouse has a high neck and bow arranged like a jabot. Bodices were often cut and draped to look like a jacket, and, as here, made with a panel in a contrasting colour.

W. STRAW, *Grocer, Tea Dealer & Provision Merchant*,
102, MARKET PLACE, WORKSOP.

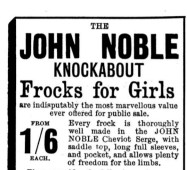

direct from the manufacturers. John Noble of Manchester, for example, was advertising 'beautifully finished' tailor-mades for half a guinea (10s 6d) in 1896 (228). His advertisement stresses that the suits were made in his 'own Factories, where over 1,000 well-paid Workers are employed under the strictest conditions of Sanitation and Cleanliness' – just in case the customer assumed that because they were cheap they had been made in a sweatshop.[83] Hartley & Company's Yorkshire Warehouse in Leeds sent out samples of its materials on mail order forms in the Edwardian period (229). A 'stylish blouse' made from 'Lintaf', a fabric 'finer than linen', available in a wide range of colours, cost only 2s 3d, with postage 3d extra. The novelist Arnold Bennett was not impressed by the quality of these mass-produced garments. When he attended a talk given by H.G. Wells at the Times Book Club in 1910 he found that the women in the audience 'deemed themselves elegant . . . being far back from the rostrum I had a good view of, the back of their blouses, chemisettes and bodices. What an assortment of

228 Half-guinea suits were available ready-made direct from the manufacturers, John Noble of Manchester, undercutting the price charged by department stores. Although sizing was somewhat vague – a choice of four lengths – the stylish product, degree of choice and a carriage charge of only sixpence meant that this method of shopping was effortless and very reasonable.

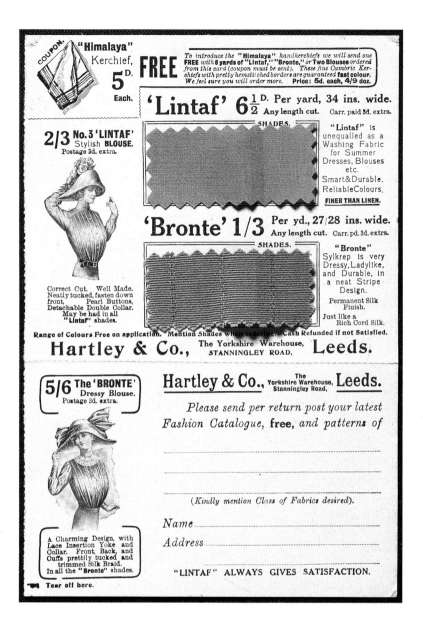

229 Hartley & Co., 'the Yorkshire Warehouse', manufactured a wide range of inexpensive fabrics for blouses, dresses, coats, motoring coats and 'Charming Fabrics for Evening Wear'. They also sold some ready-made items like blouses, and gave quotations for making up clothes from their own fabrics.

pretentious and ill-made toilettes! What disclosures of clumsy hooks-and-eyes and general creased carelessness!'[84]

Caley's in Windsor, eventually acquired by the John Lewis partnership, was established in 1813 by a Miss Caley. Originally selling millinery and haberdashery and offering an exclusive dress-making service, the shop's rapid expansion during the century mirrored the increased prosperity of the town. A railway was opened in the late 1840s and trade also benefitted from the patronage of the Royal Family when they were in residence at Windsor Castle. The Caleys continued to add more departments until, in 1866, they described themselves as 'Silk Mercers, Linen Drapers, Lacemen, Furriers, Florists etc. to the Queen'. By this time they were providing the entire clothing requirements of the wealthy residents of the town and surrounding areas. They also sold mourning clothes and operated an undertaking service.

Although there was a rapid growth of department stores throughout Britain – early

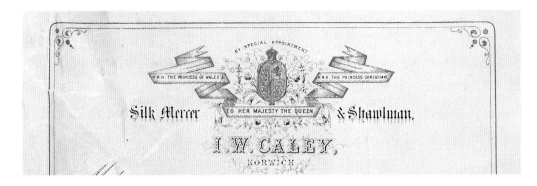

230 In 1860 I.W. Caley opened a high-class retailing establishment in Norwich, selling silks, haberdashery, shawls and ladies' clothing. It had dressmaking and mantle-making departments, and fashionable clothes and accessories were imported from the Continent. As this letter-head shows, it received the royal warrant, and remained one of the most exclusive establishments in Norwich until 1914.

231 This corset would have stood, under a glass dome, on a shop counter. Embroidered on the filled-in top section of the corset, alongside crossed French and British flags, are the words 'The Celebrated CB Corsets – Corsets de Première Qualité'. The manufacturer was Charles Bayee & Company from London Wall who, according to an advertisement in *The Ladies' Field* of 1905, manufactured tailor-made corsets ranging in price from 10s 6d to three guineas.

The finest French fabrics were used – hence the Gallic connection – to make the corsets as 'easy fitting as a perfectly cut kid glove', thus giving 'a complete absence of pressure upon the respiratory organs'.

pioneering examples being Bainbridge's of Newcastle-upon-Tyne, Kendal Milne & Faulkner of Manchester and Caley's of Norwich (230) – drapery and millinery largely remained in the hands of individual shopkeepers and the small-scale retailer prevailed right through to 1914. One such establishment, Edwin Hide's Drapery Emporium of Southend on Sea, Essex, was the scene of H.G. Wells's apprenticeship from 1881: he left two years later, halfway through his training. Renaming it as Edwin Shalford's Drapery Bazaar of Folkestone in his novel *Kipps* (1905), he gives a fascinating insight into the day-to-day running of a shop, the way the customers were treated, the types of material sold, methods of displaying the garments and accessories and the latest device for taking cash – an overhead change carrier which shot around the ceiling of the shop to a cashier's desk. In *Kipps* the owner of the store praised the 'Fishency of the System', which he estimated saved him a large amount of money every year. Wells also describes how the male shop assistants were distinguished by their clothes: junior apprentices wore short black coats and turn-down collars and were kept busy running errands, cleaning and packing parcels. At sixteen Wells himself was promoted to serving the less important customers and taking goods out on approval and so was allowed to wear the uniform of a more senior assistant: a black morning coat with tails and a high stand-up collar. One of Kipps's duties was to fetch the dummies from the Costume Room and take them to the window, where they would be dressed and then displayed:

> They crossed a large room full of the strangest things Kipps had ever seen. Lady-like figures, surmounted by black, wooden knobs in the place of the refined heads one might have reasonably expected, stood about with a lifelike air of conscious fashion. 'Costume Room,' said Shalford. . . . They discovered two young ladies, taller and fairer than any of the other young ladies, and with black trains to their dresses, who were engaged in writing at a little table.[85]

By the end of the century a wide variety of dummies and other gadgets, specially designed to display all manner of merchandise – even underwear was displayed – were available to the shopkeeper, so adding to an already cluttered shop interior (231).

Shop-windows were crammed with all the 'innumerable whim-whams and fribble-frabble of fashion', creating 'museums of fashion in plate glass cases' in the grand London stores.[86] This conspicuous display of goods, their prices clearly marked, was a deliberate marketing ploy. The passer-by, impressed by the quality and range of goods in the windows, would then be tempted to go in and buy something. The system of price

232 Packaging of objects as small as pins and needles could be extremely attractive. The items illustrated here include a card needlecase, *c.*1850, in the form of a fold-out box with a central satin pin-cushion. Inside the box are four packets of different-sized sewing needles in card slots, decorated with cut-outs of fashionable beauties. Next to it is another paper needlecase from 1850–70, decorated with pastoral scenes. It contains steel pins and four packets of assorted Sharps of Alcester needles. There are two ivory tape measures and one made of bone.

The elaborate contraption in the background is a brass sewing tree, *c.*1870, which has twelve bobbins for accommodating spools of silk thread. To the right of it is a workbox, *c.*1800–30, made from papier-mâché covered with gilt paper. Under the lid is a tiny drawer with a silk ribbon draw-pull containing a silk thread holder and a needlecase.

ticketing is described in some detail in Arnold Bennett's novel *The Old Wives' Tale*, about two sisters, daughters of a draper, in a drab town in Staffordshire:

> Heavy oblong tickets for flannels, shirtings, and other stuffs in the piece, smaller diamond-shaped tickets for intermediate goods, and diamond-shaped tickets (containing nothing but the price) for bonnets, gloves and flim-flam generally. The words 'lasting', 'cheap', 'stylish', 'novelty', 'choice' (as an adjective), 'new', and 'tasteful' exhausted the entire vocabulary of tickets.[87]

The reason for the crowded and diverse displays in the windows of the drapers' shops was explained by Charles Knight, editor of *London*, in 1851:

> The principle of competition has been driven further in the drapery business than in most others, hence the linen-drapers' shops exhibit the effect which this competition produces more strikingly perhaps than most others. The rise of the cotton manufacture in England has had much to do with this matter; for when woollen fabrics were the staple of English dress, the comparative costliness prevented any very eager competition, and the fabrics themselves were not of so showy a character . . . the immense consumption of cotton in female dress has been the chief moving power towards the production of the present remarkable display in the drapers' shops.[88]

The Costume Room of Edwin Hide's Drapery Emporium was modest compared to the Model Gown Departments to be found in smart London stores like Marshall & Snellgrove, or Debenham & Freebody. These departments sold made-to-order clothes which were sewn in their own dressmaking workrooms. In time, however, ready-to-wear departments were established in these stores, expanding rapidly and outstripping made-to-order. At Peter Robinson in 1891, for example, takings from the ready-made were £18,641, with made-to-order trailing behind at £12,729.[89]

One reason for this trend was the fact that the really high-class clientèle still preferred to purchase their clothes in the elegantly-appointed premises of the 'Court Dressmaker'. These establishments, run on the lines of a French couture house, comprised a salon, fitting rooms and workrooms. As they did not advertise and were only recommended by word of mouth, they possessed an impenetrable air of snobbishness and exclusivity. Their customers would never have considered paying cash and so the prospect of going to a large store to find an attractively-priced garment was not an enticing one. There were also many smaller businesses and private dressmakers in the West End who were used by society ladies for making garments to be worn on social occasions not considered important or grand enough to merit the considerable outlay required for an outfit from a Court Dressmaker.

The ability of the fashionable London dressmaker to dominate and influence her customers certainly impressed Mary Elizabeth Lucy of Charlecote when, in 1865, she wanted to purchase a wedding dress and trousseau for her future daughter-in-law, Christina Cameron Campbell. On arriving at Mrs James's premises in Hanover Square she found 'it was difficult to say no to anything she recommended'.[90]

> 'Oh! Miss Campbell will look so charming in this dove coloured silk, to travel in, you know; then here is a lovely blue silk which would so become her, then this pink is so exquisite it would so suit her fine complexion, and then oh! Miss Campbell must have this buff creation. I have just made a dress of the same for Princess Mary of Cambridge [who married the Prince, later Duke, of Teck. Their daughter, May, became Queen Mary in 1910.] I make all her things, she is such a darling, only she is too large.' And so her tongue ran on till she would run you up such a bill that would make you cry out, as the Princess of Wales [Princess Alexandra] is reported to have done when she saw her first milliner's bill. 'Oh, Heaven forgive me for such extravagance!'[91]

The wedding dress they eventually chose, made from 'the richest white silk, covered with the most exquisite tunic of Brussels lace looped up the front with large bunches of orange flowers and true-lovers' knots of white satin', was seen to best advantage as Mrs James 'acted lady's maid on the occasion; so every fold sat in its right place'.

Private dressmakers, or 'modistes' as they liked to call themselves, were found in towns and cities throughout Britain and the prices they charged depended on the standing and status of their customers. From the 1870s the development of the Stevengraph process of weaving silk meant that dressmakers could sew a woven silk label inside their creations, bearing their name and address (233). Some of the clothes worn by the Marchionesses of Bristol from 1870 to 1907 have been transferred from the family home, Ickworth in Suffolk, to the National Trust's Conservation Workroom,

233 A number of garments in the Killerton collection have survived with their labels still attached. Woven into the waistband of a silk afternoon dress (206), *c.*1889, are the words 'Peter Robinson Mourning Warehouse, Regent Street'. Advertisements for similar dresses suggest that this garment would have cost between 5 and 6½ guineas. The bodice, shaped by ten narrow bones, has black silk facings and a brown twill lining. A protective dress shield is still in place inside each armhole.

which is at Blickling Hall, Norfolk, and their labels show that they patronised H.J. & D. Nicholl's of 114–20 Regent Street, Worth and Woolland's of 95–107 Knightsbridge. The last, opposite Albert Gate in Hyde Park, had originally supplied servants with their uniforms and other necessities, but as the store gradually went up-market its original brick premises were replaced with a new and imposing stone edifice in 1899. By this time the establishment was regarded as one of the most fashionable in London and was particularly renowned for its exquisite tea-gowns. H.J. & D. Nicholl's were men's tailors with a very large department for ladies, in which 'creative designing' was done. It was an expensive and superior establishment which held Royal Appointments to the Queen and British and foreign royalty and, unusually for that time, had two branches in Liverpool and one in Manchester.[92]

The 1850s had witnessed the emergence in Paris of the first true house of haute couture, a development which led once again to France becoming the unrivalled leader of world fashion. It was, perhaps surprisingly, headed by an Englishman, Charles Frederick Worth, who had served an apprenticeship at Swan & Edgar and, after a brief period at Lewis & Allenby, the most famous silk mercer's in London, had settled in Paris working as a shop assistant selling textiles, shawls and ready-made gowns. In 1858 Worth opened his own premises at 7 rue de la Paix, at a particularly propitious moment

in the history of French fashion. The heady days when the ladies of Napoleon I's court were elegantly clad by Leroy in gold- and silver-encrusted silks and velvets had long since gone. As no outstanding designer had succeeded him, fashion passed into the hands of a series of uninspired dressmakers, who concerned themselves with making minor alterations to established styles rather than creating fashions that were bold and innovative. Worth's first important client was the Princesse de Metternich and when she wore his clothes at court they caught the eye of Eugénie de Montijo, Napoleon III's Empress and fashion leader of Europe during the Second Empire (1852–70).

The combination of a brilliant designer and a beautiful empress inspired fashions of great opulence and sumptuousness. When Ellen Terry visited Paris in 1867, she was struck not only by the beauty of the Empress, whom she described as 'looking like an exquisite wax-work', but also by the consummate sense of style of the Parisian ladies: 'Oh, the beautiful slope of women at this period! They looked like lovely half-moons, lying back in their carriages. It was an age of elegance – in France particularly – an age of luxury.'[93]

Worth's genius lay in his ability to predict the kind of fashions that would become popular and introduce new styles before women realised they were bored with existing ones. He established the couturier as a figure of power and international influence, dressing the nobility and royal families of Russia, Austria-Hungary, Spain and Italy. He was recognised throughout the moneyed world as being an arbiter of taste and this unrivalled position meant that he could charge huge sums of money for his creations. Intended to be symbols of wealth, Worth's gowns were 'brilliant statements of conspicuous consumption'.[94] Lady Curzon, for one, had nearly all her clothes made by the House of Worth, including the spectacular Coronation Durbar gown (see p.250). After Worth's retirement in the late 1880s the business was carried on by his sons and a branch was opened in Grosvenor Street, London, in 1900. Paul Poiret included the House of Worth and that founded by another Englishman, Redfern, in his list of the great Parisian couture houses of the 1890s. Redfern was a tailor who began his illustrious career by making ladies' yachting clothes in Cowes on the Isle of Wight. He opened a couture house at 26 Conduit Street as well as branches in Paris, and he enjoyed an unrivalled reputation for the excellence of his tailored suits and costumes for country pursuits like hunting and shooting.

Although the department stores offered the shopper as many as 27 different departments, including separate sections for items like hosiery, lace, shawls, furs, gloves, parasols, millinery, underwear and mourning, high society continued to patronise shops that dealt exclusively in one item. Describing the experience of visiting such a shop in the 1870s Lady Jeune, an early writer on consumer affairs, remembered it as being a 'solemn and dreary affair' as compared with the present (1890s):

> There was little or no display in the windows. Each shop had its own speciality, and the more expensive and costly its goods, the more unremittingly conservative was the way of carrying on its business. Jones sold the best silks, Smith the best gloves, Brown the best bonnets, Madame X was far and away the only good milliner and dressmaker. . . . We bought our goods at these various shops, and dutifully followed in the steps of our forefathers, paying for things at the end of the year, for no well-thought-of firm ever demanded or expected more than a yearly payment of debts.[95]

High-class stores operated a policy of 'serving through'. This meant that when the customer arrived at the door a senior employee, formally dressed in a black morning coat, would greet them at the doorway and summon a shop-walker to take them to the appropriate counter, where there would be a bentwood chair to sit on. The assistant behind the counter would then attempt to locate and display the items that the customer wanted to see. When a choice had been made and the transaction noted, another assistant would wrap it up neatly in paper and the whole operation would be repeated in reverse. Such shops catered for the carriage trade so that a lady or gentleman, accompanied by a footman in full livery, could be driven to the shop in their carriage, which would wait outside until business had been completed.

As the most fashionable time to shop was between 2 and 4 o'clock in the afternoon and as all the fashionable shops were concentrated in the West End of London, so there were appalling traffic jams. The most congested was Regent Street, and the chaos that ensued when shoppers, omnibuses, coaches and horseriders merged together is the subject of an engraving that appeared in *The Illustrated London News* in 1866 (234). Such congestion in Regent Street and the narrower Bond Street caused many shop owners to advertise alternative streets which gave access to their premises. *The Graphic* of 1889 carried an advertisement for Peter Robinson's Mourning Warehouse which stated that another carriage entrance was available in Argyll Street should Regent Street be blocked.

In 1875 Arthur Lazenby Liberty obtained half a shop, 218A Regent Street. Calling it East India House, he filled it with a selection of 'soft delicate coloured fabrics of the East', carefully arranged so that their subtle patterns and rich colours were seen to advantage. Inside the shop there were 'cheap and artistic porcelains for House Decoration. Persia, India, China and Japan. Cabinet specimens from 6d to 100 guineas.'[96] Liberty had learnt his trade as an employee of Farmer and Roger's Great Shawl and Cloak Emporium in Regent Street, where his Oriental Bazaar department, selling Japanese ceramics, silks and bric-à-brac, became the most profitable in the store. Liberty's imagination had been fired by the International Exhibition of 1862, which had shown the arts and crafts of Japan to the general public for the first time. The Japanese lacquer, bronze and porcelain items on display were from the private collection of Sir Rutherford Alcock, the first British Minister in Japan.

Liberty's enthusiasm was shared by many of the leading designers, architects and artists of the day, who flocked to the Bazaar to buy the blue and white oriental china and imported silks, their soft, muted colours contrasting with the harsh colours and strident patterns of contemporary designs. His artistic friends encouraged him to open his own shop to cater for those who shared his taste. Emboldened by the immediate popularity of his shop, Liberty acquired larger premises and, in 1884, opened dressmaking workrooms which designed and made 'aesthetic gowns'. Liberty's loose-flowing dresses were made from unusual, hand-woven materials: delicate muslins and filmy gauzes from India; subtly-coloured silks from China and Japan; and soft woollens from Kashmir. These were arranged in graceful folds that complemented the natural lines of the body. Each design had a name, such as 'Greek' or 'Medieval', hand-embroidered with appropriate motifs. According to the 1896 catalogue: 'The majority of designs are purposely not confined to any particular mode or style and for this reason can never be "unfashionable".' Beautifully-produced catalogues of Liberty's gowns show that they were relatively expensive. The Countess of Bristol, for example, would have had to pay 9 guineas for the tea-gown she purchased in 1897 (see 208).

Liberty's also displayed a range of 'Beautiful and Inexpensive' art fabrics for dressmaking and furnishing so that those customers who could not afford to buy anything ready-made could make their own. The Costume Department could supply the home embroideress with silks and original designs for costume and furnishings, and if the customer made an appointment she could even have private lessons in embroidery techniques. One of the most popular materials that Liberty's sold was its 'Umritza' (from Amritsar) cashmere, woven in England from East Indian wools in a wide range of colours and much cheaper and more durable than the original. Embroidered shawls in 'Umritza' were particularly successful: two yards square, they ranged in price from 84s to 10 guineas. Having persuaded British manufacturers to reproduce oriental designs and fabrics in England, Liberty decided to set up his own printing works at Merton Abbey in Surrey so that fabrics could be hand block-printed in the traditional way. A silks catalogue of *c*.1895 shows that a piece (7yds) of silk woven in India and dyed and printed at Merton cost 28s 6d with half-pieces cut without extra charge. The customer who wanted something really special would choose from a 'Persian silk in woven designs – very rare 10 guineas per piece of about six yards' and a 'saffron silk design woven by hand with many coloured silks and little jewels' for 12 guineas a yard.[97] The peacock and the sunflower were the main motifs of the aesthetic movement and 'Peacock Feather' roller-printed cotton designed by Arthur Silver for Liberty's in 1887 has been a best-seller ever since.

235 An elegant ensemble, uncharacteristically restrained for Lucile, made from fine dark grey worsted trimmed with matching bands and buttons. It is lined throughout with satin in bold black and white stripes. The hat, 1910–11 from Woolland's in London, has a plaited black straw brim, a grey chiffon-covered crown, grey and black piping and a black feather.

A rather different success story was that of Mrs Lucile (Lucy) Wallace, a society dressmaker who designed clothes for her friends. Her 1888 divorce, according to her sister Elinor Glyn, left her 'all but penniless, and with a child to provide for. With wonderful courage she set herself to build up a dress-making business.'[98] In 1895 she rented a shop and workrooms at 24 Old Burlington Street, between Bond Street and Regent Street. She had already gained a reputation for her exquisitely-decorated tea-gowns, called 'Personality' dresses, so the venture was an immediate success. Her customers were both flattered and intrigued by the idea of having a unique garment designed to suit their personalities. Exclusivity was also ensured by the fact that Lucile's designs were not repeated, and the customer could choose from a series of coloured sketches designed just for her. Lucile's dressmaking business expanded until, by the turn of the century, it was one of the great couture houses in London – with branches later in New York (1910) and Paris (1912) – employing hundreds of people.

In 1897, when the enterprise moved to the larger and grander premises of 17, later 23, Hanover Square, her dressmaking establishment became the couture house 'The Maison Lucile', and Lucile, who had always had difficulty in coping with the financial side of the business, took on Sir Cosmo Duff-Gordon as a partner. Her clientèle numbered some of the grandest ladies in the land, including Margot Asquith and the Duchess of York (later Queen Mary). The business was turned into a company and in 1900 Lucile married Sir Cosmo. She wrote in her autobiography that she 'was told that nobody would know me if I "kept a shop". It would be bad enough for a man but for a woman it meant social ruin . . . I could never be presented at Court, because I was in "Trade".'[99] In fact, her ownership of the House of Lucile did not affect her social standing very much. The reason Lucile could not be presented at court, despite the fact that her husband attended court functions, was because she had been divorced.

Lucile endeavoured to make a visit to her premises an enjoyable social occasion, unlike the regimented and formal atmosphere that was usual in the Paris couture houses and Court Dressmakers. Her clients were invited to relax over tea and to feel that they were visiting a private drawing-room. Mothers were encouraged to bring their daughters to be dressed for the season, and it was not long before Lucile opened a special department for débutantes' dresses. Hers was the first couture house in London or Paris to cater for this group, for Lucile had realised that 'fashions were created for older women, and were only adapted for the *jeune fille*, often very unsuitably at that'.[100]

Dismissing the conventional attitude that the trying on and selecting of clothes was a secretive and private experience, Lucile came up with the entirely novel idea of a 'mannequin' parade, which would be as entertaining to watch as a play. 'I would have glorious goddess-like girls, who would walk to and fro dressed in my models, displaying them to the best advantage to an admiring audience of women.'[101] Lucile trained six beautiful and statuesque girls, not one of whom weighed less than eleven stone, and staged the first-ever fashion parade to a highly-appreciative audience that included Margot Asquith, Lillie Langtry, Ellen Terry and Princess Alice of Battenburg. Each 'Gown of Emotion' had its own picturesque name, 'The Sighing Sound of Lips Unsatisfied', for example, was a 'soft gray chiffon veiling an underdress of short pink and violet taffeta, shadowed and unreal', and all the dresses were worn with carefully-chosen and colour-coordinated accessories – another innovation. Cecil Beaton said of Lucile that

236 (*left*) In 1833 Peter Robinson opened a shop at 103 Oxford Street, thirty years later he had acquired a block of six shops, and by 1900 almost all the island site in the north-west corner of Oxford Circus. This photograph, taken in 1910 before the redevelopment of the Circus, shows how each department has its own, cluttered window-display. In addition, there was another branch at 214 Oxford Street, a boy's outfitting department at 278 Regent Street, and the famous Mourning Warehouse at 256–262 Regent Street.

237 (*right*) From the turn of the century, the needs of motorists, male and female, were well catered for by the fashion industry. In 1905 Burberry published the 'Burberry Proof Kit XVI', in which all manner of garments were illustrated, including 'cold-excluding, rain-resisting and dust-proof clothing'. Motoring coats could be composed of up to four layers of warm material for winter wear, and a lightweight silk gaberdine for summer. Other vital accessories were specially designed hats (with dust-proof veils for ladies), caps, gauntlet gloves and goggles. The 'Fashionable Motor Wraps' illustrated here are from Robinson & Cleaver's catalogue of 1907.

her 'artistry was unique, her influence enormous' and that her ultra-feminine creations were 'masterpieces of intricate workmanship'. She 'worked with soft materials, delicately sprinkling them with bead or sequin embroidery, with cobweb lace insertions, true lovers' knots, and garlands of minute roses. Her colour sense was so subtle that the delicacy of detail could scarcely be seen at a distance, though the effect she created was of an indefinable shimmer.'[102]

Another late-Victorian dressmaking establishment to make its mark on the London shopping scene was set up by J.J. Fenwick in 1891. Fenwick's had been the most exclusive dressmaking shop in Newcastle-upon-Tyne in the 1880s. Its handsome shop-front, designed by an eminent architect, attracted much attention as it contained only a few elegant outfits and furs in contrast to the windows of the drapery stores, filled with a cluttered confusion of ticketed goods and dummies. Convinced that he had an excellent retailing package, Mr Fenwick conceived the audacious plan of opening a branch in one of the most exclusive shopping streets in London, at 62 and 63 New Bond Street, and was very successful.

Daring though Fenwick might have been, it would have been unthinkable for him to have opened in Old Bond Street, as 'between Old and New Bond Street was an impenetrable social barrier that nobody ever attempted to cross'.[103] In the Edwardian period the carriage trade continued to remain aloof from the stores that catered for 'general trade', preferring to patronise the exclusive shops in that 'really aristocratic street',[104] just as their parents and grandparents had done before them. The hatter Frederick Willis remembered that to see those Edwardian women 'in their glory one had to be in Old Bond Street between the hours of four and six in the afternoon. The street was full of their carriages, and there was an air of reverence in the shops as they entered.' He also recalled that 'no man of discrimination would dream of buying his hat at a big store. The really smart hatters were accommodated in small, old-fashioned shops.'[105]

There was still a clear demarcation between those stores that attracted the carriage

trade and those that did not, and in Oxford Street the new department stores of Bourne & Hollingsworth, opened in 1902, and Selfridges, in 1909, definitely belonged to the latter category. An employee of Peter Robinson recalled that 'Oxford Street was a superior shopping street until Bourne & Hollingsworth brought the general trade and then Selfridges. We were family drapers . . . the carriages would drive up and the duchesses would step out. Customers would discuss Sunday's sermon with you, give all their family news, and say their married daughter would be in during the afternoon.'[106]

I have concentrated on shopping for female clothes in this chapter. Unlike earlier centuries, when men's fashions were just as elaborate, if not more so, than those of their wives and sisters, the variety of shops, and the pleasures that men took in shopping for their clothes were evident. But in Victorian times men's clothes had taken on a more austere style, with muted colours prevailing. Thus the aristocrat and the man of substance would resort to their tailors. For those who could not afford such a luxury, factory production of clothing made available ready-made suits. In Leeds, for example, there were seven or eight such factories in 1881, by 1892 there were 54.

Such an increase in output led to the establishment of shops for men and boys selling ready-made clothes and these grew into multiple shop groups much like the high street chain stores of today. By 1900 there were at least 22 such groups with over 50 branches each. The most famous, Hepworths, G.A. Dunn and Bradleys of Chester, offered a comprehensive range of ready-made garments at very competitive prices. The department stores also catered for the male shopper. Harrod's policy of making shopping a sociable occasion included men, as there was a grandly-furnished Gentlemen's Club in which they could meet and relax. According to the 1895 Harrod's catalogue there were five departments for men on the first floor in which all manner of goods, from smoking caps and umbrellas to bespoke boots and shoes, were available. There was even a special dyeing and cleaning service for gentlemen and their shoes could be repaired on the premises.

Frederick Willis worked in an exclusive gentlemen's hat-shop during the Edwardian period. He was immensely proud of the hats that he sold and the fact that his aristocratic customers were 'proud to wear a hat with the imprint of one of the classic makers'. Such high-quality goods, when dispatched to the far corners of the Empire, had a distinct patriotic value for they were 'ambassadors for English craftsmanship'. Elaborating on this theme he explains that the gentleman who came from the 'top drawer' was 'an Olympian, as imperishable (we thought) as the British Navy and the little bits of red dotted all over the map of the world. How little we then thought that the Olympian had only a few more years to run before he became as extinct as the Regency bucks.'[107]

The future of shopping for clothes, for men and women, lay not in tasteful premises but in the glittering, Aladdin's cave of parvenus like Selfridges.

CHAPTER SEVEN

Swaddling to Sailor Suits: Children's Clothes

In the sixteenth century, producing children was regarded as the main duty of any married woman, whatever her class. Upper-class ladies, intent on securing the dynastic line, were accustomed to having their portrait painted in an advanced state of pregnancy. One such was Mildred, the wife of Sir William Cecil (later Lord Burghley), painted during her pregnancy in 1564. For this portrait she wore a modified version of fashionable dress; the usual rigid understructure was altered to accommodate her swollen stomach. That pregnant ladies continued to wear stomachers, unboned, or more lightly boned, is confirmed in a letter written to Henry Wriothesley, 3rd Earl of Southampton, by his wife Elizabeth Vernon in 1599: 'Sweet my Lord let your man Foulke buye me a stomacher of scarlet half a yard broad and as long at least, lined with plush, to keepe my body warm a days which I must ride. I send you word I growe bigger and bigger every day.'[1]

If mother and baby survived the ordeal of childbirth, they would put on their best clothes and received visitors in bed. The famous early seventeenth-century portrait of the Cholmondeley Sisters in the Tate Gallery records this event (239). Both ladies wear white arched hoods, while the swaddled babies are covered with embroidered mantles which match the stomachers worn by their mothers. The mantles were probably the bearing cloths, which would be wrapped round the babies when they were taken to church to be baptised.

The swaddling of babies was a universal practice until the early eighteenth century. The baby was dressed in a shirt or other small garment and bandages were wound over it spirally the length of the baby's body. A biggin, or small cap, was placed on the baby's head and its physical needs were catered for with a tailclout, the Elizabethan and Stuart version of a nappy. Lady Anne Clifford's diary for 13 December 1619 reads: 'My Lord gave me three shirts to make clouts of.' But any joy at the birth of a son, Thomas, on 2 February 1620, was short-lived as he died on 26 July.[2]

During the day the swaddling would be removed from time to time so that the baby could be fed and washed and have the opportunity to exercise its limbs. This process is

238 The younger children of Charles I: James, Duke of York, Princess Elizabeth and Henry, Duke of Gloucester. Henry, aged eight when the portrait was painted, is still not breeched. He wears an apron over his richly-braided doublet and long skirts. James is dressed in the height of fashion, wearing Spanish hose and high-waisted, long-legged breeches that end below the knee, where they are closed by fancies – elaborate trimmings composed of loops of ribbon. The lavish frills attached to his boothose spill out over his bucket-topped boots. Elizabeth is dressed in adult fashion, with a beautiful lace falling collar called a whisk.
(Sir Peter Lely, 1647, Petworth)

239 Already cocooned in their swaddling and elaborately embroidered robes, the babies of the Cholmondeley sisters are also wrapped in red mantles embroidered in gold that are carried right over their heads. Their mothers are dressed identically in their finest clothes, with the pattern of the embroidery on their stomachers echoing that on the babies' robes.
(British School, *c*.1600–10, Tate Gallery)

described in detail in Dialogue V of *The French Garden*, a French/English conversation manual written by Peter Erondell in 1605 and dedicated to 'Madame Elizabeth Barkley', wife of Sir Thomas Berkeley, to whom Erondell gave French lessons. The lady of the house says to the nurse: 'Unswaddle him, undoe his swaddling bands, give him his breakfast whilst I am heere. . . . Wash him before me, have you cleane water?' When the nurse has washed him thoroughly she is instructed to 'swaddle him again. But first put on his biggin and his little band with an edge, where is his little petticote? Give him his coate of changeable taffeta, and his sattin sleeves: Where is his bibbe? Let him have his gathered Aprone with stringes, and hang a Muckminder [handkerchief] to it: you need not yet to give him his Corall with the small golden chayne, for I believe it is better to let him sleepe untill the after noone.' A coral (see **51** and **241**), with or without attached bells, was a good luck charm and was also used as a rattle and for teething. When the bedding in the cradle has been rearranged the nurse is told to rock him to sleep. His mother kisses him and leaves, saying 'God send thee good rest, my little Boykin'.[3]

When the swaddling was discarded after four or six weeks the child was 'short-coated' – clothed in a 'frock', a waisted garment which just covered the feet. This custom caused Charlotte de la Trémoille, the French wife of James Stanley, later 7th Earl of Derby, some anxiety in 1628, for she had 'already in two of my letters asked you for frocks for him, for he is very big for his age; and they are needed the more that in this country children are short-clothed at a month or 6 weeks old, I am considered quite out of my senses that he is not yet short-coated'.[4]

False hanging-sleeves were attached to the armholes of the frock and these could be used as leading strings to guide the child's first faltering steps. Boys and girls wore aprons over their gowns until they were about six or seven years old, but by the time a boy was about five the bodice section of his gown would be shaped like a doublet and the girl's gown began to follow fashion. Arabella Stuart, Bess of Hardwick's grand-daughter, was twenty-three months old when an unknown artist painted her portrait (**240**), showing her wearing remarkably grown-up clothes.

240 Arabella Stuart aged nearly two: a portrait painted for her grandmother, Bess of Hardwick. Her waisted gown, with its fashionable tabbed wings, is embroidered all over with flowers. On the sleeves these flowers have pearl-shaped drops fastened in their centres. The doll she holds wears a dress that had been in vogue a few years earlier, and is probably a 'fashion doll'. (Unknown artist, 1577, Hardwick Hall)

Lady Anne Clifford's diary provides a fascinating insight into children's clothes in the early seventeenth century. Anne always refers to her daughter Margaret as 'the Child'. On 23 January 1617, at the age of three, 'the Child put on red baize coats' and the discarded baby clothes were given to the steward's wife. (Baize was a lightweight, open woollen material, not unlike flannel.) It was time for more shaped garments, so on 28 April 1617 'for the first time the Child put on a pair of whalebone bodies'. The entry on 1 May 1617 is also an important one for Anne, as she cut Child's leading strings off and 'made her use togs alone, so as she had two or three falls at first but had not hurt with them'. Leading strings tended to be made from a stout material, as is evident from a letter in the Verney collection, dated 1715, in which the writer requests 'Cousen Peg to buye me a pair of leading strings for Jak, there is stuff made on purpose that is very strong for he is so heavy I dare not venture him with a common Ribin'.[5] Jack (John) was then nearly four years old.

241 Four of Sir Thomas Lucy's thirteen children. The three girls and their little brother are all wearing bodices and skirts from the same white and gold brocade. The youngest child is propped up in a chair with a red blanket draped across his lap: he wears a biggin over a tightly-fitting coif, and an apron with a bib over the bodice. The girl next to him appears to be aged about two. She has sham hanging-sleeves attached to her bodice and a lace-trimmed collar turned down over the bib of her apron. Her hair is arranged in a way often seen in portraits of this date, with a central lock brushed back from the forehead over the lace-edged cap, to be caught in at the back of her head. Her accessories are a coral suspended on a chain and her pet bird.

The two girls holding hands are dressed identically: their bodices have wings, from which fall hanging-sleeves, and the V-shaped waistline is defined by a striped ribbon tied in a bow. Lace has been used as a standing band, and as trimming.
(After Cornelius Johnson, 1619, Charlecote Park)

On 2 May 1617 Anne noted that 'the Child put on her first coat that was laced with lace, being of red baize', but by 15 May 'the Child put on her white coats and left off many things from her head, the weather growing extreme hot'. Another milestone in Margaret's life was noted with pride on 1 January 1619: 'This day the Child put on her crimson velvet coat laced with silver lace, which was the first velvet coat she ever had.' Now that the little girl was nearly five years old she would begin to be dressed in miniature versions of her mother's clothes.[6]

There is a charming portrait at Charlecote Park, painted by an unknown artist and dated 1619, of four of Sir Thomas Lucy III's thirteen children, Margaret, Constance and Bridget, and their baby brother (**241**), which gives a good idea of how children were dressed at this time. The two girls holding hands are probably among the seven children in a Lucy family portrait painted about ten years later (see **50**). In contrast to the stiff dummy-like figures of the Lucy children, the family of George Villiers, 1st Duke of Buckingham, has been depicted in a more naturalistic way in a portrait dated 1628, after Gerrit van Honthorst (see **51**). The baby, George, is straining to escape from his mother's arms and one of the leading strings is clearly visible under her hands. The coif is closely fitted to his head and a coral hangs around his neck, attached to a blue ribbon.

Once a boy reached the age of six or seven he would discard his gown and be breeched. As this meant that he would now wear the same clothes as an adult man, it was an important occasion for the whole family. In 1679 Anne, Lady North described the breeching of her six-year-old grandson, Frank (Francis), to his father, Sir Francis North (later 1st Baron Guildford).

You cannot believe the great concerne that was in the whole family here last Wednesday, it being the day that the taylor was to help to dress little Frank in his breeches in order to the making an everyday suit by it. Never had any bride that was to be drest upon her wedding night more hands about her, some the legs, and some the arms, the taylor butt'ning, and others putting on the sword, and so many lookers on that had I not a finger amongst them I could not have seen him. When he was quite dreste, he acted his part as well as any of them. . . . They are very fitt, everything, and he looks taller and prettyer than in his coats [petticoats].[7]

Lely's portrait of the three younger children of Charles I was painted during the Civil War in 1647, while Algernon Percy, 10th Earl of Northumberland, had custody of them, and it shows that the youngest boy Henry, born in 1639, had not yet been breeched (238). A few years after Frank North was breeched his grandmother wrote that she had sent him off to school with some relief, for if he did not go to school every day her house 'would be too little for him'.[8]

An invaluable source of information about an earlier, Elizabethan, schoolboy can be found in a conversation manual written by a French teacher, Claude de Sainliens, published in 1571. A refugee from religious persecution, Sainliens took the English name of Hollyband and opened a school for the sons of London merchants 'In Paules Churcheyard, hard by the signe of the Lucrece'. The dialogue entitled 'Getting up in the morning' describes the dressing of a schoolboy called Francis, 'a late riser', by his maid Margaret. The boy summons her to bring his clothes and the man-servant is bidden to bring water so that he can wash his face and hands. He stresses that it must not be water from the River Thames as it is 'troubled'. (The river water was so polluted that when a German tourist fell into the Thames in 1598 he found he could not rid his clothes of the smell.) The dialogue continues:

> *Margaret*: Ho Fraunces, rise and get you to schoole: you shal be beaten, for it is past seven . . .
> *Francis*: Margerite, geeve me my hosen: dispatche I pray you: where is my doublet? brying my garters, and my shooes: geeve me that shooyng horne.
> *Margaret*: Take first a cleane shirte, for yours is fowle.
> *Francis*: Make hast then, for I doo tarie too long.
> *Margaret*: It is moyst yet, tary a little that I may drie it by the fier . . .
> *Francis*: . . . where have you layde my girdle and my inckhorne? where is my gyrkin [jerkin] of Spanish leather of Bouffe [buff – ox-hide]? Where be my sockes of linnen, of wollen, of clothe? Where is my cap, my hat, my coate, my cloake, my kaipe [cape], my gowne, my gloves, my mittayns, my pumpes, my moyles [mules], my slippers, my handkarchif, my poyntes [metal-tagged ribbon or lace ties for attaching doublet to hose], my sachell, my penknife and my bookes? Where is all my geare? I have nothyng ready: I will tell my father.

Once he has all his 'geare' he goes downstairs to his father's shop and says his prayers. Then he sets off to school where, by eight o'clock, he will have started his lessons.[9]

Parents would expend much time and effort ensuring that their children were dressed in a way that befitted their social status. But dressing a child in a miniature version of

242 (*left*) The children of John Taylor. Brook wears a purple version of Ashe Windham's fashionable coat (see 88), with similar gold clasps. The timeless quality conveyed by the clothes worn by the other seated boy, and the loose brocade dressing-gown worn by the boy holding the baby, contrasts with the extremely fashionable shape of their elongated, chiselled shoes. The seated girl wears a loosely-draped, grey satin nightgown over a low-cut smock, in a style reminiscent of Lely's ladies of some thirty years earlier. Her hair, however, is arranged in the latest fashion, twisted onto the top of her head with loops of pearls.
(John Closterman, 1696, Beningbrough Hall)

243 (*above right*) Henry and John Harpur wear coats with their fullness concentrated into side pleats. Waistcoat and coat are different lengths, with large flapped pockets positioned at a higher level than earlier fashions dictated. Henry has all the necessary accessories for a gentleman: a beaver tricorne hat tucked under the arm, a pair of plain leather gloves, and black leather shoes with elongated, square toes and distinctive, stacked wooden heels. He wears his cravat in the casual Steinkirk style, named after a battle fought by the French in 1692, loosely tied with the ends twisted into a buttonhole of the waistcoat, or pulled to the side of the coat by a brooch. The matching breeches are narrow in cut with stockings rolled over them at the knee, a fashion that lasted until the mid 1730s.
(Charles D'Agar, 1718, Calke Abbey)

244 (*right*) Detail from a portrait of the Edgar sisters. The older, Elizabeth, is wearing a bodice with a tucker – a frill of muslin or lace which edges the low neckline. The sleeve has a frilled cuff above the elbow, and the frilled sleeve of the smock worn underneath shows below. Both girls wear gauze aprons – Elizabeth's is delicately embroidered along the hem – and their hair is arranged in a practical yet very pretty way, tied back with a ribbon decorated with a pompom of flowers.
(Arthur Devis, 1762, Upton House)

adult dress meant that children's clothing was restrictive and complex, and accessories like gloves and muffs were as important a part of a child's costume as that of an adult's. In 1647 Mary Verney wrote a letter to her husband Ralph, living in exile with their two children in France. Mary was in London, endeavouring to get the sequestration order on Claydon lifted (see p.88). Although she had just given birth to a son, she still found time to worry about buying gloves for an older one, Edmund: 'I think you had best take a glove of my boy Mun's and cutt the bigness of it in paper . . . and I will buy some gloves for him here.' Other accessories she had sent had not fitted and Ralph, knowing Mary would be tempted to spend money that they did not have, wrote that she should refrain from doing so unless she 'can find a real bargain for they are ordinarily cheaper here than with you, and wee must take the thriftiest way'.[10]

The conventions of portrait painting in the second half of the seventeenth century often demanded a timeless style of dress which had little connection with everyday fashionable clothing. Children's portraits seldom escaped this stylisation and so provide little information about a difficult period in the history of dress. In most of the portraits from this period the children are nearly all dressed like their parents, in pseudo-classical garments and indeterminate swags of drapery. A portrait group of children that exploits all the conventions of baroque theatricality is John Closterman's 1696 painting of the the children of John Taylor of Bifrons Park, Kent (242). The group is contrived as a play on the Taylor motto 'Fama candida rosa dulcior' – fame is sweeter than a white rose. The seated boy, Brook Taylor, who became a famous mathematician, would appear to prefer to be crowned with a laurel wreath, indicating fame and achievement, rather than to receive the white roses that are being dispensed by the goddess-like figure of his sister

in the centre. Brook's interests are indicated by what seems to be a recorder in his hands and a sheet of music on the floor in front of him.

In some National Trust houses there are likely to be items from christening sets. At its christening the baby would wear a white satin robe open down the front, its bodice shaped by vertical tucks, and a matching set of cap, headpiece, bib, sleeves and mittens. When the daughter of Georgiana, Duchess of Devonshire, was christened Georgiana Dorothy on 12 August 1783, no expense was spared, and Georgiana wrote to Lady Elizabeth Foster on the same day that: 'The little girl's christening suit was of one piece of Brussels lace made there on purpose, and the finest I ever saw.'[11]

The philosopher John Locke's influential book *Thoughts concerning Education* (1693) was based on the premise that man was born with the natural right of freedom and, as he possessed this right from birth, swaddling was wrong because it deprived a child of its physical freedom. Pamela, the heroine of Samuel Richardson's successful novel *Pamela* (1740–1), endorses these views, too, when she says: 'How has my heart ached many and many a time when I have seen poor babies rolled and swathed, ten or a dozen times round, then blanket upon blanket, mantle upon that; its little neck pinned down to one posture . . . a miserable little pinnioned captive.'[12] By the middle of the eighteenth century swaddling was no longer supported by intellectual or medical opinion and, according to a doctor writing in the *Lady's Magazine* of 1785, 'the barbarous custom . . . is now almost universally laid aside'.[13]

But caps were still an important part of the baby's wardrobe as they were worn day and night from the time the baby was born. It was another hundred years before Locke's revolutionary idea that children should sleep bare-headed at night became accepted practice. These caps often had an insertion worked in a type of needlepoint lace known as 'holie-point', and so fine is the exquisite workmanship of this lace that it can only be fully appreciated when viewed through a magnifying glass. Nineteenth-century examples of 'holie-point' work can be found in the collection at Killerton, in the National Trust Conservation Workroom at Blickling Hall and in the Kay-Shuttleworth collection at Gawthorpe Hall.

In the eighteenth century boys exchanged the long skirts of their frocks and aprons (see **116**) at the age of four for a scaled-down version of adult dress, and an example of this can be seen in Charles D'Agar's portrait of Henry and John Harpur (**243**), painted in 1718. Girls wore a version of their mother's clothes from about the age of two, and even at this tender age they would be fitted for boned bodices. When Arthur Devis painted his delightful portrait of Elizabeth and Charlotte Edgar of Red House Park, Suffolk, in 1762 (**244**) a somewhat simpler style had come into vogue.

The informal style and loosely-cut suit worn by the boy in Johann Zoffany's portrait, *c*.1765, of the Woodley family (see **115**) would have met with approval from John Locke, and from Jean-Jacques Rousseau, whose writings also had a profound effect on the way people thought about the upbringing and education of children. Both men advocated the idea that the physical and social needs of children should be considered separately from those of adults and that choice of clothing should be governed not by status, but by practicality. As Rousseau put it in *Emile*: 'Before the child is enslaved by our prejudices his first wish is always to be free and comfortable. The plainest and most comfortable clothes, those which leave him most liberty, are what he always likes best.'[14]

This revolutionary concept, that children should have a distinctive costume suited to their particular needs and requirements rather than a scaled-down version of their parents' clothes, gathered pace during the 1770s. It is from this period that 'the slow emergence of the modern child may be traced, for it is reasonable to suggest that the youngsters brought up and dressed in the likeness of their elders may have "grown up" more quickly than they would otherwise have done'.[15] During the 1770s girls wore long frocks and sashes until they were in their teens, instead of discarding them at the age of three or four for a boned bodice and skirt. From the 1760s a loose-fitting coat made from a light-weight fabric and a shirt worn open at the neck provided a boy with a practical version of his father's country suit, and it was intended for, and subjected to, energetic use (see 115).

In the 1780s an entirely new silhouette was devised, called a skeleton suit because of its close fit. The trousers were cut to come high above the waist, in contrast to the low-slung breeches, and were fastened onto the bottom of a short jacket with buttons. With the collar of the jacket turned back to the shoulders, the frilled shirt collar was fully visible. These suits were acknowledged to be an English innovation and were illustrated in a German fashion magazine of 1787, *Journal des Luxus und der Moden*, bearing the caption 'comfortable and functional clothing for children based on the theories of John Locke'.[16] It was an eminently practical garment and was soon worn by children of all classes in Britain until its final demise (see 248) in the 1840s. The suit was worn until the boy was about eleven, when he would progress to a tailcoat, breeches and waistcoat – also left open at the neck with the collar turned back to the shoulders, thus again affording a display of the shirt collar with its frilled edging. Worn with natural shoulder-length hair it was a style which anticipated the informal male fashions of the early nineteenth century. This transition can be seen in a portrait of the sons of Sir Richard Croft painted in 1803 by Sir William Beechey (see 245).

An old skeleton suit seen on a second-hand dealer's stall in London's Monmouth Street, near Covent Garden, was even the subject of one of Charles Dickens's *Sketches by 'Boz'* (1836–7):

> It was a patched and much soiled skeleton suit, one of those straight blue cloth cases in which small boys used to be confined before belts and tunics had come in and old notions had gone out, an ingenious contrivance for displaying the full symmetry of a boy's figure by fastening him into a very tight jacket . . . then buttoning his trousers over it, so as to give his legs the appearance of being hooked on just under the arm-pits. . . . It had belonged to a town boy, we could see, there was a shortness about the legs and arms of the suit, and a bagging at the knees, peculiar to the rising youth of London streets.[17]

Cutting a garment so that it displayed 'the full symmetry' of a boy's figure might be aesthetically pleasing, but replacing silk and wool with cotton and linen fabrics meant that the garment gave little protection against the cold, it had less elasticity and it certainly got dirty more quickly.

Neo-classical fashions for men and women in the early nineteenth century were paralleled by those worn by children, with muslin and fine cottons remaining the popular choice. The two young sons of Lydia, Lady Acland in Sir Thomas Lawrence's portrait of

245 The sons of Sir Richard Croft. Francis, aged three, is seated second from left, wearing a white dress and a soft, lace-edged muslin cap embroidered in white and trimmed with a blue ribbon. Thomas, aged five, busy blowing bubbles, has progressed to a skeleton suit. His older brother Herbert, aged ten, wears a coat, breeches and unbuttoned waistcoat. Herbert's sad expression and somewhat isolated position in relation to the group may be due to the fact that this is a posthumous portrait. He died in 1803, while a pupil at Westminster School. (Sir William Beechey, 1803, Croft Castle)

1817–18 (see **151**) wear the high-waisted muslin frocks that were standard wear for boys and girls in their first two or three years of life, but this type of fashionable 'natural' clothing could not have been very practical and must have been quite injurious to health during the winter months.

It is apparent from surviving garments that boys were 'breeched' much earlier by the nineteenth century, and that the transition from babyhood to boyhood was made at the age of two, when skirts were exchanged for a tunic-style dress with matching trousers. The combination of dress and trousers remained popular for boys and girls until the end

246 (*left*) A boy's suit, composed of matching dress and trousers, made 1830-5 from heavy cream cotton printed with tiny brown crescents. The collar, cuffs, edges of the skirt and hem of the trousers are accentuated by brown wool braid embroidered in a loop design. The collar of the dress forms epaulettes over the short, full puffed sleeves.

247 (*above*) Before they reached the age of six or seven, boys were put into knickerbockers and jackets cut, as in this example in a photograph of the Lemann children, 1864, to come just below the knee and pleated into a band. The shirt collar, worn with a bow-tie, is turned down over the collarless jacket. The boy wears long stockings and ankle-length boots. When boys grew older, this ensemble would be exchanged for long trousers and a short jacket. His sister wears a fairly plain dress with a softly pleated bodice and low-set puff sleeves. Her hair is drawn back into an 'Alice' band.

of the century, with the trimming differentiating the sexes. Girls' clothes were trimmed with lace and frills, while boys had buttons, tabs and braid, as in a boy's suit made between 1830 and 1835 (**246**). The bold use of trimming is also shown in a fashion plate from the *Gazette of Fashion*, 1857 (see **184**), which features boys' dresses and trousers alongside the latest men's fashions. Before a boy was six or seven this ensemble would have been exchanged for knickerbockers and jacket (**247**).

248 (*above left*) As children's dress once again copied adult in style, it was frequently included in fashion plates, as in this example from *Petit Courier des Dames*, 1841. Girls' dresses copied the line of ladies' evening dress, including the uncomfortably low neckline that cut across the shoulders and pinioned the arms to the body. One boy, holding a butterfly net, wears the skeleton suit in its final form, whereas the younger boy holding the hoop wears a knee-length pelisse-style dress with trousers and a broad-brimmed hat with an ostrich feather.

249 (*above right*) This beautifully-finished white cotton piqué dress follows the *polonaise* fashion of the 1870s. The bustle effect has been created by an apron-style overskirt edged with pleated fabric, while the bodice and sleeves are trimmed with gathered ruffles of the same fabric.

Frills, lace and ruching are more apparent in an 1841 fashion illustration of girls' dresses (**248**). A dress from a similar period is worn by the daughter of the Reverend Calvert R. Jones in an 1845 photograph (see **166**), which shows that even girls' clothes were supported by stiffened petticoats to achieve a fashionably domed shape. Such styles would have been worn with short socks and flat, side-buttoned, toe-capped boots. The increased width of women's skirts in the 1850s was echoed in those worn by young girls, but their short skirts, distended by stiffened petticoats and, after 1856, mini crinolines, revealed the bottom half of the body, so it had to be covered with long pantalettes. These were loose drawers with frills round the bottom of each leg, worn from about 1825 to the mid-1850s.

Children's clothing, following adult fashion through the Victorian period, was extremely elaborate and highly decorated and all female fashions had their junior version, as in a child's copy of the *polonaise* style of the 1870s (**249**). This dress is typical of the best white frocks worn at children's tea-parties. As Arnold Bennett observed in his novel *The Old Wives' Tale*: 'Weeks of labour, thousands of cubic feet of gas, whole nights stolen from repose, eyesight and general health, will disappear into the manufacture of a single frock that accidental jam may ruin in ten seconds.'[18]

Although some small girls continued to wear miniature versions of adult fashion in the 1880s, the general trend was to move towards simpler and more practical clothes. By the end of the decade smocking (see **251**) had become an extremely popular decorative device for children's clothes and though first employed on the yoke soon extended to other areas of the dress. Such dresses, when worn by toddlers and young girls, would have a soft, broad sash draped around the hips. A sash was also worn with the popular Princess-line dress but older girls, from the age of ten to fourteen, discarded the sash and wore the dress with a double skirt (**250**), as portrayed by the Prince of Wales's three

daughters. The alternative to this style, a loosely draped jacket and closely pleated skirt, is worn by the Princesses' unknown companion.

Despite these developments, getting dressed and undressed was still a slow and laborious process. Recalling her childhood at Hardwick Hall at the turn of the century Lady Maud Baillie, daughter of the 9th Duke of Devonshire, remembered that 'each activity meant a change of clothing, and the lacing up, or unlacing, of high laced boots. All clothing was under the supervision of the nanny, and was therefore kept on the nursery floor at the very top of the house. The idea of keeping coats downstairs or near the schoolroom was unheard of.'[19] Gwen Raverat found that the most time-consuming chore in her childhood was the continual buttoning and unbuttoning of the layers of clothes. 'There must have been something aristocratic about buttons in those days, for everything that could possibly button and unbutton was made to do so; buttons all down the front of one's nightgowns, buttons on the sleeves, buttons everywhere. That anonymous genius, who discovered that clothes could be slipped over one's head, had not yet been born; nor had his twin brother, who discovered elastic.'[20]

Even in this century very young boys and girls were dressed identically in frilly dresses, usually trimmed with broderie anglaise, and their hair was left to fall in natural

250 (*above left*) Maud, Louise and Victoria, daughters of the Prince and Princess of Wales, are depicted standing on a bridge over the Debdon Burn at Cragside, Northumberland. The Princesses' pale lilac summer dresses have a centre front opening decorated with bows, and a tie-back skirt with back draperies in the same colour. Tightly buttoned boots and stockings were standard wear, whatever the season. (H.H. Emmerson, 1884, Cragside)

251 (*above right*) The girl's black wool dress from 1900–5 would have been worn when the family was in mourning. It has a large frilled collar and smocking on the cuff and on the skirt below the yoke. It is worn under a plain white pinafore with a frilled cap sleeve. The boy's wool sailor suit was made *c.*1910 to fit a seven-year-old. It still has its original price tag – 32s 6d.

252 A photograph of the Bankes family of Kingston Lacy, taken in 1908. Daphne and Viola wore comfortable loose-fitting blouses and skirts, but their large hats must have been difficult to keep on. Their brother, Ralph, and mother, Henrietta, wore stylish versions of the workman's cap, and Ralph had a matching reefer coat and gaiters buttoned up the side.

curls around the face. For older girls in the late Victorian and Edwardian periods the standard daytime costume was a pinafore dress and blouse, always worn with thick black stockings and tightly-buttoned boots, and for boys it was often a sailor suit (251). The pinafore dress was destined to have a long life as it evolved into the gym-tunic, which was worn at school for games lessons to become, by 1910, standard school uniform. An alternative dress, widely worn by older girls, was a yoked dress made from white cotton with a wide sash at the waist, detailing on the collar and tight-fitting cuffs. In his account of his Edwardian childhood, *Cricket in the Grass*, Kenneth de Burgh Codrington remembered a hot summer day:

> Eleanor was wearing another of her white broderie anglaise frocks, full in the skirt and wide at the shoulder, tied with a blue sash. On a chair by her lay her large floppy leghorn straw hat, also tied with a blue ribbon. There were a great many other girls of thirteen dressed exactly like that in England on that clear August Sunday. And they and Eleanor would continue to be dressed like that until the close of their seventeenth year, when they might be given a party frock from London, probably bought in Westbourne Grove.[21]

Gwen Raverat did not have fond memories of the clothes she wore at that time: 'It fairly makes my heart bleed to see photograph after photograph of ourselves as children playing in the garden in high summer always in thick, black, woolly stockings and high boots. We wore too, very long full overalls with long sleeves, and of course hats or caps of some sort.'[22] As ladies' hats acquired gargantuan proportions in the first decade of the twentieth century, girls' hats also went through a similar escalation in size, like the disproportionately large hats worn by Daphne and Viola Bankes (252). Viola recalled in her book *A Kingston Lacy Childhood* (1986) that many undergarments were worn under her seemingly simple costume of blouse and skirt:

We always wore Jaeger combinations in soft creamy-grey wool, 'Wool next to the skin' being an inflexible rule in those days. They had short sleeves and came down to our knees. Under our petticoats we also wore cotton knickers made at home and long black stockings, like little nuns. Parisian, flesh-coloured stockings did not come in till 1912. Our sleeves were fastened tightly by a strap with one button. At first our frocks and pinafore were white which was then thought a very hygienic colour for children, as it showed the dirt.[23]

Viola also wrote about when they went for walks: 'Children were never expected to do anything for themselves, in those days, if they had maids. So we would stretch out our legs for Alice or Winnie to fasten the hooks on our high button boots, then, weather permitting, we would set off, with Nurse and the nurserymaid in their grey coats, nurserymaid pushing the pram, Nanny walking majestically behind.'[24]

Albert Edward, Prince of Wales, had launched the idea of the sailor suit for children when the tailor who outfitted sailors of the Royal Navy made him one in 1846 when he was five. By the turn of the century sailor suits were a popular outfit for boys (see 251) and girls (253) of all ages. In winter the boy's suit, with wide-legged trousers and front flap fastening, was made from navy blue wool, and in summer from a stout white cotton with blue facings.

There may have been little variation between the classes in children's clothing, but it

253 (*above left*) Winifred Armstrong wore a girl's version of the sailor suit in this photograph, *c.*1902, but any comfort offered by the loose top and skirt must have been dispelled by the thick-ribbed stockings, laced boots and hat. Her brother William wore a loosely-cut, matching jacket, waistcoat, knickerbockers and a cricketing cap.

254 (*above right*) According to Liberty's advertisement in the 18 September issue of *The Ladies' Field* of 1909, this girl's coat could be teamed with a huge hat of 'velveteen, with soft beaver felt brim, trimmed with a bow of ribbon' and a substantial fur muff. The hat cost £2 7s 6d, the muff, if made of mole skin, 18s 6d, and of squirrel, £1 5s 0d. The total cost of the ensemble, if squirrel was chosen, was £9 13s. Accessories were available in as wide a range of styles for girls as for their mothers.

255 In a photograph taken on 19 September 1915, the girl, identified as Juliette, wears a cotton tunic edged with white bobbles over a matching skirt with central box pleat. It is a strikingly simple outfit, but is decorated with very delicate embroidery and two panels of drawn work. The itchy black stockings, lace-up boots and massive hats that were the bane of Edwardian girls, have gone for ever, replaced by the comfortable combination of socks, strap shoes and a soft, squashy hat.

would have been quite easy to determine the social status of the wearer by the quality of his or her clothes. As much attention was focused on what the children wore as on the clothes of their parents. Kenneth de Burgh Codrington points out: 'It was the quality of our clothes that really distinguished us from the children of the lower orders with whom we did not play, not the cut or pattern, for we all wore identical overalls and pinafores and knickerbockers.'[25]

A child whose clothes were purchased from Liberty's would certainly have been marked out as having wealthy and very stylish parents. As with the female fashions there, their range of children's clothes was distinguished by exquisite fabrics, hand-embroidered decoration and 'picturesque old-world' designs. A girl's cream silk satin coat purchased from them, *c.*1909, is a beautiful example with its elegant simple shape and the embroidery on net on the collar and cuffs (254). An advertisement for Liberty's in *The Ladies' Field* of 18 September 1909 features a very similar coat, with the information that it was available 'In velveteen (100 colours) lined with silk and interlined. Collar and Cuffs hand-embroidered on Shantung Silk. Suitable for a girl twelve years of age. £5 19s 6d.'[26]

The First World War had as decisive an effect on clothes for children as it had upon ladies' fashions. For children of all ages, restrictive and formal clothes were replaced by practical garments. The number of servants available to help children on and off with their clothes had, of course, dwindled dramatically with the war. And at last children's basic requirements were recognised, that a garment should be easy to take on and off, should not impede movement, and should be easy to clean.

The romper suit was introduced for toddlers. For girls frilly knickers, starched flounced petticoats, fancy white dresses, long ringleted hair, picturesque hats and black stockings were exchanged for straight-cut, low-waisted dresses, short white socks and shoes (255). Hair was either cut short in a bob or arranged in pigtails. Boys traded their stiff collars and knickerbocker suits for jerseys and shirts with soft collars that could be teamed with either shorts or flannel trousers.

This change must have been blessed release to children of that generation, although it had come too late for Gwen Raverat, who failed to see any charm in the clothes that she was forced to wear during her Edwardian childhood:

> I thought all my clothes horrible. I can't remember liking a single coat or hat or frock in all my youth, except for one pinafore with pink edges. There is a theory that we always admire the present-day fashions, and think those which are recently past vulgar, till lapse of time gives them a period romance again. This cannot be true . . . all the fashions from 1890 to 1914 seemed to me then, and seem to me still, preposterous, hideous and uncomfortable.[27]

One labour more, then muse of mine
That broughtest dorset into birth
And before you leave us, enter
To record our old Carpenter.
Tis threescore years, then young in gram...
When here, at first, he held an hamm...
Under his Father, dead long since
Who was entitled = The black Prince.

A Raiser this indeed of Houses,
That has already had four Spouses.
And if the Present, dont survive,
Hopes to rebuild them up to five;
From these bold strokes, arise a race
Of Princes to adorn the place,
Who thrive beneath their parent stock,
And make good Chipps from that old block.

*Thalia the dancing
sportive sister of the
nine.

Ed. Prince Æt. 75. 1792.

Old Charles Prince the presen...
Ed... Father was the Carpente...
at Firbeck, in M.r Mellers ti...
who was used to call him the
Black Prince, being a black ...
dark com...

CHAPTER EIGHT

Dress Suitable to their Station: Clothes for Servants

The term livery comes from the Old French *livrer*, originally meaning to hand over food and clothes to servants and retainers. A seventeenth-century ballad on the wearing of livery runs:

> The Nobles of our Land
> Were much delighted then,
> To have at their command
> A crue of lustie Men,
> Which by their Coates were knowne,
> Of Tawnie, Red or Blue,
> With Crests on their sleeves showne,
> When this Old Cap was new.[1]

From medieval times, in noble households in England, livery colours, picking out the two most prominent colours in the coat-of-arms of a noble family, might be worn by anyone who served in any way, and were not restricted to those who had a specific duty or post in the household. At this period a noble household could range from personal attendants who were well-born – including young men from another noble family who were learning the courtesies of life – to the most menial servants. Superior gentlemen servants would wear the livery colours on their hat, hood or gown. Lower servants would have their clothing provided by their employer, so that when they went abroad with their master, or came before his guests, they would wear full livery colours with an embroidered badge on the breast, back or sleeves.

Sumptuary laws were passed during the reigns of Richard II (1377–99) and Henry IV (1399–1413) to try to control the wearing of livery by limiting it to menial servants, in an attempt to cut down on private armies of retainers. But these efforts did not prove effective, for sumptuary legislation continued to be promulgated, including a series of ten proclamations issued between 1559 and 1597 by Elizabeth I (see p.27). These attempted to define exactly what fabrics, furs and trimmings could be worn by each

256 Edward Prince, the carpenter at Erddig in the late eighteenth century. He wears a heavy wool coat that is too small for him, a stiff leather apron and a black hat, the wide brim of which would afford protection from the elements. The house at Erddig can be seen in the distance, while Prince's virtues are extolled in the verse by Philip Yorke I.
(John Walters of Denbigh, 1792, Erddig)

rank of society. Servants were not allowed to wear silk, although an amendment passed
in 1597 permitted the Queen's servants, and those of noblemen and gentlemen, to wear
'Badges and cognizances or other ornaments of velvet and silk' on their livery coats and
cloaks. The household accounts for 1611–2 for Francis Manners, 6th Earl of Rutland,
record that the blue coats worn by his servants were embroidered with a peacock. The
upper servants had a velvet ground, costing 6s, whereas the lower servants had their
peacocks embroidered on a satin ground at a cost of 5s.

New liveries would also be ordered for special occasions, such as a royal visit. Lord
Rutland ordered his liveries with their peacocks ready for James I's visit to Belvoir
Castle in 1612. When Elizabeth I made a royal progress to Lord North's home at Kirt-
ling, near Cambridge, in 1578, North spent £23 3s 8d on tawny cloth for new livery, and
£9 on coats for his servants, which were worn with gold neck chains and the badge of the
family embroidered on the left sleeve.

257 (*opposite*) Queen Elizabeth I being carried amid her officers of state, courtiers and servants, all of whom are attired according to rank. Six Knights of the Garter lead the procession: second from the left is George Clifford, 3rd Earl of Cumberland (father of Lady Anne Clifford, p.63); next to him is the Lord Chamberlain, Lord Hunsdon, carrying his white rod of office; holding the Sword of State is Gilbert Talbot, 7th Earl of Shrewsbury (step-son and son-in-law of Bess of Hardwick, p.24).

Behind the Queen's chair stand three elderly gentlemen who are 'grooms of our coaches or litters'. Their livery comprises red tunics embroidered in gold with the royal arms, matching breeches and black skull-caps. Lining the route are twelve Gentlemen Pensioners wearing their uniform of a black cloak and a gold chain of office. Each holds a halberd issued from the Royal Armoury.

On the right hand side there are eight ladies of the court, and it is likely that the figure in the foreground, clad in shimmering white and silver, is one of the Queen's Maids of Honour. (Attributed to Robert Peake, *c*.1600, Sherborne Castle)

As summer and winter liveries formed part of the wages for every servant, this biannual provision represented a substantial financial outlay. This is why Rowland Whyte felt the need for some clarification from his master, Sir Robert Sidney, when he was entrusted with purchasing livery in London in 1597. He wrote, 'How many yards you will bestow in a cloak, what trimming, what colour?'[2] Servants taken into smaller households also received clothing as part of their wages. John Dee, the mathematician and astrologer, noted in his diary on 29 September 1595: 'Margery Stubble of Hounslow, our dry nurse, entered into the yere of her service beginning on Michelmas Day, and is to have £3 her yeres wages and a gown cloth of russet.'[3]

The return of Charles II in 1660 was marked in some style by the 5th Earl of Bedford, who ran up a bill of £245 2s 0d at the mercer, woollen draper, silkman, milliner, hosier, tailor, haberdasher and cutler. This was for 'several extraordinary liveries' for his male servants who were on public display: the coachman, three grooms, the postilion and his six footmen. The postilion assisted the coachman when he was driving four or more horses, while footmen at this period were employed to run on foot by the side of the master or mistress when out riding or in a carriage.

Although many servants were still required to run a noble household in the seventeenth century, the large number of gentlemen attendants had disappeared. Upper servants now meant the steward, butler, valet, groom of the chambers, clerk of the kitchen and, in time, the housekeeper, who were dressed much like their employers. The discarding of their livery was regarded as a rise in status and social advancement. Lower servants, like the coachman and the footman and, on large estates, the park keeper and gamekeeper, continued to wear the family livery. In smaller households, provision of new livery to estate workers was more erratic – as they were rarely inside the house or on public view. This attitude is clearly stated in a letter written by Sir John Verney of Claydon in 1698, refusing to give his keeper a new livery: 'I gave him one last year, there is no reason which I should give one a livery that doth not wait on me nor my wife ten times in a year.'[4]

Even modest households would provide livery if they could afford to do so. When Samuel Pepys was given his first important post, he immediately ordered some livery for his solitary male servant, recording the event in his diary on 23 March 1662: 'This morning was brought to me my boyes fine livery, which is very handsome, and I do think to keep to black and gold lace upon gray, being the colour of my armes for ever.'[5]

To complement the livery of coachmen and postilions, the family coach and horse trappings, and even the sedan-chairs, would be decorated in the family colours, embellished with the coat-of-arms. When Sir John Verney married for the second time in 1692, he decided to alter his coat-of-arms to incorporate those of his new wife. He wrote: 'I have put side glasses in my Coach, and taken off the red tassels from my harness and put on white ones and also white trappings on ye bridels and made new liveries for my servants, the Arms I will alter shortly by putting her Coate with mine.'[6]

Lady Verney, writing to her stepson Ralph in 1704, gives some idea of the cost of livery. She warned him that he would have to spend about £150 a year if he wanted to compete with Sir Edward Denton who 'has a very rich Leverys a making at your tailor ... a whole cloth a laced with Crimson Yellow and Gold, the breadth of your Hand and made full-laced like the Queen's'.[7]

Of the Conditions of this Negro,
Our information is but meagre,
However here, he was a Dweller,
And blew the horn for Master Mellor.
Here, too he dy'd, but when or how
Can scarcely be remember'd now.
But that to Marchwiel he was sen
And had good Christian interment.
Pray Heav'n may stand his present frie
Where black or white distinctions, en
For sure on this side of the grave
They are too strong, twixt Lord & Slav
Here also liv'd a dingy brother,
Who play'd together with the other
But of him, yet longer rotten?
Every particular's forgotten,
Save that like Tweedle-dum & di
These but in notes, could eer agree
In all things else, as they do tell y
Were just like Handel and Corelli
O had it been in their life's course
T'have met with Massa Wilber force,
They woud in this alone have joine
And been together of a mind,
Have raisd their horns, to one high
And blown his Merits, to the Moon

258 The black coachboy at Erddig, wearing a very smart livery, comprising a red waistcoat and a green jacket with red revers and cuffs. The edge of both garments is liberally trimmed with silver lace and silver buttons. (Unknown artist, 1730s, Erddig)

Ralph's son, also Ralph, 2nd Earl Verney, was a flamboyant character, whose coach-and-six was escorted round the country by 'a brace of tall negroes, with silver French horns . . . perpetually making a noise, like Sir Henry Sidney's Trompeters in the days of Elizabeth, blowing very joyfully to behold and see'.[8] It was considered something of a status symbol at this time to have a black servant, and this is why they are so frequently included in family portraits (see **74** and **98**).

At Erddig, hanging in the servants' hall, is a striking portrait of a black coachboy, clad in smart livery, holding the horn that he would have blown whilst riding on a coach

(258). This is traditionally held to be the coachboy employed by John Meller, owner of Erddig in the early eighteenth century. Recent research, however, suggests it might be an inn sign which was later adapted by Philip Yorke I to fit in with his collection of servants' portraits (see p.294). He added a poem in the 1770s admitting 'our information is "but 'me'gre'"' about the boy, but it was certain that if he had 'met with Massa Wilberforce [the philanthropist MP William Wilberforce who campaigned for abolition of the slave trade]' he would have blown his horn to praise 'his merits to the Moon'. The status of negro servants in England was that of slaves until 1772, when employers were no longer allowed to keep them against their will. Before 1772 they were required to wear closely-fitting collars engraved with the name and dwelling of their master, so that they could be identified if they escaped. A collar can be seen in Kneller's portrait of Captain Thomas Lucy and his page at Charlecote (see 74).

In the eighteenth century livery for household servants tended to be made from cloth, serge or plush, and consisted of a collarless knee-length coat liberally trimmed with gold or silver braid and buttons stamped with the employer's crest, a long waistcoat, knee-breeches and white silk stockings (see 265). The coat was usually made in two colours, with the collar, lapels and cuffs contrasting with the main colour, but matching the waistcoat. The distinctive 'shoulder' knot was worn on the right shoulder. It was a bunch of cord or braid loops that was sometimes tipped with ornamental metal tags. The knot was such an intrinsic part of livery that a footman was often referred to as a 'Knight of the Shoulder Knot'. If the footmen wore their own hair, it had to be powdered: otherwise a wig was worn at all times. When dressed in his formal attire, the footman wore a bag wig, a square black silk bag enclosing the queue of the wig, drawn in at the nape of the neck by a running string concealed by a black bow.

In the early part of the eighteenth century, the footman still retained his outdoor function, as a running servant. His out-of-doors livery consisted of a great coat that fell below the knees and a tricorn hat, sometimes trimmed with gold braid, and even with a cockade. He often carried a long cane with a gold or silver top containing a mixture of eggs and white wine to sustain him as he ran through the streets. A running footman could cut an impressive figure. In George Farquhar's play, *The Beaux' Stratagem*, 1707, a servant when asked about the footman's livery, replies: 'Livery! Lord, Madam I took him for a captain, he's so bedizen'd with Lace, and then he has . . . a silver-headed Cane dangling at his Nuckles . . . and has a fine long periwig tied up in a bag.'[9]

The difficulty in distinguishing between gentlemen and servants in livery was particularly acute for foreign visitors, creating problems of identification and etiquette. When Count Kielmansegge was entertained by the Duke of Newcastle at his London home in Lincoln's Inn Fields in 1761–2, he found that 'At least ten to twelve servants out of livery waited upon us, of whom the majority wore long wigs, which would naturally make it difficult for a stranger to distinguish between guests and servants. Now all these people, in spite of their fine clothing, expect their tips when you leave, but to a gold-laced coat you cannot offer a solitary shilling.'[10]

Fashion influences took place in reverse, too, at this time. Two garments from the working man's wardrobe, the frock-coat and the greatcoat, made the transition from practical garments to fashionable wear. The frock-coat had acquired fashionable status by the 1740s, followed shortly by the greatcoat, with its large collar and wide cuffs. The enduring quality of greatcoats can be seen in an unusual survival of servants' livery at Erddig (259). Hanging in the butler's pantry are two greatcoats, or box coats, that belonged to the Yorkes' coachman (see p.295). In the 1790s another working man's outer garment, the coachman's caped greatcoat (260) was similarly elevated in status and became an essential part of the gentleman's wardrobe. Ladies also wore caped overcoats when travelling in inclement weather. The one illustrated here (261) is made from close wool of a felt-like texture, so thick that the edges of the coat have been left unbound as they do not fray. It would certainly have offered protection from the cold. When the greatcoat was no longer fashionable, George Augustus Sala wrote sadly in 1859 of its demise:

> But where is the great coat – the long, voluminous wide-skirted garment of brown or drab broad cloth, reaching to the ankle, possessing unnumbered pockets. . . . This venerable garment had a cape, which, in wet or snowy weather, when travelling outside the 'Highflyer' coach, you turned over your head. Your father wore it before you, and you hoped to leave it to your eldest son. Solemn repairs – careful renovation of buttons and braiding were done to it, from time to time. A new great coat was an event – a thing to be remembered as happening once or so in a lifetime.[11]

Erddig was given to the National Trust by the last of the Yorkes, Philip III in 1973. It is not a particularly fine house architecturally, but it has two great assets – a fine collection of early eighteenth-century furniture, and a uniquely rich archive of inventories, letters, household accounts and information about the servants, kept by the Yorke family since 1733, when Simon Yorke I inherited the estate from his uncle, John Meller. (The eldest Yorke sons were invariably called Simon or Philip, hence the numbering to identify individuals.)

The information about the servants employed by the Yorkes not only includes details in the household accounts, but also portraits of them with tributes in verse, which now hang in the servants' hall at Erddig. The first set of portraits was painted for Philip Yorke I in the 1790s by John Walters of Denbigh. The second set was commissioned by his son Simon II in 1830 from an anonymous painter. Later generations are recorded in daguerreotypes and photographs. As Merlin Waterson explains in his book about Erddig, 'there was nothing unusual about a country-house owner having expensive portraits painted of his horse, his prize-winning bulls or his dogs – they, after all, were the product of careful breeding like their owners – but to extend the treatment to generations of servants was thought to be a symptom of extreme eccentricity'.[12]

As livery was replaced on a regular, usually annual, basis, it was not worn until it was in a state of total disrepair, but departing servants would often take their livery with them and recirculate garments on the second-hand clothes market, where they would gradually be reduced to tatters. We have good reason, therefore, to bless the eccentricity of the Yorkes, as the portraits provide a very rare chance of visually tracing the development of the dress of household servants since the eighteenth century.

At Erddig livery was given only to the footmen, coachmen, grooms and postilion – again, the servants most likely to be on public view. In 1776, for example, Philip Yorke noted that he took on a new coachman on the understanding that he would receive £20 a

259 These nineteenth-century livery coats, called box coats, were worn by the footmen, generations of whom have inscribed their names on the wall of the butler's pantry at Erddig. They would have been worn with top hats, the bands of which matched the braid decoration on the coat collar and cuffs. Double-breasted box coats were also worn by the coachman, with a top hat with cockade and top boots.

260 (*above*) From the late eighteenth century, and throughout the nineteenth, the coachman's bulky coat with its layers of capes afforded him some protection from the elements. He always wore breeches and, when on the box of the coach, jack boots or gaiters. A coachman in service in the nineteenth century would be expected to wear a wig and a top hat. The lady bidding adieu to a traveller in *The Departure* wears the typical dress of a working woman – mob cap, folded kerchief and a long apron fastened over a bedgown.
(George Morland, 1792, Upton)

261 (*right*) An example of fashion borrowing from occupational dress. This wool caped coat dating from 1820-30, and thought to be for a lady, has an overlapping front and buttons from neck to hem. Four layers of capes cover the high-waisted belt and the high collar of the caped section has beige velvet slots around it, possibly to fasten a scarf. Beige velvet has also been used to line the collar and its concealed front tab fastening, and there is a slit opening in the side of the coat with a flap buttoned at the centre.

year in wages, plus a 'full suit of livery with plush breeches 1 pair Buckskin breeches Waistcoat and Frock Greatcoat and boots in every second year and to provide himself out of his said wages with a frock coat for common work allow him also a jacket when neat'.[13] The estate workers at Erddig, therefore, did not wear livery, and a portrait of Edward Prince, the carpenter, painted in 1792, shows him in working clothes (see 256).

The last member of the Erddig staff to wear livery was John Jones. Originally employed as a coachman, in time he combined the roles of carpenter, gardener and estate foreman. By 1943, when a photographer from *Picture Post* came to the house, Jones was the estate odd-job man and, at the photographer's request, he donned his long-relinquished livery – a coat, with a collar decorated with braid, and top hat (see 259), and posed for a photograph with the only other remaining member of staff, the housekeeper, Lucy Jones (no relation).

Unlike their male counterparts, female servants in the eighteenth century did not wear livery or uniform. It was an established practice that the maid should be given the cast-off clothes of her mistress and, in the event of her death, part or all of her wardrobe. When the Countess of Bristol died in 1741, her husband, John Hervey, 1st Earl, wrote to their son:

> I am glad to find that you have delivered to Williams all the things which were your poor mother's and which by a customary sort of right are now due to every common servant in her place; but as her merit and services for near 18 years have been of the most uncommon kind, that consideration alone would have entitled her to any favour out of the ordinary course of proceedings between executors and residuary legatees.[14]

Just as confusion between a gentleman and his liveried servants could cause problems, so the similarity in appearance of a mistress and her personal maid or waiting woman could give rise to embarrassing social situations. Daniel Defoe wrote in 1725: 'I remember I was put very much to the Blush being at a Friend's House and by him required to salute the Ladies, and I kiss'd the chamber jade [hussy] into the bargain for she was as well dressed as the best.'[15]

Typically, a country woman's working dress in the eighteenth and early nineteenth centuries would have comprised a cotton or linen bedgown, petticoat and apron. The bedgown was a three-quarter-length loose wrapping jacket that was worn over a petticoat of wool or linen. As it had no fastening, it could be secured about the waist by apron strings. This arrangement can be seen clearly in an 1803 print, *The Rapacious*

262 An 1803 print showing the unedifying spectacle of a zealous agent carrying out an eviction order. The wife of the evicted tenant is wearing a red bedgown over a blue quilted petticoat, which has been pulled round, fastened at the back and held in place at the waist by the apron. The lady next to her has a similar combination. The tenant is wearing a plain smock (see pp.301–3) under a loose, shapeless coat. His son, kneeling, wears a smock with a simple back opening that has a small area of decoration around it.

steward or the Unfortunate tenant (262). The bedgown probably originated as a kind of dressing jacket, but it was also worn by millworkers in Lancashire, who could have the price of it deducted from their wages.

Until the latter part of the eighteenth century, when cheap, factory-made suits and trousers provided him with a fashionable alternative, the traditional garb of a countryman was a smock (see p.302) worn with breeches made from leather, corduroy (a stout, ribbed cotton material introduced in 1795) or linen, with leather gaiters to protect the lower part of the leg. These garments were made at home and passed on from one generation to the next. It was a costume eminently suited to the wear and tear of country life, and breeches and gaiters were to reappear in the nineteenth century in the wardrobe of the country gentleman (see 136). Whether he wore a tailored Norfolk suit or matching jacket and knickerbockers of the finest wool, he would team them with leather gaiters or thick socks and stout leather shoes (see 207).

In the nineteenth century, the rather informal relationship between family and servants in matters of dress gave way to stricter and more prescribed forms of service. The housekeeper, the senior female servant of the house, would not wear uniform, but was usually dressed in black, carrying the symbol of her authority, a ring of keys to all the rooms, closets and cupboards for which she was responsible. Sarah Wells, the mother of H.G. Wells, was promoted from lady's maid to housekeeper at Uppark in Sussex in 1880. Her son, in his *Experiment in Autobiography* (1934), says that she looked the part when she 'assumed a lace cap, lace apron, black silk dress and all the rest of it', though he rather disloyally went on to say that she was 'perhaps the worst housekeeper that was ever thought of'. Unfortunately Sarah 'did not know how to plan work, control servants, buy stores or economise in any way.'[16] Inevitably her incompetence could not be tolerated and in 1893 Sarah was given a month's notice, at seventy-one years of age.

Mary Webster, the housekeeper at Erddig for more than thirty years, was photographed in the mid-1850s prominently displaying her badge of office, a bunch of keys (263). Philip Yorke II wrote an accompanying poem:

263 Mary Webster, housekeeper at Erddig, photographed in the mid-1850s. Her plain black dress has a very full skirt, a rather coarse-looking checked woollen shawl and a white lace cap threaded with wide black ribbon.

> Upon the portly frame we look
> Of one who was our former Cook
> No better keeper of our Store
> Did ever enter at our door.[17]

Her skill at financial management stood in strong contrast to Sarah Wells's. When she died in 1875, to the amazement of all, her will revealed she had saved £1,300.

Under the command of the housekeeper came the housemaids, who cleaned and tidied the house. For morning work, nineteenth-century maids would wear print dresses with a cap and apron, then change after lunch into black dresses, with a clean apron and frilly cap for their afternoon and evening duties.

The parlourmaid was a somewhat superior maid-servant who, in the absence of a footman, was expected to wait at table and usher in the guests. As she would be seen by all who visited the house, she was expected to be smartly dressed at all times. The importance placed on the parlourmaid's appearance is stressed by Arnold Bennett in *Anna of the Five Towns*, 1902, a novel about life in the Potteries at the turn of the century. When Anna is invited out to tea, she is suitably impressed by the maid who answers the door wearing 'black alpaca with white wristbands, cap, streamers, and embroidered apron (each article a dernier crie from Bostock's great shop at Hambridge)'.[18] Like the housemaids, the parlourmaid wore a print dress with cap and apron in the morning, and after lunch a black dress, the style of which conformed to fashion, a fresh apron and cap. By the end of the nineteenth century, she wore a distinctive starched and frilled apron with a bib secured by cross-straps behind.

The lady's maid did not usually come under the aegis of the housekeeper, but was employed directly by her mistress. As in the previous century, she did not wear a uniform but expected to be fashionably, though not flamboyantly, dressed. Before her elevation to housekeeper, Sarah Wells had been lady's maid to Lady Fetherstonhaugh and her sister, Miss Bullock, at Uppark. She was more admirably equipped for this role, as she had served a four-year apprenticeship with a dressmaker and had taken lessons in millinery. A knowledge of fashion and dressmaking was essential for a lady's maid, as she was required to dress and undress her mistress, put out suitable clothes for whatever activity she might be engaged in during the day, wash her lace and fine linen and keep her wardrobe in an immaculate state of repair. In her autobiography, *Edwardian Daughter*, Sonia Keppel recalled all the tasks her mother's maid had performed, and how surprised she was that her mother managed to cope when deprived of her services in 1914. She remembered the maid 'setting out her underclothes under their lace cover; kneeling on the floor to put on Mamma's stockings, lacing Mamma into her stays (as though she were reining in a runaway horse); doing her hair; pinning her veil on to her hat; buttoning up her gloves; putting her powder and cigarettes and money into her bag. And, behind the scenes, washing, ironing, mending.'[19]

Another female member of staff who was usually directly answerable to the mistress of the house was the children's nurse. She wore a print dress in the morning and a soberly-coloured dress with cap and apron in the afternoon. The severity of the nurse's headwear is indelibly linked in Frances Crompton's mind with discipline and obedience, when remembering her childhood in the 1890s: 'We consider nurse a very cross person. . . . Her aprons are as stiff as the nursery tea-tray, besides being the same plain shape, and she will wear the tightest and sternest caps that were ever seen . . . her caps were all strictish, but her Sunday cap was savage.'[20]

When the children were old enough, they would pass from the care of the nurse to the governess who undertook their early education. The governess was expected to have a ladylike but unassuming appearance. Usually a gentlewoman in reduced circumstances, the governess was socially superior to the nurse, but was not, unlike the lady's maid, entitled to her employer's cast-off clothing.

For male servants, too, the contrast between the dress of upper and lower ranks became more marked in the nineteenth century. The butler was now the head male servant in the household. He continued to wear a sober version of fashionable dress. Lord Hamilton, describing the menservants employed by his parents at Chesterfield House in London in the 1860s, recalled the butler, Burgh, in a 'short frock-coat of the day, unbuttoned, and the natural majesty of his appearance was enhanced by a pointed grey "Imperial" [a small tuft of hair left growing beneath the lower lip, so-called because the Emperor Napoleon III wore one]'.[21] In the 1870s the butler's uniform was

264 The household staff of Cragside pose in their best off-duty clothes, 1890s. By the end of the century women could choose between a tailored jacket, blouse and skirt, and a day dress. The blouses and dresses worn here have high collars, gigot sleeves, narrow waists defined by a belt, and flared skirts. The practice of lining all fabrics gave a strong definition to the silhouette and the extra weight and body this added to the skirts is particularly noticeable in those worn by the seated girls in the foreground. The central figures in the group, the imposing lady in a black satin dress and the stern-looking man in a morning suit, are likely to be the most senior members of the household staff, the housekeeper and the butler.

standardised as a version of his master's evening dress – black tailcoat and trousers, stiff white shirt and tie.

Under the butler came the footmen, no longer fulfilling their running duties, but carrying out a whole host of tasks within the house. They still wore livery when on duty, and were thus clad in a fossilised version of eighteenth-century fashion. In grander establishments there were four sets of livery: 'undress' and 'full dress' for indoors, and the same for outdoors. Footmen, being seen in public more than any other member of staff, were often chosen for their looks rather than their character, so that their expensive livery could be seen to best advantage. Lord Hamilton remembered:

> [they] were noble and impressive figures, but it must be owned that their moral worth was not always on a par with the magnificence of their physical deportment. They were always engaged by Burgh, who was more concerned with their physique and more especially with the contour of their calves than with the whiteness of their souls. As the livery to which a recruit succeeded was very expensive, it was first and foremost essential that newcomers should be of stock size, so as to slip into their legacies without any straining of buttons or loose ungainly flaps.[22]

Lanhydrock in Cornwall has been the home of the Robartes family for four hundred years. In 1881, following a disastrous fire, Thomas Agar-Robartes, later 6th Lord Clifden, rebuilt the house to the highest standards of comfort of the time: it now provides a fascinating example of a late Victorian house with all its service quarters intact. Part of the top floor was the realm of the footmen, and their bedrooms and livery room have recently been redecorated to show how they would have looked in the 1880s and 90s. Sadly, there is little remaining of Robartes' livery, apart from some footmen's striped waistcoats, appropriately in the Cornish colours of gold and black (see 3). But the National Trust has been lent the very complete liveries of male servants from another

265 When John S. Tregoning of Landue was appointed High Sheriff of Cornwall in 1904 he purchased new liveries for his footmen, coachman and postilion from a local tailor in Truro. The splendid suits, in the family colours of blue and silver, and the coachman's coat have been loaned to the National Trust and are now displayed in the footmen's wardrobes on the top floor at Lanhydrock. This livery room has recently been redecorated to show how it would have looked in the late nineteenth century. The only surviving livery of the Robartes family of Lanhydrock is shown in 3.

266 John S. Tregoning, High Sheriff of Cornwall, 1904-5, with his chaplain, footmen, coachman and postilion in their new liveries. Full dress livery such as this was a fossilised version of eighteenth-century court dress. The sloped-back coat is reminiscent of the cut of coats in the 1770s (119), as are the distinctive trimmings of buttons and braid. The knee-length coat was worn with a long waistcoat, knee-breeches, white silk stockings, buckled shoes and, in this instance, a cockaded top hat. The employer's crest, once embroidered on the coat, is now stamped onto the buttons.

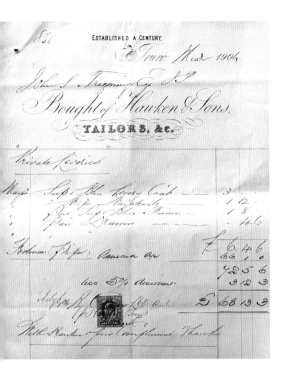

267 (*above*) All the Landue livery was purchased from Hawken & Sons, an old-established firm of tailors in Truro. Livery could also be ordered from a number of specialist outfitters in London – the Robartes bought theirs from Simpson & Son, South Audley Street.

268 (*right*) A late nineteenth-century photograph of the gardening staff at Petworth. Each man displays the main tool of his trade and the miscellany of equipment includes the very latest model of lawnmower and the more traditional spade, rake and trowel. Proudly seated in the middle, the head gardener is smartly dressed in a wool suit and, unlike the dusty bowler hats held by the others, his pristine bowler is balanced on his knee.

Cornish country house, by the Tregonings of Landue, and these, in their blue and silver splendour, hang in the footmen's wardrobes at Lanhydrock (265).

Just as Lord North prepared for the visit of Elizabeth I in 1578 by ordering new livery, and Lord Bedford marked the Restoration of Charles II by lavish spending on servants' clothes, so John S. Tregoning celebrated his appointment as the High Sheriff of Cornwall in 1904 by fitting out his footmen, coachman and postilion in new liveries (266). The garments hark back to those specified by Philip Yorke I a century and a half earlier. For the footmen, jacket with shoulder knot, waistcoat, plush breeches, greatcoat and hat; for the coachman, plush breeches; for the postilion, breeches in velvet.[23] Even the blue and yellow rosettes to adorn the horses survive. All this livery was purchased from Hawken & Sons, Tailors, of Truro, for the sum of £68 13s 3d (267).

Although Tregoning patronised a local Cornish tailor, livery was often ordered from specialist shops of which there were many in London. One of the most prestigious was owned by T.S. Freeman and Sons at 18 Fenchurch Street and another was Thomas Townend of 110 Oxford Street.

At Petworth in Sussex, like Erddig, there is another good collection of images of servants. Petworth was the home in the mid-nineteenth century of George Wyndham, 1st Lord Leconfield, whose daughter-in-law compiled an album of photos of about thirty of the servants in the household. The album bears the title 'All the dear servants at Petworth when I came there', and they pose, sometimes rather self-consciously, in their best clothes. In the 1880s and 90s a local photographer, Walter Kevis, also took group pictures of the different household departments wearing their working clothes. Perhaps one of the most interesting is that of the gardening staff (268).

An earlier photograph, *c*.1860, shows two men and a boy surveying a fallen tree in the park at Petworth. One man wears a suit and a top hat, the other a smock and a bowler hat. The countryman's smock, generally thought of as an ancient garment, in fact has a fairly short history. It dates from the mid-eighteenth century, and evolved from a loose

protective overgarment, generally made of cotton or linen, worn by men working with horses or labouring on the land (269). As the century progressed, the embroidered area on the smock became larger, the patterns more complex. Smocks seem to have been confined to the south of England and the Midlands, with distinctive regional variations in shape. They were available in different colours and quality of linen, determined by the type of work the wearer was involved in – the coarser and simpler garments being used for heavy work, the finest linen smock reserved for Sunday best.

An average smock required about 8 yards of twilled cotton cloth or linen. Its shape was identical to that of a shirt, so it was easy to cut out and sew together. But it was cut very full so that the volume of material could offer total protection to the wearer. To control this fullness, the fabric was gathered up into pleats, which were then embroidered with white or buff thread. The most finely worked smocks were the ones least worn, and most likely therefore to survive.

Smocks were also produced commercially in towns centred around factories that produced the cloth. At Newark-on-Trent in Nottinghamshire ten smock-makers were listed from 1819 to 1872. The linen was woven in Newark, dyed locally, and the smocks made and sold in the town. Designs for the embroidery, stamped on sheet metal pattern printers, are still in existence.

Smocks declined when inexpensive, mass-produced fashionable clothes became generally available. They were seen as old-fashioned garments, worn only by the elderly, though traditionalists like Gertrude Jekyll and the novelist Thomas Hardy deplored the fact that young countrymen had forsaken their durable smocks and corduroy breeches for cheap and shoddy versions of the middle-class suit. Hardy observed that the great change took place between the 1850s and 80s, by which time it was no longer possible to distinguish between urban men and rural men merely by the colour of their clothing.

270 This delightful sketch by Claire Avery, from *Vogue*, May 1914, transforms what was once the functional dress of the working countryman into a fashionable garment that is as chic as it is practical. The next year, the smock made the cover of *Vogue*.

Countrymen, who formerly wore 'whitey-brown flecked with white' were now 'as dark as a London crowd. . . . Formerly they came in frock coats and gaiters, the shepherds with their crooks, the carters with a zone [girdle] of whipcord round their hats, thatchers with a straw tucked into the brim and so on. Now . . . there is no mark of speciality in the groups, who might be tailors or undertakers for what they exhibit externally.'[24]

But smocking now had acquired fashionable status, employed on tea-gowns produced by Liberty's in the late 1880s. An article written by Mrs Oscar Wilde on the 'fashionable revival of this difficult craft' for *The Woman's World* in 1890 explained that 'the artistic modistes had to send their delicate "Liberty" silks down to humble cottages in this county [Sussex] and in Dorsetshire where a few conservative rustics still adhere to the old smock frock.'[25] Smocking was also used extensively in children's clothing, and a beautiful silk smock, *c*.1910, made for a child by a Liberty's outworker can be seen in the Kay-Shuttleworth collection at Gawthorpe Hall.

The final apotheosis of the smock from working-man's uniform to female fashion garment was encouraged by the actress Ellen Terry, who had always favoured loose-fitting smocked dresses and had the smocks made locally to her home in Kent, Smallhythe Place, in a variety of vivid colours. She wore them with a blouse and skirt and flat sandals. Her daughter Edie, a 'highly imaginative stage costumier and a notable Suffragette',[26] also adopted this combination for everyday wear and daringly wore the smock with baggy trousers. When an American friend, Claire Avery, an artist who worked for *Vogue*, visited Ellen and Edie at Smallhythe, she was very impressed by their clothes. In May 1914 an anonymous article appeared in *Vogue* about the smock being an eminently suitable garment for gardening. It had been discovered in England by some unnamed artists who 'brought the smock habit back to America to their garden loving friends, who live in them during the Long Island summer, and bring them into town in winter'.[27] Claire's accompanying sketch (270) confirmed the smock as an enduring fashion garment.

A cartoon published in *Punch* in 1912 depicts an old man in a smock talking to a lady in a carriage, who is looking at the receding figure of a fashionably-dresssed girl in an identical hat. Her Ladyship asks, 'Isn't that my gardener's daughter, Giles?' He replies, 'Yes, yer ladyship; Quite a mistake, touching my 'at to 'er. Why she's as poor as I be.'[28]

Mistaken identity between master and servant, mistress and maid, has been a theme of this chapter, but this was now a general trend rather than an embarrassing incident. On the eve of the First World War, with increased opportunities for employment outside service and profound changes in the social climate, it was becoming difficult to determine a person's station in life by their clothes.

Notes

INTRODUCTION

1. Cecil Beaton, *The Glass of Fashion*, Weidenfeld and Nicolson, 1954, pp.1-3.
2. Ibid., p.232.
3. Gustave Doré and Blanchard Jerrold, *London: A Pilgrimage*, London, 1872, pp.35-6.
4. James Lees-Milne, *People and Places. Country House Donors and the National Trust*, John Murray, 1992, p.219.
5. Ibid.
6. Alice, Lady Fairfax-Lucy, *Charlecote and the Lucys*, Oxford University Press, 1958, p.248.
7. National Trust Guide to Beningbrough Hall, 1992, p.33.

CHAPTER ONE

1. Horace Walpole, *Anecdotes of English Painting in England*, 2 vols, 1828, London, I, p.85.
2. Edward Hall, 'The Triumphant Reign of Henry VIII', quoted in James Lees-Milne, *Tudor Renaissance*, Batsford, 1951, p.20.
3. Report from the Venetian ambassador Giustinian, 'Giustinian's Dispatches', II, p.312. Quoted in J.S. Brewer, *The Reign of Henry VIII from his Accession to the Death of Wolsey*, ed. James Gairdner, 1884, I, pp.8-10.
4. Letter written to Ulrich von Hutten, Antwerp, 23 July 1519, quoted in J. Huizinga, *Erasmus of Rotterdam*, trs. F. Hopman, London, 1952. See also J.B. Trapp and H.S. Herbruggen, 'The King's Good Servant', *Sir Thomas More*, National Portrait Gallery, 1977, no.26.
5. Muriel St Clare Byrne, ed., *The Lisle Letters*, 6 vols, Secker and Warburg, 1983, III, no.698.
6. Ibid., IV, no.895.
7. Ibid., IV, no.896.
8. Ibid., IV, no.906.
9. Ibid., IV, no.908.
10. Ibid., IV, no.871.
11. Ibid.
12. Ibid., IV, no.872.
13. Ibid., VI, Appendix E, pp.189-210.
14. Ibid., VI, p.184.
15. Privy Purse Expenses Princess Mary 1536-44, Ms.Royal 17B xxviii, British Museum. See also A.J. Carter, 'Mary Tudor's Wardrobe', *Costume*, 1984, no.18, pp.9-29.
16. *The Lisle Letters*, op. cit., I, no.81.
17. Report of England made by Giacomo Soranzo, Calendar State Papers, Venetian, V, 1534-54, no.934.

18. William Shakespeare, *Henry VIII*, V.iv.33-5, from the Arden edition, ed. R.A. Foakes, Methuen, 1957.
19. William Harrison, *A Description of England in 1577-8*, ed. F.J. Furnivall, London, 1889, p.148.
20. *The Epigrams of Sir John Harington*, ed. N.E. McClure, University of Pennsylvania, 1925, p.207, no.364.
21. Harrison, op. cit., p.197.
22. Quoted in Victor von Klarwill, *Queen Elizabeth I and some Foreigners*, trs. T.N. Nash, Bodley Head, 1928, p.376.
23. Ben Jonson, *Every Man out of his Humour*, I.ii.40-2, from *The Works of Ben Jonson*, ed. C.H. Herford, P. Simpson and E.M. Simpson, 11 vols, Oxford, 1925-52, III.
24. John Eliot, *The Parlement of Prattlers*, 1593, reissued by Fanfrolico Press, 1928, Dialogue 1, 'The Uprising in the morning'.
25. Philip Stubbes, *Anatomy of Abuses in England in 1583*, ed. F.J. Furnivall, New Shakespeare Society, 1882, p.53.
26. A.L. Rowse, *Simon Forman: Sex and Society in Shakespeare's Age*, Macmillan, 1974, p.93.
27. Nicholas Hilliard, *A Treatise Concerning the Arte of Limning*, ed. R.K.R. Thornton and T.G.S. Cain, Carcanet New Press, 1981, p.87.
28. Sicile, Herald of Alphonso V, King of Aragon, *Le Blason des couleurs en Armes Liurées et deuises*, 1526, trs. by R[ichard] R[obinson] with the title *A Rare True and Proper Blazon of Coloures and Ensignes Military with theyre Peculiar Signification*, 1583, quoted in M.C. Linthicum, *Costume in the Drama of Shakespeare and his Contemporaries*, Oxford, 1936, p.17.
29. R. Hakluyt, *The Principal Navigations, Voyages, Traffiques and Discoveries of the English Nation*, 12 vols, Glasgow, 1589, III, p.249 seq.
30. Harrison, op. cit., p.148.
31. Walpole, op. cit., I, p.251.
32. Thomas Nashe, *Christ's Teares over Ierusalem*, 1593, from *The Works of Thomas Nashe*, ed. from original texts by R.B. McKerrow, Blackwell, 1966, II, p.151.
33. Stubbes, op. cit., p.51.
34. George More, *A True Discourse concerning the certain possession and dispossession of seven persons in one family in Lancashire*, 1600. Quoted in G.B. Harrison, *A Second Elizabethan Journal*, Routledge, 1938, p.177-8.
35. Ibid.
36. Stubbes, op. cit., p.60.
37. Ibid., p.33.
38. Nashe, op. cit., p.142.

39. John Lyly, *Midas*, 1592 from *The Plays of John Lyly*, ed. Carter A. Daniel, Associated University Press, 1988, p.201.
40. Stubbes, op. cit., p.55.
41. *The Diary of Baron Waldstein. A Traveller in Elizabethan England*, trs. and annotated by G.W. Groos, Thames and Hudson, 1981, p.77.
42. Calendar State Papers, Foreign, 1575-7, no.1470, p.596.
43. Janet Arnold, *Queen Elizabeth's Wardrobe Unlock'd: the Inventories of the Wardrobe of Robes prepared in July 1600*, ed. from Stowe MS.557 (British Museum), MS LR 2/121 PRO (Public Record Office), MS. V.b.72, Folger Library (Washington), Maney, Leeds, 1988.
44. Sir Henry Norris replied from Paris on 1 March 1566, 'As for a tailor for the Queen, my wife and I will do what we may', Historic Manuscript Commission, Report on the Pepys Ms. preserved at Magdalene College, Cambridge, 1911, p.99.
45. Cobham to Walsingham, 22 Jan. 1581/2, PRO S.P.78/7, no.12, quoted in Roy Strong, *Portraits of Elizabeth I*, Oxford University Press, 1969, p.21.
46. William Shakespeare, *Much Ado about Nothing*, II.iii.16, from the Arden edition, ed. A.R. Humphreys, Methuen.
47. A.L. Rowse, *Raleigh and the Throckmortons*, Macmillan, 1967, p.100.
48. Ibid., p.160.
49. Stubbes, op. cit., p.55.
50. T. Middleton and T. Dekker, *The Epistle, The Roaring Girl*, 1611, from *The Revels Plays*, ed. P.A. Mulholland, Manchester University Press, 1987, p.68.
51. Muriel St Clare Byrne, *The Elizabethan Home, discovered in Two Dialogues by Claudius Hollyband and Peter Erondell*, Methuen, 1949, *The French Garden*, 1605, Dialogue I, 'The Rising in the Morning', pp.36-40.
52. Janet Arnold, 'Lost from Her Majesties Back', *Costume Society*, Extra Series no.7, 1980, p.60.
53. Thomas Platter, *Travels in England, 1599*, trs. C. Williams, Cape, 1937, p.192.
54. Arnold, *Queen Elizabeth's Wardrobe*, op. cit., pp.77-80.
55. Dedication to Sir William Cecil, John Gerard, *The Herball or General History of Plants*, 1597, British Library. Gerard had superintended Cecil's garden for twenty years. See also George Wingfield Digby, *Elizabethan Embroidery*, Faber & Faber, 1963, pp.36-43.
56. 'New Year's Day Present List 1584', ed. J. Nevinson, *Costume*, 1975, no.9. See also J. Arnold, 'Sweet England's Jewels', from *Princely Magnificence. Court Jewels of the*

Renaissance 1500-1630, Debrett's Peerage Ltd in association with the Victoria and Albert Museum, 1981, pp.31-40.
57. Eliot, op. cit., Dialogue 4, 'The Goldsmith'.
58. The Cheapside Hoard in the Museum of London, the stock of a London jeweller dating from about 1600, includes a number of unset stones – topaz from Brazil, Indian rubies and diamonds, Persian lapis lazuli, and peridot from the Red Sea.
59. T. Dekker, *The Seven Deadly Sinnes of London*, 1606, The Percy Reprints, no.4, Blackwell, 1922, p.44.
60. Platter, op. cit., p.156.
61. John Stow, *The Annales or generall Chronicle of England beginning first by Maister John Stow and after him continued and augmented . . . by Edmond Howes*, London, 1615, pp.867-9. See also his *The Survey of London*, 1598, ed. C.L. Kingsford, London, reprinted from the revised text of 1603, 2 vols, Oxford University Press, 1908, reprinted 1971.
62. There is a portrait of Hobson in the Long Gallery at Montacute painted in 1629 when he was 84 years old. Apparently he insisted on letting out horses only in their proper turn, hence the meaning of the phrase 'Hobson's choice' – this one, or none.
63. Dekker, op. cit., p.37.
64. Fynes Moryson, 1617, quoted in *London in the Age of Shakespeare; An Anthology*, ed. L. Manley, Croom Helm, 1986, p.43.
65. Sir William Davenant, quoted in John Bedford, *London's Burning*, Abelard-Schumann, 1966, p.18. The appearance of these towering wooden façades can be gauged from one that is preserved in the Victoria and Albert Museum – the home of Sir Paul Pindar, built in Bishopsgate in the 1620s. When the house was demolished in 1890 the façade was saved and transferred to the Museum.
66. Letters of Philip Gawdy, Ms. Egerton 2804, British Museum. Printed by The Roxburghe Club, London, 1906, no.148, ed. I.H. Jeayes, p.50.
67. John Florio, *His first fruits which yeelde familiar speech*, London, 1578, Ch.19.
68. John Gage, *The History and Antiquities of Hengrave*, London, 1822, pp.213-4.
69. Eliot, op. cit., Dialogue 3, 'The Mercer'. See also Linthicum, op. cit., chapters on silks and woollen cloth, pp.110-27 and 53-91.
70. William Shakespeare *I Henry IV*, III.iii.65-70, from the Arden edition, ed. A.R. Humphreys, Methuen, 1974. Dowlas cost about 9 pence a yard, see Linthicum, op. cit., pp.92-103.
71. P. Clabburn, *The National Trust Book of Furnishing Textiles*, Penguin, 1988, p.239.

72. Stow, *The Survey of London*, op. cit., I, p.345.
73. Gawdy, op. cit., p.41.
74. Ibid., p.62.
75. Ibid., p.121.
76. J.W. Burgon, *The Life and Times of Sir Thomas Gresham*, 2 vols, 1839, I, p.35.
77. William Shakespeare, *1 Henry IV*, op. cit., I.iii.35.
78. Robert Greene, *A quip for an upstart courtier*, 1592, Scolar Press facsimile, 1971.
79. Thomas Heywood, *A Critical Edition of The Faire Maide of the Exchange*, III.ii.69-72, ed. K.E. Synder, Renaissance Drama Series, Garland Publishing, New York and London, 1980.
80. Jonson, op. cit., IV.vi.79.
81. De L'Isle and Dudley MS at Penshurst, Historic Manuscripts Commission, 1925, I, p.263.
82. Eliot, op. cit., Dialogue 7, 'The Shoemaker'.
83. Sir Thomas Overbury, 'A Country Gentleman' from *A Book of Characters*, published in *The Miscellaneous Works of Sir Thomas Overbury*, ed. E. Rimbault, London, 1890, p.66.
84. Shrewsbury tradesman's invoice from *Shropshire Archaeological and Natural History Transactions*, 1879, II, p.400.
85. *The Lisle Letters*, op. cit., IV, no.848.
86. Robert Greene, 'The Art of Cony-Catching', 1591, published in *Rogues, Vagabonds and Sturdy Beggars. A New Gallery of Tudor and Early Stuart Literature*, ed. A.F. Kinney, University of Massachusetts Press, 1990, p.167.
87. William Shakespeare, *Love's Labour's Lost*, V.ii.406-14, from the Arden edition, ed. R. David, Methuen, 1951.
88. William Shakespeare, *The Winter's Tale*, IV.iv.220-28, from the Arden edition, ed. J.H.P. Pafford, Methuen, 1963.
89. M. Spufford, *The Great Reclothing of Rural England, Petty Chapmen and their wares in the Seventeenth Century*, Hambledon, 1984, pp.172-7.
90. Gerard, op. cit., p.1008.

CHAPTER TWO

1. Anon poem, early seventeenth century. *The Oxford Dictionary of Nursery Rhymes*, ed. I. and P. Opie, Oxford University Press, 1958, p.52, also suggests that this rhyme might refer to the effects of the Elizabethan Poor Laws, and that the 'velvet gowns' could be stolen property.
2. Anon, 'The meeting of gallants at an ordinarie or the walkes in Powles', 1603, black-letter copy in Bodleian Library, ed. J. Halliwell, Percy Society, 1841.
3. Ibid.
4. Scaramelli to the Doge and Senate, Calendar State Papers, Venetian, X, 1603-7, no.66, 28 May 1603.

5. *The funeral obsequies of Sir All-in-New fashions*, Douce Prints Portfolio 138, no.89, c.1625-30, Bodleian Library, printed in Shakespeare Survey 11, 1958.
6. T. Middleton, *Father Hubburd's Tales*, 1604, from *The Works of Thomas Middleton*, ed. A.H. Bullen, London, 1885-6, VIII, p.71.
7. 'Extracts from Prince Henry's Wardrobe Accounts 1607-8', *Archeologia*, XI, 1794, pp.88-94.
8. Quoted in Roy Strong, *Henry Prince of Wales and England's Lost Renaissance*, Thames and Hudson, 1986, p.12.
9. Letter from Lord Thomas Howard printed in Sir John Harington, *Nugae Antiquae . . . original papers in prose and verse*, 3 vols, London, 1779.
10. Strong, op. cit., p.222.
11. Roy Strong, *The English Icon: Elizabethan and Jacobean Portraiture*, Routledge and Kegan Paul, 1969, p.56.
12. Ibid.
13. Strong, *Henry Prince of Wales*, op. cit., p.225.
14. 'Warrant to the Great Wardrobe on the occasion of Princess Elizabeth's wedding', *Archeologia*, XXII, 1836. See also Valerie Cumming, 'The Trousseau of Princess Elizabeth', *Collectanea Londiensia*, no.2, 1978. There are many portraits of Elizabeth at Ashdown House, Oxon, a National Trust property built in the early 1660s by her devoted supporter, the 1st Lord Craven.
15. Ms. Stowe 557, British Museum. Frontispiece, extract from the *Journal of Sir Simonds d'Ewes*, dated 21 January 1620. See also: Thomas Fuller's *The Worthies of England*, 1662 edition, p.193, quoted in H. Wheatley, *London Past and Present*, London, 1891, III; and Arnold, *Queen Elizabeth's Wardrobe*, op. cit., pp.174-5.
16. *The Letters of John Chamberlain*, ed. N.E. McClure, 2 vols, American Philosophical Society, Philadelphia, 1939, II, no.322, 27 March 1619, p.224. Chamberlain's letters, from 1597 to 1627, were frequently addressed to Sir Dudley Carleton, English ambassador at Venice and later The Hague. Chamberlain lived near St Paul's Cathedral but there is 'no indication that he followed a profession, engaged in business, or held public office'.
17. Strong, *Henry Prince of Wales*, op. cit., p.16.
18. Quoted in D.N. Durant *Arabella Stuart*, Weidenfeld and Nicolson, 1974, p.135. Some idea of her taste in jewellery can be gauged from a portrait, after van Somer, 1617, now on display at Montacute. The jewellery is described in *Princely Magnificence*, op. cit., p.21.
19. Scaramelli to the Doge, Calendar State Papers, Venetian, X, op. cit., no.91, 10 July 1603.
20. Edward Hall, *Chronicle: The Union of the two Noble Families . . .*, original edition 1548, 1809 edition, ed. Sir H. Ellis, p.526.

21. S. Orgel and R. Strong, *Inigo Jones. The Theatre of the Stuart Court*, 2 vols, University of California Press, 1973, I, p.111.
22. Ibid., I, p.191.
23. T. Middleton and T. Dekker, *The Honest Whore*, Part I, III.i.42-5, from *The Dramatic Works of Thomas Dekker*, ed. Fredson Bowers, Cambridge University Press, 1955, p.59.
24. Middleton, *Father Hubburd's Tales*, op. cit.
25. Quoted in Roy Strong, *The Elizabethan Image. Painting in England 1540-1620*, Tate Gallery, 1969, no.142; see also Roy Strong *The English Renaissance Miniature*, Thames and Hudson, 1984, pp.180-4.
26. Overbury, 'An Amorist', op. cit., p.10.
27. Anon, *The Return from Parnassus*, 1606, III.iv, from Dodsley's *Old English Plays*, London, 1874-6, IX.
28. Quoted in J. Jacob and J. Simon, *The Suffolk Collection, Catalogue of Paintings*, Greater London Council, no.3. An inventory of Sackville's clothes and their relationship to this portrait are discussed in Peter and Ann McTaggart, 'The rich wearing apparel of Richard, 3rd Earl of Dorset', *Costume*, no.14, 1980, pp.41-5.
29. Jacob and Simon, op. cit.
30. *The Diary of the Lady Anne Clifford*, introduced by Vita Sackville-West, Heinemann, 1923, edited from an eighteenth-century transcript of the original manuscript. See also: Martin Holmes, *Proud Northern Lady. Lady Anne Clifford, 1590-1676*, Phillimore, 1975; and *The Diaries of Lady Anne Clifford*, ed. D.J.H. Clifford, Alan Sutton, 1990.
31. *The Diary of the Lady Anne Clifford*, op. cit., p.42.
32. Ibid., letter dated 29 November 1616.
33. Ibid., pp.71 and 79.
34. Ibid., p.45.
35. Some of these items were on loan to the Victoria and Albert Museum in the early 1930s and were described briefly by John L. Nevinson in his article 'New Material for the History of Early 17th century Costume in England', *Apollo*, no.20, 1934. The nightgown has been fully described with drawings, photographs and a pattern diagram by Janet Arnold in *Patterns of Fashion: The cut and construction of clothes for men and women c.1560-1620*, Macmillan, 1985, pattern no.37. Pattern no.36 in this book is the loose gown from Hardwick Hall, see 26.
36. *Memoirs of the Verney Family*, ed. Lady F.P. Verney and M.M. Verney, 4 vols., 1892-9, I, pp.67-8.
37. The English merchant John Watchin obtained a formal certificate of Sir Francis Verney's death which he forwarded, with his effects, to Claydon, where they are still preserved. His staff, inlaid with mother-of-pearl crosses, now hangs below his portrait there.

For further information about the family see: Sir Harry Verney, *The Verneys of Claydon. A seventeenth century English family*, Maxwell, 1969; Peter Verney, *The Standard Bearer: The Story of Sir Edmund Verney*, Hutchinson, 1963.
Relationships within the Verney family are discussed in Miriam Slater's *Family life in the Seventeenth century. The Verneys of Claydon House*, Routledge and Kegan Paul, 1984.
38. St Clare Byrne, *The Elizabethan Home*, op. cit., The French Garden, Dialogue VIII, 'At the Royal Exchange', pp.57-60.
39. Ben Jonson, *The Devil is an Ass*, I.vi.30-4, from Herford and Simpson, op. cit., VI.
40. Roy Strong, 'Charles I's Clothes for the years 1633 to 1635', *Costume*, no.19, 1985, pp.73-89.
41. Quoted in Aileen Ribeiro, *Dress and Morality*, Batsford, 1986, p.81.
42. Quoted in David Piper, *Van Dyck*, Collins, 1968, p.20.
43. Ibid.
44. 'The Four Seasons by Wenceslaus Hollar', introduced by John Nevinson and Ann Saunders, Costume Society, Extra Series no.6, 1979.
45. K. Sharpe, *The Personal Rule of Charles I*, Yale University Press, 1992, p.238.
46. Quoted in J.T. Cliffe, *The Puritan Gentry. The Great Puritan Families of Early Stuart England*, Routledge and Kegan Paul, 1984, p.143.
47. Ribeiro, op. cit., p.85.
48. Lucy Hutchinson, *Memoirs of the Life of Colonel Hutchinson*, ed. James Sutherland, Oxford University Press, 1973, p.43.
49. 'Letters of the Lady Brilliana Harley', Camden Society, Old Series, 1854, no.58.
50. Taylor Downing and Maggie Millman, *Civil War*, Collins and Brown, 1991, p.83.
51. Ribeiro, op. cit., p.83.
52. *Memoirs of Sir John Reresby, 1634-89*, ed. J.J. Cartwright, Longmans, Green & Co., 1875, p.37; reprinted Royal Historical Society, 1991, pp.21-2.
53. Historic Manuscripts Commission, Seymour Papers 1532-1686, IV, Longleat MS, 4 November 1603.
54. Quoted in Diana de Marly, 'Fashionable Suppliers 1660-1700. Tailors and Clothing Tradesmen of the Restoration Period', *Antiquaries Journal*, 1978, LVIII.ii, p.334. The value of stock held by mercers in the Exchange could be very high: see R.G. Lang, 'London's Aldermen in Business 1600-25', Guildhall Miscellany, III, no.1, 1969, pp.242-64, where that of Edward Ryder was valued at £3,267 in 1592.
55. Quoted in F.C. Chalfont, *Ben Jonson's London. A Jacobean Placename Dictionary*, The University of Georgia Press, 1978, p.55.
56. Ben Jonson, *Epicene*, I.iii.35-9, from Herford and Simpson, op. cit., V.
57. Heywood, op. cit., II.i.261-8.

58. T. Tomkis, *Lingua*, 1607, from Dodsley, op. cit., 1874-6, IX, p.426.
59. Printed in 'Poetical Miscellany', ed. J.O. Halliwell, Percy Society, 1845, IV, p.11.
60. 'Letters of the Lady Brilliana Harley', op. cit., no.68.
61. Extract printed in Rachel Weigall, 'An Elizabethan Gentlewoman', *Quarterly Review*, no.215, 1911, p.125.
62. Nathaniel Bacon, MS Steward's Account 1587-97, Centre for East Anglian Studies, University East Anglia, quoted in Clabburn, op. cit., p.212.
63. 'Extracts from Prince Henry's Wardrobe Accounts', op. cit.
64. Quoted in G.P.V. Akrigg, *Jacobean Pageant; or, the Court of King James I*, London, 1962, p.87.
65. *The Letters of John Chamberlain*, op. cit., I, no.167, 23 February 1613 to Sir Ralph Winwood.
66. Ibid., I, no.166, 18 February 1613 to Alice Carleton.
On 2 November 1617 Lady Anne Clifford wrote in her diary that she sent Queen Anne the 'skirts of a white satin gown all pearled and embroiderd with colours which cost me fourscore pounds without the satin', op. cit., p.80.
67. Anon, *Sir Giles Goosecap*, 1606, II.i, Tudor Facsimile Texts, 1912.
68. *Memoirs of the Verney Family*, op. cit., I, p.256.
69. Her niece, the gifted poetess Anne Killigrew, published a poem about the incident in 1686, *On my aunt Mrs A. K[irke] Drown'd under London Bridge in the Queen's Bardge Anno 1641*.
70. Ben Jonson, *Epicene*, II.v.66, from Herford and Simpson, op. cit.
71. John Webster, *Anything for a Quiet Life*, I.i.300-8, from *The Complete Works of John Webster*, 4 vols, ed. F.L. Lucas, Chatto and Windus, 1927, IV.
72. *The Letters of John Chamberlain*, op. cit., II, no.294, 20 April 1618 to Sir Dudley Carleton.
73. R.G. Lang, op. cit.
74. T. Dekker, *The Guls Horne-Book*, 1609, reprinted by the Stratford-on-Avon Library, ed. E. Pendry, 1967, no.4, p.234.
75. Ibid.
76. Dudgin Powell, 'Coach and Sedan, Pleasantly disputing for place and precedence. The brewers cart being Moderator', 1636.
Sedan chairs continued to be used during the Commonwealth. According to the accounts of Sir Richard Brownlow of Belton, payment was made 1653-4 to a 'Coachmaker that lives at the Peacock in St. Martin's Lane for a sedan, for sedan men's coats', from *Records of the Cust family. Series II. The Brownlows of Belton 1550-1779*, ed. Lady E. Cust, 1909, p.139.
77. See Belton House, Lincolnshire, Blickling Hall, Norfolk, and Calke Abbey, Derbyshire.

78. *Memoirs of the Verney Family*, op. cit., II, p.234.
79. 'The House and Farm Accounts of the Shuttleworths of Gawthorpe, 1582-1621', 4 vols, ed. John Harland, Chetham Society, 1856-8.
80. Ibid., XXXIII, Steward's Accounts 1 July 1608-6 November 1613, pp.175-83 and 184-5.
81. A caroche was purchased from Richard Eastwood for the journey back to Lancashire and he received 30s 'for his paynes' and for training the horses, and it cost threepence to stable the horses in London. Repairs to the vehicle during the journey came to 22s 4d, and there was another separate account for the 'Carriage and horses, their food, shoeing and ostlers etc.'.
82. During the second half of the century the village of Islington became a popular residential choice for middle-class Londoners. It had clean country air and was surrounded by pastures on which cattle grazed. In the late eighteenth century the Peacock Inn, in what is now Islington High Street, was the first stop out of London for the northern stage coaches that commenced their journey from the Bull and Mouth Inn at St Martins-le-Grand.
83. *Memoirs of the Verney Family*, op. cit., I, p.234.

CHAPTER THREE

1. *The Diaries of Samuel Pepys*, ed. Robert Latham and William Matthews, 11 vols, Bell and Hyman, 1969-83, 16 May 1660, I, p.143.
2. Ibid., 23 May 1660, I, p.155.
3. Diana de Marly, op. cit., p.235.
4. Arthur Bryant, *King Charles II*, Collins, 1968, p.84.
5. Anon, *England's Joy*, 1660. Harleian Miscellany, VII, 1810.
6. *Memoirs of the Verney Family*, op. cit., III, p.242.
7. Lesley Edwards, 'Dres't Like a May-Pole. A Study of Two Suits of c.1660-62', *Costume*, 1985, no.19, pp.75-93.
8. *Memoirs of the Verney Family*, op. cit., IV, p.167.
9. *The Diaries of Samuel Pepys*, op. cit., 6 April 1661, II, p.66.
10. Ibid., 24 May 1660, I, p.156.
11. John Evelyn, 'Tyrannus or the Mode', Costume Society Reprint, edited from 1661 edition by J.L. Nevinson.
12. *The Life and Times of Anthony Wood*, 5 vols, Oxford Historical Society, 1891-1900, 18 October 1665.
13. *The Diaries of Samuel Pepys*, op. cit., 26 April 1667, VIII, p.181.
14. *The Life and Times of Anthony Wood*, op. cit., December 1663.
15. Evelyn, op. cit.
16. *The Diaries of Samuel Pepys*, op. cit., 28 October 1665, VI, p.281.

17. Ibid., 13 October 1666, VII, p.320.
18. Ibid., 15 October 1666, VII, p.324.
19. Ibid., 17 October 1666, VII, p.328.
20. *The Diaries of John Evelyn*, ed. E.S. De Beer, Oxford, 1955, III, p.465. See also Diana de Marly, 'King Charles II's Own Fashion. The Theatrical Origins of the English Vest', *Journal Warburg and Courtauld Institute*, XXXVII, 1974.
21. César de Saussure, *A Foreign View of England in the Reigns of George I and George II*, John Murray, 1902, pp.112-13.
22. Diana de Marly, 'Some Aristocratic Clothing Accounts of the Restoration period in England', *Waffen und Kostümkunde*, 1976, XVIII, p.105 and *The Diaries of Samuel Pepys*, op.cit., 1 July 1665, VI, p.114.
23. I am indebted to Cherry Ann Knott for this and subsequent information about George Vernon's accounts. Some of the Vernon estate papers are deposited in the Derbyshire County Record Office, Matlock, others remain in the possession of Lord Vernon.
24. Quoted in National Trust Guide to Sudbury Hall, 1992, p.19. See also S. Stevenson and D. Thomson, *J.M. Wright. The King's Painter*, Scottish National Portrait Gallery, 1982.
25. In 1672 William Russell, 5th Earl of Bedford paid his wigmaker £54 10s 0d for four wigs, costing £20, £18, £10 (a periwig for riding) and £6 respectively. An old periwig was cleaned and repaired at a cost of 10s. This was, however, exceptionally extravagant as his annual outlay was usually £20. G. Scott Thompson, *Life in a Noble Household 1641-1700*, Cape, 1937, p.341.
26. *The Diaries of Samuel Pepys*, op. cit., 3 November 1663, IV, p.362.
27. Ibid., 8 November 1663, IV, p.369.
28. Ibid., 29 March 1667, VIII, p.136.
29. Quoted in R. Corson, *Fashions in Hair*, Peter Owen, 1971, p.225.
30. John Gay, 'Trivia', I.iii.55-8 from *John Gay. Poetry and Prose*, ed. V.A. Dearing and C.E. Beckwith, Oxford English Texts Series, 1974.
31. Portraits of ladies wearing a variety of nightgowns can be seen in Oliver Millar, *Sir Peter Lely*, National Portrait Gallery, 1978.
32. *The Diaries of Samuel Pepys*, op. cit., 1 May 1667, VIII, p.193.
33. Ibid., 18 June 1662, III, p.113.
34. Quoted in Oliver Millar, *The Tudor, Stuart and Early Georgian Pictures in the Collection of Her Majesty the Queen*, 2 vols, Phaidon, London, 1963, II, pp.124-5.
35. The incorporation of classical dress in portraits is discussed by Diana de Marly in 'The Establishment of Roman Dress in Seventeenth-Century Portraiture', *Burlington Magazine*, July 1975, pp.442-51. Also in Diana de Marly, 'Undress in the Oeuvre of Lely', *Burlington Magazine*, November 1978, pp.749-50.

36. 'Extracts from the Executors Account Book of Sir Peter Lely', *Burlington Magazine*, November 1978, pp.747-9.
37. Quoted in Millar, *The Tudor, Stuart and Early Georgian Pictures*, op. cit., p.125.
38. Additional Ms. (anon) 22,950 f.41, British Museum, quoted in M. Whinney and Oliver Millar, *English Art 1625-1714*, Oxford University Press, 1957, p.174.
39. *The Diaries of John Evelyn*, op. cit., III, pp.589-90.
40. Quoted in Millar, *The Tudor, Stuart and Early Georgian Pictures*, op. cit., p.124.
41. *The Diaries of Samuel Pepys*, op. cit., 18 June 1662, III, p.113.
42. John and Mary Evelyn, *Mundus Muliebris; the Lady's Dressing-Room Unlock'd*, 1690, ed. J.L. Nevinson, Special Publication of the Costume Society, no.5, 1977.
43. *The Diaries of Samuel Pepys*, op. cit., 11 August 1667, VIII, pp.381-2.
44. Ibid., 12 June 1666, VII, p.162.
45. Ibid., 30 March 1666, VII, p.85. Nightgowns and banyans are discussed in Margaret Swain's 'Nightgown into Dressing-gown. A study of Men's nightgowns in the Eighteenth-century', *Costume*, 1972, no.6, pp.10-21.
46. G. Scott Thompson, op. cit., p.342.
47. Quoted in Adrian Tinniswood, *Historic Houses of the National Trust*, The National Trust, 1991, p.126.
48. Ibid., p.127.
49. de Marly, *Fashionable Suppliers*, op. cit., p.337.
50. E. Ashmole, 'The Institution, Laws and Ceremonies of the Most Noble Order of the Garter', 1676, quoted in Alan Mansfield, *Ceremonial Costume*, A. and C. Black, 1980, p.59.
J.M. Wright's portrait of Charles II in Garter robes (**69**) is dated by Millar, *The Tudor, Stuart and Early Georgian Pictures*, op. cit., no.285, p.129, as from the 1660s, but Valerie Cumming, *Royal Dress: Image and Reality 1580-1986*, Batsford, 1989, fn.13, p.208, questions this date. According to the Stevenson and Thomson catalogue of the Wright exhibition, at the Scottish National Portrait Gallery, op. cit., the shape of the wig merits the later date of c.1676.
51. G. Scott Thompson, op. cit., p.332.
52. G. Scott Thompson, op. cit., pp.332-3.
53. G. Scott Thompson, *The Russells in Bloomsbury 1669-1771*, Jonathan Cape, 1940, p.114.
54. Quoted in C.W. Cunnington, *Handbook of English Costume in the Seventeenth Century*, Faber & Faber, 1955, p.168.
55. Cumming, op. cit., p.42.
56. Quoted in Cumming, op. cit., p.46 from *The Letters of Horace Walpole*, ed. H. Paget Toynbee, London, 1903, IV, p.409.
57. Alexander Pope, *Windsor Forest*, from *The Poems of Alexander Pope*, ed. J. Butt, Methuen, 1968, p.208.

58. G. Scott Thompson, *Life in a Noble Household*, op. cit., pp.83-90.
59. Quoted in A. Ribeiro and V. Cumming, *The Visual History of Costume*, Batsford, 1989, p.24.
60. Quoted in Anne Buck, *Dress in Eighteenth-Century England*, Batsford, 1979, p.192.
61. R. Campbell, *The London Tradesman*, 1747, David and Charles Reprints, 1969, p.259.
62. In 1685-7 Elizabeth Percy, Duchess of Somerset, patronised the milliner Samuel Tuer of Pall Mall, and William Tuer supplied Queen Mary II, 1689-90. Elizabeth's accounts for those years, in the archive at Petworth, are reproduced in de Marly, 'Some Aristocratic Clothing Accounts', op. cit., p.113.
63. Quoted in E. J. Burford, *Royal St. James's. Being a Story of Kings, Clubmen and Courtesans*, Hale, 1986, p.50.
64. Gay, op. cit., ii.267-70.
65. Quoted in J. Bowle, *John Evelyn and His World*, Routledge and Kegan Paul, 1981, p.111.
66. Another source suggests that it was the tailor Robert Baker who made a fortune from the pickadils he sold in his shop in the Strand. He invested his money in one and a half acres of open land and in c.1612 built himself a house near the windmill (hence Windmill Street). The name, Pickadilly, first applied to his house, and was eventually used to describe the whole area and, in particular, a famous ordinary. By the end of the seventeenth century the area had been built over.
67. *The Lisle Letters*, op. cit., III, no.544.
68. Letter of student quoted in 'Clare College. Letters and Documents', J.R. Wardale, Cambridge, 1903.
69. *The Diaries of Samuel Pepys*, op. cit., 3 September 1665, VII, p.210.
70. de Marly, *Fashionable Suppliers*, op. cit., p.334.
71. *The Diaries of Samuel Pepys*, op. cit., 4 April 1665, VI, p.73.
72. Ibid., 26 July 1665, VI, pp.170-1.
73. de Marly, *Fashionable Suppliers*, op. cit., p.335.
74. *The Diaries of Samuel Pepys*, op. cit., 17 May 1662, III, p.84.
75. Quoted in E. Ewing, *Everyday Dress 1650-1900*, Batsford, 1984, p.20.
76. John Stow, 'Survey of London: brought down from 1633 to the present time by John Strype', 2 vols, London, 1720.
77. *The Diaries of Samuel Pepys*, op. cit., 25 June 1663, IV, p.199.
78. Ibid., 21 November 1660, I, p.298.
79. Thomas Vincent, 'God's Terrible Voice in the City', London, 1667, quoted in Bedford, op. cit., p.77.
80. *The Diaries of Samuel Pepys*, op. cit., 23 October 1667, VIII, pp.496-7.
81. Ibid., 12 December 1666, VII, p.404.
82. Ibid., 27 June 1668, IX, p.42.

83. Simon Ford, 'London's Resurrection', 1669 from *The New Oxford Book of Seventeenth-century Verse*, ed. A. Fowler, 1991, p.572.
84. *The Diaries of Samuel Pepys*, op. cit., 26 September 1666, VII, p.296.
85. Quoted in E. J. Burford, *Wits, Wenches and Wantons. London's Low Life. Covent Garden in the Eighteenth Century*, Hale, 1986, p.11.
86. de Marly, 'Fashionable Suppliers', op. cit., pp.341 and 348.
87. *The Diaries of Samuel Pepys*, op. cit., 27 January 1664, V, p.27.
88. Daniel Defoe *The Complete English Tradesman*, London, 1726, pp.235-7.
89. Campbell, op. cit., p.227.
90. Cust, op. cit., pp.167-69.
91. *The Diaries of Samuel Pepys*, op. cit., 1 May 1669, IX, p.540.
92. Scott Thompson, *Life in a Noble Household*, op. cit., p.88.
93. John Oldham, 'A Satyr, in Imitation of The Third Juvenal', 1683, from *The New Oxford Book of Seventeenth-century Verse*, op. cit., p.770.
94. Quoted in Mary Cathcart Borer, *The British Hotel Through The Ages*, Lutterworth Press, 1972, p.59.
95. Spufford, op. cit.
96. *The Journeys of Celia Fiennes*, ed. C. Morris, Cresset Press, 1947. See also C. Hill, *The Illustrated Journeys of Celia Fiennes*, Macdonald, 1993.
97. Rosalind K. Marshall, 'Conscience and Costume in seventeenth-century Scotland', *Costume*, 1972, no.6, pp.32-5.
98. Quoted in ibid., p.34.
99. Ibid.
100. Ibid.

CHAPTER FOUR

1. Sir Walter Raleigh, 'The Lie' from *Silver Poets of the Sixteenth Century*, ed. G. Bullett, Dent, 1967, p.293.
2. Frances, Countess of Hertford and Henrietta Louisa, Countess of Pomfret, *Correspondence, 1736-1741*, London, 1805, II, p.184, quoted in Buck, op. cit., p.17.
3. James Cawthorne, 1736, quoted in C. W. Cunnington and P.C. Cunnington, *Handbook of English Costume in the Eighteenth Century*, Faber & Faber, 1972, p.14.
4. Campbell, op. cit., p.197.
5. Richard Rush, *Residence at the Court of London*, ed. B. Rush, London, 1872, p.324-5, quoted in Barbara Burman Baines, *Fashion Revivals from the Elizabethan age to the present day*, Batsford, 1981.
6. Robert Lloyd, 'The Cit's Country Box', 1757 from *The Penguin Book of Everyday Verse. Social and Documentary Poetry 1250-1916*, ed. D. Wright, 1976, p.341.
7. William Cowper, *The Poetical Works of William Cowper*, ed. H.S. Milford, Oxford University Press, 1934, Book IV, 534-42.

8. Jean Jacques Rousseau, *Emile*, Everyman edition, Dent, 1993, Book V, p.395.
9. *The Works of Sir Joshua Reynolds*, ed. E. Malone, London, 1798, I, p.237.
10. Reynolds, 7th Lecture to Royal Academy, 1776, from *Fifteen Discourses Delivered in the Royal Academy by Sir Joshua Reynolds*, Dent, pp.98-128.
11. Henry Fielding, *Amelia*, London, 1751.
12. Her embroidery and flower mosaics are amply illustrated in Ruth Hayden, *Mrs Delany: Her Life and Her Flowers*, Colonnade, 1980.
13. Quoted in Natalie Rothstein, 'God Bless This Choye', *Costume*, 1977, no.11, p.67.
14. Mary Granville, Mrs Delany, *The Autobiography and Correspondence*, ed. Lady Llanover, 6 vols, 1st series, London, 1861-2, II, p.147.
15. Ibid., II, p.580.
16. Henry Fielding, *Tom Jones*, 1749.
17. Other portraits can be found in *Polite Society by Arthur Devis 1712-87. Portraits of the English Country Gentleman and his Family*, Harris Museum and Art Gallery, Preston, 1983.
18. Pierre Jean Grosley, *A Tour to London, or New Observations on England and its Inhabitants*, trans. T. Nugent, London, 1772, p.254.
19. There is a lady's worsted woollen cloth riding jacket in the Snowshill collection (SNO 709). Dated 1720-50 it has matching velvet collar and cuffs, buttonholes of silver thread and silver buttons.
20. From Henrietta Countess of Suffolk, *Letters . . . 1824*, II, p.98.
21. *London in 1710. From the Travels of Zacharias Conrad von Uffenbach*, trans. W.H. Quarrell and M. Mare, London, 1934, p.106.
22. *The Purefoy Letters 1735-1753*, ed. G. Eland, Sidgwick and Jackson, 1931, II, no.448.
23. The quilted jacket and petticoat (**107**) and a *pet-en-l'air* from the Snowshill collection are illustrated in Janet Arnold, *Patterns of Fashion. Englishwomen's dresses and their construction c.1660-1860*, Macmillan, 1972, pp.30-1.
See also Kay Staniland, 'An Eighteenth-century Quilted Dress', *Costume*, 1990, no.24, pp.43-54.
24. Quoted in Valerie Steele, 'The Social and Political Significance of Macaroni Fashion', *Costume*, 1985, no.19, p.102.
25. James Lees Milne, *People and Places*, op. cit., p.219. See also R. W. Ketton-Cremer, *Felbrigg: The Story of a House*, National Trust, 1962.
26. Clothes described in P. Clabburn, 'A Countryman's Wardrobe. Costume at Felbrigg Hall', *Country Life*, 18 December 1980.
The coat belonging to the suit of fine brown needlecord, c.1735-40, is an early

example of protective clothing. A linen under-sleeve, sewn into the lower part of the sleeve, buttons round the wrist to stop rain running up the arm while shooting. Another useful feature is two deep poacher or hare pockets in the lining.
27. Quoted in *The Swagger Portrait: Grand Manner Portraiture in Britain from Van Dyck to Augustus John 1630-1930*, Andrew Wilton, Tate Gallery, 1992-3, no.28.
28. Quoted in Fairfax-Lucy, op. cit., p.204.
29. Ibid.
30. Ibid., p.219. For a detailed account of the festivities see C. Deelman, *The Great Shakespeare Jubilee*, M. Joseph, 1964.
31. Delany, op. cit., 2nd series, 1862, I, p.490.
32. *The Swagger Portrait*, op. cit., no.31.
33. J.R. Planché, 'Souvenir of the Bal Costumé, 6 June 1845, Buckingham Palace'. See also: 'Conservation of Two English eighteenth century court mantuas', 11C Studies in Conservation; J. Arnold, 'A Silver Embroidered Court Mantua and Petticoat c.1740', *Costume*, 1972, no.6, and 'A Mantua 1760-5', *Costume*, 1973, no.7.
34. Cumming, op. cit., p.78.
35. Buck, op. cit., p.13.
36. Louis Simond, *Journal of a Tour and Residence in Great Britain During the Years 1810 and 1811*, 2 vols, Edinburgh, 1817, I, p.208.
37. Delany, op. cit., 2nd series, 1862, II, p.524.
38. Steele, op. cit., p.94.
39. Ibid., p.102.
40. Ibid., p.103.
41. Ibid.
42. Quoted in Roy Porter, *The Pelican Social History of English Society in the Eighteenth Century*, Penguin, 1982, p.202.
43. Ibid., p.203.
44. Ibid., p.251.
45. Carl Philip Moritz, *Journeys of a German in England in 1782*, trans. and ed. R. Nettel, Cape, 1965, p.138.
46. Madame du Bocage, *Letters Concerning England, Holland and Italy*, London, 1770, I, p.61.
47. Quoted in Porter, op. cit., p.249.
48. Grosley, op. cit., p.35.
49. de Saussure, op. cit., p.74.
50. Quoted in Buck, op. cit., p.158.
51. Quoted in John Pudney, *Crossing London's River*, Dent, 1972, p.30.
52. Gay, op. cit., ii.67-9.
53. For a business operated from rented lodgings, information about any distinguishing features of the house and the location of its back entrance was essential. Hence a 1670s bill for a doctor operating in the Strand 'over against Exeter House (that is now pulling down), between the Golden Cock and the Blew Anchor, at a Bookseller's House, where you will see Two handsome Blew Balconies, gilded; but you are desired

not to come to him the shop way, for there is a very fine conveniency to come the back way in the Savoy Alley; the first door on your left hand, near the Church, where you will see a Blew Balcony, gilded, and a Green Lanthorn with a candle in it at night.' Quoted in C. J.S. Thompson, *The Quacks of Old London*, reprinted Barnes and Noble, 1993, p.163.
54. Description of a signboard that was hung outside the shop of mercer Joseph Trigge of Ludgate Street in 1742. Quoted in A. Heal, *The Signboards of Old London Shops in the Seventeenth and Eighteenth Centuries*, Batsford, 1947, reprinted 1988, p.134.
55. de Saussure, op. cit., p.81.
56. Heal, op. cit., p.136.
57. N. Rouquet, *L'État des Arts en Angleterre*, Paris, 1755, pp.185-6, quoted in B. Sprague Allen, *Tides in English Taste 1619-1800*, Cambridge, Mass., 1937.
58. *The Female Tatler* by Mrs Crackenthorpe (Mrs Mary de la Rivière Manley), quoted in Alison Adburgham, *Shopping in Style. London from the Restoration to Edwardian Elegance*, Thames and Hudson, 1979, p.42.
59. Although the lighting in major thoroughfares like Oxford Street was effective, elsewhere it was uncertain and spasmodic and continued to be until the advent of gas lighting in the next century. When walking in badly-lit and pot-holed streets at night, it was essential to be accompanied by a link-boy.
60. Sophie von la Roche, *Sophie in London 1786*, trans. and ed. Clare Williams, Cape, 1933.
61. Buck, op. cit., p.170.
62. Grosley, op. cit., p.106.
63. *The Spectator*, January 1712, no.277.
64. Wrest Park Papers L/30/9/3/6,7. Some of the Hardwicke family papers from Wimpole Hall are kept at the Bedfordshire County Record Office at Wrest Park.
65. Ibid., L/30/9/3/40.
66. Ibid., L/30/11/122/72. See also Janet Arnold, 'The Cut and Construction of Women's Clothes in the Eighteenth Century' from *Revolution in Fashion, European Clothing 1715-1815*, The Kyoto Costume Institute, 1989, and Abbeville Press, 1990, pp.126-34.
67. Natalie Rothstein, 'Textiles in the Album' from *Barbara Johnson's Album of Fashions and Fabrics*, Thames and Hudson, 1987, p.30. See also Rothstein, *Silk Designs of the Eighteenth Century in the Victoria and Albert Museum*, Thames and Hudson, 1990.
68. Lady Mary Coke, *The Letters and Journals of Lady Mary Coke*, 1889-96, I, pp.114-19.
69. Wrest Park Papers, op. cit., L/30/11//122/72.
70. Samuel Richardson, *Clarissa*, Penguin, 1985, p.621.

71. Lady Louisa's *Memoirs* were published in 1827, and a selection from her *Letters* in Edinburgh in 1899. Extract quoted in R. Bayne-Powell, *Eighteenth-Century London*, John Murray, 1937, p.60.
72. Sir Walter Besant, *London in the Eighteenth-Century*, A. and C. Black, 1902, p.303.
73. Whenever possible a garment made from an expensive silk would be altered and brought up to date. A beautiful jacket in the Snowshill collection (SNO 45) clearly demonstrates this process. The brilliant yellow silk patterned with flowers was made in 1715-20. Between 1730 and 1750 sections of this material, possibly left over from a dress, were joined together to make a jacket with elbow-length sleeves. It was altered between 1777 and 1780 when ruched silk gauze trimming was added to the sleeves and edges. Detachable sleeves were then attached, and these fasten tightly around the wrist with hooks and eyes.
74. G. Scott Thompson, *The Russells in Bloomsbury*, op. cit., pp.259-79.
75. Burford, *Wits, Wenches and Wantons*, op. cit., p.80.
76. Ibid., p.60.
77. Ibid., p.21.
78. Ibid., p.149. The shop was at the sign of the 'Green Canister', seven doors from the Strand on the left-hand side.
79. Quoted in *The London Encyclopaedia*, ed. B. Weinreb and C. Hibbert, Macmillan, 1983, p.74.
80. Scott Thompson, *Russells in Bloomsbury*, op. cit., pp.260-1.
81. Ibid., p.275.
82. Fielding, *Tom Jones*, op. cit.
83. J.F. Smith, *Nollekens and his Times*, 1829, I, footnote p.116.
84. Campbell, op. cit., p.207.
85. Wrest Park Papers, op. cit., L/30/9/81/11.
86. Buck, op. cit., p.163.
87. *The Purefoy Letters 1735-53*, op. cit., II, no.457.
88. Ibid.
  Information about London carrier departure and arrival times, and their tariffs, could be found in printed timetables. One was 'The Shopkeeper's and Tradesman's Assistant', 1768, which listed all the towns in England providing a carrier service, and each town was accompanied with the name of an inn and time of departure from London, the distance in miles and the fare.
89. Quoted in Porter, op. cit., p.241.
90. Sir J. Hawkins, *The Life of Samuel Johnson*, London, 1781, ed. B.H. Davis, 1962, p.113.
91. Quoted in National Trust Guide to the Assembly Rooms, Bath, 1994.
92. M. Williams, *Lady Luxborough Goes to Bath*, Basil Blackwell, 1945.
93. Ibid.

94. The Rev. James Woodforde, *The Diary of a Country Parson, 1758-1802*, 5 vols, ed. J. Beresford, London, 1924-31, I, p.313. See also an illustrated selection of extracts, *A Country Parson, James Woodforde's Diary 1759-1802*, Oxford University Press, 1985. For a detailed discussion of the materials and garments purchased by Woodforde see Buck, op. cit., pp.79-82 and P. Clabburn, 'Parson Woodforde's View of Fashion', *Costume*, 1971, no.5.
95. Woodforde, op. cit., IV, p.108. The stock list of a milliner's shop in Norwich is reproduced in P. Clabburn, 'A Provincial Milliner's Shop in 1785', *Costume*, 1977, no.11, pp.100-112. The list is so detailed that 'it is possible to visualise the layout of the shop. It tells what was in the right- and left-hand windows, and what was in the drawers and boxes, so presumably all the other listed items were on display'.
96. Woodforde, op. cit., V, p.392. Miss Ryder occasionally provided Nancy with gowns. Nancy also dealt with the milliner Miss Stevenson of Greek Street, London.
97. Woodforde, op. cit., IV, p.239.
98. Woodforde, op. cit., I, p.332.
99. The *Diary of Nancy Woodforde* for 1792 is in the *Woodforde Papers and Diaries*, ed. D.H. Woodforde, Peter Davies, 1932, p.46. Extracts from Nancy's diary are printed in *The Englishwoman's Diary*, ed. H. Blodgett, Fourth Estate, 1992, pp.35-85.
100. Trevor Fawcett, 'Bath's Georgian Warehouses', *Costume*, 1992, no.26, pp.32-9.
101. Heal, op. cit., Plate XLIX. According to the trade card this warehouse was situated in the middle of the Strand almost opposite Exeter Change.
102. Fawcett, op. cit., p.35.
103. Ibid., p.38. See also Beverly Lemire, 'Developing Consumerism and the Ready-made Clothing Trade in Britain 1750-1800', *Textile History*, XV, 1984, pp.21-41.

CHAPTER FIVE

1. National Trust Guide to Quarry Bank Mill and Styal, 1988.
2. Ibid. See also Beverly Lemire 'Fashion's favourite: the cotton trade and the consumer in Britain, 1660-1800', Oxford University Press for the Pasold Research Fund, 1991, Pasold Studies in Textile History, no.9.
3. Three of the scenes, 'Telemachus with Minerva disguised as Mentor shipwrecked on the island of Calypso', 'Juno with her peacock' and 'the nymph Echo changing into a sound' have been taken from illustrations in the 1785 edition of *The Adventures of Telemachus* published in London. The fourth illustration, 'Telemachus seated at a table telling his story to Calypso and the nymphs', was engraved by Frances Eginton, after Gavin Hamilton, and published on 1 September 1796. There is a length of the

same fabric, plate-printed in sepia, in the Victoria and Albert Museum (T.152-1964) and another in the Henry Francis du Pont Winterthur Museum, Delaware, USA (T.1049).
4. Richard Brinsley Sheridan, *The School for Scandal*, Penguin, 1988, II.i., p.207.
5. Campbell, op. cit., p.289.
6. *The Journal of Samuel Curwen, Loyalist*, ed. A. Oliver, Salem, Massachusetts, 1972, II, p.930, quoted in Buck, op. cit., p.56.
7. Ribeiro and Cumming, op. cit., p.32.
8. *Extracts from the Correspondence of Georgiana, Duchess of Devonshire*, ed. Earl of Bessborough, John Murray, 1955, p.91, letter to her mother, Countess Spencer, 14-18 August 1784. Queen Marie Antoinette, a family friend of the Spencers, had always taken a great interest in Georgiana and her position as the 'Queen of this frivolous yet highly civilised society'. In 1777 Countess Spencer had written to her daughter from Fontainebleau saying how much the Queen talked about her and that she hoped she would visit her in Paris.
9. Quoted in Jacob Larwood, *The Story of London Parks*, London, 1877, p.249.
10. Elizabeth Foster, *Dearest Bess, Extracts from Elizabeth Foster's Journals and Correspondence*, ed. D.M. Stuart, London, 1955, p.48.
11. Ibid., p.52.
12. Quoted in Vyvyan Holland, *Hand-coloured fashion plates, 1770-1899*, Batsford, reprinted 1988, p.43.
13. von la Roche, op. cit.
14. Foster, op. cit., p.77.
15. James Peller Malcolm, *Anecdotes of the Manners and Customs of London during the Eighteenth Century with a Review of the State of Society in 1807*, London, 1808, p.448.
  The specific influence of classical taste on fashion is discussed by J. Arnold in 'The Classical Influence on the Cut, Construction and Decoration of Women's Dresses c.1785-1820', from the proceedings of the Fourth Conference of the Costume Society, 'The so-called Age of Elegance: Costume 1785-1820', 1970.
16. Jane Austen, *Mansfield Park*, Everyman's Library, 1992, p.222.
17. *Jane Austen's letters to her sister Cassandra and others*, collected and ed. R.W. Chapman, Oxford University Press, 1952, no.30.
18. James Peller Malcolm, op. cit., p.448.
19. Quoted in Nancy Bradfield, *Costume in Detail 1730-1930*, Harrap, 1968, reprinted 1989, p.86.
20. Woodforde, op. cit., V, p.200.
21. Ibid., V, p.401.
22. There are a number of examples in the Snowshill and Killerton collections. A selection of those from Snowshill, 1800-60, have been illustrated by J. Arnold, *Patterns of Fashion*, op. cit., pp.50-1.

23. *Mistress of Charlecote, the Memoirs of Mary Elizabeth Lucy*, ed. A. Fairfax-Lucy, Gollancz, 1983, pp.30-1.
24. Ibid.
25. James Laver, *Dandies*, Weidenfeld and Nicolson, 1968, p.36.
26. Nora Waugh, *The Cut of Men's Clothes 1600-1900*, Faber & Faber, 1964, p.112.
27. George Augustus Sala, *Gaslight and Daylight*, Chapman and Hall, 1859, V, p.63.
28. James Peller Malcolm, op. cit., p.449.
29. A 'pink' frock-coat in the Snowshill collection (SNO 694) has the raised monogram LHC on its buttons, the letters stand for Louth Hunt Club. The coat, and a pair of hunting breeches of the same date, 1840s, are said to have belonged to Mr Brook, an Irish amateur jockey who died in 1852.
30. Quoted in *They saw it happen 1689-1897*, ed. Charles Edwards, Blackwell, 1958, p.282.
31. Quoted in Penelope Byrde, *The Male Image: Men's Fashion in England 1300-1970*, Batsford, 1979, p.86. Sala is also quoted, saying that 'next to Count d'Orsay' Dickens was 'the choicest and most tastefully dressed dandy in London'.
32. Sarah Levitt and Jane Tozer, *Fabric of Society. A Century of People and Their Clothes 1770-1870*, Laura Ashley, 1983, p.100.
33. Ibid.
34. George Augustus Sala, *Twice around the Clock*, Houlston and Wright, 1859, p.83.
35. Richard Philipps, *The Picture of London*, 1803 edition, London, quoted in A. Adburgham, *Shops and Shopping 1800-1914*, Barrie and Jenkins, 1989, p.5.
36. Simond, op. cit., quoted in Porter, op. cit., p.53.
37. *Jane Austen's Letters*, op. cit., no.15. For Jane Austen see also: Penelope Byrde, 'Dress and Fashion', from *The Jane Austen Handbook*, ed. J. David Grey, Athlone Press, 1986, pp.131-4; Penelope Byrde, *A Frivolous Distinction. Fashion and Needlework in the Works of Jane Austen*, Bath, 1979; Anne Buck, *The Costume of Jane Austen and her Characters*, from 'The so-called Age of Elegance', op. cit.
38. Campbell, op. cit., p.301.
39. Conditions and regulations for tailors and seamstresses are discussed in Madeleine Ginsburg's 'The Tailoring and Dressmaking Trades, 1700-1850', *Costume*, 1972, no.6, pp.64-71, where there is also further information about the slop trade and Moses, pp.67-8. See also Melina Godman, 'Everyday Tailoring in the 1820s', *Costume*, 1989, no.23, pp.80-5.
40. E.P. Thompson, Eileen Yeo, *The Unknown Mayhew: Selections from the Morning Chronicle 1849-50*, Harmondsworth, 1984, pp.200-1. Quoted in Elizabeth Wilson and Lou Taylor, *Through the Looking Glass*, BBC Publications, 1987, p.43.

41. *Punch*, 1842, IV, p.167.
42. Francis Place, MS Autobiography, 1824, British Museum, Add.MSS 35142. Reprinted as *The Autobiography of Francis Place*, ed. M. Thrale, London, 1972, p.201.
43. Ibid., p.215.
44. William Wordsworth, *The 14-Book Prelude*, ed. W.J.B. Owen, Cornell University Press, 1985, lines 157-67, p.141.
45. James Peller Malcolm, op. cit., p.473.
46. Ibid.
47. Writing in 1829 the sculptor Joseph Nollekens describes a shop-front in St Martin's Lane that 'has one of the very few remaining shop-fronts where the shutters slide in grooves; the street door frame is of the style of Queen Anne, with a spread eagle, foliage and flowers curiously and deeply carved in wood over the entrance'. Quoted in Smith, op. cit., II, p.228.
48. Mary Robinson, 'London's Summer Morning' from *Eighteenth-century Women Poets*, ed. R. Lonsdale, Oxford University Press, 1989, p.473.
49. Rudolph Ackermann, *Repository of the Arts*, London, 1809, I, no.3.
50. Ibid.
51. *The Reminiscences and Recollections of Captain R.H. Gronow*, 2 vols, Nimmo, London, 1900, I, p.44.
52. Adburgham, *Shops and Shopping*, op. cit., p.101.
53. Jane Austen, *Northanger Abbey*, ed. R.W. Chapman, Oxford, 1933, p.28.
54. *Jane Austen's Letters*, op. cit., no.69.
55. Ibid., no.33.
56. Ibid., no.69.
57. Ibid., no.83.
58. Ibid., no.117.
59. Ibid., no.82.
60. Ibid., no.60.
61. Ibid., no.69. This letter was written on 18 April 1811 when Jane was staying at her brother's house in Sloane Street, and the dressmaker concerned was a 'young woman in this Neighbourhood'.
62. Ibid., no.38.
63. Fashion illustrations reproduced in *Ackermann's Costume Plates; Women's Fashions in England 1818-1828*, ed. S. Blum, Dover, New York, 1978.
64. Quoted in Adburgham, *Shops and Shopping*, op. cit., p.29.
65. Ibid., p.30.
66. Ibid., p.33.
67. Ibid., p.35.
68. According to a bill dated 1857, they operated a 'Wholesale and Retail Silk Warehouse. Carpet and General Furnishing Warehouse. Funerals furnished'. Faulkner died in 1862 and the firm became Kendal, Milne, & Co. Kendals was taken over by Harrods after the First World War and was purchased by the House of Fraser in 1959. There is a collection of bills for a wide variety of items purchased at Kendals from the 1850s to the 1870s at Platt Hall, Manchester. See Levitt and Tozer, op. cit.

69. The Quadrant colonnades were removed in 1848. The largest late-Georgian shop-fronts to survive until the twentieth century were nos 10, 11 and 12 Coventry Street, but these were demolished with the rest of the north side of the street in 1914.
70. John Tallis, *Tallis's Street View*, London, 1837-8, quoted in Adburgham, *Shops and Shopping*, op. cit., p.12.
71. Ibid.
72. Ibid., p.13.
73. A copy of the Guide in the National Art Library shows that many mercers and linen drapers had shops in Henrietta Street and New Bond Street. Coopers at 113 New Bond Street supplied the Royal Family with linens and another Cooper, at 28 Pall Mall, supplied them with silks. There were also a number of warehouses, selling lace, trimmings and materials.
74. There is a pair of black satin shoes dating from the late 1830s in the Snowshill collection (SNO 112). A label inside states 'F. Marsh, Maker and importer of French boots and shoes, 148 Oxford Street, opposite Bond Street'. Printed paper labels bearing the name of the maker and his premises were used from the late eighteenth century.
75. *The Letters of Horace Walpole*, op. cit., XIV, p.447.
76. Adburgham, *Shops and Shopping*, op. cit., p.99.

CHAPTER SIX

1. Fairfax-Lucy, *Mistress of Charlecote*, op. cit., p.93.
2. Quoted in Asa Briggs, *Victorian Things*, Batsford, 1988, p.56.
3. Quoted in Avril Lansdell, *Fashion à la Carte 1860-1900*, Shire, 1985, p.17.
4. Quoted in Avril Lansdell, *Wedding Fashions 1860-1980*, Shire, 1986, p.303.
5. Quoted in Levitt and Tozer, op. cit.
6. Sonia Keppel, *Edwardian Daughter*, Hamish Hamilton, 1958, p.14.
7. Waugh, op. cit., p.114.
8. *The Tailor and Cutter*, London, 13 May 1897.
9. Shaw, the designer of Cragside, was the pioneer of an 'eclectic, romantic style of architecture which did not belong to any one period but drew on a range of sources', Tinniswood, op. cit., p.250.
10. *The Tailor and Cutter*, 20 May 1897.
11. Diana de Marly, *Fashion for Men. An Illustrated History*, Batsford, 1985, p.113.
12. Quoted in Levitt and Tozer, op. cit., pp.161-2.
13. Frederick Willis, *A Book of London Yesterdays*, Phoenix House, 1960, p.154.
14. Elinor Glyn, *Romantic Adventure*, Nicolson and Watson, 1936, p.74.
15. Fairfax-Lucy, *Mistress of Charlecote*, op. cit., p.78.

16. *Punch*, 25 March 1865, reproduced in C. Walkley, *The Way to Wear 'em. 150 Years of Punch on Fashion*, Peter Owen, 1985, p.36.
17. Jane Welsh Carlyle, *I too am here. Selections from her letters*, eds. A. and M. McQueen Simpson, Cambridge University Press, 1977, p.230.
18. Monsieur Hippolyte Taine, *Notes on England*, 3rd edition, London, 1872, p.68. He was describing the clothes worn by the 'wealthy middle classes' in Hyde Park on a Sunday.
19. According to contemporary advertisements the 'Ondina' was 'so light and compressible' that it 'might almost be rolled up and carried in the pocket'.
20. Taine, op. cit.
21. The complex construction of dresses in 1876 is apparent from the following comment: 'It is now quite impossible to describe dresses with exactitude; the skirts are draped so mysteriously, the arrangement of trimmings is usually one-sided and the fastenings are so curiously contrived that after studying any particular toilette for even quarter of an hour the task of writing down how it is all made remains hopeless.' Quoted in C.W. Cunnington and P.E. Cunnington, *Englishwomen's Clothing in the Nineteenth Century*, Faber & Faber, 1937, p.279.
22. Quoted in Walkley, op. cit., p.51.
23. Ibid.
24. Quoted in Elizabeth Aslin, *The Aesthetic Movement*, Ferndale, 1981, p.148. The subject of artistic and rational dress is also explored in S.M. Newton's *Health, Art and Reason*, John Murray, 1974.
25. Ibid.
26. Quoted in National Trust Guide to Belton House, 1992, p.30. Adelaide, the daughter of the 18th Earl of Shrewsbury, married the 3rd Earl of Brownlow in 1868. They had no children and devoted themselves to the restoration of Belton and its gardens. Adelaide's keen interest in embroidery led her and her mother-in-law, Lady Marion Alford, to join the Committee which founded the first School of Art Needlework in 1871. Queen Victoria became patron of the School in 1875, when it was known as the Royal School of Needlework. In 1903 the School moved to the permanent premises that it still occupies, in Kensington, London.
27. Ibid.
28. Lillie Langtry, *The Days I Knew*, New York, 1925, p.37, reprinted Redberry Press Ltd, 1989, p.27.
29. Dorothea Mapleson, quoted in J. Birkett and J. Richardson, *Lillie Langtry. Her life in words and pictures*, R. Shuff Ltd, 1979.
30. The Professional Beauty made a living out of her good looks and ability to be an amusing and witty companion. This was necessary as the 'PB' did not possess a great fortune and did not come from the higher echelons of society. By the 1870s, when the Cabinet photograph (6 × 4in) became

popular and was large enough to display in a shop window, there was a great demand for photographs of beautiful women dressed in the latest fashions. PBs also made money by appearing in advertisements and endorsing products. See Sandra Barwick, *A Century of Style*, Allen and Unwin, 1984, pp.27-47.

31. Countess of Warwick, *Life's Ebb and Flow*, Hutchinson, 1929, p.46.

32. Lord Ernest Hamilton, *Old Days and New*, Hodder, 1923, p.105.

33. Wilson and Taylor, op. cit., p.53. Viscountess Harberton formed the Society in 1881 with Mrs King, author of *Women's Dress in Relation to Health*.

34. *Punch*, 2 June 1883. Quoted in Walkley, op. cit., p.170.

35. Quoted in Wilson and Taylor, op. cit., p.59.

36. Quoted in Lou Taylor, *Mourning Dress. A Costume and Social History*, Allen and Unwin, 1983, pp.156-7.

Paramatta, when woven with a worsted weft and cotton warp, was a cheap alternative to the more expensive bombazine.

37. Quoted in Adburgham, *Shopping in Style*, op. cit., p.165.

38. Taylor, op. cit., p.162.

39. Keppel, op. cit., p.53.

40. Quoted in Joanna Smith, *Edwardian Children*, Hutchinson, 1983, p.171.

41. *Exchange and Mart Selected Issues 1869-1948*, David and Charles Reprints, 1970.

42. Ibid.

43. Quoted in Taylor, op. cit.

There is a sizeable collection of all types of mourning dress at Killerton, and a black muslin white spot 'half mourning' dress (SNO 445), worn by the widow of the actor William Charles Macready, in the Snowshill collection.

44. Lord Ernest Hamilton, *The Halcyon Era. A rambling reverie of now and then*, John Murray, 1933, pp.42-3.

45. de Marly, *Fashions for Men*, op. cit., p.112.

46. Taylor, op. cit., p.121.

47. Hamilton, *Halcyon Era*, op. cit., p.132.

48. Keppel, op. cit., p.23.

49. Catalogue of exhibition 'American Women of Style', Costume Institute, Metropolitan Museum, New York, 1975.

50. Nigel Nicolson, *Mary Curzon*, Weidenfeld and Nicolson, 1977, pp.39-40. See also Barwick, op. cit., pp.89-94.

51. Beaton, op. cit., p.69.

52. Barwick, op. cit., pp.72-7.

53. Glynn, op. cit., pp.69-70.

54. Ibid.

The Prince of Wales and his circle encouraged and endorsed the custom of leaving London for the country on a regular Saturday-to-Monday basis, but it did not become an established form of entertainment for the upper classes until the middle of the 1890s. The first appearance of the term 'week-end' was in *The Times* in 1892.

55. Beaton, op. cit., p.7.

56. Anthony Masters, *Nancy Astor. A Life*, Weidenfeld and Nicolson, 1981, p.54.

57. Vita Sackville-West, *The Edwardians*, Virago, 1983, p.39.

58. Gwen Raverat, *Period Piece. A Cambridge Childhood*, Faber & Faber, 1952, p.259.

59. Hamilton, *Halcyon Era*, op. cit., p.44.

60. Levitt and Tozer, op. cit., p.155.

61. Sackville-West, *The Edwardians*, op. cit., p.140.

62. Beaton, op. cit., p.9.

63. Nicolson, op. cit., p.167.

64. Ibid., p.180.

65. The Museum of Costume, Bath, has a collection of the clothes Lady Curzon wore in India. See also *Lady Curzon's India. Letters of a Vicereine*, ed. J. Bradley, Weidenfeld and Nicolson, 1985.

66. Quoted in C.W. Cunnington, *English Women's Clothing in the Present Century*, Faber & Faber, 1952, p.81.

67. Lady Diana Cooper, *The Rainbow comes and goes*, Rupert Hart-Davies, 1958, reprinted Michael Russell, 1980, p.61.

68. Paul Poiret, *My First Fifty Years*, trs. Stephen Haden Guest, Gollancz, 1931, p.63.

69. Ibid., pp.89-90.

70. Quoted in Cunnington, op. cit., p.97.

71. Ibid., p.129.

72. Miranda Seymour, *Ottoline Morrell. Life on the Grand Scale*, Hodder and Stoughton, 1992, p.88.

73. Langtry, op. cit.

74. R. Pankhurst, *Sylvia Pankhurst. Artist and Crusader*, Virago, 1979, p.63.

75. Quoted in Cunnington, op. cit., p.129.

76. Langtry, op. cit.

77. H.G. Wells, *Experiment in Autobiography*, 1934, reprinted Faber & Faber, 2 vols, 1984, I, p.83.

78. Charles Dickens, *The Uncommercial Traveller*, no.XXIV, 'An Old Stage-Coaching House', from *The Oxford Illustrated Dickens*, Oxford University Press, 1987, p.241.

79. *The Lady's World*, 1886, quoted in Adburgham, *Shops and Shopping*, op. cit., p.231.

80. Raverat, op. cit., p.93.

81. Quoted in Adburgham, *Shops and Shopping*, op. cit., p.128.

82. Madeleine Ginsburg, *Victorian Dress in Photographs*, Batsford, 1982, p.17.

83. Factory production of clothes and the continued use of sweated labour are discussed in E. Ewing, *History of Twentieth Century Fashion*, Batsford, 1986, pp.48-61.

84. Quoted in Wilson and Taylor, op. cit., p.46.

85. H.G. Wells, *Kipps*, Everyman, Dent, 1993, p.26. Wells also described this episode in his *Experiment in Autobiography*, op. cit.

86. Sala, op. cit., p.77.

87. Arnold Bennett, *The Old Wives' Tale*, Hodder and Stoughton, 1931, p.89.

88. Charles Knight, ed., *London*, V, Henry G. Bohn, 1851, quoted in Adburgham, *Shops and Shopping*, op. cit., p.96.

89. Ibid., p.208.

90. Fairfax-Lucy, *Mistress of Charlecote*, op. cit., p.131.

91. Ibid.

92. Adburgham, *Shops and Shopping*, op. cit., p.78.

93. Ellen Terry, *Memoirs*, Gollancz, 1933, p.57.

94. Levitt and Tozer, op. cit., p.155.

95. Lady Jeune, 'The Ethics of Shopping', *Fortnightly Review*, Jan 1895, quoted in Adburgham, *Shops and Shopping*, op. cit., p.146.

96. Advertisement, c.1875, reproduced in B. Morris, *Liberty Design 1874-1914*, Chartwell, 1989, p.10; see also Adburgham: *Shopping in Style*, op. cit., p.157; *Liberty's: A biography of a shop*, Allen and Unwin, 1975; and *Liberty's 1875-1975. Catalogue of an Exhibition to Mark the Firm's Centenary*, HMSO, 1975.

97. Morris, op. cit., p.17. Thomas Wardle, the Leek silk printer and dyer who was already printing textiles for William Morris, also produced a wide range of silks in artistic colours for Liberty's. His wife founded the Leek Embroidery School in 1879 and sold its embroideries at her own shop in Leek, and to Liberty's. There is a large collection of this embroidery in the Kay-Shuttleworth collection, Gawthorpe Hall.

98. Glyn, op. cit., p.54.

99. Lady Duff-Gordon, *Discretions and Indiscretions*, Jarrold, 1932. Lucy could not be presented at court because she had obtained a divorce from her husband James Kennedy in 1888, 'a fact that Lucy bitterly resented for the rest of her life', from Meredith Etherington-Smith and Jeremy Pilcher, *The 'It' Girls, Lucy, Lady Duff-Gordon, the Couturière 'Lucile', and Elinor Glyn, Romantic Novelist*, Hamish Hamilton, 1986, p.65.

100. Quoted in Etherington-Smith, op. cit., p.74.

101. Ibid., p.75.

102. Beaton, op. cit., pp.31-2.

103. Willis, op. cit., p.126.

104. Ibid., p.146.

105. Ibid., p.152.

106. Adburgham, *Shopping in Style*, op. cit., p.170.

107. Willis, op. cit., p.154.

CHAPTER SEVEN

1. Quoted in A.L. Rowse, *Shakespeare's Southampton*, 1965, Macmillan, p.139.

2. *The Diary of Lady Anne Clifford*, op. cit., p.83. The Earl also recycled his clothes to provide furnishings for Knole. In 1617 Anne wrote: 'About this time my Lord made the Steward alter most of the rooms in the house, and dress them up as fine as he could, and determined to make all his old clothes in purple stuff for the Gallery and Drawing Chamber.' See Clabburn, *The National Trust Book of Furnishing Textiles*, op. cit., p.73.

3. St Clare Byrne, *The Elizabethan Home*, op. cit., *The French Garden*, Dialogue V, 'In the Nursery', pp.49-51.

4. Mary C. Rowsell, *The Life Story of Charlotte de la Trémoille, Countess of Derby*, Kegan Paul, 1905, p.38.

5. Margaret Verney, *Verney Letters of the Eighteenth Century*, 2 vols, 1930, II, p.131.

6. *The Diary of Lady Anne Clifford*, op. cit., p.111.

7. Roger North, *The Lives of the Norths*, London, 1679, quoted in P. Cunnington and A. Buck, *Children's Costume in England 1300-1900*, A. and C. Black, 1965, pp.71-2.

8. Ibid.

9. St Clare Byrne, *The Elizabethan Home*, op. cit., *The Frenche Schoolemaister*, Dialogue I, 'Getting up in the Morning', pp.1-2.

10. *Memoirs of the Verney Family*, op. cit., II, pp.310-1.

11. *Extracts from the Correspondence of Georgiana, Duchess of Devonshire*, op. cit., p.62.

12. Quoted in Cunnington and Buck, op. cit., p.104.

13. Ibid.

14. Rousseau, op. cit., Book II, p.109.

15. Gordon Roe, *The Georgian Child*, quoted in Elizabeth Ewing, *History of Children's Costume*, Batsford, 1977, p.44.

16. Plate from *Journal des Luxus und der Moden*, Wiemar, 1787, II, British Library.

17. Charles Dickens, *Sketches by 'Boz'*, 'Meditations in Monmouth Street', from *The Oxford Illustrated Dickens*, op. cit., p.75. Henry Mayhew's *London Labour and the London Poor*, 4 vols, London, 1851-2, also contains vivid and detailed descriptions of the second-hand clothes trade in Monmouth Street, Rosemary and Petticoat Lanes and Seven Dials.

18. Bennett, op. cit., p.89.

At Charlecote there is an earlier purple velvet party dress that belonged to Mary and George Lucy's eldest son William Fulke Lucy, and the fancy dress worn by Caroline Chichester in 1849 is displayed at Arlington Court, Devon next to a portrait of her wearing the same dress.

19. National Trust Guide to Hardwick Hall, 1989, p.45.

20. Raverat, op. cit., pp.263-4.

21. Kenneth de Burgh Codrington, *Cricket in the Grass*, Faber & Faber, 1959, p.170.

22. Raverat, op. cit., p.262.

23. Viola Bankes, *A Kingston Lacy Childhood. Reminiscences of Viola Bankes*, collected by Pamela Watkin, Dovecote Press, 1986, p.11.

24. Ibid.

25. Codrington, op. cit., p.44.

26. Two of the twelve coloured plates in Liberty's lavish costume catalogue *Dress and Decoration*, 1905, featured clothes for children: 'Freda', a white satin frock with matching cap; and 'Marjorie', an Empire-style brown velvet coat with an ostrich feather trimmed hat. The 'Mab' smock became one of Liberty's most popular garments when the seven-year-old Lady Elizabeth Bowes-Lyon wore one in 1907. 'It was a stock pattern, very expensive, and we were all kept very busy with them . . . it was still being made when I left Liberty's in 1924.' Reminiscences of an employee of Liberty's quoted in Clare Frances Lloyd, 'Liberty's Embroidery Workroom', *Costume*, 1976, no.10, pp.86–90.
27. Raverat, op. cit., p.255.

CHAPTER EIGHT

1. 'Times Alteration', a seventeenth-century ballad from the Roxburghe collection.
2. De L'Isle and Dudley MS, op. cit., 1934, II, p.265.
3. *Diary of John Dee*, Camden Society Old Series, 19, 1842, p.54.

4. *Verney Letters*, op. cit., I, p.34.
5. *The Diaries of Samuel Pepys*, op. cit., 23 March 1662, III, p.50.
6. *Memoirs of the Verney Family*, op. cit., IV, p.468.
7. *Verney Letters*, op. cit., I, p.173.
8. Quoted in National Trust Guide to Claydon, 1992, p.36.
9. George Farquhar, 'The Beaux' Stratagem, III.i.70-3, from *The Works of George Farquhar*, ed. S. Strum Kennedy, 2 vols, Clarendon Press, 1988.
10. Count Frederick Kielmansegge, *Diary of Journal to England in the Years 1761-1762*, 1902, p.53. See also Ann Buck, 'The Dress of Domestic Servants in the Eighteenth Century', *Costume*, 1979, no.13.
11. Sala, *Gaslight and Daylight*, op. cit., p.59.
12. Merlin Waterson, *The Servants' Hall. The Domestic History of a Country House*, National Trust, 1990, p.2.
13. Ibid., p.169.
14. J. Hervey, *Letterbooks*, London, 1894, III, pp.272-3.
15. Daniel Defoe, *Everybody's Business is Nobody's Business*, London, 1725, p.17.
16. Wells, *Experiment in Autobiography*, op. cit., I, p.110.

17. Waterson, op. cit., p.80.
18. Arnold Bennett, *Anna of the Five Towns*, London, 1902, p.86.
19. Keppel, op. cit., pp.110-1.
20. Frances E. Crompton, *The Gentle Heritage*, London, 1893. Quoted in P. Cunnington, *Costume of Household Servants From the Middle Ages to 1900*, A. and C. Black, 1974, p.117.
21. Hamilton, *Halcyon Era*, op. cit., p.67.
22. Ibid., p.68.
23. In the Trust's Textile Conservation Workroom at Blickling there is a child's suit of livery. It came from Felbrigg and is thought to have belonged to 'Gla' Windham (1840-66), 'the strange little son of the house' who 'spent much of his time in the servants' hall, and was given a little suit of livery – blue coat, red waistcoat, red plush breeches – in which he waited at tables', Ketton-Cremer, op. cit., p.247.
24. Thomas Hardy, *The Dorset Farm Labourer Past and Present*, London, 1884. Quoted in Diana de Marly, *Working Dress. A History of Occupational Clothing*, Batsford, 1986, p.109. See also, Rachel Worth, 'Thomas Hardy and Rural Dress', *Costume*, 1995, no.29, pp.55-67.

There are two late-nineteenth-century smocks in the Snowshill collection, SNO 195, made from cotton twill, and SNO 196 made from cream linen. In the Kay-Shuttleworth collection there is a very fine one with elaborate embroidery. There are also several children's smocks, of which one, c.1800, is in the Museum of Childhood at Sudbury. A number of articles and books have been written on this subject, including A. Buck, *The Countryman's Smock*, Folk Life, 1963 and M. Hall, *Smocks*, Shire Album no.46, Buckinghamshire, 1972.
25. *The Woman's World*, III, 1890, p.223. Oscar Wilde became editor of *The Lady's World* in 1887 and changed its name to *The Woman's World*.
26. Lees-Milne, *People and Places*, op. cit., p.112.
27. Quoted in Barwick, op. cit., pp.102-5. Claire Avery's friendship with Ellen and Edie is recounted by Edna Woolman Chase in *Always in Vogue*, Gollancz, 1954, pp.76-7.

A number of Terry's stage costumes and an early tea-gown are kept in the collection at Smallhythe. See also Valerie Cumming, 'Ellen Terry: an Aesthetic Actress and her Costumes', *Costume*, 1987, no.21, pp.67-74.
28. Reproduced in Walkley, op. cit., p.43.

List of Plates

Select Bibliography

Other relevant or useful books are referred to in the Notes.

General

Adburgham, A., *Shopping in Style. London from the Restoration to Edwardian Elegance*, Thames and Hudson, 1979

Arnold, J., *Patterns of Fashion. Englishwomen's dresses and their construction c.1660-1860*, Macmillan, 1972

Baines, B., *Fashion Revivals from the Elizabethan age to the present day*, Batsford, 1981

Bradfield, N., *Costume in Detail 1730-1930*, Harrap, 1968, new edition, 1989

Byrde, P., *The Male Image: Men's Fashions in England 1300-1970*, Batsford, 1979

Cumming, V., *Royal Dress: Image and Reality 1580-1986*, Batsford, 1989

Cunnington, P. and Lucas C., *Costume for Births, Marriages and Deaths*, A. and C. Black, 1981

de Marly, D., *Fashion for Men. An Illustrated History*, Batsford, 1985

Ewing, E., *Everyday Dress 1650-1900*, Batsford, 1984, paperback, 1989

Langley Moore, D., *Fashion through Fashion Plates 1771-1970*, Ward Lock, 1971

Levitt, S. and Tozer, J., *Fabric of Society. A Century of People and Their Clothes 1770-1870*, Laura Ashley, 1983

Mansfield, P., *Ceremonial Costume*, A. and C. Black, 1980

Ribeiro, A., *Dress and Morality*, Batsford, 1986, paperback, 1990

Ribeiro A. and Cumming V., *The Visual History of Costume*, Batsford, 1989

Squire, G., *Dress, Art and Society 1560-1970*, Studio Vista, 1974

Swann, J., *Shoes*, Batsford, 1982

Taylor, L., *Mourning Dress. A Costume and Social History*, Allen and Unwin, 1983

Victoria and Albert Museum, Department of Textiles and Dress, *Four Hundred Years of Fashion*, Victoria and Albert Museum and Collins, 1984

Waugh, N., *Corsets and Crinolines*, Batsford, 1987

Waugh, N., *The Cut of Men's Clothes 1600-1900*, Faber & Faber, 1964

Waugh, N., *The Cut of Women's Clothes 1600-1930*, Faber & Faber, 1968

Gorgeous Attyre 1500-1603

Arnold, J., *Patterns of Fashion. The cut and construction of clothes for men and women c.1560-1620*, Macmillan, 1985

Arnold, J., *Queen Elizabeth's Wardrobe Unlock'd*, Maney, Leeds, 1988

Ashelford, J., *Dress in the Age of Elizabeth I*, Batsford, 1988

Ashelford, J., Visual History of Costume series, *The Sixteenth Century*, Batsford, 1983, reprinted 1993

Cunnington, C.W. and P., *Handbook of English Costume in the Sixteenth Century*, Faber & Faber, 1970

Linthicum, M.C., *Costume in the Drama of Shakespeare and his Contemporaries*, Oxford, 1936, reprinted Hacker Art Books, New York, 1972

Nevinson, J.L., *Catalogue of English Domestic Needlework of the Sixteenth and Seventeenth Century*, Victoria and Albert Museum, 1938

Wingfield Digby G., *Elizabethan Embroidery*, Faber & Faber, 1963

Careless Romance 1603-1660 and Wigs & Drapery 1660-1720

Cumming, V., Visual History of Costume series, *The Seventeenth Century*, Batsford, 1984, reprinted 1987

Cunnington, C.W. and P., *Handbook of English Costume in the Seventeenth Century*, Faber & Faber, 1955, reprinted 1973

Uniformly Elegant 1720-1780

Buck, A., *Dress in Eighteenth-Century England*, Batsford, 1979

Cunnington, C.W. and P., *Handbook of English Costume in the Eighteenth Century*, Faber & Faber, 1972

Revolution in Fashion, European Clothing 1715-1815, The Kyoto Costume Institute, 1989 and Abbeville Press, New York, 1990

Ribeiro, A., *Dress in Eighteenth Century Europe 1715-1789*, Batsford, 1984

Ribeiro, A., Visual History of Costume series, *The Eighteenth Century*, Batsford, 1983

Ribeiro, A., *Fashion in the French Revolution*, Batsford, 1988

Rothstein, N., *Silk Designs of the Eighteenth Century in the Victoria and Albert Museum*, Thames and Hudson, 1990

Perfect Cut & Fit 1780-1850 and Tyranny of Fashion 1850-1914

Adburgham, A., *A Punch History of Manners and Modes 1841-1940*, Hutchinson, 1961

Adburgham, A., *Shops and Shopping 1800-1914*, Allen and Unwin, 1964, paperback, Barrie and Jenkins, 1989

Barwick, S., *A Century of Style*, Allen and Unwin, 1984

Byrde, P., *Nineteenth Century Fashion*, Batsford, 1992

Buck, A., *Victorian Costume and Costume Accessories*, Ruth Bean, 1984

Cunnington, C.W. and P., *Handbook of English Costume in the Nineteenth Century*, Faber & Faber, 1970

Ewing, E., *History of Twentieth Century Fashion*, Batsford, 1986

Foster, V., Visual History of Costume series, *The Nineteenth Century*, Batsford, 1986

Ginsburg, M., *Victorian Dress in Photographs*, Batsford, 1982, paperback, 1988

Levitt, S., *Fashion in Photographs 1880-1900*, Batsford, 1991

Walkley, C., *The Way to Wear 'em, 150 Years of Punch on Fashion*, Peter Owen, 1985

Wilson, E. and Taylor, L., *Through the Looking Glass*, BBC Publications, 1987

Children's Clothes

Cunnington, P. and Buck, A., *Children's Costume in England 1300-1900*, A. and C. Black, 1965

Ewing, E., *History of Children's Costume*, Batsford, 1977

Kevill-Davies, S., *Yesterday's Children. The Antiques and History of Childcare*, Antique Collector's Club, 1991

Rose, C., *Children's Clothes since 1750*, Batsford, 1989

Clothes for Servants

Cunnington, P., *Costume of Household Servants From the Middle Ages to 1900*, A. and C. Black, 1974

de Marly, D., *Working Dress. A History of Occupational Clothing*, Batsford, 1986

Girouard, M., *Life in the English Country House. A Social and Architectural History*, Yale University Press, 1978

Hartcup, A., *Below Stairs in the Great Country Houses*, Sidgwick & Jackson, 1980

Lummis, T. and Marsh, J., *The Woman's Domain. Women and the English Country House*, in association with the National Trust, Viking, 1990

Waterson, M., *The Servants' Hall. The Domestic History of a Country House*, National Trust, 1990

Index